WAF

A Perilous Twenty-First Century

Wade Shol, Ph.D.

Security Studies Press

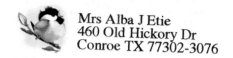

Mrs Alba J Etie
460 Old Hickory Dr
Conroe TX 77302-3076

WARNING

"We are not in the presence of a simple problem..."
Rear Admiral Alfred Thayer Mahan

To May Etie,

with kind regards,

Wade Hsu

23 April 2009

Security Studies Press
Lincoln, Nebraska

Copyright 2007, Security Studies Press

First published in 2007 by Security Studies Press,
650 J Street, Suite 405
Lincoln, Nebraska 68508
www.securitystudies.us

Security Studies is a registered trademark of Security Studies Press.

Manufactured in the United States of America.

Library of Congress Control Number: 2007936397

Shol, Wade A.
Warning: A Perilous Twenty-First Century/ Wade Shol

p.   cm.

Includes bibliographic references and index.

2007
1. International Studies
2. National Security
3. World History
4. United States History
5. Strategic Studies

ISBN: 978-0-9797539-0-9

For Laura, Ian and Susan

In Memory of Rear Admiral Alfred Thayer Mahan

United States Navy

Table of Contents

Preface

Sir Winston Churchill's description of Russia as "a riddle wrapped in a mystery inside an enigma" summarizes well the subject of national grand strategy. Attempting to open one provocative strategic door during the course of this research often resulted in disclosure of two more. Failure to unlock those soon ended with four more appearing out of nowhere. This piling on process continued until progressive policy ideas of our modern era were discarded, and grand strategy's historic legends arrived with a set of keys to the security studies crypt. Their designs, easily discarded by today's world of fast thinking and even faster bungling, were dusted off and incorporated with care and respect. Expressions of gratitude must start with the Sarah Scaife Foundation for providing financial encouragement during this journey's research phase. Their record of assistance for higher education is rock solid, and I am thankful for the trust and support.

Name-calling begins by conveying appreciation, or curse, to Dr. Colin Gray of the University of Reading. During one of many frank and open diplomatic sessions he made a challenge to "think what sea power will look like one hundred years from now." This launched a seagoing adventure that often seemed like a one-way trip to nowhere. Dr. Gray's guidance is a testament why so many professionals seek his counsel. His message that my approach would take ten years haunted my senses numerous times. Equal worthiness, or wrath, goes to Dr. Harold Rood, Professor Emeritus at Claremont McKenna College. He served as navigator on turbulent seas, and had the bad fortune of introducing me to Dr. Gray in 1998. In modern times, where scholars' frantically pound away at keyboards seeking to "publish or perish," Dr. Rood can be found standing over a map, magnifying lens in hand, and eloquently contemplating geostrategic possibilities. The entire scholastic community should strive to emulate his standard. He epitomises the meaning of academic excellence and is a legend of high order. I am fortunate to serve in the company of these two great men. They are rare breeds among today's 'enlightened' epoch.

Writers reaching this point know the list is long of those who contribute. My colleagues at the Universities of Hull and Reading comprised an eclectic colloquium from many fabulous countries. Their security perspective allowed me to view the global arena from outside America's box. My American colleague, Dr. Brian Auten, helped maintain focus through a trying research process. He kept willing paper shredders from tempting reach on several occasions. My POW/MIA contact, Bruce Petty, used his skill as an author and diplomat to warn of writing perils over the horizon. I paid a price for not always listening. Dr. Michal Rozbicki at St. Louis University gave valuable insight on politics behind the Iron Curtain. His knowledge brought tasty realism to many conversations. The Republic of the Philippines was well represented by Vic Bellosillo. His insight on Southeast Asia's geopolitical climate reinforced my view of a vacuum caused by America's military departure several years ago. Another good friend and colleague, Lee Mestres, gave incomparable advice while editing the end product. He noted the benefit behind adding savory red political meat for readers to chew on. His trademark is a sharp eye, gleaned from years of dedicated service with the Central Intelligence Agency. The man is a national treasure. Another piercing eye came from Joanne Sprott, who put her former US Air Force Intelligence Officer skills to use deciphering bits and pieces into a fine index for referencing types. It had to be an excruciating challenge that requires a special breed.

British hospitality during my residency at St. Mary's Church in Cottingham, East Yorkshire, will not be forgotten. The United Kingdom faced ordeals throughout the twentieth century that would cause any other nation to implode. Each British citizen is a walking symbol of what 'tough' is all about. They deserve our complete respect. Remaining gracious hosts to those from far away parts is an admirable character trait. It was also a pleasure to experience such wonderful folks at Montgomery College in Conroe, Texas. Staff and students whose presence graced my classroom during this project's final three years were a refreshing timeout from mankind's horrid history. All made me feel right at home in an exquisite academic environment.

A venture this excruciating cannot occur without collateral damage. I accept responsibility for all gaffes. Readers may, at times, feel buried by citations that span vast cultures and civilizations. Clocks start ticking before the first millennium BC. Quotations could challenge some readers based on contemporary writing styles. Those who proofed the book found a second reading even more grabbing. Technique and theory leap from pages with ease on the next visit, and after reading historic and futuristic events in later chapters. Remarks, old and new, act as jigsaw puzzle pieces to form a picture. Effort must be taken to grasp each writer's line of reasoning. My task occasionally involved guiding details from fine scholars toward a proper destination. This is expected since national grand strategy's striking picture dominates the scholastic gallery. Formulating sea power's next of kin; land, air, and space power into this family portrait required attention to detail. Satisfaction is gained from meticulously combining the efforts of professional colleagues to produce new and lasting definitions.

History is broadly covered and not confined to sea power. Grasping national grand strategy requires consideration of the entire political kingdom. People must study the content in all its complexity. Political coercion is constantly at work. It is, for example, ironic that final touches were being applied on 01 May 2007. Rabble-rousing socialist and communist faithful stayed busy that day with their annual march, fiercely clinching a fist while demanding worker bondage. Few noticed the charades, instigated and staged by menacing political forces lurking in dark shadows. Most people were preoccupied doing jobs as productive members of society, bringing us to one group in particular.

The key to unlocking national grand strategy's most dramatic door was found among employees at Union Pacific Railroad. These men and women reflect the highest tradition of America's work ethic. Countless flights taken on United Airlines between Los Angeles and London consistently traveled over the Great Salt Lake Basin. Directly below sat Promontory, Utah, site of the golden spike that symbolized connection of the transcontinental railroad. This would play a crucial role to another connecting point, which became that "missing link" for defining sea power. The bridge to definitions created by this research exposed itself on one particular flight as I viewed the Rocky Mountain splendor from 39,000 feet. Mr. John Landers, Senior Director, and Vice President, Mr. Steve Barkley, deserve my deepest thanks for allowing me onboard to witness firsthand how the "real world" works. Every Union Pacific employee deserves America's respect and I am privileged to experience that environment in which they thrive.

Last, but certainly far from least, I owe appreciation to my wonderful family. An undertaking of this degree is an arduous ordeal that will test the grit of those you hold dear. My own encounter turned out no different. This project could not have happened without their support and they showed as strong a conviction in me as my own toward the book's merit.

As for all those mentioned and others I should have, I am eternally grateful.

W.S.
Veterans Day
11 November 2007

Control

You only need study Lenin and Mao
to gain the adrenalin and know how.
Give me control of their cash
and I will give them the lash.
Give me control of the schools
and I will make them fools.
Give me control of elections
and I will make the selections.
Give me control of the laws
and I will force them to crawl.
Give me control of the press
and I will rule the West.
There were a few who attempted to save
all those who have since become enslaved.
Welcome my friends to this great tragedy
known by states as national grand strategy.

- Wade Shol

The Present is the Past

"Whether you like it or not, history is on our side. We will bury you."
- Nikita Sergeyevich Khrushchev (15 September 1959).

Dateline:
Houston, Texas
22 November 2004

The Gulfstream III corporate jet began its flight from Love Field in Dallas. The trip went smooth and appeared uneventful. Approaching Houston's Hobby Airport seemed a painless exercise. Sunrise was underway and flying conditions excellent. A morning fog bank maintained a low ceiling. Such layers were not unusual for fall weather along coastal regions. Hurricane season kicked off three months earlier and the annual ritual of tropical storms thrashing cities was in bloom. In earlier times these weather patterns were considered Mother Nature's cyclical phase. In a "progressive" era of political climatology, free market forces deserved blame. The aircraft came in on schedule for its 6:15 AM arrival and VIP pick-up at Hobby Airport. Ultimate destination happens to be Ecuador for a speaking engagement to a group of people now stigmatized by the enlightened left as evil entrepreneurs. The Gulfstream's crew was top drawer quality for Business Jet Services, the Dallas-based private charter service. Both pilots and flight attendant had logged a cumulative sum totaling tens of thousands of flying hours. Nothing less would be expected for the high-ranking person making this trip. He had been transported numerous times by the same company and crew. They were thoroughly "vetted" for security reasons.

Descent toward Hobby's runway #4 from five miles came at textbook altitude and rate of decline. At three miles out, approximately sixty seconds before landing, the plane suddenly took a faster downward gradient than cockpit landing instrumentation or airport guidance systems would normally allow. The Hobby air traffic controller supervising this approach immediately attempted to make contact and, without waiting for acknowledgment, proceeded to inform the crew they were prematurely descending below 400 feet. No response came and several seconds later the aircraft clipped a light tower reaching a height of just over 125 feet. Fortunately the aircraft's speed and direction propelled it into an open field where it exploded on impact. Minor debris littered the Sam Houston Parkway. The crash spared commuter traffic and no injuries were reported.

A preliminary survey of the scene revealed no answers. National Transportation Safety Administration (NTSA) officials dispatched a team from Washington, DC to conduct a thorough examination. Plane crashes may be infrequent, but not unusual. There is almost always a logical explanation. The traveling public must be reassured the friendly skies are full of joy and happiness. Aircraft instrumentation and airport guidance systems would be a primary focus of NTSA investigators. Analysis of crew and aircraft history is considered standard procedure. This process would not be easy since the light tower and subsequent explosion shattered the aircraft into thousands of pieces. No problems were communicated by the crew to air traffic controllers at either Love or Hobby Airport during the trip. Trouble did not surface until a few seconds before landing. Approach records showed a five mile range and altitude of 1,500 feet as monotonous procedure. Lack of response to the controller's warning indicated the crew believed they were in good hands. Pilots instinctively maintain a close eye on instrumentation panels while on a runway approach. It is reasonable to assume the crew thought their course was correct until the tower suddenly stared at them through the cockpit windshield.

The crash provided rapid-fire rush hour news for radio and television talk shows that would otherwise be left to discuss mundane things like Thanksgiving turkey, or celebrity gossip of a dysfunctional nature. The VIP could not help wonder what happened as his limousine proceeded home. Arrangements had to be made for the trip's cancellation, with people to call and condolence letters to write. Under such circumstances, a shot of Bailey's to go with that morning coffee is certainly in order. He'd been in several close calls before. This included having his own aircraft shot out of the sky over Pacific waters during World War II, and serving as a bombing target for Saddam Hussein's agents while visiting Kuwait. If a cat truly did have nine lives, then this particular one managed to compile an impressive number. Nothing, however, could prepare him for realization that his flight crew, which he personally knew, ended up buried under flaming wreckage that produced dark clouds of smoke visible from miles away.

The following day's *Houston Chronicle*, known by less flattering names among the region's political right, headlined the crash with a gruesome wreckage photo. Front-page coverage contained a lengthy report warranting continuation inside the broadsheet. That spread provided further news of eyewitness accounts and preliminary theories. The immediate facing page comprised a dedicated smorgasbord of international events, which included Iran's latest and greatest denial of uranium enrichment. A strategically centered large photo and article noted the political climate over Ukraine's presidential election. Titled, "Thousands denounce runoff," had a subtitle referencing Russia's man beating Ukraine's native son, Viktor Yushchenko. Accusations were flying that Moscow operatives rigged the process. This stirred up an impressive mob. Some saw the whole charade as just another day of political monkey business by Kremlin thugs. Control in Kiev is considered essential to ensure Ukraine remained within Moscow's sphere of influence. Yushchenko, who barely survived a previous poisoning attempt by Russian assassins, demanded a new election. International agencies monitoring the debacle allege blatant voter fraud. Labels come cheap whether it is called the Union of Soviet Socialist Republics, Russian Federation, or Commonwealth of Independent States. Some things never change.

Upon finishing inside coverage of the Hobby crash, and reviewing Ukraine's political turmoil on the facing page, readers are confronted by a particular photograph in the lower right-hand corner. This person is tossing a soccer ball in the air, observing its flight with a grin, and keeping an open hand to catch the descent. The Reuters photograph is a stunning shot, catching the act at a precise moment. Some would immediately recognize the individual as Vladimir Putin, KGB alumnus and current President of the Russian Federation. A colorful subtitle, "Eye on the ball," perfectly describes the unusual photo and is also a fitting headline for events at Hobby.

Those who believe nation-states will take extreme measures to ensure their continuation and survival cannot help being captivated by this layout editing. In current times, however, everyone is a foreign policy expert. Anyone who suspiciously identifies this anomaly is simply ridiculed and classified as just another conspiracy fanatic. Such analysis, at least in the West, is triumphantly slandered by masses living in hedonistic denial. Thanks to a 'civilized' world's belief that evil intent is never aimed at people in free and open societies, advancing sinister motives are quickly dismissed and put to rest. People do not have time for acts of state. There are far more important things to do like party, go on vacation, or spend endless hours at the local shopping mall. All mankind must understand that world politics is about group hugs, rock concerts for military disarmament (of the West), and back-scratching tyrants so they will not act harshly.

There is, however, something easily missed by factions who take pleasure ridiculing those warning of foreign dangers. Is the date significant? Assistance is provided by turning the headline page and viewing a moving A3 photo. It is a service remembering the *'forty-first'* anniversary of John F. Kennedy's assassination. This occurred on 22 November 1963, and in Dallas where the destroyed Business Jet Services aircraft originated. The A3 photo subtitle, "JFK tragedy remembered," should cause reflection over plane crash coverage from previously read pages. JFK's murder comprised a political hit of global proportions. National security experts who possess real-world experience contemplate ways certain nations send their sensitive diplomatic messages. Some will be relieved knowing a vast majority of people will simply discard the event. Far more of their colleagues will express frustration over a cult of denial permeating apathetic political elites, and the thundering herd they lead. Perhaps this plane crash is a prearranged message to keep your hands off Ukraine. After all, the recipient of that message could very well be the VIP arriving for a doomed flight to Ecuador. He is none other than George Bush, *"forty-first"* President of the United States. You were warned.

WARNING

"Of men who have a sense of honor, more come through alive than are slain, but from those who flee comes neither glory or any help."
- Homer, *Iliad*

Part I

Offense

"Knowledge thus established is, I apprehend, the material with which the historian has to deal, out of which he has to build-up the artistic creation, the temple of truth, which a worthy history should aim to be. Like the material of the architect it will be found often refractory; not because truth is frequently unpleasant to be heard, especially by prepossessed ears, but because the multiplicity of details, often contradictory, not merely in appearance but in reality do not readily lend themselves to unity of treatment. It becomes thus exceedingly difficult to present numerous related truths in such a manner as to convey an impression which shall be true."

Alfred Thayer Mahan (Capt., USN), "Subordination in Historical Treatment," *Annual Report of the American Historical Association* (1902).

Chapter One

Introduction

"There is a distinct difference between education and intelligence. A person may be educated, but not intelligent. A person may be intelligent, but not educated. Once in a while you may be fortunate enough to find an individual who is both. However, if that person is both educated and intelligent, and they also happen to know the difference between the two...then you have really discovered someone."
- Harold W. Rood

"Words mean different things to different people." While a popularly used statement, it does not justify acceptance and, in fact, admonishment is warranted. Sea, land, air, and space power have suffered similar fates by falling victim to variances in meaning. National security's chain of policy-strategy-tactics has been subjected to an enormous degree of imagination over what constitutes an acceptable template. This has left experts locked in a raging battle while adjusting to a constantly evolving world. Damage from progressive ideas or, "diversity in strategic culture," among national security ranks has been a catastrophic exercise for those failing to grasp complexities of national grand strategy. Obedient ones blindly jumped onboard the latest fad and often paid dearly. Those aware and respectful of the trade's history and tradition usually came out victorious. Harold Rood's comment has similarities to problems surrounding a clear grasp of national grand strategy. Additionally, it serves as an analogy to national grand strategy's four products known as sea, land, air, and space power. National grand strategy performs a crucial role building consensus for various words and definitions created by this thesis. "Word puzzles" are not unique. Commenting to students engaged in studying peculiarities of international relations, K.J. Holsti wrote an analogy similar to semantic problems burdening sea and land power for centuries:

> If by now the reader is confused over the use of the terms *international relations, international politics,* and *foreign policy,* he or she joins the company of most experts in the field. There are many

definitions of these terms but little agreement upon which are the most adequate or where the distinctions among them lie. This lack of consensus is no doubt related to the problem of organizing devices. How one defines these terms is largely influenced by what one wants to investigate, and what one investigates is largely a function of a particular approach, model, or theory.[1]

Terminology addressing sea, land, air, and space power has suffered like forms of punishment. The practice is complicated by maritime power, naval power, and sea power, which are routinely intermingled to a degree they are mistaken to mean the same thing.

Holsti's observation is also reflected in an amusing explanation by George Kennan concerning the diplomatic community: "The central function for the diplomat is to serve as a sensitive, accurate, and intelligent channel of communication between one's own government and another one."[2] An overabundant stock of government officials exist to explain post-conciliation floggings because "in the international arena ambiguity may be counterproductive – and dangerous."[3] An awareness of nuclear annihilation can assist in grasping the importance of that statement. Kennan's own record illustrates many diplomatic breakdowns from his dealings with the Soviet Union.[4] With centuries of ham-fisted precedence to go by, individuals in both government and private sectors remain vulnerable to transmission snafus. An additional handicap of politics deals with those gifted at slinging words with cunning deception. Attempting to clarify intricacies of complex global events to a domestic audience is replaced by a Machiavellian process of merely telling the mob what they want to hear. Fortunately, discrepancies surrounding a perfect definition for sea power involve honest confusion over fundamentals. This is far more palatable than doing business with shifty lawyers and politicians.

The next several pages dissect and reconstruct national policy, grand strategy, strategy, and tactics. This process is accomplished under strict principles established by the world's great strategic thinkers. Research kicks off by first sweeping redundant and inappropriate chatter from national grand strategy's overburdened landscape. Only then can sea power surface and be explained in context with historic impact. Sea power's co-conspirators, which are comprised of land, air, and space power, enter the fray because of their tight relationship. All four interact on a professional level to achieve national policy objectives.

Research Challenge

New discoveries are common in any field, and certain revelations can shake theoretic stability. Research is especially challenging if a discipline is vague or novel. Oddly, definitions for sea and land power fall under this quandary even though they have been part of mankind's experiment for thousands of years. Air and space power are pristine additions that appeared in more recent decades. However, understanding both is already on equal footing with sea and land power. Difficulty defining sea and land power has to do with the era each was born, nurtured, and raised in. Both developed centuries before any attempt occurred to distinguish the phenomena.

Rear Admiral Alfred Thayer Mahan's research serves as the primary mechanism supporting this mission. Mahan's broad-based thoughts on sea power are exposed in Chapter 1 of his classic work, *The Influence of Sea Power upon History*. It is within Chapter 1, titled "Discussions of the Elements of Sea Power," that a foundation is retrieved.[5] Mahan's most famous book is actually a combination of two separate themes. Material from part one may be considered essential fundamentals comprising sea power.[6] The second part, which takes up the book's vast bulk, largely involves an investigation of naval and maritime affairs from 1660 to 1783.[7] Content is primarily a military history of events at sea that helped determine action on land. Many who attempted to define sea power based on Mahan's work were diverted by naval and maritime technicalities in Part II. This created a disregard toward sea power's role in broader national power terms.

Confusion over sea, land, air, and space power is underscored by Judsen Jusell and William Johnsen. Their discovery discloses a common theme of all four powers. Jusell found "space power" used for the first time in 1964. The earliest official definition occurred in 1988.[8] William Johnsen's findings are even more shocking. Johnsen could not locate an official definition for land power prior to 1998.[9] This is an omission of great consequence. Land power has existed for centuries, making such an oversight unprecedented. Johnsen seeks extra mileage with another relevant contribution:

> Land power historically has defeated sea power by taking enemy harbors and sea ports from the land. Additionally, ground-based anti-ship missiles have considerable potential to influence operations at sea; especially in the littoral regions. That influence undoubtedly will increase as technology improves.[10]

This research will contradict Johnsen's claim. Land forces used for "taking enemy harbors and sea ports," are actually elements of sea power since their objective is to influence events at sea. Naval ships launching cruise missile strikes at Taliban bases in Afghanistan, for example, are assets of land power during that time and mission. Admiral Mahan serves as project coordinator and spring-board for multiple reasons. His work came closest to meeting definitional totality but, as Paul Kennedy noted, he left behind just enough temptation to lead his successors astray:

> Ever since Captain Mahan wrote his seminal books at the end of the last century, the term [sea power] has become a commonplace in the language of naval men, politicians, strategists and historians: yet it remains difficult to define precisely in a few words, and even the writers who have attempted it have usually hastened to add many provisions and further comments in acknowledgment of the complexity of the topic. It is noticeable that Mahan himself did not seek to define what sea power is at the beginning of his studies, but preferred instead to show its nature by historical examples and commentary in order to prevent it remaining 'vague and insubstantial.'[11]

Mahan places his scholarly brethren in a state of frustrating confusion. Why did he come so close to a definitive *tour de force* and yet walk away from an encore? By choosing summary over precision, fundamentals over technical detail, and spatial growth over stagnation, Mahan preferred describing sea power as a foundation supported by six unwavering footings:

- Geographic Position
- Physical Conformation
- Extent of Territory
- Number of Population
- National Character
- Character of Government[12]

Geography's influence upon Mahan in four of six traits is clear. The remaining two features, which are national character and character of government, carry great consequence but they cannot be quantified. This research classifies what is called "power resources" as essential sea power components. They are derivatives of Mahan's six characters and each is widely known from previous discussions.[13] Power resources have not, until now, been enshrined into a cohesive bond supporting all four power generators.

Power resources comprise two categories consisting of fundamental and fluid factors. Each is an underlying feature that enables states to design, create, deploy, and engage a power generator with authority. Characteristics include obvious ones, such as geography, time, and natural resources. Some are crafty, such as a willingness to fight, intelligence, and logistics. Each power resource possesses three subcategories (elements). Elements give resources strength. Willingness to fight, for example, is a power resource composed of elements called war history, culture, and solidarity. Power resource modeling provides analytical tools to understand and measure sea power. It includes quantitative and qualitative features to assist strategic thinkers.

Mahan has suffered havoc from critics able to exploit hindsight. This is a common theme for many strategic legends. Targets are often unable to mount a defense due to biological time-clocks. Professional allies are left to defend the honor and manhood of their ancestor. Though predecessor research is worthy of selective modification based on changing parameters in the modern era, each legend's contribution remains a solid foundation. Mahan sets atop the enemy acquisition list, primarily because of his broad theoretical principle surrounding sea power. Detractors get wrapped around stale specifics having nothing to do with Mahan's superseding thesis. This is a common theme for politics and history:

> Of the difficulty here existing history bears sufficient proof. Not merely the discovery of new evidence, but different modes of presenting the same facts, give contradictory impressions of the same series of events. One or the other is not true; neither perhaps is even closely true. Without impeaching the integrity of the historian, we are then forced to impeach his presentment, and to recognize by direct logical inference that the function of history is not merely to accumulate facts, at once in entirety and in accuracy, but to present them in such ways that the wayfaring man, whom we now call the man in the street, shall no err therein.[14]

Academic research is tasked with finding answers to where, what, how, and why something happens the way it does. How, for example, did Lech Walesa, creator of Poland's Solidarity movement,

thrive on the world stage at the shipyard in Gdansk?[15] Why were
"dissident leaders" able to proliferate in East Bloc countries when the
Soviet Union has a long and colorful history of squashing such naughty
behavior?[16] What caused US Central Intelligence Agency (CIA) assets
to miss forecasting the Communist Bloc's collapse? Instead, America's
premier intelligence service became the butt of jokes on the late-night
comedy circuit. Considering the chummy relationships between senior
Cable News Network (CNN) executives and Soviet leaders - which
included establishing the Good Will Games - accepting CIA's passive
poise seems a safer bet. Perhaps it is worth contemplating if any change
of political substance has taken place:

> Among leading European politicians the percentage of those involved
> in Communist, pro-Communist, leftist or even terrorist activity is
> shocking. Socialist (to say the least) rites are reflected in political
> correctness. Membership in the Communist Party or of a terrorist
> organization is no obstacle to the highest positions and most
> prestigious honors. A clear sign of the times. It is hard to imagine
> President Eisenhower calling Nikita Khruschchev "a man with whom
> he could do business." And how, by comparison, could one explain
> the declaration of President of the United States George Bush,
> regarding the Soviet Chekist, now holding the office of President of
> the Russian Federation, Vladimir Putin, that he is a man worthy of
> esteem?[17]

The surface is often an illusion for nastier things below. An 84
year-old Nazi in Buenos Aires can be arrested at a hospice while
gasping for air in an oxygen tent, and yet a Communist is viewed as
"progressive." The West must rejoice with collective singing, though
the faithful followers of Marx outclassed Hitler by murdering over five
times as many people (200,000,000). These figures are not relevant
because it is the thought that counts. They did it for the environment.

Perhaps the CIA did not miss a thing, while John Q. Public
lapped up Communist Bloc gala events like a Hollywood matinee.[18]
Could an attempted *coup d'état* in the Union of Soviet Socialist
Republics (USSR) during August 1991 possibly be staged? The coup
leadership's freshly starched shirts and finely tailored suits had all the
wholesome markings of a Chinese laundry. Why did Moscow allow
Western reporters inside city limits to report on an underway rebellion?
Traditionally, the foreign press is always first to disappear when this
form of regime change is put in practice.

Tradition vs. Revision

Grueling investigations can produce disturbing results. A scholar may feel abandoned or academically betrayed because their discovery is not a "correct" outcome sought by supporters. This particularly applies to politics because scholars must backtrack, correct records, amend memoirs, or challenge news reports. Carefully groomed reputations are at stake. It should not come as a surprise when people are held accountable.[19] Academic research must ensure truth is not sacrificed for political convenience. Unfortunately, political convenience became a problem in the West during tense Cold War events. Fear of political instability routinely became an excuse for not correcting misperceived "facts." A scholar thinks in terms of decades and centuries. They see more harm not immediately rectifying a foggy affair. Lyndon Johnson, for example, justified avoiding Soviet-Cuban sanctioning of John F. Kennedy's assassination by arguing revelation "could lead us into a war that could cost forty million lives."[20] He informed Warren Commission investigators that "speculation about Oswald's motivation should be cut off, and we should have some basis for rebutting the thought that this was a Communist conspiracy."[21] A supposedly unbiased presidential murder investigation wound up fixed before even getting started.[22]

There is danger the opposite extreme could occur from over-zealous aggression.[23] Most scholars will not admit relativism is a utopian figment of their imagination. Every person possesses bias and yet it is routinely exploited by a nihilist to cover their historical "findings."[24] Political shenanigans are often found hiding within those discoveries. The ideal scholar restrains personal bias, while aware it does exist. Mahan's warning over recording facts remained germane throughout the twentieth century. Guenter Lewy identifies a pattern by so-called "progressive" intellectuals who have absorbed uncharacteristic motives in research appearing politically suspicious:

> During much of human history, intellectuals – individuals concerned with ideas and ideals – have functioned as guardians and defenders of traditional values. In modern times on the other hand, it is generally agreed, intellectuals have exhibited a pronounced tendency to criticize the established order of things.[25]

Changes noted by Lewy reaches a zenith with contemporary events. Policy issues and political battles normally contained within the public domain infect the academy to a degree that a 'proper' hypothesis becomes fact. Political correctness rules the day, tainting an arena for unbiased scholarly research. Studying art, poetry, chemistry, or math should be straightforward pursuits.[26] Practicing politics in a classroom subjects students to a constantly changing environment of uncertainty. Politics is incorporated in art, for example, so that art becomes controversial for artistic village people.[27] It still remains politics behind the art which causes controversy.[28] Those in a faculty who rebel against the traditional order are routinely portrayed as enlightened and progressive. They have seen a better way and everyone should get in proper order.[29] This elite view, as Thomas Sowell argues, is transposed from "ivory towers of academe" to institutions of political power:

> The quest for cosmic justice via the judiciary – law as an "agent of change," as it is often phrased – quietly repeals one of the foundations of the American Revolution. It reduces a free people to a subject people, subject now to the edicts of unelected judges enforcing "evolving standards" and made more heedless by their exalted sense of moral superiority. It is one of the most dangerous of the many ways in which towering presumptions are a threat to the freedoms of Americans.[30]

A traditional scholar is placed in a very difficult negotiating position with a revisionist. The latter is fully aware of a traditionalist's position. The traditionalist, however, may not know where a revisionist stands. Revisionism has the grace of time and patience on its side. Those supporting revision win because of incremental approaches with time.[31] A revisionist wins when "compromise" is reached. They must only return at a later date to demand another compromise. Transition takes place to a newly established center, which is relabeled as middle ground. That new position of "moderation" may have once been a far left radical point.[32] Either way, the traditionalist has lost hold as a bastion of continuity. They may pay dearly for opposing the "unbiased" left.[33] A traditionalist who survives often compromises for the sake of stability. A revisionist, who is never on solid ground, made a minor adjustment that is still considered a victory:

> Towards the preservation of your government, and the permanency of your present happy state, it is requisite, not only that you steadily discountenance irregular oppositions to its acknowledged authority, but also that you resist with care the spirit of innovation upon its principles, however specious the pretexts. One method of assault may

be to effect, in the forms of the Constitution, alterations which will impair the energy of the system, and thus to undermine what cannot be directly overthrown.[34]

George Washington's farewell address to the American people is a warning often ignored by those too terrified of the consequences.

Chapter Two

Fundamentals

"A day on the ground somewhere will teach you more than a year of flying over it."
- Thomas E. Ricks, *Making the Corps*

Mahan frequently warned about the academic path of least resistance. Unfortunately, vague and misleading definitions from the start made that path too tempting to avoid. Attempts to reverse course developed into a daunting task because of vast numbers heading down the slippery slope. Missing a defining target for all four power generators and supporting resources came about for multiple reasons:

- Confusion over application of sea, land, air, and space power is compounded by the passage of time and a tolerance of fashionable ideas.
- Work of substance is discarded as outdated and creates a tendency to digress into new material of little value.
- Too many definitions of enormous variance have come into existence causing sharp disagreement.
- A serious definition is glossed over as time goes by and more chatter is added by developments having little substance.
- Analysis becomes skewed by cosmetic events, which opens the door to alternative agendas and erroneous parameters.

This state of affairs is expected based on development of sea power's growing curve before anyone attempted a definition. It is not unusual for scholars to debate political issues for years, decades, and even centuries. Carl von Clausewitz's *On War*, for example, has been disputed since 1815. Jon Sumida reflected on his own experience while conducting arduous research of Mahan's fundamental concepts:

> In 1989, Colin Gray argued that 'a reconsideration of Mahan is overdue.' During 1995 and 1996, the author of the present essay, under the auspices of the Woodrow Wilson International Center for Scholars in Washington DC, was able to devote a full year to a

systematic reconsideration of all Mahan's books, prompted by his own misgivings about the basic accuracy of the existing interpretation of Mahan's writing, and knowledge that these doubts were shared by others. The goal of the inquiry was to answer two fundamental questions: Did Mahan's books at any level represent a coherent body of thought, and if so, what was its nature.[1]

Sumida came close to identifying a single solution for virtually every contradiction surrounding Mahan. The answer to his questions is found in a concise definition for sea power. Sumida's frustration, combined with a vast quantity of existing definitions, makes clear why Mahan must be reconsidered. Though they can fill several pages, no definition provides the scope and flexibility to fulfill sea power's needs.

Background

Collateral issues of little value caused people to wrongly divorce sea power from its marriage with the other three power generators. This mistakenly led to disengagement from national grand strategy's incubator. As a result, each member of the power generator harem got separated by a wall high enough to conceal commonality. Domiciles in the vehicle of national grand strategy became dislodged from reality. It is within national grand strategy that sea power is bred, grown to maturity, and housed. Consequences are seen in a propensity of states to position each power generator in strategic arenas. This has the opposite effect of inflexible walls separating each power generator. A wall belongs, but that barrier goes between grand strategy and strategy. This is justified to prevent cross-border incursions which can camouflage strategic and grand strategic differences.

Sea, land, air, and space power exist to accomplish tasks set forth by policy-makers. *Policy is the art and science of using logic and reason to create decisions and set direction for implementation of national grand strategic designs.* Sea power is a mainstay of national grand strategy and couching national grand strategy under the facade of strategy jeopardizes power generator options. Williamson Murray and Mark Grimsley expand on this by considering Liddell Hart's definition for strategy:

> The concept of "strategy" has proven notoriously difficult to define. Many theorists have attempted it, only to see their efforts wither beneath the blasts of critics. B.H. Liddell Hart's well known

definition – "the art of distributing and applying military means to fulfill the ends of policy" – may suggest the limitations of the definitional approach, for this forthright but unhappy example restricts the word strictly to *military* affairs, whereas in practice strategy operates in a much broader sphere.[2]

Murray and Grimsley confirm national grand strategy's contractual obligation. Resource allocation for tactical theatres is an assignment of strategy. Hart's definition identifies national grand strategy and strategy as a package, which is wrong. Murray and Grimsley's characterization of strategy's broader area of interest reinforces sea power's contribution at all times. This includes areas not restricted by a military, naval, or maritime context. National grand strategy warrants separation from strategy because each possesses unique traits. This domain surpasses Hart's purely military orientation.

National policy is created and dictated by those holding power. It involves soliciting ideas, reviewing suggestions, deciding on a position, building support through consensus (voluntary or forced), and crafting a statement of purpose. In an ideal world it drives bureaucratic machinery. Theoretically, elected officials receive a mandate based on policy proposals presented during an election campaign. In reality, a number of factors determine systemic success or failure. These include bureaucratic motion, form of government, ideology, and leadership characteristics. Constitutional republics are faced with the real possibility dirty laundry may be exposed. Enemies seeking exploitation avenues eagerly await these opportunities.[3] Dictatorships, on the other hand, have no problem cracking a whip. Getting 97% turnout at polls is a simple exercise and, amazingly, 99.9% of those voting choose the party in power. The remaining .1% are labeled "counter-revolutionaries" and escorted to re-education camps. Constitutional republics face burdens of checks and balances, which is insurance from the abuse of power. Checks and balances can cause stagnation and malaise to the relief of those believing in limited government.

Policy goals risk ending with the wrong interpretation. Opening statements from Chapter 1 underline that danger. A policy definition from the previous page achieves in fewer words the same goal as a "proposed course of action of a person, group, or government within a given environment providing obstacles and opportunities which the policy was proposed to utilize and overcome in an effort to reach a goal or realize an objective or a purpose."[4] Policy-formulation environments can blossom into hostile cat fights. Various special interest groups vie for influence, countermanding each other in route to winning the taxpayer funded prize.[5] National policy may be attached to ideological mechanisms. A Marxist economy may seem intoxicating for some because policy is tied to a governing institution gleefully claiming to be looking after the toiling masses (Dictatorship of the Proletariat). Realism takes a pragmatic approach in policy-making processes (Richard Nixon), while idealism concentrates on moral principle (Jimmy Carter). The better administration can balance both.

Policy-making in free societies can be a monumental challenge. Those devising policy must be alert for public sensitivities. This is complicated by a free media and press, which often have their own agenda. Growth in news-based opinion polling has managed to create an entire industry. Polls become the news. Opinions of the press and public are seldom made with all facts in hand, yet points of view are freely given.[6] An administration sensitive to opinion polling may make poor policy decisions over a desire to follow media spin. Rare is the national leader who did not take into consideration public opinion.

This relationship to sea power is found at the point where policy and national grand strategy meet. National grand strategy incorporates policy and directs it toward power generators. Power resources are allocated based on national policy, and a plan of action takes shape. Political leadership in a multi-party democracy must maintain concern for public support. A wise competitor patiently looks for signs of intent at the national policy level. If political leaders fear polling results, then an adversary benefits by manipulating opinion.

Connecting national grand strategy with physical acts of war is often wrongly inferred. Edward Mead Earle's definition is dangerously close to that view: "That which so integrates the policies and armaments of the nation that the resort to war is either rendered unnecessary or is undertaken with the maximum chance of victory."[7] Earle describes the atmosphere between national grand strategy and strategy with a follow-on statement: "It is in this broader sense that the word strategy is used in this volume."[8] The line separating strategy and national grand strategy is blurred by insinuating that strategy overlaps national grand strategy's dominant theme. Geoffrey Sloan successfully distinguishes this dividing line with his definition of national grand strategy:

> The process of planning, co-ordinating and directing the use of all resources of a nation or an alliance – social, political, economic and military – towards the attainment of a political objective.[9]

A minor word addition is appropriate. Adding "creating" to his mix of "planning, coordinating and directing," firmly encases national grand strategy's package. Alastair Buchan prematurely reinforced Sloan by arguing "the real content of strategy is concerned not merely with war and battles but with the application or maintenance of force so that it contributes most effectively to the achievement of political objectives."[10] Buchan takes strategy to a line where, once crossed, it becomes national grand strategy. Sir Julian Corbett crossed that line by describing strategy in context of national grand strategy:

> The last thing that an explorer arrives at is a complete map that will cover the whole ground he has traveled, but for those who come after him and would profit by and extend his knowledge his map is the first thing with which they will begin. So it is with strategy.[11]

Corbett's explorer would be the nation-state, and "ground he has traveled," its history. His map serves as national policies from the past, and national grand strategy enabled those policy objectives to be fulfilled. National grand strategy is energy that allows a course of action to continue. It is a preparatory and implementation process which can take a long time to develop. Less patient types will be frustrated. National grand strategy is less susceptible to rapid shifts seen at strategic and tactical levels. A naval fleet, for example, can take several years to design, finance, and build. In the 1980s US Secretary of the Navy (SECNAV), John Lehman, announced plans for a 600-ship fleet. It approached that figure in the years that followed. But, by the end of the decade, the goal backfired and started heading in reverse. Decline eventually reached a point that, by 2006, half the desired fleet size remained.

What is the cost of a small fleet caught off-guard before it has time to build? Mahan's description of France's predicament should haunt anyone believing naval power is an instantaneous fling:

> The virtual annihilation of the French fleet in 1759 was indeed followed by an outburst of national enthusiasm for the navy, skillfully fostered and guided by Choiseul. "Popular feeling took up the cry, from one end of France to the other, 'The navy must be restored.' Gifts of cities, corporations, and private individuals raised funds. A prodigious activity sprang up in the lately silent ports; everywhere ships were building and repairing." The minister also recognized the need of restoring the discipline and tone, as well as the material of the navy. The hour, however, was too late; the middle of a great and

unsuccessful war is no time to begin preparations. "Better late than never" is not so safe a proverb as "In time of peace prepare for war."[12]

Difference in time between national grand strategy and strategy is stark. The same applies to tactics and strategy. Logistics support for Soviet efforts on land is a reality accurately showing profound disparity between national grand strategy and strategy. Westerners often deride the primitive nature of transportation networks in "less advanced" societies. Perceived low quality roads in the USSR during World War II turned out to be quite a quagmire for "more advanced" Germans. Arrogance can create a serious degree of overconfidence, blurring the barrier between national grand strategy and strategy. The design and poor condition of Soviet transportation systems may have been intentional. Liddell Hart identifies an interesting problem the German Army had upon encountering this scheme:

> The Allies' progress in conquering Germany benefited much from the fine network of roads available to them in the country they were invading, in the same way that the Germans had profited from the excellence of the French road system in 1940 – whereas the Germans' heaviest handicap in the invasion of Russia had been the scarcity and poorness of the roads they found there. This condition fatally multiplied the time-and-space problem which the Germans had to solve in pursuing victory there.
>
> How we are brought to reflect on one of the crucial factors, and deeper lessons, of the war. For Russia was saved less by the degree of her technical progress under the Communist regime than by the degree to which the primitive conditions of her past still persisted. If the Soviet Government had modernized its roads in the same way as other parts of its equipment a German victory would have been much more difficult to prevent. The bad roads – quickly turned into quagmires by any downpour of rain – held up the mass of wheeled transport which backed up the German tank spearheads, and did more than any human resistance to check these from overrunning the land in decisive time.[13]

Siberian oil reserves are the envy of every nation. Those reserves are worthless if a sophisticated transportation network is not in place to distribute the booty. Pipelines help solve a problem previously confined to roads and rail. While roads can remain primitive, pipelines pre-empt a need for modernization while providing leverage over those seeking your product. Should European Union (EU) behavior fail to meet Russian standards, then Moscow can simply close the pipeline valve 5,000 miles away and challenge anyone to travel that far to reopen it. This is national grand strategy, which is a more spatial management tool than strategic planning. Complexity behind keeping national grand strategy and strategy separated is largely due to strategy, which has suffered its own peculiar descriptions.

Edward Luttwak and Stuart Koehl, two highly respected strategic minds, do a remarkable job of challenging the average "Joe":

> The wisdom of war, which differs from other wisdom because the logic of war differs from normal logic. As against the linear/formal logic of everyday life, the logic of war, and more broadly of conflict, is paradoxical ("if you want peace, prepare for war") and dialectical (action yields not only a result, but also a reaction that modifies, and may utterly reverse, that result). In the realm of conflict, action cannot therefore proceed straightforwardly, but instead will normally reach a culminating point of achievement, which evokes corresponding adversary reactions so that decline ensues in the absence of additional effort.[14]

Are there any questions? Luttwak and Koehl's technical explanation invites a lot of grief. Their opening comment that "the logic of war differs from normal logic" depends on personal and cultural views of war. The clash of nations is not unusual and, in fact, it is ongoing. Therefore, the logic of war is actually quite normal, though it does not have to be a socially accepted standard of behavior. Luttwak and Koehl proceed with more clear-cut definitions:

> The art and science of developing and using political, economic, psychological, and military forces as necessary during peace and war, to afford the maximum support to policies, in order to increase the probabilities and favorable consequences of victory and lessen the chances of defeat.[15]

> A science, an art, or a plan (subject to revision) governing the raising, arming, and utilization of the military forces of a nation (or coalition) to the end that its interests will be effectively promoted or secured against enemies, actual, potential, or merely presumed.[16]

Murray and Grimsley's comment on strategy is now in a better frame of reference. Problems at tactical levels complicate strategy directly and grand strategy indirectly. Carl von Clausewitz's warning over friction is a unique tactical event easily camouflaged from untrained eyes. Alarm and panic generally ensue for the taxi squad.[17]

Tactics describes actual engagements, or contact between competing parties. Words such as "combat" are incorporated to note the clash between groups. A propensity to assume that physical carnage is involved justifies caution. Many military weapons now developed serve to demobilize an adversary's abilities without seeking mass annihilation. Tactical weapons used by law enforcement are designed to rein in aggression with little harm. Rubber bullets and tear gas disburse out-of-control mobs, while avoiding a lot of negative press. Clausewitz defines tactics as, "The use of armed forces in the engagement." This explanation may cause a mistaken belief bloodshed is a foregone conclusion.[18] The USSR helped the West discover tactical action is not confined to armed military force. They cooperated by providing several examples. Defining tactics requires consideration of asymmetric methods: *"The detailed methods used to carry out strategic designs in the theatre of actual engagement."*

Wylie Observation

The free flow of commerce on the sea is explained by J. C. Wylie using Mahan's focus on sea lanes and lines of communication. Additionally, unfettered access is imperative for the US to project military power on foreign shores. The point is epitomized by those gallant acts of US Marines during World War II:

> As it did in Mahan's writings a century ago, as it did for the United States in the middle years of this century, one nearly universal vehicle for this leverage, for extension of control today may be found in sea power, not as a policy in itself, but as a *basis* for policy. Exploitation of this capability to extend some measure of control, more often a degree of influence, from the world's great interconnecting maritime communication system, from the sea on to the land, is the great asset of sea power then and today. A kind and degree of control that may be direct or subtle, immediate or slow, forceful or benign, the variations are infinite – some measure of control or influence extended from the sea on to the land.[19]

The corollary often missed is the insignificant difference between strategic principles of supply lines at sea with those on land.

Sea lanes are the same as pipelines from Siberia and each can be a great benefit to the controlling party. This relationship is easily lost in cosmetic figures that propel analysis into complex details having little value to far greater domains of sea, land, air, and space power. Wylie combines Mahan in context with the era his work evolved and changes now underway: "It is no longer a world centered on Europe. Nothing less than a world-wide comprehension will now serve the strategist."[20] Caution must be used regarding regional dominance. A wise strategist prudently ensures a world-wide comprehension is maintained. Mahan's concern over a rising Asian power is well documented. Wylie correctly ties Mahan's earliest writings to historical events in Europe, which is where sea power primarily flourished in comparison to later world-wide exploitation. But Mahan became astute enough to realize the planet is a very big place, with a diverse culture. His vision of an Asian superpower, in fact, is now beginning to appear quite real.

Mischaracterizing sea power is a frequent exercise when its application is absorbed into naval power:

> **Sea Power** *n.* **1.** A nation having significant naval strength. **2.** Naval strength.[21]

Houghton Miffin's description is superficial and adroitly summarizes poor understanding surrounding sea power. Thompson Lenfestey provides continuity:

> **Sea Power:** A nation with a navy. Naval strength that allows a country to keep open sea-lanes between itself and its allies for the purpose of conducting trade or military operations.[22]

Absorbing sea power into naval power dominates designs of those pursuing a definition. Lenfestey's statement of "naval strength that allows a country to keep open sea-lanes" is commendable at defining command of the sea. Concentration on naval strength steers Lenfestey into "trade or military operations." This created an impression no other purpose exists. No single culprit is responsible for missing sea power's vast domain. In fact, Jon Sumida accurately states Mahan's own frustration:

> Other important concepts that Mahan also handled in a complex and therefore prone to be misunderstood way were "sea power" and

"naval power." In his work, the terms were on occasion treated as near equivalents, and blame for the tendency to conflate the two cannot, therefore, be attributed solely to careless reading. But Mahan nonetheless considered sea power and naval power to be different phenomena. Sea power was the combination of the activities of world trade generated by an international economy and world-trade defense by a national navy or transnational naval consortium. Because this phenomenon was driven by individuals or groups in search of private gain, Mahan saw it as self-sustaining. Naval power, on the other hand, was organized force created by particular governments – that is, a subset of sea power.[23]

Sumida made a direct hit. He excuses Mahan's own difficulty defining sea power because of bureaucratic machinery burdening society. This gets complicating in a democracy because those in charge of political organs may give greater priority to winning an upcoming election. Individuals can deny themselves clear sight of national security dangers for the sake of pacifying toiling masses with largess. This discomfort does not apply to totalitarian regimes:

> For Mahan the critical factor was the latter – the democratic propensity to spend inadequately on defense not only made it necessary to define naval supremacy in transnational terms in the twentieth century but prompted his formulation of political, political-economic, and governmental argument as a means of educating legislators and thus moderating their parsimony in naval matters.[24]

Mahan attempted to educate an American electorate who were struggling to see over the ocean's horizon:

> So long as the United States had no external possessions, it was comparatively easy to blind people to the usefulness of a navy, or to the necessity for it. A navy for coast defence only was then plausible, though a deceitful cry; and it was a very easy further step to say that fortifications, stationary land defences, were cheaper and more effective. On the narrow ground of passive defence, that is true; therefore, ignorance of military principles being characteristic of mankind generally, and of Americans perhaps particularly, the need of a mobile force to act offensively could not obtain recognition.[25]

US Navy Admiral Claude Ricketts came close to accurately defining sea power over 40 years ago, while also attempting to duplicate Mahan's effort at turning around public indifference:

The measure of a nation's total capability to exploit the benefits that oceans have to offer. In its far-reaching political sense it includes all assets that are employed for advantageous use of the oceans for commercial and military purposes."[26]

This is a refreshing improvement over Houghton Miffin's explanation. Admiral Ricketts addresses sea power in expansive terms, but his application of "measure" and "total" are not entirely fulfilling. Additionally, singling out "capability" should be avoided on its own. It threatens to demarcate operations from his definition by insinuating movement of force is not part of sea power's amalgamation. A "distinct difference" exists between potential energy (stored energy) found in "capability," and converting that capability into kinetic energy (energy in motion). Capability may look good on paper, and it often does depending on who is fudging the numbers. However, when put in motion it must perform according to operating instructions. An accurate definition must allow for "ability" to transform potential into practice with a degree of freedom and mastery. A "sleeping giant" needs to mobilize and commit forces necessary to win a decisive victory, especially if that adversary were to launch a surprise attack. That "sleeping giant" must maintain the peace and service requirements at sea once victory is achieved. Carl Amme explained this energy conversion by remarking "if the forms of power do not permit its use in action to achieve desirable ends, then the forms may be outmoded."[27] Amme is confirming that tons of capability may sparkle on a power-point presentation, but the inability to place assets in action makes a well-padded portfolio inconsequential.

Defining Power Generators

Deeply ingrained, well-intentioned, but inadequately developed research patterns risk compounding matters later. Though an unintended consequence, Mahan's own research got hijacked and diverted on the wrong course. Sea power then fell into a menace with scathing results. The predicament caused several vital elements to be depreciated over time and falsely labeled as superficial. Each are revised and reinforced as crucial products of national power's portfolio. Futuristic potentialities, whether social, commercial, or military, have been incorporated to show continuity. Forecasting sea power's future configuration is done to show the definition's ability to adapt. Three criteria were established to form an enduring definition:

- It must be flexible, yet maintain enough rigidity to meet the purpose of acting as a foundation.
- It must be concise, while broad enough to grab the vastness of sea power's meaning.
- It must be comprehensible, although the topic has a long record of evasive behavior.

A definition surpassing expectations of these guidelines resulted. Avoiding strict parameters allowed the invisible nature of sea, land, air, and space power to be exposed. Pressure influences events in a specified geographic domain from points not necessarily associated with that region. All four power generator definitions emphasize a relationship to each other based on three paramount realities:

- Interchanging capability of the definitions is without question. Distinguishing characteristics separating each definition is geographic domain.
- Physical objects in a geographic realm are not determining factors. The targeted geographic region of pressure application is the singular feature.
- Sea, land, air, and space power act in accordance with the art and science of national grand strategy. It is not a marriage of convenience, but a combination where a single power generator has difficulty surviving without support from the other three.

Each explanation is formulated around schools of history, geography, economics, culture, and politics. These faculties are coupled to theories of great strategic minds. Sun Tzu Wu taught us to never forget power can be evasive if that is intended by those possessing it. Sea, land, air, and space power serve as good examples. Boundaries are not constrictive, but allow room for overlap where and when warranted. *Geographic identity of sea, land, air, or space power does not always specify where activity is taking place. It is not based on the appearance of physical elements. The label purely identifies geographic location of the recipient. Pressure sources come from a complete package of elements making a contribution to influencing events. This is regardless of source or point of origin.* A region manipulated by a pressure source does not mean it is within that geographic boundary. A source can be fluid and identified as a product of any region. Classification is strictly determined by location where pressure is applied:

Sea Power: The ability to deploy the total capability of active and passive national resources for the purpose of influencing events at sea or other navigable waters associated with the sea.

Land Power: The ability to deploy the total capability of active and passive national resources for the purpose of influencing events on land.

Air Power: The ability to deploy the total capability of active and passive national resources for the purpose of influencing events in the atmosphere.

Space Power: The ability to deploy the total capability of active and passive national resources for the purpose of influencing events in space.

These definitions may seem repetitive. Similarities are many and, in reality, geography is the only item of distinction. Oxford University Press defines power as "the ability to get people [or things] to do what they would not otherwise have done."[28] Sea, land, air, and space "power" evolve from sources not inevitably in their territorial domain. Distinguishing ability and capability is important. Use of phrases, "ability to deploy," "active and passive," and "total capability," accomplishes all Admiral Ricketts sought to achieve.

Sea power is often considered something entirely confined to parameters of the sea. All four generators fall victim to geographic cages because they are habitually judged as strategic assets rather than products of national grand strategy. Those plagued with poor strategic knowledge may stand on the beach witnessing a ship cutting across the horizon. They falsely assume this graphic visual is sea power, which is restricted by limits. It is not until explosive projectiles rain down on their heads, and an amphibious force of marines is heading ashore, do these wayward souls realize what is unfolding. Sea power transformed itself into land power and those assets are simply showing up for work. Unhappy recipients on the beach gauged an observation in terms of illusionary geographic boundaries, without realizing pressure points transcend superficial lines. A submarine sent to sea to launch a satellite in space is a value belonging to space power. That does not take anything away from physical realities that the submarine serves as a "maritime" or "naval" asset. Influencing events in space simply made it a temporary instrument of "space" power. Each power generator's essence involves their service feeding national grand strategy with energy to support strategic operations.

John Noel identifies sea power as "the resources of a country in material and personnel which may influence control of the world's oceans and the air above those waters."[29] Noel generates enthusiasm until crossing geographic parameters with "the air above those waters." This has the opposite effect from examples given. The atmosphere is an entirely unique domain. Sea power assets applied to influence control over air, wherever the air may be at a given time, are products of air power. Additionally, Noel inadvertently omitted navigable inland waters from consideration by specifying oceans.

Using "influencing" in place of "pressure" for each power generator definition resulted from a desire to recognize passive features. This does not take away from pressure's value, and Mahan consistently identified its importance throughout his work:

> It is not the taking of individual ships or convoys, be they few or many, that strikes down the money power of a nation; it is the possession of that overbearing power on the sea which drives the enemy's flag from it, or allows it to appear only as a fugitive; and which, by controlling the great common, closes the highways by which commerce moves to and from the enemy's shores. This overbearing power can only be exercised by great navies, and by them (on the broad sea) less efficiently now than in the days when the neutral flag had not its present immunity.[30]

Technology available today requires only minor modification to Mahan's explanation. Stamina and relevancy remain while it is technology that eventually becomes outdated. Though referencing sea power specifically, adjustment of Mahan's explanation describes land, air, and space power as well. Fundamentals of national grand strategy maintain continuity and are not uprooted with time: "Warfare comprises everything related to the fighting forces – everything to do with their creation, maintenance, and use."[31] Those hustled by technological wizards may overlook that which does not alter the national power train. Power generator definitions honor that mainstay while allowing room for engineering advances.

Collateral Definitions

Mahan identified a clear line between strategy and tactics by distinguishing physical contact that occurs at the tactical level.[32] This environment is highly porous as opposing forces engage and disengage from contact. Power in various sizes and shapes evolves during this stage. Definitions for military, naval, and maritime power refine that categorization:

Military Power: The capability for deploying and the ability to exercise designated branches of the armed forces to fulfill military objectives set forth by the policy-making apparatus of a nation.

Naval Power: The craft of organizing, training, and equipping a maritime military force for prompt deployment and sustained combat at sea, to establish a national presence, or maintain stability.

Maritime Power: The sum of maritime assets and their ability to operate on, over, and under the sea or other navigable waters.

Three definitions reveal profound differences that clarify confusion associated with sea power. Each establishes precise limits, while holding value adding to the sum of sea power. All make sundry contributions to land, air, and space power as needed, but that is where similarities end. Military force used to influence events in atmospheric regions is considered air force. Military force used to influence activity in space is appropriately labeled space force. Sum totals of all activities conducted for purposes of dictating events in the atmosphere or space transitions into air and space power. Actual military branches assigned to specific geographic regions are identified as land force power, air force power, and space force power. This is in keeping with proper recognition of naval power. Maritime power surpasses all terms in a false belief it means the same thing as sea power. Maritime is a method of classifying physical objects having assiduity to the sea. This could apply to a ballistic missile submarine or Flipper the dolphin. A ballistic missile submarine is an asset of land power because its mission is to launch nuclear strikes against land targets. It still remains a maritime product and, because of military value, it remains a naval ship. J. C. Wylie explains this relationship by incorporating a sailor's view toward maritime application:

In the maritime pattern of thought, the sailor sees his tasks falling into two major fields, and while they are separated here simply for convenience in this discussion, one should recognize that in practice they are so closely interwoven that it is hard to tell where one stops and the other starts. One half of the task is the establishment of control of the sea which, of course, includes the depths of its waters and the air above it. The other half is the exploitation of that control of the sea toward extension of control from the sea on to the land.[33]

Military power is routinely embroiled in sea power's controversy. Military power often finds a way of becoming wrapped in all four power generators to such a degree that distinction is lost. This is identical to problems over naval and maritime power.

Work by Clausewitz truly represents a product of consistent value. Upgrading for the twenty-first century is certainly in order. An example of the tweaking needed can be found with his definition for strategy. War, as Clausewitz viewed it, came in terms of battlefield clashes by great armies. His explanation for tactics states it as "the use of the armed forces in engagements."[34] He goes on to describe strategy as "the employment of the battle as the means towards the attainment of the object of the war."[35] Allowance is needed for various types of warfare now waged by modern states. In fact, proceeding with Clausewitz would be counterproductive without a clear grasp of war. People are inclined to visualize death and destruction when the word is applied to multi-national intercourse. While physical carnage can take place, many CIA operatives would argue that war can transpire in discreet ways.

A realist believes war is a continuous exercise of international affairs. This is an accurate position, though characteristics differ. Its application is identical to rules governing tactics, strategy, grand strategy and policy. Perception is influenced by an organization, profession, and business. War is a season, in an athlete's mind. Great battles take place when teams compete. Companies strive to increase market share by waging war against each other. Policy-making's model is used in pursuit of competitive advantage. Events between nations are larger in scope, with final outcomes more costly. Sun Tzu Wu states "to win one hundred victories in one hundred battles is not the acme of skill. To subdue the enemy without fighting is the acme of skill."[36] Sun explained the purist form of winning a war and his colleagues provide additional warning:

I make the enemy see my strengths as weaknesses and my weaknesses as strengths while I cause his strengths to become weaknesses and discover where he is not strong. . . . I conceal my tracks so that none can discern them; I keep silence so that none can hear me.[37]

US Navy Admiral Hyman Rickover attempted to put Cold War events in the context of both physical and psychological aspects of war, hoping the American people could grasp a threatening Communist menace: "Most of our people cannot understand that we are actually at war. They need to hear shells. They are not psychologically prepared for the concept that you can have a war when you don't have actual fighting."[38] Rickover ran among the ranks of an incredibly small number taking time to consider Sun's analogy that "warfare is based on deception."[39] Quincy Wright defines war, sociologically, as "a recognized form of inter-group conflict involving violence."[40] Wright gives a convincing argument in support of this definition:

War is seen to be a state of law and a form of conflict involving a high degree of legal equality, of hostility, and violence in the relations of organized human groups, or, more simply, the legal condition which equally permits two or more hostile groups to carry on a conflict by armed force.[41]

Wright's definition and follow-up are in perfect unison with war's standing in this thesis, and Clausewitz would agree: "We therefore conclude that war does not belong in the realm of arts and sciences; rather it is part of man's social existence."[42] Edward Luttwak and Stuart Koehl's surgical definition of strategy is worth comparing to Wright's description for war. While Wright considers war an accepted practice of international affairs, Luttwak and Koehl note it as socially unacceptable to civilized society. Exception to Wright's version involves use of "violence" and "armed force" in his explanation. Specific words further assumptions that physical destruction must occur. War comes in a colorful array of forms. War does not consist of strict physical aggression: "Weapons are ominous tools to be used only when there is no alternative."[43] It includes a long list of methods at the disposal of competing parties. Evil intent is the same, though techniques may be different:

We maintain, on the contrary, that war is simply a continuation of political intercourse, with the addition of other means. We deliberately use the phrase "with the addition of other means" because we also want to make it into something entirely different. In essentials that intercourse continues, irrespective of the means it employs. The main lines along which military events progress, and to which they are restricted, are political lines that continue throughout the war into the subsequent peace. How could it be otherwise? Do political relations between peoples and between their governments stop when diplomatic notes are no longer exchanged? Is war not just another expression of their thoughts, another form of speech or writing? Its grammar, indeed, may be its own, but not its logic.[44]

Vladimir Lenin's comment, "Politics is but an extension of war," can now be understood by Westerners gullibly seduced while visiting the Soviet Union.[45] Those given Moscow's royal treatment witnessed majestic and glorious May Day parades through Red Square. They became intoxicated by the socialist experiment. Unfortunately, killing fields outside city limits were not on the tour schedule:

> To this day, the former Soviet Union is dotted with enormous secret graveyards, usually located on the outskirts of big cities – often in parks reserved for NKVD dachas and sometimes in abandoned mine shafts – in which the bodies of the executed victims were systematically (usually at night) buried.[46]

Understanding the countenance of war allows the "illusion" of a "Cold War" to be swept away and true horrors brought before green Western eyes. Moscow's winter blizzards blocked this vision, which has similarities to problems identifying sea power. People often envision the aura of a battleship blasting away with sixteen-inch guns when sea power is mentioned. This makes a big contribution to constraining proper understanding of a broader package. Thinking of that battleship in terms of sea power is totally missing the mark if those guns are bombarding targets on land.

Processes and Procedures

The United States serves as primary role model. This is not done out of bias, but simply because the US is currently the world's dominant sea power. Additionally, America's topography is diverse and unique. Virtually every possible condition affiliated with sea power exists somewhere within its border and along the coast.[47] By European standards the US is young and yet has a colorful sea power history. It is technologically sophisticated, powerful and, for the immediate future, an economic giant. The US may be man's last hope for projecting ideals of constitutional self-government. Discussion of the twenty-first century will reveal cracks threatening achievements with humanity's democratic experiment. The United Kingdom will also be included based on their contribution to the cause.

There is no shortage of analysis on Mahan or his work. A search for that common denominator connecting his research with contemporaries has not occurred. This link has been achieved by accurately defining sea power. Sea power's definition reinforces work by many scholars. A "missing link" to each position is found with sea power's proper categorization in national grand strategy. The same applies to land, air, and space power. Each definition withstands challenges from history, technology, geography, culture, and the future. Chosen words are flexible, while maintaining clear limits. Debate is expected, but it should be confined to a futuristic portfolio. No argument can alter any definition's foundation, which is a solid axiom:

- History is used to support research findings when a contribution applies. Evidence will challenge existing records.
- Maritime issues, methods, and motive are presented to underscore a definition's utility. This is in conjunction with sea power's fluid nature.
- Techniques are aligned to better describe application of pressure within geographic parameters. Power generators are concepts and not something built on a factory floor. They are ideals and pursuits, which remain in the same abecedarian state as when first practiced.
- National grand strategy is constructed in parallel with power generators. Their manner of existence expresses independence, but also a working relationship. This confuses those believing in separation. This doctrinal view is disassembled and physical characteristics eliminated. Pressure dictates a fluid status.
- Any fixation that technology weakens sea power is discredited. It is technology that is acclimated to support sea power and not the opposite.
- Geography and time are strongholds in an environment of few certainties. Time is measured in precise units not subject to change. Technology may provide efficient time management, but it does not alter content. With the exception of catastrophic

events, geography is a fixed asset. Time and geography explain why things happen and happen the way they do.

- Power resources determine generator success or failure. Many resources are ignored, minimized, or taken for granted. All work in unison to support a competent sea power. Financial assets provide capital for shipbuilding. Shipbuilding takes place if geography is favorable. A shipyard must be properly equipped, with a skilled workforce standing by.

- Geographic theaters are explored using sea power assets. This satisfies judicial requirements for evidence of complementary roles. Each power generator's assets can assist colleagues as an event unfolds. Trouble in a single region may cause profound spill-over sequences in another geographic domain. Loss of territory on land can deny resources for maritime assets at sea. Failure to control airspace may alter ground and sea outcomes.

The "Influence of History on Mahan" conference, held at the US Naval War College, is a fitting location to clarify sea power's strategic angle. J. C. Wylie presented three theorems to emphasize national grand strategy's center of gravity between policy and strategy:

1. Strategy is a plan for doing something to achieve some known aim.
2. The aim of strategy is some measure of control over some other individual or group. This control may be direct or indirect. It may be partial or complete. It may be subtle or obvious. It may be immediate or slow. But, whatever its characteristics may be, it should be sufficient to induce or to force its target into some status or position or action or attitude acceptable to the strategist.
3. Desired measure of control may be achieved by manipulation of a pressure point, a centre of gravity, a leverage which will control or sway or influence the situation to the advantage of the strategist.[48]

Wylie's first theorem is broad enough to adapt for either grand strategic or strategic levels. His second reflects Mahan's position on application of force and power. Wylie's third position would make Sun Tzu Wu proud. To dominate, control, or manipulate is a strategic objective not necessarily involving use of force. This occurs at the

point of transition from grand strategy to strategic application.
Decisions must be made regarding objectives.

The following chapter presents Mahan's moral fiber. Sea
power and national grand strategy are discussed in context with his
character. Connection between Mahan's principles and his theories of
national grand strategy will be presented to challenge the stable of
critics. Common threads tying most detractors fall back on a failure to
submerge power generators into national grand strategy's framework.
Strategic fixations result causing a loss of grand strategic direction.
Both *national* and *grand* are vital and warrant joint usage.[49] History
will find a correlation as discoveries unfold. Sea, land, air, and space
power rely on history while they are making history. This is a crucial
realization in the quest for definition because all four generators are
deployed on behalf of policy. National policy is where intellectual
dynamics create what is destined to be historical events. The United
States is given particular attention throughout. A futuristic analysis of
sea power's value and expected facial features will prevail toward the
end. Methodology discloses the continued value of existing theory.
This reflects Mahan's vibrant thinking:

> The genius of Caesar, in his Gallic and Germanic campaigns, built up
> an outside barrier, which, like a dike, for centuries postponed the
> inevitable end, but which also, like every artificial barrier, gave way
> when the strong masculine impulse which first created it had
> degenerated into that worship of comfort, wealth, and general
> softness, which is the ideal of the peace prophets of to-day. The wave
> of the invaders broke in, - the rain descended, the floods came, the
> winds blew, and beat upon the house, and it fell, because not founded
> upon the rock of virile reliance upon strong hands and brave hearts to
> defend what was dear to them.[50]

Is there a haunting correlation to the United States? Mahan
delivered sea power to the water's edge with enough knowledge and
intuition to complete the mission. He then decided to leave behind the
task of creating a definition with his loyal disciples.

Chapter Three

Alfred Thayer Mahan

"Be a philosopher; but amidst all your philosophy, be still a man."
- David Hume

Alfred Thayer Mahan was born in 1840 and spent his early years on the premises of the United States Military Academy (USMA) at West Point, New York. Dennis Mahan, his father, served as an instructor and grounded Alfred in a rigid reading regimen. This background evolved into religious convictions of deep impact:

> And yet more is this true if, as is commonly said, faith is failing among ourselves, if the progress of our own civilization is towards the loss of those spiritual convictions upon which it was founded and which in early days were mighty indeed towards the overthrowing of strongholds of evil. What, in such a case shall play the tremendous part which the Church of the Middle Ages, with all its defects and with all the shortcomings of its ministers, played amid the ruin of the Roman Empire and the flood of the barbarians? If our own civilization is becoming material only, a thing limited in hope and love to this world, I know not what we have to offer to save ourselves or others; but in either event, whether to go down finally under a flood of outside invasion, or whether to succeed, by our own living faith, in converting to our ideal civilization those who shall thus press upon us, - in either event we need time, and time can be gained only by organized material force.[1]

Mahan often equated his Christian faith with discussions of sea power. A religious pacifist may find his attempt to link Christianity and military action rather peculiar:

> When the religion of Christ, of Him who was led as a lamb to the slaughter, seeks to raise before its followers the image of self-control, and of resistance to evil, it is the soldier whom it presents. He Himself, if by office King of Peace, is first of all, in the essence of His Being, King of Righteousness, without which true peace cannot be.[2]

Mahan entered the United States Naval Academy (USNA) in 1857. His aquatic footprint surfaced in the fleet just as the Civil War began and while the Navy attempted to become relevant. Ironically, Mahan's public presence ended in 1914; just at the moment American sea power got in position to explode on the world stage. Half a century following publication of his magnum opus, *The Influence of Sea Power upon History*, the US Navy found itself preparing for World War II and a destiny as the greatest military machine to ever sail the seas.

Mahan saw little action of significance outside occasional rebellions in Latin America. This usually required military intervention for purposes of protecting lives and property. The first twenty years of naval service primarily consisted of research and analysis of naval history. Rear Admiral Stephen B. Luce, founder of the newly formed US Naval War College (NWC), noted Mahan's fascination and decided to further his academic enthusiasm with a faculty appointment. David McCullough notes the reason for Mahan's lack of protest:

> He [Mahan] and his father agreed that he might have done better in some other profession. By the time he was appointed to the staff of the War College, after thirty years in the service, he was still, in his own words, "drifting on the lines of simple respectability as aimlessly as one ever could."[3]

Shortly after Luce's announcement, Mahan, while serving in Lima, Peru, claimed to have a conscious awakening from God instructing him to write a treatise on sea power:

> He who seeks, finds, if he does not lose heart; and to me, continuously seeking, came from within the suggestion that control of the sea was an historic factor which had never been systematically appreciated and expanded. For me . . . the light dawned first on my inner consciousness; I owed it to no other man. . . . I cannot now reconstitute from memory the sequence of my mental processes, but while my problem was still wrestling with my brain there dawned upon me one of those concrete perceptions which turn inward darkness into light – and give substance to shadow. . . . It suddenly struck me, whether by some chance phrase of the author I do not know, how different things might have been could Hannibal have invaded Italy by sea, as the Romans often had Africa, instead of by the long land route.[4]

This treatise turned out to be *The Influence of Sea Power upon History*. The book's popularity made Mahan a household name among Americans and, globally, he became an acknowledged maritime expert. Mahan's popularity broke the celebrity meter in Great Britain where many sought validation for the British Empire. His writing became recognized as the legal argument justifying maritime supremacy.

Jomini and Clausewitz

Mahan's pursuit of a grand treatise found itself on hold in 1886 by demands of Rear Admiral Luce. Luce, an avid devotee of Antoine-Henri Jomini, wanted Mahan to teach naval tactics. He firmly believed that Jomini's, *The Art of War*, could be modified from land warfare tactics to achieve success at sea. His keen eye for Mahan's talents likely had its basis in Mahan's father, who developed into a distinguished faculty member at West Point. Unfortunately for Luce, Dennis Mahan's thinking on battle tactics and strategy did not square with his. There existed a popular belief throughout military ranks that D. H. Mahan advocated Jomini and Napoleon Bonaparte's tactical theories of warfare. These ideals championed full frontal assaults to battlefield management. Though Jomini persisted as widely accepted reading on campus, Dennis Mahan's combat engineering background made him a strong believer in fortifications.

Many contemporary scholars still believe Dennis Mahan came from Jomini stock. Brian Sullivan's review of Jon Sumida's book notes the complexity surrounding Dennis and Alfred Mahan's opinion:

> Because Mahan's father, Dennis Hart Mahan, taught at West Point for nearly fifty years and was influenced by Jomini, many scholars have emphasized the Napoleonic influence on the younger Mahan. Some have gone so far as to label A.T. Mahan "the Jomini of the sea," maintaining that both men stressed operations over strategy, insisted on a deterministic set of rules for conducting war, and argued that success in war basically amounted to seizing a superior position, then smashing one's enemy in all-or-nothing battle. Sumida agrees that there is some validity in this portrayal of Mahan's early ideas. But he emphasizes that the admiral developed far more sophisticated thinking as his grasp of war deepened. Even D.H. Mahan came to reject the idea of an all-inclusive theory of warfare, eventually arguing that the practice of war was an art, not a science, and that the study of military history was more useful than knowledge of geometry for appreciating the nature of warfare.[5]

Dennis Mahan became a mathematical genius. He achieved a successful career at West Point by applying his expertise to analysis of battle tactics and strategy. D.H. Mahan's mathematical calculations showed positive results behind defensive measures that countered mainstream strategic and tactical thinking. His findings contradicted Jomini's assault doctrine. Sumida argues that Dennis Mahan "was anti-Jominian in his distrust of systematic theory in matters of command."[6] Dennis Mahan believed, and the Civil War proved, rifles and other war-fighting products of the industrial age would render Jomini and Napoleonic philosophies archaic.

Ten months following Mahan's assignment to the NWC, Admiral Luce grew discouraged over Mahan's lack of enthusiasm for tactical writing. He wisely reduced Mahan's classroom schedule for teaching naval tactics. This allowed Mahan time to give undivided attention to researching sea power's global implications. It is here that similarities between Mahan and Clausewitz begin to surface. Like Mahan, Clausewitz firmly believed military genius is a creation of advanced civilizations. In fact, both men use the Roman Empire and France extensively as examples.[7] Ian Moffat adds to the problem of mistaken identity by also arguing that Mahan and Sir Julian Corbett actually complement each other:

> Writing in the same period was Sir Julian Stafford Corbett, a British historian. He was a meticulous researcher and became a leading maritime strategist to rival Mahan. Corbett complemented Mahan's ideas while presenting a more logical and structured argument. His development of Maritime Strategy was a necessary complement to Mahan's development of Naval Strategy. Corbett was more pragmatic and therefore, a more effective strategist than Mahan. He had studied Carl von Clausewitz and he adapted the Prussian's military theories to the maritime environment. Corbett's theories eventually became the accepted way of conducting maritime conflicts.[8]

Brian Sullivan adds explosive fuel with his summation that scholars who launched a study of Mahan ended up dissecting and serving their own agenda. Such difficulty has a lot to do with the elusive nature of Mahan's work. Recent work connecting Mahan and Corbett reveals many similarities. Variations are most often contained within geographic regions of expertise:

> Unfortunately, for many who read Mahan, the author was not the most meticulous historian nor was he necessarily able to articulate his

points concisely and consistently. Thus, the influential people who read Mahan may have misinterpreted his concepts or more likely adapted those that supported their own ideas while not following Mahan's complete lesson.[9]

Ian Moffat's observation is a classic example of an academic realignment now underway. Revelation turns full circle once Sumida's research is incorporated, and his results appear starkly different from common stereotypes. Both Moffat and Sullivan could have one-upped themselves by noting that Mahan's naval strategy and Corbett's maritime strategy are both subsets of sea power. Those who attempted to show contradictions between Mahan and Corbett were equating "apples to oranges." The same would apply to a comparison of Jomini and Clausewitz. They are not identical and do not deserve a comparative analysis. Their work is fruit derived from the same power generating orchard, but similarities end there. Their strategic traits originate from different trees. Mahan's broader expanse for sea power begins to change the dynamic entirely, and it is here that similarities begin to appear. In the storm of confusion over what, when, where, and for whom, it is ironic Corbett heaped accolades on Mahan's *The Influence of Sea Power upon History*:

> For the first time naval history was placed on a philosophical basis. From the mass of facts which had hitherto done duty for naval history, broad generalizations were possible. The ears of statesmen and publicists were opened, and a new note began to sound in world politics. Regarded as a political pamphlet in the higher sense – for that is how the famous book is best characterized – it has few equals in the sudden and far-reaching effect it produced on political thought and action.[10]

Moffat, Sullivan and Sumida identified an interesting contradiction with the status quo. Sullivan calls attention to Mahan's view of Jomini as "too absolute and pedantic for his insistence on a precise formulation of the principles of war."[11] He goes on to reinforce Mahan's position that "sea power should be used primarily to achieve strategic goals established by a navy's government."[12] These are significant facts discarded from previous debate.

Mahan's critics cover an impressive time-frame. Accusations include arrogance and aloof behavior by classmates at the US Naval Academy. Onboard ship he was considered a mediocre seaman. His most colorful experience occurred while commanding USS *Chicago*, flagship of Rear Admiral Henry Erben, Commander US European Squadron. Erben's scathing fitness reports involved such decorative comments as "interests are entirely outside the service, for which, I am satisfied, he cares but little, and is therefore not a good officer."[13] Even publishers found Mahan's writing lacking. Daggers flew from every direction. Nobody, however, accused him of poor vision. Keen insight, combined with acute abilities to think spatially, enabled Mahan to viciously address sea power's dilemma. With the likely exception of Rear Admiral Erben, previous critics began realizing Mahan's perceived character deficiencies were, in actuality, traits of a man possessing intense analytical talent. Mahan credits this ability with religious upbringing and belief in a God-given purpose for his action.

Mahan and His Colleagues

Mahan and Corbett

Mahanian doctrine's application to the spatial development of sea power is routinely misinterpreted within strict parameters of naval warfare. Mahan wrote extensively on naval matters, but this is a distinct topic within broader research dedicated to sea power. His naval views are wrongly compared to the work by Sir Julian Corbett. Mahan is not in the same academic category as Corbett's focused work on maritime strategy. Additionally, Mahan's negative view of Jomini's absolute approach squares with his writings on sea power. Corbett's work held many similarities to Mahan, but for a different purpose. Those placing geostrategic constraints around Mahan create a false mystic on matters such as amphibious operations. Perception of differences existing between Mahan and Corbett is not helped by Mahan's work on Lord Horatio Nelson. This dovetails Sullivan's argument that scholars parceled material which fit their own agenda. Sumida draws attention to Mahan's criticism that amphibious operational theory is "the pernicious practice of jeopardizing the personnel of a fleet, the peculiar trained force so vitally necessary, and so hard to replace, in petty operations on shore."[14] Mahan makes a "distinct difference" with "fleet personnel" involved in operations on shore. Sumida notes Mahan's amphibious view but with an interesting caveat:

> In books written before and after the Farragut biography, Mahan criticized Admiral Horatio Nelson's advocacy of amphibious operations in support of land campaigns and, in general, opposed overseas expeditions. But these views were applied to circumstances

in which the opposing side possessed – the capacity to dispute sea command. Mahan reasoned that in such a case any attempt to project power from water to land risked naval assets that were needed to preserve the general control of the oceans, upon which all depended. When the maintenance of maritime lines of communication was not an issue, he had no objection to using naval force in combination with an army to achieve a military objective, and well understood that such action could have great strategic value.[15]

Comparison between Mahan and Corbett is frequently locked on a blue-water verses power projection ashore mindset. This is not representative of their true nature. Mahan's resistance to amphibious force involved concern over fleet personnel becoming subservient to an already underway land campaign. He did not oppose amphibious operations for other strategic reasons. A bureaucratic threat existed toward relegating naval operations to a situation jeopardizing fleet action. Sumida adds that Mahan believed amphibious operations violated "the fundamental principle of concentration of force, and by posing logistical burdens that diverted effort away from dealing with an opponent's main fleet, they risked skilled manpower."[16] But Mahan had priorities and once the enemy's battle-fleet had been dispatched, amphibious operations could be executed. This is sound strategy.

Mahan's early position toward amphibious operations is largely based on his analysis of Nelson. Obviously the science, or art, of US Marine Corps methods incorporated in the twentieth century developed into a far more advanced process. The days of a ship's crew piling off sailing vessels, and paddling rowboats ashore to assault well-defended fortifications had, by the twentieth century, joined the ranks of other long forgotten tactical operations. Additionally, supporting a land campaign already underway, while simultaneously fighting an enemy armada for sea control, is suicide. This has no similarity to invading a Pacific island where control of surrounding waters is complete. Mahan would be in total agreement that islands are vital once transformed into aircraft carriers capable of unleashing a bomber's wrath onto wayward souls occupying enemy territory. His "positive" views of joint sea and land operations contradict the status quo:

> He [Mahan] ended the main narrative of *The Influence of Sea Power upon History* with an account of the British defeat at Yorktown in 1781. The outcome of this battle had been determined by the reinforcement of American and French armies by sea, and also by French naval control of surrounding waters, which prevented a

British fleet from relieving the besieged British army. In the book that made his reputation, Mahan thus used the survival of what was to become imperial Rome and the creation of the United States as powerful historical testaments to the transcendent value of naval force in support of military operations.[17]

Mahan reinforces amphibious operations by noting fleet actions during the Civil War. These were carried out with troops embarked to rotate with those garrisoned ashore:

> The United States in the Civil War stationed her fleets off the Southern ports, not because she feared for her own, but to break down the Confederacy by isolation from the rest of the world, and ultimately by attacking the ports. The methods were the same; but the purpose in one case was defensive, in the other offensive.
> The confusion of the two ideas leads to much unnecessary wrangling as to the proper sphere of army and navy in coast-defence. Passive defences belong to the army; everything that moves in the water to the navy, which has the prerogative of the offensive defence. If seamen are used to garrison forts, they become part of the land forces, as surely as troops, when embarked as part of the complement, become part of the sea forces.[18]

It is an attribute that France helped win Yorktown by gaining control over surrounding waters. This minimized risk factors associated with facing far superior British maritime operations. Had France not interfered by way of the Chesapeake, history ashore probably would have turned out differently. Academic variations of Mahan's opinion on amphibious efforts should be scrutinized. The USMC Basic Officer Course (BOC) maintains an accredited module titled "Principles of Amphibious Operations." It pointedly emphasizes Mahan's influence. The course syllabus goes so far as to identify Mahan's impact on the General Board of the Navy (1900):

> Influenced by Mahan's ideas and the lessons learned from the Spanish – American War, this board decided to establish a permanent force capable of seizing and defending advance bases. The Marine Corps was chosen to perform this (amphibious) mission of seizing and defending advance bases.[19]

The USMC curriculum outline continues with commencement of amphibious training on islands in the Caribbean and Pacific from

1901 to 1914.[20] Fantasies run wild believing Mahan incapable of stopping such an exercise. He rose to icon status throughout American society, as well as a great part of the world. When Mahan spoke, people listened. While the USMC ran rampant carrying out amphibious training, Mahan had already served on the Commission to Report on the Reorganization of the Navy Department, Board of Visitors at the United States Naval Academy, Senate Commission on Merchant Marine, and the Naval Strategy Board during the Spanish-American War, when 600 Marines conducted an amphibious invasion to seize a Spanish coaling station. During this period Mahan provided valuable input to the War Department for the US Army's landing by sea at Daiquiri. This enabled US forces to capture Santiago, Cuba.[21] He certainly held a favorable position to protest amphibious operations. Because of his popularity, political elites would have flirted with disaster to deny him redress over grievances.

Sir Halford Mackinder, a legendary skeptic of Corbett's maritime power thesis, argued that sophisticated shoreline defenses and land transportation would devalue maritime capabilities. Things have not turned out that way. Even Geoffrey Sloan, a staunch supporter of Mackinder, noted that virtually all 600 amphibious landings during World War II were successful. The number and frequency is equivalent to a landing every 3-4 days.[22] This occurred just as Mackinder revised his heartland theory to include the North Atlantic. Even Mackinder became aware that technology held as much value at sea as on land. Clicking a mouse on a war-wagon sailing at "greater than thirty-knots" seems wiser than in a fixed target like the Pentagon.

Mahan and Mackinder

It would not be intellectually healthy if Mahan's work went unchallenged. Sir Halford Mackinder's equivalent but opposing examination came about while Mahan expressed his own geostrategic theories. Mackinder moved on land while Mahan sailed the high seas. Differences depended on geographic preference. Mahan and Mackinder were otherwise identical in many ways.[23] Margaret Tuttle Sprout shows Mackinder developing into what many came to consider a second coming of Clausewitz, and a noble counter-stroke to Mahan's work:

> It is one of the strange quirks of history that the American naval officer whose doctrines became the guiding principles of the world's leading sea powers should have inadvertently provided inspiration for the creation of an antithetical theory of land power. Had the grand

strategy of Haushofer and Hitler succeeded, it would have spelled the doom of sea power as Mahan understood. And as the modern world has been largely predicated upon British and more recently upon Anglo-American control of the seas, the results of a Nazi victory would have been revolutionary far beyond their best hopes and our worst fears.[24]

Mahan's similarity with Clausewitz instead exposes a relationship to Mackinder. Sumida makes it possible to label Mahan "Clausewitz of the sea," just as Mackinder is the same on land. Differences between Clausewitzian camps involves turf: "Sir Halford Mackinder had always contended that control by a military state of long stretches of the European coast line would nullify British control of the seas – a contention which was enthusiastically taken over by Haushofer and the geopoliticians."[25] Colin Gray combines Mackinder and Mahan's theories to show how little history has changed:

> Mahan's U.S.-continental frame of personal reference for the world (notwithstanding his anglophilia and the focus on the Royal Navy in his histories) in important ways made for a sounder comprehension of trends in the balance of power than was expounded by Mackinder. But Mackinder's theoretical framework, organized around the enduring opposition between whichever power or coalition controlled, or threatened to control, the Eurasian continental Heartland and the ocean-facing states, was fundamentally correct. The persisting historical pattern of conflict between continental powers striving to achieve hegemony on land and coalitions organized by offshore sea powers for the purpose of thwarting those repeated bids for hegemony has been too steady to be dismissed as a passing phase or an accident of particular circumstances.[26]

World Wars I & II, and the ensuing Cold War depended on North Atlantic lines of communication to thwart a dominant Eurasian land power. Like Mackinder, Mahan possessed an awareness of technology's impact on communications. It evolved into a matter of land against sea, and Mahan's geostrategic vision grew frigid:

> As a wilderness gives place to civilization, as means of communication multiply, as roads are opened, rivers bridged, food-resources increased, the operations of war become easier, more rapid, more extensive, but the principles to which they must be conformed remain the same. When the march on foot was replaced by carrying troops in coaches, when the latter in turn gave place to railroads, the

scale of distances was increased, or if you will, the scale of time
diminished; but the principles which dictated the point at which the
army should be concentrated, the direction in which it should move,
the part of the enemies position which it should assail, the protection
of communications were not altered.[27]

Profound geostrategic differences between Mahan and
Mackinder did not prevent either from generating enormous attention.
Mahan became the salvation for future US policy and grand strategic
designs. Without the counterbalance provided by Mahan, doom and
gloom associated with Mackinder's sea power position may have
generated enough publicity to deny public support. Fortunately for the
US, Mahan's historical synopsis included enough documentation to
command attention.

Mahan and Nelson

Mahan deeply admired British Admiral Horatio Nelson's
leadership qualities. Nelson's talent at frustrating the French was not an
isolated circumstance. Britain's success involved a valuable link
between skill and historical events:

> Nevertheless, a vague feeling of contempt for the past, supposed to be
> obsolete, combines with natural indolence to blind men even to those
> permanent strategic lessons which lie close to the surface of naval
> history. For instance, how many look upon the battle of Trafalgar, the
> crown of Nelson's glory and the seal of his genius, as other than an
> isolated event of exceptional grandeur? How many ask themselves
> the strategic question, "How did the ships come to be just there?"
> How many realize it to be the final act in a great strategic drama,
> extending over a year or more, in which two of the greatest leaders
> that ever lived, Napoleon and Nelson, were pitted against each other?
> At Trafalgar it was not Villeneuve that failed, but Napoleon that was
> vanquished; not Nelson that won, but England that was saved; and
> why? Because Napoleon's combinations failed, and Nelson's
> intuitions and activity kept the English fleet ever on the track of the
> enemy, and brought it up in time at the decisive moment.[28]

Trafalgar was not the result of a solitary event and incredible
stroke of luck. It symbolized a nationwide effort toward achieving
maritime supremacy which spanned centuries. Nelson posthumously
earned the title as British sea power's crowning symbol:

> The breadth and acuteness of Nelson's intellect have been too much overlooked, in the admiration excited by his unusually grand moral endowments of resolution, dash, and fearlessness of responsibility. Though scarcely what could be called an educated man, he was one of close and constant observation, thereby gaining a great deal of information; and to the use of this he brought a practical sagacity, which coped with the civil or political questions placed before it, *for action*, much as it did with military questions – for, after all, good generalship, on its intellectual side, is simply the application, to the solution of a military problem, of a mind naturally gifted therefore, and stored with experience, either personal or of others.[29]

Harold Rood's opening comment has linkage to Mahan's study of Nelson. Nelson possessed a high degree of intelligence and an instinctive aura in battle. The legend this trait creates far surpasses that left by more highly educated individuals. Rood's comment links a "distinct difference" between education and intelligence with a great military leader from the past. There is a vast parade of educated individuals who have a difficult time making a decision.[30] Highly intelligent individuals who willingly accept responsibility know the importance of remaining alert for that moment when immediate action is required.[31] Intelligent people are aware that when "the enemy presents an opportunity, speedily take advantage of it."[32] Mahan admired the British sailor's ability to act quickly, while making life miserable for his French counterpart:

> Historically, good men with poor ships are better than poor men in good ships; over and over again the French Revolution taught us this lesson, which our own age, with its rage for the last new thing in material improvement, has largely dropped out of memory.[33]

A skillfully endowed nation can circumvent disadvantages in certain areas with a stellar display in other fields. Some fail in the process of trying. Britain has shown there is no substitute for superior seamanship. A solid economic foundation existed at the time and was able to support the expense associated with maritime endeavors. Initial outlays provided an attractive return on the taxpayer's investment. British naval power allowed commerce to take place on the seas without molestation. Mahan saw many similarities between Great Britain and the US. He believed an Anglo-American maritime alliance would solve the burden of cost.[34] Once again, another proposal showed up ahead of time with similar versions developing relevancy in recent years.[35] A maritime alliance, like any other agreement of multi-national character, is based on mutual interest:

> Although I am convinced firmly that it would be to the interest of Great Britain and the United States, and for the benefit of the world, that the two nations should act together cordially on the seas, I am equally sure that the result not only must be hoped but also quietly waited for, while the conditions upon which such cordiality depends are being realized by men.[36]

Grasp of future threats is again provided with Mahan's description of dangers posed with a unified China:

> It may perhaps be for the welfare of humanity that the Chinese people and territory should undergo a period of political division, like that of Germany anterior to the French Revolution, before achieving the race patriotism which, in or epoch, is tending to bind peoples into larger groups than the existing nationalities. The issue is one that passes human foreordainment; but the contemplation of the two alternatives is not amiss to the preparation of the statesman.[37]

Mahan and Rickover

Mahan viewed many technological pursuits as endeavors in blindness and crazed enthusiasm for style. The Soviet Union's stellar record at choosing superior strategic intelligence over techno-hype is a testament to Mahan's belief. His skepticism had staying power. It infiltrated the ranks of America's military leadership and remained contagious for decades. Remnants existed as late as the 1980s with the best example coming from Admiral Hyman Rickover. As head of the US Navy's nuclear propulsion program for over thirty years, he lost a bureaucratic battle with then Secretary of the Navy, John Lehman.[38] Rickover, acting on behalf of Mahan's old school, and Lehman, representing a new order, often locked horns over budget allocation. The long feud started when scientists at Los Alamos, New Mexico complained to Lehman that Rickover refused to fund research proposals on experimental propulsion plants. Rickover held a stellar record managing the taxpayer's investment and it left an overpowering mark on his offspring:

> I have never met a man who worked harder or evidenced less interest in material possessions than Admiral Rickover. His life was devoted to the job.

He worked long hours in Spartan surroundings, shunning fancy
clothes, cars, and furniture. He had no stewards. He traveled tourist
class.
Admiral Rickover could have retired in 1952 at three-quarters pay
and made a fortune in the private sector. But he stayed on serving his
country for another thirty years. That's when he designed and built
the nuclear propulsion plant for *Nautilus* and for all the ships that
today comprise 40 percent of our major combatants.[39]

The clash climaxed on 08 January 1982 during Rickover's
farewell visit to the Oval Office: "Mr. President [Ronald Reagan], that
piss-ant [John Lehman] knows nothing about the navy."[40] Mahan, like
Rickover, did not hold technology in low esteem. Both men simply
believed in more vigilant approaches to allow sober consideration of
strategic effect. This is a reflection of very smart shopping. Each grew
disturbed by a perceived willingness by others to supplant naval
strategy with technology.[41] One example is Mahan's concern over
foreign ports. Entertaining vacationing political elites on "fact-finding"
missions did not justify defense expenditures for those ports.[42] Mahan's
rationale rose over concern for deployed naval fleets. Passing from sail
to steam propulsion made this paramount. The technology required new
strategic considerations; a need for fuel far from home waters:

> A long-range steam navy needed coaling stations. The farther from
> home U.S. warships were deployed, the greater the need for secure
> overseas bases. Thus, implicit in the need to exclude European states
> from the Caribbean and to protect the west coast, was the need for
> forward bases. Congressional isolationists were correct. Building a
> long-range naval force would open up the prospect of colonial
> expansion.[43]

Ship replenishment did not involve a fresh idea for existing
strategy, but coaling stations were new concepts and coal developed
into an essential ingredient:

> For fuel is the life of modern naval war; it is the food of the ship;
> without it the modern monsters of the deep die of inanition. Around
> it, therefore, cluster some of the most important considerations of
> naval strategy. In the Caribbean and in the Atlantic we are confronted
> with many a foreign coal depot, bidding us stand to our arms, even as
> Carthage bade Rome; but let us not acquiesce in an addition to our
> dangers, a further diversion of our strength, by being forestalled in the
> North Pacific.[44]

Steam propulsion enhanced the dependency on foreign ports, and just when the US Navy's commitments in Asia were enlarging. Stations were scarce and the options comprised taking bases by force, or negotiating treaties with governments to replenish the fleet.

Rickover's nuclear power followed fossil fuels as the next generation of propulsion design. Mahan would have embraced this technological marvel, but not because of impressive bells and whistles on the control panel. Nuclear power is a great achievement of mankind, and it offers unsurpassed strategic and tactical advantage to the fleet. Its application in naval operations provides unlimited freedom of action. No other energy source can offer such flexibility. A host of benchmarks must exist to support its use. This includes adequate supplies of brain power. It takes the US Navy over three years to fully train a nuclear propulsion plant operator, and the cost surpasses $50,000. An educated workforce is necessary to maximize nuclear power's utility. This also applies to those filling support roles ashore. Knowledgeable shipyard personnel are required to replace reactor fuel cells, perform high pressure welds on reactor fluid systems and, most importantly, understand why detailed procedures should be followed.

Mahan and the Panama Canal

Mahan firmly believed the United States to be honorable and, therefore, the American people had a global destiny based on their Christian heritage. This included a moral aspect to stand up for justice and righteousness:

> Power, force is a faculty of national life; one of the talents committed to nations by God. And this obligation to maintain right, by force if need be, while common to all states, rests peculiarly upon the greater in proportion to their means. So viewed, the ability speedily to put forth the nation's power, is one of the clear duties involved in the Christian word "watchfulness," readiness for the call that may come, whether expectedly or not. Until it is demonstrated that evil no longer exists, or threatens the world, which cannot be obviated without the recourse to force, the obligation to readiness must remain; and where evil is mighty and defiant, the obligation to use force, that is, war arises.[45]

Mahan lacked political muscle to promote his theories. This became solved by his relationship with Theodore Roosevelt. Roosevelt believed a naval force of global reach was needed to defend itself against European meddling. He held a steadfast belief in both the Monroe Doctrine and Mahan's publications: "I think I have studied your books to pretty good purpose."[46] Roosevelt received an appointment as Assistant Secretary of the Navy following William McKinley's 1896 presidential election. A zealous nature turned into high-energy maintenance for Secretary of the Navy, John Long. No finer example of two opposites existed. Long, a sophisticated Massachusetts statesman took events in stride and followed America's tradition of isolationism. Roosevelt, on the other hand, believed America's future depended on global power projection to show the world a new international player had arrived. Mahan's pen helped Roosevelt push for new naval doctrine which transcended small vessels designed for coastal defense. Long's instruction that Roosevelt ran the show in his absence was like passing a child keys to the candy store.[47]

The Spanish-American War propelled Mahan to primacy with badly needed physical evidence. It provided Roosevelt political justification why taxpayer dollars must be dedicated to an offensive naval fleet. Realities of world politics had finally arrived at America's front door:

> Except Russia and Japan, the several nations actively concerned in this great problem rest, for home bases, upon remote countries. We find therefore two classes of powers: those whose communication is by land, and those who depend upon the sea. The sea lines are the most numerous and easy, and they will probably be determinative of the courses of trade. Among them there are two the advantages of which excel all others – for Europe by Suez, from America by way of the Pacific Ocean. The latter will doubtless receive further modification by an isthmian canal, extending the use of the rout to the Atlantic seaboard of America, North and South.[48]

Immediately following the Spanish-American War, the United States launched an aggressive maritime expansion program with support from all socioeconomic classes. This unprecedented transition caught many by surprise, including Europe's political elite. Spain had the unfortunate luck of losing its position in the Philippines and Caribbean Sea region, which included the highly cherished islands of Cuba and Puerto Rico. American ships and political influence spanned the Pacific and Atlantic Oceans. The Caribbean Sea and Central America fell under its control, while a notable presence blossomed in

South America. Positive relations with Great Britain took shape during this period, which coincided with British concern over Germany's desire to build a first-rate blue-water navy. Mahan's Anglo-American alliance began to show some leg. Inspiration is traced to John Knox Laughton, an instructor at Britain's Royal Naval College in Portsmouth. His introduction to Mahan came through Rear Admiral Luce. Luce grew impressed by Laughton's own desire to incorporate Antoine-Henri Jomini's theories on land warfare into naval tactics. Laughton assisted Luce in establishing the US Naval War College and this resulted in Laughton becoming a professional confidant throughout Mahan's career.[49]

The crowning touch to Roosevelt and Mahan's relationship did not come by way of a floating vessel. Their commonality is symbolized on land by construction of the Panama Canal. Its completion eliminated the perilous and lengthy Cape Horn route around South America. Mahan served as Roosevelt's ammunition for promoting construction. To Roosevelt's credit, he regularly referenced Mahan in letters to political figures, articles in journals, and during speeches to community organizations.[50] Name-dropping Mahan was a priceless commodity.

The US government initially favored a waterway running across Nicaragua. Panama entered the fray when France offered to sell their interest. The financial risk grew as America created a suffocating presence. The US possessed a railroad running from the Gulf of Mexico to the Pacific. Even Mahan once defended the line during a Panamanian rebellion. A canal across Nicaragua combined with a railroad in Panama showed resolve at dominating transportation between two shores. Construction began in 1904 and its completion ten years later announced America's status as a major player on the global stage. The United Kingdom wholeheartedly supported the effort and, as a result, relations were cultivated on all fronts. American's traditionally viewed Great Britain as just another European power seeking to protect an empire. Lack of response by other Europeans to challenge America's drive across the isthmus served as acknowledgment and acceptance. Even Denmark jumped on the acceptance bandwagon by willingly selling its interest in the Virgin Islands on the eve of World War I. This denied Germany a naval base in the eastern Caribbean. Doubt over who controlled the Western Hemisphere was settled.

When the US Congress approved construction of a canal, provisions were added for a permanent military garrison in Panama. Fortification on land became a priority to protect both investment and strategic gain. A direct relationship between sea and land power is obvious. Many mistakenly saw a troop deployment as proof of an unnecessary boondoggle. Military leaders, however, correctly assessed the Canal's importance and its necessity for sea control in both Caribbean and Pacific Ocean waters. Maintaining land forces in Panama, even today, is vital to shipping arteries from both bodies of water. Operations through the isthmus must not stop.[51] The waterway is on land, but its pressure application is at sea. As a result, Mahan found himself launching counter-offensives against critics over cost:

> In your issue of April 11 Park Benjamin endeavors to exploit what he apparently conceives to be a contradiction between two statements of mine with reference to (1) the fortification of the Panama Canal, which I advocate, and (2) the ultimate dependence of the canal upon the navy for its secure possession by the Nation, which I affirm. To a careful civilian reader even the quotations from my writings, by which Mr. Benjamin endeavors to substantiate an inconsistency, will carry the refutation which to any military man is apparent at once.[52]

Congress did not hesitate to support Mahan's argument by, several years earlier, creating a treaty enshrining defense of the isthmus into doctrine:

> In 1901 the second Hay-Pauncefote Treaty conceded fortification rights to the United States, abrogating the earlier agreement on neutrality. With that, Britain gave the United States a free hand on the isthmus.[53]

Forming a sphere of influence that involves sea power and a broad range of assets took shape as Mahan continued counter-punching Park Benjamin's charges:

> I pointed out that in such a case the navy would be tied to the canal, unable therefore to be used anywhere else, because the position, being unfortified, could be seized without difficulty in the absence of the fleet. The expediency of fortification was supported further on the grounds of economy, in that it would cost less than two battleships, while two battleships alone would be insufficient for defense, not to speak of the impolicy of detaching two ships from the fleet under most circumstances. These are A, B, Cs of naval strategy.[54]

Mahan closes by taking a shot at the opposition party, while arguing service branch coordination is not unusual:

I can assure the readers of *The Times* that this reciprocal relation of fortification and mobile force are mere commonplaces of the military art. This they can ascertain from any military friend, whether navy or army. I should have imagined Mr. Benjamin to be familiar with them, save for his letter. It is in some degree vexatious to have to repeat commonplaces in reply to commonplace blunderings, but there is some compensation in the belief that such controversy serves to keep before people the calamity with which the Nation is threatened by the seeming resolve of the Democratic Party in Congress to arrest the growth of the navy.[55]

Some things never change. Mahan's relationship to Clausewitz reappears through support of fortifications. His promotion of a combined army and navy defense of the Panama Canal contradicts the preponderance toward Mahan serving solely as a blue-water advocate. It is a reflection of Clausewitz's argument that "successful closure of war requires grasp of national policy. Here strategy and policy coalesce."[56] Mahan looked at work in Panama from a perspective not purely naval, but from a position of national policy and grand strategy. This involves more than a single power generator (two at the time). Unfortunately, such things as the Panama Canal seem to fall by the wayside in contemporary debates. Geostrategic utility appeared to be sacrificed for diplomatic back-scratching when the US formally turned over its control at the end of the twentieth century. Panama, in an attempt to show appreciation, wasted no time flipping their newly acquired authority. Bill Gertz identifies the lucky recipient as Hutchinson-Whampoa, a Hong Kong shipping firm tied to the People's Republic of China (PRC). Political elites acted indifferent to warnings by those burdened with protecting America's geostrategic advantage:

> China's goals in Panama are to ensure unrestricted access to the markets and natural resources of Latin America and to promote China as a potential political and economic alternative to the U.S. In my view, the impact of Chinese commercial interests in Panama is less a local threat to the Canal and more a regional threat posed by expanding Chinese influence throughout Latin America.[57]

Evidence is clear that Communist China seeks to challenge American influence in the Western Hemisphere:

> The heroic struggle now being waged by the people of Panama against U.S. aggression and in defence of their national sovereignty is

a great patriotic struggle. The Chinese people stand firmly on the side of the Panamanian people and fully support their just action in opposing U.S. aggression and seeking to regain sovereignty over the Panama Canal Zone.[58]

Hutchinson-Whampoa obtained control of the Canal's two main ports, one on each side of the isthmus. This occurred with great skill and in typical Sun fashion.[59] The firm won the contract when Panama put those facilities out to "competitive" bidding. This amusing process achieved favorable results with sums of cash lining the pockets of Panamanian officials.[60] Nobody seemed to consider what Mahan or Roosevelt's thoughts might have been, especially in light of the past 40 years:

> The flames of revolution are raging in United States imperialism's 'backyard'. The Latin American people's armed struggle against United States imperialism and its lackeys continues to develop. The struggle of the Latin American students against tyranny and persecution is steadily expanding.[61]

Such exciting displays of propaganda are not new to Latin America. The US deserves thanks for building the Panama Canal and opening its waterway to all who desired transit. There are not many nations that would be so gracious with their enormous personal investment. President William H. Taft's inaugural address on 04 March 1904 glorified Mahan's influence on American foreign policy which, unfortunately, seems to have died on Capital Hill:

> A modern navy can not be improvised. It must be built and in existence when the emergency arises which calls for its use and operation. My distinguished predecessor [Theodore Roosevelt] has in many speeches and messages set out with great force and striking language the necessity for maintaining a strong navy commensurate with the coast line, the governmental resources, and the foreign trade of our Nation; and I wish to reiterate all the reasons which he has presented in favor of the policy of maintaining a strong navy as the best conservator of our peace with other nations, and the best means of securing respect for the assertion of our rights, the defense of our interests, and the exercise of our influence in international matters.[62]

Substantial credit for the legacy described by President Taft belongs to Rear Admiral Mahan.

Land and Sea

The Influence of Sea Power upon the French Revolution and Empire served as Mahan's follow-on version to *The Influence of Sea Power upon History*. Jon Sumida notes Mahan took far greater care portraying sea power:

> Sea power, in other words, was in this volume transformed from a desirable policy option for certain countries into a self-sustaining system made up of both formal and informal elements. In these terms, it was not simply a political instrument but a new phenomenon that unconsciously but nonetheless effectively integrated the actions of the state with those of self-interested individuals and private corporations.[63]

Mahan stresses sea power's broad capacity by identifying Great Britain's substantial political-economic position following periods of war with France:

> The strength of Great Britain could be said to lie in her commerce only as, and because, it was the external manifestation of the wisdom and strength of the British people, unhampered by any control beyond that of a government and institutions in essential sympathy with them. In the enjoyment of these blessings, - in their independence and untrammeled pursuit of wealth, - they were secured by their powerful navy; and so long as this breastplate was borne, unpierced, over the heart of the great organism, over the British islands themselves, Great Britain was – not invulnerable – but invincible. She could be hurt indeed, but she could not be slain.[64]

Colin Gray underscores sea power's ripple effect on national grand strategy by distinguishing Napoleon Bonaparte's march to Russia. Gray correctly argues that the Royal Navy's maritime blockade along the European coast doomed Napoleon.[65] British sea power did not defeat Napoleon at sea as Gray notes, but it did accomplish this task on land. Britain's naval might forced Napoleon into Russia's graveyard where, over the course of history, so many uninvited guests have been put to rest. Williamson Murray subconsciously supports Mahan and Sir Julian Corbett's relationship by absorbing Napoleon's eastward journey into the maritime mix:

According to Corbett, land and maritime operations did not represent separate theaters existing independently of each other, but rather were together intertwined with the political, strategic, and operational framework within which conflicts take place. Unlike Mahan, Corbett understood that naval warfare occurred within this larger context. The storm-tossed squadrons of the Royal Navy may have played a crucial role in Napoleon's (q.v.) defeat, but only the great armies fighting on the Continent finally accomplished the emperor's overthrow.[66]

Mahan and Corbett were both aware of the political, strategic, and operational framework. Murray's concentration on "naval warfare" should not be construed as more broadly based sea power. He is agreeing that Corbett's maritime utility serves greater justice as a resource of land power. This clarifies previously discussed issues over attempts to lattice Corbett and Mahan into a single camp. Mahan also had connections to land power, but that occurred by way of sea power and not, as Murray noted, with strictly naval power. "The Mahanian challenge lay ahead."[67]

Part II

Defense

"Communications are probably the most vital and determining element in strategy, military or naval. They are literally the most radical; for all military operations depend upon communications, as the fruit of a plant depends upon communication with its root. We draw therefore upon the map the chief lines by which communication exists between these two centres and the outside world. Such lines represent the mutual dependence of the centres and the exterior, by which each ministers to the other, and by severance of which either becomes useless to the others."

Alfred Thayer Mahan (Capt., USN), "The Strategic Features of the Gulf of Mexico and the Caribbean Sea," *Harper's New Monthly Magazine*, Vol. XCV, no. DLXIX (October 1897).

Chapter Four

Critical Mass

"Revisionism is the opium of the people."
- Mao Zedong

Colin Gray once wrote that "academics are apt to expend undue energy on trivial matters of definition."[1] This statement is correct in most cases. There does exist, however, circumstances requiring a high degree of care and analysis. Mahan duplicates Gray's remark by expressing his own frustration with attention given to insignificant detail:

> The rejection of details, where permissible and understandingly done, facilitates comprehension, which is baffled by a multiplication of minutiae, just as the impression of a work of art, or of a story, is lost amid a multiplicity of figures or of actors.[2]

Sea power does not suffer from a lack of energy spent developing a definition. The variety of explanations causes some to conclude that seeking perfection may be unrealistic. Mahan would agree with Gray's remark over "undue energy on trivial matters of definition." Defining sea, land, air, and space power, on the other hand, is not "trivial." In a publication two years prior, Gray noted that "a satisfactory definition of air power has proved elusive. Since sea power too has evaded a firm definition, it is probably the case that the difficulty is a systemic one."[3] Gray got it exactly right, but stopped short by excluding land and space power. His comments, in conjunction with Mahan's own view, are not contradictory. Problems both men address relates to an obsessive infatuation over detail, which caused many in pursuit of an answer to run astray.

Mahan ranks among the world's most popular recipients of criticism. The number and caliber of people making his enemies list is an astonishing collective of broadly-based professionals. Mahan's situation is unique, for an equal number of supporters charge to his defense. This group believes opponents failed to grasp his overriding thesis and, instead, wound up submerged in those details so eloquently identified by Gray. It is impossible to recognize and refute each and every digression off Mahan's path. Dispelling charges and various categories of disagreement is accomplished by exterminating a select cadre of sacrificial lambs. Their contribution is duly noted and treated with utmost respect.

Case Study One: Man is a Land Animal

Sir Halford Mackinder's heartland theory argued that land transportation and technological advances would depreciate sea power's value.[4] Therefore, it could be legitimately argued that sea power held no further utility as a contributor of national strength.[5] Mackinder's theoretic origin is located on the Eurasian continent. Mackinder identified a geostrategic region in Central Eurasia that allowed topography to insulate it from the outside. He considered this the center of global power, and any nation gaining control stood a good chance of ruling the world. Some of the planet's largest and most diverse natural resource reserves are housed here. Climate is ideal for growing abundant agricultural goods. Thanks to technology, land transportation made it reasonably efficient to tap these resources from numerous continental locations. Hypothetically, the most powerful continental state gaining access to the region could ultimately dictate terms for all Eurasia. Controlling Eurasia would be the grand prize leading to global domination.

Mackinder's theory became official in January 1904. His paper, titled "The Geographic Pivot of History," found its way to Britain's Royal Geographical Society in London. It quickly caused a stir for a nation solidly dedicated to maritime power.[6] Heartland ideals soon suffered a setback when, in May 1905, Imperial Russia's naval fleet got permanently parked on the Sea of Japan's bottom. Russia represented Mackinder's heartland jewel. The performance, compliments of Japan's Imperial Navy, occurred at the Battle of Tsushima Straits in a way that "neither Trafalgar nor the defeat of the Spanish Armada was as complete–as overwhelming."[7] This well-timed event provided powerful momentum to Mahan's theory of maritime supremacy, just as Mackinder started making headway against him. In 1919 Mackinder's equivalent opus to Mahan's *Influence of Sea Power upon History* found its way into the publishing world under the title *Democratic Ideals and Reality*. It achieved for land power what Mahan managed to do for sea power:

> The heartland for the purposes of strategical thinking includes the Baltic Sea, the navigable Middle and Lower Danube, the Black Sea, Asia Minor, Armenia, Persia, Tibet and Mongolia. Within it, therefore were Brandenburg-Prussia, and Austria-Hungary as well as Russia – a vast triple base of manpower, which was lacking to the horse-riders of history. The heartland is the region to which under modern conditions, sea-power can be refused access.[8]

The United States Navy and Marine Corps successfully showed how maritime power can access the "heartland" during recent military operations in Afghanistan: "It is about as far from the sea as a potential battlefield can get, yet our ability to reach it from the sea probably has been decisive."[9] Power projection delivered into the belly of Asia from the Indian Ocean is a task that would have enthralled Mackinder.

Definitions developed by this research consider both Mahan and Mackinder for geostrategic purposes. Both men held identical views toward Russian attempts to dominate what Mahan called the "middle strip." This strip extended across land from the Mediterranean Sea, Turkey, and Persian Gulf to the Sea of Japan. Mahan believed Russia possessed enough power and geostrategic position to conquer the region. The concept, first promoted by Mahan in 1901, occurred three years before Mackinder formally announced his own theory. Primary difference between Mahan and Mackinder is in Mahan's advocacy of a US, British, German, and Japanese maritime alliance to check Russia's move. Mahan's inspiration for a united front developed from observing over 100,000 Russian troops stationed in Mongolia when the Boxer Rebellion ended in 1900. This force remained on station to move into China throughout the 1930s and World War II.

Mackinder's theoretic shortcoming is found in technology. He failed to recognize identical contributions apply when incorporated into geostrategic responsibilities of a maritime power:

> Today armies have at their disposal not only the trans-continental railway but also the motor car. They have, too, the aeroplane, which is of a boomerang nature, a weapon of land-power as against sea-power ... In short, a great military power in possession of the heartland, and of Arabia could take easy possession of the crossways of the world at Suez.[10]

Technology works both ways and Christopher Fettweis alludes to Mackinder's error by failing to consider the identical benefits made available to all power generators:

Mackinder seemed to ignore the fact that to the extent these geographical formations protected a Heartland power, they also prevented it from projecting outward. Walls tend to keep residents in as effectively as they keep invaders out. The geographical boundaries of the Heartland, to the extent that they were ever obstacles, would have hampered any attempt to use it as a springboard for hemispheric domination.[11]

In fairness to Mackinder, those same technologies could work to the Heartland power's benefit. This allows walls of isolation to be broken and power projected outward. Achieving technological parity could turn geographic advantage toward the Heartland. Geoffrey Sloan's review of Mackinder's heartland version closes with a remark that "it can be argued that the heartland theory has no more utility."[12] Sloan continues by actually presenting evidence of convergence underway between Mackinder and Mahan's theories:

> As we move into the twenty-first century, new geographical perspectives will emerge that may be different from the geographical perspective of the twentieth century ... the heartland theory has left a theoretical legacy which can be utilized to outline the geographical perspective of the twenty-first century.[13]

Certain nations possess a wealth of natural resources. Some do not possess appropriate technology or political stability to access these valuable assets. There are also plenty of states with little to offer. They must resort to lesser standards of living, development of international trade, if there is anything of value to trade, or be subjected to conquest if they possess anything worth going after. Mackinder's reference to natural resources in the Heartland must be given consideration for the era surrounding his theoretic proposal. Offshore oil wells and oil fields of enormous reserves are now in places not previously known. Alloy metals have appeared defying anything in existence when the twentieth century began. These materials allowed Neil Armstrong to set foot on the Moon, exactly half a century after Mackinder's publication of *Democratic Ideals and Reality*. How would he respond to space and the entire stable of geostrategic possibilities?

Mackinder's legacy can be found in the North Atlantic where he devised his Midland Ocean. It is similar to his heartland theory but with application at sea and outside Central Asia. A direct connection between Mahan and Mackinder begins to build. This theoretical basis is better understood viewing Mackinder's heartland theory as a moving ameba. A geostrategic power center evolves around the world as great nations come and go, as new oil fields are discovered, and as new technologies appear, just as railroads did to ignite Mackinder's geographic instinct. The power center's location can be planted in the Pacific Ocean just as easily as the Caspian Sea. It is here that fundamental power resources and elements impacting Mahan's philosophy disburse from national grand strategy to also influence Mackinder's theory.

Case Study Two: It's the Economy Stupid

Sea power's benefit to national prosperity and world politics is proven beyond doubt. For whatever reason, a substantial number of people remain unconvinced and even hostile. Paul Kennedy contributes to the cause by arguing British sea power suffered from hype. In Kennedy's view, economic wealth wins wars and sea power tends to drain national economies.[14] His thesis, *The Rise and Fall of British Naval Mastery*, is a critique of Great Britain's economic decline which he believes resulted from a sustained effort to maintain maritime supremacy in support of colonial empire. This argument forces a consideration of England's economic condition and legacy if not for maritime supremacy. William Maltby provides accurate opposition:

> Mahan and Corbett noted long ago that France thereby gave up any claim to command of the sea, although it could regain that command if it wished as the American Revolutionary War showed. The French turn to commerce raiding made an English global strategy not only possible but necessary. England's wealth depended upon trade, and the new policy threatened it on a worldwide basis as never before. England had to protect its trade at all costs, and the disbanding of the French battle fleet released English ships from their traditional duties in the Channel.[15]

Britain's destiny would have quickly ended at the cliffs of Dover were it not for the Royal Navy. Analysis of British maritime power typically begins at a point that reaches a desired conclusion.[16] Kennedy's conclusion would have to start data mining at the pinnacle of success.[17] Everything can then be measured in a downhill spiral as Great Britain enters a black hole of no return. It is not difficult to find examples where sea power appeared to burden a nation's treasury. Kennedy is justified bringing attention to the possibility of such an event taking place.[18] But these cases involve situations where financial health collapsed from revenue shortfalls and economic conditions outside sea power's control.[19] There is no hard evidence sea power's complete package caused a catastrophic demise. Those in support of Kennedy's argument overlook sea power's position within national grand strategy's zone of control. They never left the strategic arena. Outcomes for states in decline often occur from incompetence, mismanagement, or just bad luck. Failure did not result from wise and well-managed investment in sea power. Not even Mackinder could refute Mahan's long-standing defense of maritime transportation: "Notwithstanding all the familiar and unfamiliar dangers of the sea, both travel and traffic by water have always been easier and cheaper than by land."[20] Kennedy actually validates power generators and the relationship to each other, linkage to power resources, and significance of each element to national power in general:

> An economic giant could prefer, for reasons of its political culture or geographical security, to be a military pigmy, while a state without great economic resources could nonetheless so organize its society as to be a formidable military power.[21]

A number of reasons exist why a well-stacked portfolio would not become a viable force of power. Clausewitz describes Kennedy's comment in very eloquent terms: "Theory becomes infinitely more difficult as soon as it touches the realm of moral values."[22] Form of government and political leadership is often a reflection of moral values. Allowance for dreaded surprises must be made when formulating policy and implementing national grand strategy. Moral values are also a vital consideration. This issue is easily discarded in contemporary times as a cacophony of hedonistic groups scream for mainstream acceptance of their behavioral choices.

Mahan managed to build an impressive portfolio of critics from Kennedy's economics sector. Mark Shulman, by coincidence a student of Kennedy, does wonders echoing calls by those who refuse to consider sea power's long-range geostrategic advantages:

> An examination of navalism's first dozen years affords insights into the dynamics of militarism, the degree to which politics, pork, and strategy are linked, and the interrelatedness of various social discourses in the early Progressive era. It also places the fame and impact of Mahan and his writings into a context from which his

successors too quickly removed him. The cost of mounting him upon a pedestal has been paid many times over by the nation. In the past century, the Mahanian navy has proven to be the single most expensive organization ever, a status toward which it had been launched by 1893.[23]

Shulman's focus on expense fails to calculate far greater security costs for not pursuing offensive sea control. This is, expectedly, along the same lines as Kennedy's analysis of Great Britain. A European puppet regime in Mexico, for example, is enough to concern any national security advisor. Abraham Lincoln could not allow the Confederacy to align with European powers. Not only would an alliance achieve sovereignty for the South, but not much would remain of the United States. This prototype applies to the Western Hemisphere vis-à-vis the Monroe Doctrine, which is easily discarded in current times.[24] Shulman's infatuation over cost echoes the theme of critics. It ignores a far more significant return on investment. That reward became known as the American century.

Shulman's thesis launches an assault on political elites for promotional measures taken during the nineteenth century's final decade. The effort successfully fueled public support behind building a maritime portfolio. Criticism again avoids alternative outcomes.[25] No other operational substitute existed to defend the Monroe Doctrine, and this has not changed. The life-span for America's most important national security policy position of the nineteenth century would have been incredibly short, ending in 1859 rather than 1959 when Fidel Castro overthrew the Batista regime in Cuba. The US could not defend South American allies without maritime lift. Lack of criticism in scholarly circles toward the pacifist movement shows bias. Identical tactics were used by that group to influence public opinion.[26] Politics is a war of ideas and each side may resort to unsavory methods in pursuit of victory. Shulman's position is obvious. Fortunately, the pacifist cause lost. Mahan's work can take major credit for saving the United States in the twentieth century.

Case Study Three: Alumni Association

Mahan used history to dramatize his research curriculum: "A study of the military history of the past, such as this, is enjoined by great military leaders as essential to correct ideas and to the skilful conduct of war in the future."[27] He did commit errors and often found himself confronted with similar puzzling questions faced by later maritime scholars. As a result, his work has not significantly advanced since addressing the American Historical Association in 1902. Mahan's work has managed to be as controversial as the ruckus over Cold War analysis.[28] Brian Sullivan identifies a common joke at, of all places, the Naval War College: "The adoption of his [Mahan's] ideas by Germany, Italy and Japan doomed their surface fleets to defeat in the two world wars."[29] Martin van Creveld contributes to Mahan's critics by arguing he failed to recognize German use of submarines in World War I:

> Reared as they were on Mahan's theories concerning the need to seek out and destroy the enemy's battlefleet, the Germans in particular took time to realize that the submarines' best targets were not warships. However, once this happened and Unrestricted Submarine War was declared, the possibility of defeating Britain by starvation became very real indeed.[30]

Mahan did believe the enemy's battle fleet should be destroyed, but this comprised a small part of greater philosophical vision. Even Mahan would argue a number of different factors had to be taken into consideration, including use of submarines to achieve maritime objectives. This reflects D. H. Mahan's strategic belief, which was far less mechanized than perceived: "Cadets called him 'Old Cobbon Sense' (a nasal infection impaired his pronunciation) because of his injunctions to use judgment and common sense rather than rely on the rote application of so-called principles of war."[31] This philosophy transformed to Alfred and bewilders those believing Mahan held the title, "Jomini of the sea."[32]

Methods employed to dominate the sea can be argued indefinitely. These are specifics and a good topic for power lunches. Sea power is the cumulative sum of all national assets used to influence events at sea. None is sole arbiter of sea power. Brian Sullivan characterizes this problem by unknowingly identifying peculiar and contradictory views of many historians:

> George Baer and other historians have pointed out the admiral's ideas did not guide American naval strategy in World Wars I and II nor the Cold War. In the Atlantic – Mediterranean theater, including the post-1945 era, the Navy concentrated on convoy protection and amphibious operations. In the Pacific, it focused on amphibious warfare as well as battle fleets only when they sought out our forces or as an adjunct to landings by the Army or Marines.[33]

An A-6 Intruder pilot may have taken exception upon departing an aircraft carrier in the eastern Mediterranean Sea during the 1980s. This point carries even greater relevance if the cargo included a 150-kiloton nuclear device, with orders to head for the Black Sea. Operating tempo for the US Sixth Fleet in the Mediterranean during the 1980s does not lend credence to Baer's comment from his otherwise outstanding book, *One Hundred Years of Sea Power*.

Describing Mahanian doctrine in strict confines of the sea digresses away from the main thrust of his thesis. In assessing where Germany, Japan, and Italy went terribly wrong with sea power, reference is found in the power resources from Chapter 6. Maritime or naval power is not the dominant theme. Superior management of resources explains the achievement of British and American sea power against their opponent. The Germans, Japanese, and Italians did not realize *sea power* had land-based requirements. Only from land can states support a maritime and naval effort beyond the horizon: "Maritime excellence can be developed and sustained only if there is an absence of intense competition for scarce resources with the army."[34] Germany's main deficiency comprised geographic destiny, Japan's problem involved a lack of natural resources, and Italy's difficulty came from manpower and industrial production.[35] The deficiencies are all land-based and none are strictly military related.

Mahan believed dominating an entire geographic region involved those connecting domains as well (hence sea power). Amphibious operations conducted during WWII are perfectly aligned with his doctrine. Conquest of islands served a critical purpose by providing logistics support to the fleet, air patrol over the Pacific, and bombing operations against a seafaring island nation. It is difficult to believe Mahan would not approve. In the context of those definitions created by this thesis, Baer's comment regarding Mahan's influence in World War I and II, and the Cold War is mischaracterized. Not only were Mahan's views of "sea power" properly applied, but they remained a priority until the twentieth century's ending.

Case Study Four: US Navy Propaganda

Russell Weigley is among those who consider Mahan simply an organ for the Office of Naval Public Affairs. Francis Duncan shows this group of critics cutting a path through Mahan's work immediately upon his passing in December 1914:

Although Mahan was widely read in his own day, he was criticized severely in the period after the First World War. Louis M. Hacker, in an article published in 1934 in *Scribner's Magazine* considered him as "a philosopher of death and destruction," and added, "To regard Mahan seriously as a great historian or thinker is therefore an absurdity." Others have added that Mahan's thought was inconsistent, while the late Professor Charles A. Beard, one of the most prominent of American historians, has written that the so-called "philosophy of Mahan" is no philosophy at all, but a collection of assertions and contradictions vitiated by sentiments including acceptance of British naval supremacy as a moral good.[36]

Soviet Fifth Column operations were alive and well early in the twentieth century. Weigley takes point for those labeling Mahan a propaganda mouthpiece of the military establishment. Weigley discredits himself by using his own intellectual pomp to make an anti-Mahan case: "Within the United States, however, there were forces stirring which would push the interests of the country outward, and which through the projection of American ambitions and activities overseas might involve the country in international competition, perhaps including military competition."[37] This précis has all the beauty of *Pravda*. There is no sinister motive behind Mahan's effort, unless patriotism has been declared a crime.

Focusing on *naval* power is a treacherous journey without adding Mahan's national grand strategy paradigm to the debate. A horrendous research quagmire results from labeling Mahan a maritime sales agent. Weigley continued to lay into Mahan by attaching and then disengaging from the "Jomini of the sea" label. This is followed up by accusations questioning Mahan's ability to even grasp strategic theory:

Even as younger and more progressive officers came to recognize the shortcomings of Mahanian strategic thought, the Navy had to pay homage to Mahan because its public and political image depended on him. Thus his ideas survived the criticism they encountered in his later years, and after his death in 1914 he gained renewed stature as the high priest of American navalism, whose strategic teachings were its holy writ.[38]

Weigley's use of "progressive" should be a warning. Mahan's contribution became far greater than a US Navy promotional product. Weigley would benefit by reconsidering the referenced history. The United States overcame numerous dire threats to its survival, and instruments of sea power played critical roles in suppressing these challenges. Fortunately for those who believe in freedom of the pen, which may include Weigley, Nazi Germany and the Soviet Union were denied their self-perceived right to world domination. Mahan's vision and the US Navy/Marine Corps were significant players. Weigley's assault continues with the addition of railroads:

> Railroad systems had too much replaced coastal waterways as the medium of transportation within Europe. Mahan did not concede that the change since Napoleon's day was so drastic, but his failure to do so is another evidence of his excessive reliance on the past to guide the strategy of the future.[39]

Documentation of successful maritime and naval action against land power throughout the twentieth century is quite clear. It somehow escapes Weigley's keen analysis. Weigley's critique has merit, but only where navigable waterways are nonexistent. That does not cover much territory and a globe of the planet reveals an awful lot of blue.

Case Study Five: The Strategic Legends

Jon Sumida has identified a prevailing problem arising from anti-Mahan methodology:

> Mahan is often portrayed – because of misreadings of fragments of his writing, or all too often upon no reading of the original texts at all – as a purveyor of truisms about naval strategy and doctrine. The resulting caricature is frequently either misapplied or dismissed as outdated.[40]

Sumida makes the same accusation of Weigley that Weigley makes of Mahan. The difference is the accuracy of Sumida's charge. Sumida's correlation is starkly similar to the diverse definitions now being compassionately put out of their misery. He elevates his explanation to scholars of Carl von Clausewitz. That focus is on two particular notes by the German military strategist in promoting his consideration to rewrite *On War*. Excitement became fixated on analysis of each letter's content and, like the treatment of Mahan, scholars failed to contemplate his work spatially. This identical problem exists with sea power, and matches Sumida's criticism of surgical attempts to slice and dice both Mahan and Clausewitz:

Nineteenth century readers of Clausewitz ignored his arguments on the superiority of the defense over the offense. Britain's leading military theorist of the twentieth century, Basil Liddell Hart, portrayed Clausewitz "as a relentless advocate of mass and the offensive." The critical essays in the standard English language edition of On War fall in between: while Peter Paret says nothing on the subject, Michael Howard and Bernard Brodie acknowledge Clausewitz's views while not making much of them.[41]

Sumida recognizes a prevailing problem. It explains why establishing exacting definitions has been a hindrance. Explanations for sea, land, air, and space power are presented for public consumption based on "highly selective reading." Caution is warranted when applying broad context because of a desire to correlate spatial programming with "doctrine." Doctrine is a concept attached to directional purpose and has closer affinity to policy-making. Sumida distinguishes the danger of inappropriate use because Mahan believed doctrine caused bureaucratic overkill to a degree that it threatened military operations:

> The imposition of a common set of action principles, he argued in 1911, meant that "within a pretty wide range there will be in a school of officers a certain homogeneousness of intellectual equipment and conviction which will tend to cause likeness of impulse and of conduct under any set of given conditions. The formation of a similar habit of thought, and of assurance as to the right thing to do under particular circumstances, reinforces strongly the power of co-operation, which is the essential factor in military operations." But Mahan was conscious of the tendency of doctrine to interfere with the exercise of intelligent judgment, which to him was also of critical importance. "The French word *doctrinaire*, fully adopted into English," he thus wrote, "gives warning of the danger that attends doctrine; a danger to which all useful conceptions are liable," which was the propensity to exaggerate "the letter above the spirit, of becoming mechanical instead of discriminating."[42]

Again, evidence shows Mahan fell in tune with Clausewitz rather than Jomini. A Look at Jomini's definition of grand tactics reveals sharp differences with Mahan's own view on defense and fortifications:

> The art of posting troops upon the battle-field according to the accidents of the ground, of bringing them into action, and the art of

fighting upon the ground, in contradistinction to planning upon a map.[43]

Jomini's description is contained within a model of offensive military action. He supports his statement with an eight point reinforcement that includes lines of battle, offensive and defensive positioning, maneuvering for attack, and arrangement of troops.[44] Jomini and his disciples did a marvelous job confusing people over the distinctions between tactics, grand tactics, and strategy. Grand tactics is not given application for this research because of the commingling danger with strategic and tactical responsibilities.

Case Study Six: Problems of Definition

The file on scholars attempting to explain sea power is as thick as the list containing definitions. Bernard Brodie identifies sea power as "The sum total of those weapons, installations, and geographical circumstances which enables a nation to control transportation over the seas during wartime."[45] Passing examination reveals something worthy of merit based on mainstream criteria. This is particularly true since it originated from Brodie. Name recognition has its benefit. Brodie, by way of his definition, is either indirectly critical of Mahan's work or ignoring his explanation in *The Influence of Sea Power upon History*. Concentration on naval and maritime elements is a path countless others have taken.[46] Brodie supports the status quo by granting single source consideration to the wartime environment. Specifying his view on what warrants wartime matters, or eliminating "during wartime" entirely would cure the traveling public's fixation on things that go bang. War is an accumulation of acts in an ongoing state of affairs and sea power is a crucial factor in war. Utilizing the word "war," without distinguishing a peacetime role, threatens sea power's importance by people who consider its contribution minimal during periods of non-violence. Sea power affords allies a large degree of interaction as states seek to get along. This cannot be ignored.

Brodie's air power explanation also contradicts spatial domains that upset national grand strategy's configuration: "That force of aircraft and missiles which is operated more or less independently of ground and naval forces for generally independent purposes."[47] His air power definition is used here to defend the power generator model's overriding thesis. Brodie's remark is in the context of an air power association with strategy and tactics. He states the definition "does *not* imply or prejudice any position on the so-called 'tactical use' of aircraft, either as to its importance or the methods of pursuing it. The use of air power in support of ground or naval operations simply forms a different subject."[48] Attaching this disclaimer should be a warning. Integrating physical objects (aircraft and missiles) is a primitive exercise for complex processes. Power resources influencing atmospheric regions determine air power identity. Tools deployed to exert that pressure are far more extensive than aircraft and missiles. Aircraft and missiles do, however, provide value associated with defining "air force power."

Brodie's approach to sea power omits such factors as economics, industrial might, and manpower.[49] These are essential ingredients clearly emphasized by Mahan. Sea power is the foundation for naval power, which serves as an instrument of foreign policy. Sea power is vital to a nation's grand strategy portfolio at all times and, yes, especially when war does get physical. Products of sea power make a valuable contribution when non-violent conflict is underway between parties. Naval and maritime power offer great advantages in the maintenance of peace.[50] The ability to project formidable naval forces at will is an insurance policy for avoiding physical aspects of war.[51] Brodie's argument appears quite similar to Mackinder: "If in the future the greater part of ocean transport is carried in aircraft rather than in ships, or if the transfer of men and commodities across the seas becomes unimportant, sea power as such will cease to have meaning."[52] Contributions made by air assets take on increasingly significant responsibility for sea power's success each year. If air assets are supporting events in the geographical environment of the sea, then those instruments belong to sea power. Finally, sea power's value to national grand strategy far surpasses the "transporting men and commodities across the seas."

Case Study Seven: Unconventional Perspectives

Don DeYoung illustrates an intriguing idea with the hypothesis that only two real powers exist (sea and land), while air and space power are actually supporting forces.[53] This amusing position has merit considering air and space power's short life-cycle. His reasoning behind air and space forces acting in support of land and sea power may apply at the tactical level. In fact, Mahan could be used to support

DeYoung's contention tactically, but would then obliterate him at the strategic level: "From time to time the superstructure of tactics has to be altered or wholly torn down; but the old foundations of strategy so far remain, as though laid upon a rock."[54] Colin Gray, a proactive advocate of air and space power, unknowingly provides an explanation of DeYoung's view:

> The environmentally conditioned worldviews of the sailor and the soldier continue to challenge the coherence of national and coalition military strategy. On their mental world maps, soldiers tend, understandably, to see more or less extensive lakes surrounded by land (the dominant feature). In contrast, sailors tend to see islands, more or less extensive in scale, surrounded by water (the dominant feature).[55]

Logic exists in De Young's geostrategic map and frame of reference. His treatment of efforts to dominate the atmosphere and space, however, minimizes contributions "from" the surface. Additionally, his use of "force" insinuates strict military approaches to sea, land, air, and space power. DeYoung's argument has strength if only horizontal approaches to power generating theory existed. But power can flow vertically just as easily as it does horizontally.

DeYoung raises two questions worth considering. Could the sea be dominated and controlled using only air and space forces? If so, would these be considered elements of air or sea power? The answer to the first question is "yes" with a caveat. Each situation must be judged on specific environments relative to the action (tactics), and the aptitude of available assets. The second answer is "no" and "yes." Objectives would be the deciding factor. In this particular case, that priority would belong at sea. DeYoung's air and space force, in context with the sea, belong to sea power if that is where their assignment is fulfilled. This model can be reversed to show naval forces exerting "pressure" in the atmosphere or space. This vertically propels those products into the realm of air and space power.

DeYoung's hypothesis can be turned upside down by applying numerous scenarios. Land power could be considered land force based on his same argument; its purpose is to support air and space power. Land, in other words, exists to provide air bases, launch pads, resources, and logistics support for both powers. Brigadier General William "Billy" Mitchell used similar philosophical vision to promote air forces during debates in the 1920s; he proposed that if and when produced, aircraft carriers should belong to the Army Air Service.[56] This gives an appearance that naval "force" exists as an instrument supporting air power. Vertical realities of power challenge DeYoung's position. Another example could be an argument land power is actually land force, whose purpose is to support sea power. This horizontal approach argues land assets, such as industrial capability, logistical support facilities, and natural resources serve to support sea power. Additionally, if the sea can be dominated from the air, then there is no reason why atmospheric regions cannot be dominated from the sea. Possibilities are endless.

Case Study Eight: Military Focus

The blast of critics marching in lockstep with a mission to dissect Mahan is an impressive roster covering the ideological spectrum. George Quester adds beef to NWC jokes by focusing on Japan's situation during World War II:

> While lacking in larger numbers of aircraft carriers and battleships, the United States Navy in World War II had one other weapon to deploy in facing the Japanese advance: the submarine. She used this weapon very effectively against Japan from the outset, indeed more effectively than the Germans anti-British campaigns in either World War. U.S. submarines sought to sink Japanese merchant shipping. While the United States had entered World War I in protest against Germans unrestricted submarine warfare, it was ironic that the United States Navy was directed, on the day after Pearl Harbor, to engage in such unrestricted submarine warfare against Japan.
>
> Apart from issues of civilization and a moral regard for the rights of civilians, this departure, and the substantial accomplishments of the U.S. submarine attacks in greatly reducing the flow of food and oil and other materials back to Japan across the Pacific, raises a question about the impact of Mahan, the strategic theorist, on the U.S. Navy? The answer again seems fairly clear. This element of the war was more analogous to the exploits of John Paul Jones and U.S. commerce raiders in the War of 1812, than to the dramatic fleet actions of Nelson.[57]

Quester may not have realized Mahan's support in 1896 for submarine research and development: "In our present unprotected condition, the risk of losing the money by reason of the boat's being a failure is more than counterbalanced by the great protection the boat would be if a substantial success."[58] Russell Weigley expectedly supports Quester by accusing Mahan of "ignoring the emergence of a threat which in 1917 was to come close to ruining Great Britain and thereby gravely endangering the United States."[59]

Weigley and Quester fixate on a single naval instrument. Dedicated criticism based on narrowly focused tools is a common trait. Both men do a fine job noting the success of US submarine warfare capabilities operating within parameters of *naval* strategy. But submarines were just one of multiple reasons Japan lost the war. Focusing on a singular issue betrays the entire sea power package. In a conversation with General Douglas MacArthur following Japan's surrender, General Hideki Tojo identified three reasons why Japan lost. US submarines were appropriately identified as a factor. The two other reasons include America's ability to leap-frog around Japanese garrisons. The third and most unacknowledged truth by Mahanian critics involved abilities associated with *Essex*-class carriers to operate at sea for months without a need for harbor anchorage to replenish.[60] These factors comprise far more than Quester's submarines.

Submarines are singular contributions to naval power. They are important assets to Mahan's sea power tenet. *Essex*-class carrier abilities to remain underway for extended periods frustrated Japan's attempt to find, isolate, and accost. According to Tojo, the surface fleet made an impact far beyond subsurface activity. Actions taken by America's submarine fleet in the Pacific were effective as specific *naval* operations contributing to sea power's vast realm. Submarine action damaged Japan's once marveled manufacturing base by hitting supply ships. Land warfare works in similar ways. Heavy armor divisions are the equivalent on land to Mahan's main battle fleet at sea. Special Forces units are the equivalent of submarines and ambushes are a perfectly acceptable means for attacking the enemy.

Quester's view toward civilians and commerce in war must be harshly evaluated on Machiavellian terms of unrestricted warfare:

> For it must be noted, that men must either be caressed or else annihilated; they will revenge themselves for small injuries, but cannot do so for great ones; the injury therefore that we do to a man must be such that we need not fear his vengeance.[61]

Those operating on the seas under a flag representing their nation during war are not innocent, regardless of redundant attire. Innocent civilians often do not apply when great nations collide and brute force becomes the order of the day. If war must remove a despot acting against standard norms of international behavior, chances are good it is because civilians failed to take matters in their own hands.[62]

Quester successfully notes tactical specifics associated with a military theatre, but sea power's broad expanse in context with his statement prevents coordination and linkage. Submarine pinging by Quester is in an identical league as other assets used to gain command of the sea. Admiral Vern Clark explains this in precise form:

> They [U.S. Navy sailors] knew of the numerous basic training centers that had been established in the United States that soon would be churning out sailors and soldiers by the thousands. They knew of the shipyards, airplane factories, and armament manufacturers that were gearing up to produce new weapons of war. And they knew, in the early days of June 1942 with the war barely six months old, that they, with their three carriers and escort forces barely half the size of the approaching Japanese fleet, were the only force standing between Japan and victory. With the odds stacked against them, they were prepared to fight and, if need be, die in service to the nation.
> Sailors and Marines of all ranks, through skill, determination, and remarkable courage, and despite heavy odds, won that battle [Midway]. In the air, on the sea in surface engagements, and beneath the surface as our submarines engaged the enemy, all facets of the U.S. Navy combined to deliver the most decisive victory of World War II in the Pacific.[63]

Think Big

Sir Walter Raleigh summarized sea power's enormity with his statement, "Who commands the sea commands commerce, who commands commerce disposes of the riches of the world and thereby dominates the world itself."[64] This is classic Mahanian doctrine and could have served as an inspirational quote. Peter Padfield alluded to this in his defense of Mahan:

> Mahan's explanation was rather fuller: traffic by water was and had always been easier and cheaper than by land – a principle that holds good for most commodities even after the development of railways, motorways and air transport – hence the use and control of the sea lanes was the central link in the chain of exchanges whereby wealth was accumulated. And wealth was, of course, the sinews of war.[65]

There are a large number of features involved in Sir Walter Raleigh's statement. If states overlook national grand strategy's arena where sea power thrives, then they will miss valuable contributions that could have advanced the effort. Grand strategy's submersion in a single package labelled "strategy" disrupts national security's power generator train. This seduces and disorients people as they commence applying various theories. Results have been devastating for far more than Germany, Japan, and Italy. Napoleon Bonaparte would wholeheartedly agree.

Chapter Five

National Power

"Does it seem as if a child will be born?"
- Message to Tokyo from Japanese ambassador to the United States (27 November 1941).

"Yes, the birth of a child seems imminent. It seems as if it will be a strong, healthy boy."
- Reply from Tokyo (29 November 1941).

National grand strategy places its capability in motion based on the strategic needs of policy objectives. Strategy evolves as grand strategy's power generators distribute power resources in strategic channels. Appropriate channels are determined at the policy level. The strategic channel goes active upon receiving those mechanisms delegated to it by grand strategy.[1] Once grand strategy's energy goes kinetic, strategy must be ready to incorporate that power for allocation to surgical action (tactics). This substantiates problems with the earlier definition by Claude Ricketts. A power generator definition must indicate that connecting transition from capability to kinetic deployment. A center of power serves as a rendezvous point for all four power generators. Once converged, they then get released into a strategic theater. Three strategic channels exist comprised of peaceful guardian, passive hostile, and active hostile.[2] Peaceful guardian is warranted where conditions are stable and maintaining an existing order desired. This is most often accomplished by a show of strength, but without creating fear or intimidation. Peaceful guardian is the most desired, but seldom functions without a show of force. Nations often find themselves operating on two strategic channels. Passive hostile is preferred over the active hostile strategic channel, but effectiveness is in question. Passive hostile pressure may include political, economic, and cultural isolation, either as singular events or in combination.

Giving the passive hostile category more muscle through international solidarity has been disappointing when dealing with repressive regimes. Military force was ultimately required to rid Iraq of Saddam Hussein, thirteen years following his eviction from Kuwait.

Fidel Castro had no difficulty remaining the designated tyrant for life in Cuba. This occurred even as Cuban citizens lived in squalor, fully aware of the good times to the north. People of Burma have been subjected to oppressive military rule for years, while that nation gets absorbed into the People's Republic of China's sphere of influence.[3]

Political and economic bias runs amuck in a passive hostile strategic channel. Playing favorites is profoundly shown by Western inaction against the PRC, a state annually qualifying among the five most oppressive regimes. Several questions arise concerning the international community's record for selectively incorporating a passive hostile channel: Is financial gain and stock performance more important than moral compass? Does hypocrisy exist toward various dictatorships? Why is Communist China fawned over by Western political and business elites, while the Republic of China government on Taiwan is treated like a deadly virus? Totalitarian states survive despite foreign policy rhetoric proudly proclaiming a dictatorship is "feeling the heat" of economic sanctions.[4] Passive hostile strategic operations are simply prevailing fashion statements with purely cosmetic results.

Taking their cue from past experience with Nazi Germany and the USSR, many Western democracies and companies have again incorporated free-wheeling trade practices with those planning their destruction. State suicide seems to be a noble calling for some. The Cold War highlighted countless displays of deranged acts by officials pushing for development of Soviet trade. Econo-lawlessness routinely carried on while gross acts of international behavior took place. A profound example followed downing of Korean Airlines Flight 007 in 1983: "When it comes to transfer of valuable free world technology that will strategically benefit the Soviet Union, it was during the Reagan Administration that the floodgates were opened."[5] Even an allegedly weak Carter administration took a more hard-line approach following the Soviet invasion of Afghanistan and KGB orchestrated overthrow of the Shah of Iran. Ironically, the Department of State energetically pushed for continued business fondling. State won out over a Department of Commerce decision recommending trade sanctions against the USSR following the KAL massacre.[6] America and its allies then continued to compete against each other for business as if nothing happened. Identical behavior is seen today with the People's Republic of China.[7]

Energy Distribution

Without all four power generators acting in conjunction with each other, national grand strategy can easily fail to meet expectations of policy-makers. National grand strategy is the distributor of energy held by a center of power binding power generators together. National grand strategy harnesses the atom (center of power) containing a nucleus of protons (sea power) and neutrons (land power), while electrons (air and space power) orbit about. It deploys energy in accordance with national objectives. Each generator is dependent on and supportive of the others. Like an atom, an imbalance between particles can cause severe consequences. Collectively, power generators determine the center of power's value. A nation's center of power kinetic force originates from national grand strategy's design. Colin Gray's reference to military force summarizes the relationship between all four generators:

> Land power, sea power, air power, and space power are distinguishable, even though the potency of each typically depends upon the performance of one or more of the others; each (with the exception of space power) embraces well-established activities that would appear to belong more properly to another (e.g., navies with their own small armies and air forces); and each contributes more or less strategic effectiveness overall to the course and outcome of deterrence and war. It is possible to recognize the uncertainty of the margins between, say, sea power and air power, or land power and air power, as well as the synergism's for improved performance that exist among the geographically specialized forces.[8]

Gray describes strategy as "the bridge that connects the threat and use of force with policy or politics."[9] A worthy point based on prevailing themes surrounding a three-pronged policy-strategy-tactics triad. Splitting this process further allows national grand strategy's distinguishing characteristics to surface. Gray's explanation can be presented in two parts, making national grand strategy the bridge connecting threats and use of force with policy. It is strategy that serves as the management firm supervising grueling applications of force, while tactics is the actual tortuous ordeal. Gray's definition is specifically tooled for military application, but force is applied in a number of ways. Economic strain and diplomatic pressure are two points of duress, though success is sometimes dubious.[10] Strategy may not be strictly military driven but, if a state wishes to enhance survival chances, the ability to unleash military force must be ready as a final option: "War for a non-aggressor nation is actually a nearly complete collapse of policy."[11]

Each channel becomes a political act when put in motion. Strategic analysis is a unique world in that no two situations are identical: "He changes his methods and alters his plans so that people have no knowledge of what he is doing."[12] The profession is unlike any other. Lawyers are fixed to law, surgeons use set procedures in operating rooms, and chemical engineers know what will happen by mixing certain ingredients improperly. A strategist faces a portfolio of many uncertainties. Though primitive, a foundation does exist. Alteration of the environment is constantly changing and, therefore, basic theoretic tools help prevent a lot of grief. Transition from theory to reality is incredibly dramatic and success is critical to job security because of the outcome for losing. Nations can rise and fall based on strategic designs. For the loser, there is often no recourse but to succumb to the victor's imposition, and hopefully they implement lenient treatment.

Similarities and Differences

The United States considers the Atlantic, Pacific, and Caribbean Sea as boundaries worth securing. It deploys naval force powerful enough to guarantee that priority. Rulers of the Roman Empire failed to make waterways and naval operations a main concern. Legions on land were the primary instruments of national defense, while anything at sea belonged to the supporting cast. This forced an empire upon a republic and it marked the start of a very long slide. Rome's legions gained fame as they became the essence of national power's military stick. Mahan's first principle condition for sea power comes to mind and, unfortunately for Rome, this crucial piece of information was not yet in print for the ruling elite to heed:

> It may be pointed out, in the first place, that if a nation be so situated that it is neither forced to defend itself by land nor induced to seek extension of its territory by way of the land, it has, by the very unity of its aim directed upon the sea, an advantage as compared with a people one of whose boundaries is continental. This has been a great advantage to England over both France and Holland as a sea power.

The strength of the latter was early exhausted by the necessity of keeping up a large army and carrying on expensive wars to preserve her independence; while the policy of France was constantly diverted, sometimes wisely and sometimes most foolishly, from the sea to projects of continental extension. These military efforts expended wealth; whereas a wiser and consistent use of her geographical position would have added to it.[13]

A nation is in peril if a vast bulk of defense allocation must be dedicated to securing continental land boundaries. The United States provides a paradigm of the right mix, contingent on stable north-south borders. Europe's topography is extremely diverse, with climates to match. It is as unforgiving today as 2000 years ago for Rome, 200 years ago for France, or in the twenty-first century for the European Union. Geographic position was Mahan's primary consideration for power projection. Ramses would agree by claiming geostrategy has been a factor since the parting of the Red Sea. Geostrategic necessity required overseas bases to sustain the US Navy's forward fleet as the twentieth century unfolded. This is the motivation behind Mahan's argument for annexing the Sandwich Islands:

> By no premeditated contrivance of our own, by the cooperation of a series of events which, however dependent step by step upon human action, were not intended to prepare the present crisis, the United States finds herself compelled to answer a question – to make a decision – not unlike and not less momentous than that required of the Roman senate, when the Mamertine garrison invited it to occupy Messina, and so to abandon the hitherto traditional policy which had confined the expansion of Rome to the Italian peninsula.[14]

A touch of comparative elasticity on Mahan's part is apparent. It is perfectly legitimate to argue another power such as Japan would make a move on the islands if the United States had not beaten them to the punch. While treatment of vanquished natives falling to imperialism can lead to unfavorable outcomes, a lot depends on who is conducting territorial acquisition. America's long-range geostrategic requirements in the Pacific Ocean benefited more than just people from the lower forty-eight states. A unique US position took place by the way native populations were offered citizenship and integration into America's political system. Inhabitants were allowed full-fledged membership, with all the rights and freedoms of everyone else. This unprecedented event was accomplished by a democratic republic harnessed to real constraints of constitutional law.[15] The native populace, as a result of this alien concept called federalism, achieved freedoms unimaginable, even under their own independent ruler.

Wise administrations consider geographic circumstances before taking action. Pursuing policy requires that resource allocation be tied to the state's geographic position:

> The military or strategic value of a naval position depends upon its situation, upon its strength, and upon its resources. Of the three, the first is of the most consequence, because it results from the nature of things; whereas the two latter, when deficient, can be supplied artificially, in whole or in part. Fortifications remedy the weaknesses of a position, foresight accumulates beforehand the resources which nature does not yield on the spot; but it is not within the power of man to change the geographical situation of a point which lies outside the limit of strategic effect.[16]

Mahan's comment must be considered in the context of the year made. Many argue the advent of nuclear weapons has limited strategic advantages associated with geography. Nikita Khrushchev's 40 mile high mushroom cloud on 30 October 1961 allegedly proved this point. An astute strategist counters that nuclear strategy, like all military strategy, is a two-way street. Geographic advantage may appear insignificant following the fireworks display, but it does still exist. Geography's importance to power generation and national grand strategy is without question. Nobody can intellectually argue the Suez Canal does not remain a valuable geostrategic chokepoint. The same pressure point that caused the British Empire to contract in the 1950s existed 200 years ago in relation to Egypt and the Nile River. Suez served the British at sea as Euro-tunnel does today for land transport across the English Channel:

> Egypt, despite the jealousy of France, has passed under English control. The importance of that position to India, understood by Napoleon and Nelson, led the latter at once to send an officer overland to Bombay with the news of the battle of the Nile and the downfall of Bonaparte's hopes. Even now, the jealousy with which England views the advance of Russia in Central Asia is the result of those days in which her sea power and resources triumphed over the weakness of D'Ache and the genius of Suffren, and wrenched the peninsula of India from the ambition of the French.[17]

Mahan used the geostrategic importance of Suez in comparison to a canal across Panama. As a chokepoint, Panama could cause profound negative effects similar to the British experience with Suez.[18] A similar fate occurred in Egyptian waters when Nelson dispatched the French fleet at the mouth of the Nile in 1798, leaving Napoleon to exclaim, "Italy is lost!"[19] Captain Amme's description of kinetic energy stands out when connected to Mahan's remark that force is "power in action." Sea power's long arm stretched across the Mediterranean from the Nile to the boot of Italy. Power in motion (kinetic energy) must be stated equally to potential because each is a "distinct" feature of sea power. Deployable naval, land, and air forces provide coercive muscle for national power's entire package. They feed political authority to all three strategic channels. Additionally, peace through strength, while having military connotations, can include such resources as financial sway: "Indeed, it was at the Bank of England that the Empire was effectively lost."[20] Each strategic channel is of no value if the willpower does not exist when political wants and needs arise.

The War of the Spanish Succession demonstrated the imprint England's inferior maritime force left on a more "capable" Spain possessing little political willpower:

> Spain, the nation before which all others had trembled less than a century before, was now long in decay and scarcely formidable; the central weakness had spread to all parts of the administration. In extent of territory, however, she was still great. The Spanish Netherlands still belonged to her; she held Naples, Sicily, and Sardinia; Gibraltar had not yet fallen into English hands; her vast possessions in America – with the exception of Jamaica, conquered by England a few years before – were still untouched.[21]

Differences between Spain and England are classic displays of sea power passivity in conjunction with an "ability" to release military force:

> The noiseless, steady, exhausting pressure with which sea power acts, cutting off the resources of the enemy while maintaining its own, supporting war in scenes where it does not appear itself, or appears only in the background, and striking open blows at rare intervals, though lost on most, is emphasized to the careful reader by the events of this war and of the half-century that followed. The overwhelming sea power of England was the determining factor in European history during the period mentioned, maintaining war abroad while keeping

its own people in prosperity at home, and building up the great empire which is now seen; but from its very greatness its action, by escaping opposition, escapes attention.[22]

Mahan's use of "pressure" strikes at the heart of this thesis and resulting definitions for all four power generators. "Military sea power" enabled Great Britain to advance an entire stable of sea power assets during its intercourse with the world. The active hostile strategic channel is the political zone for vicious human behavior and where previous threats of military force actually materialize.

Implementing national policy may appear straightforward. But cerebral challenges, such as Clausewitz's friction, will surface once events unfold. Rotating from national grand strategy (distribution of assets), to the process of strategy (application of those assets) marks a transition from macro to micro levels.[23] This phase is critical and those responsible for grand strategy must be certain adequate resources exist to fulfill strategic objectives. Individuals tasked with pursuing strategic objectives must make certain planning and requests for support are complete enough to ensure success. Once strategy's operational sphere is entered, then the situation becomes susceptible to rapid and volatile shifts. Without adequate assets to identify and deal with unusual developments during the strategic phase, which can result from tactical outcomes, then damage may reverberate back to national grand strategy in a hurry.[24] No nation desires to find themselves in this "blow-back" position and the Germans, Japanese, and Italians showed why. When reverse force has crossed that barrier separating strategy from national grand strategy, the entire national policy process is put at risk of unraveling. Too many failed to understand national grand strategy's importance and the role of power generators in determining success or failure.

National grand strategy is worthy of distinction as a crucial link in the popularly labeled policy-strategy-tactics chain for those reasons just described. Clearly separating grand strategy into a unique category reinforces all four power generators. Accurate power generator definitions can be extracted by firmly establishing this strategic train. Dennis Drew and Donald Snow summarized a viable case purely by accident:

> Grand national strategy thus emerges as the process by which the appropriate instruments of power are arrayed and employed to accomplish the national interest. Thus, the building blocks of grand

national strategy are the goals or national interests that are to be served and the instruments that may be used to serve those ends.[25]

Drew and Snow describe this process as "grand national strategy." Verbal structure aside, they anchor their point to power resources as the main generators within national grand strategy's arena. Their comment is dedicated to political, economic, and military instruments. These are power resources supporting sea, land, air, and space power. Power generators are driving forces for national grand strategy, bringing life to the policy incubator. Power resources act as intricate parts, while maintaining close ties to geography, a resource colleague. Colin Gray, in fact, focuses on geography's priority with his creation of four working propositions:

- All politics is geopolitics.
- All strategy is geostrategy.
- Geography is 'out there' objectively as environment or 'terrain.'
-   Geography is also 'within us', in here, as imagined spatial relationships.[26]

Several reasons are given for overlooking national grand strategy's presence in the past. The most prevalent involved ease at describing processes in terms of a simplified policy-strategy-tactics triad.[27] This compounded matters over time and omitting national grand strategy became second nature. Another explanation states continuity and cohesion of the process is better understood by compressing as many titles as possible. This defense argues that policy advancement is complicated enough. A third reason concerns convenience when attempting to describe an activity in a way that does not hinder expedient presentation. All are reasons associated with efficiency but, as a result, become less efficient over time: "All too often, tactics has masqueraded as strategy."[28] Keeping national grand strategy under a general title of strategy prevents complete grasp of grand strategy's contribution to national objectives. Imagine the chaotic horde of a system where national grand strategy is buried in strategy while tactics is simultaneously "masqueraded as strategy." Nations cannot afford the loss of grand strategy's identity. Responsibility as that crucial "enabler" between policy and strategy is far too critical to survival.[29]

A large number of tangents can alter strategy's transformation. Failure to maintain control when events unfold exacerbates survival chances of theoretical designs. Contingency planning is of utmost importance: "Attack may be changed into defense and defense into attack; advance may be turned into retreat and retreat into advance; containing forces may be turned into assault forces, and assault forces into containing forces."[30] It is impossible to know what may go through an on-scene commander's mind or that of anyone else engaged in direct tactical contact.[31] Tactics enables a strategist to witness moral, physical, geographical, mathematical, and statistical elements preying on strategy.[32] Clausewitz's "friction" and so many other challenges rise to the surface in rapid order.[33] Life can become disoriented from that point forward. Physical sciences have difficulty dealing with such uncertainties. Their work is confined to the material and a propensity that it does not exist if it cannot be quantified. Clausewitz argues moral values cannot be ignored because they are the foundation bringing life to a quantifier's material.[34] His point is observed firsthand when opposing forces get unleashed.

Failure of Germany in World War I and the Axis Powers in World War II involved an infatuation over naval operational theory that blinded otherwise keen leadership. Gray's comment over expenditures of "undue energy on trivial matters" has appropriate application. Japan, Germany, and Italy did not get it and attempting to connect their blunders to Mahan's overriding thesis is itself misguided:

> Certainly Mahan's cogently argued theses did not lead to the establishment of institutions such as Staff and War Colleges, where the principles he propounded could be analysed in relation to contemporary political, economic and technical developments, and so assist in formulating sound strategy. Rather did his gift for gripping narrative, his plangent rhetoric, and his genius for creating an image by a simple, telling phrase (such as 'those far-distant, storm-beaten ships upon which the Grand Army never looked'), cause his British readers too often to remember the phrase and forget the reasoning, often accompanied by cautious and discretionary qualifications which lay behind it.[35]

Disregard for "Discussion of the Elements of Sea Power" in *The Influence of Sea Power upon History* doomed Germany, Japan and Italy. Though each of General Tojo's three points laid out to General MacArthur can be consolidated into naval power, they are wrapped inside a single package called sea power and tied to national power. Martin Van Creveld's reference to Great Britain's starvation chances during World War I is in line with Mahan's larger view of sea power. A strangle-hold of that magnitude is a climactic display of an adversary's national grand strategy and sea power might: "Of the items wholly unconnected with engagements, serving only to maintain the forces, supply is the one which most directly affects the fighting."[36]

Japan, Germany and Italy suffered from an inability to demarcate where planning and "group-think" meetings end, and the art of resolute leadership takes over: "Even with the violence of emotion, judgment and principle must still function like a ship's compass, which records the slightest variations however rough the sea."[37] This is an excellent Clausewitzian reinforcement that emphasizes "art" in the intercourse of war.[38] The "Jomini of the sea" must have been confused during his AHA speech. "Art" is used a dozen times in reference to the historical profession.[39]

Transport This

Transportation is a power resource with physical characteristics based on geographic destiny. Transportation makes a vital contribution to national power regardless of specific methods used. Union Pacific Railroad (UPR), an American Fortune 150 company, serves as a perfect example of Mahanian doctrine while simultaneously reinforcing technological advances promoted by Mackinder. UPR provides a connecting link with Mahan's principles of sea power by way of a rail network equivalent to navigable tributaries where those waterways do not exist. Trains transport commodities overland where ships cannot go. This contributes to sea power's value. Were it not for UPR's ability to transport cargo, off-loaded from merchant ships, then Pacific Ocean seaports would become choked by backlogged freight. The bottleneck would reverberate across the world's oceans.

Railroad and coastal intermodal facilities of today have become a vital transportation link for economic growth in agricultural products, mineral resources, energy products, and manufactured goods. This includes military hardware destined for and returning from overseas. Sea power's position in this "link" is getting greater consideration because of estimates showing merchant shipping surpassing a 300% growth rate over the next twenty-five years.[40] Union Pacific Railroad's ability to transport products in a highly safe manner, while keeping an eye on future demand, is a positive reflection of their corporate environment.

Union Pacific's transportation system is extremely complex and sophisticated. Entire network comprises almost 40,000 miles of track. Major east-west arteries stretch from seaports in Los Angeles, California, to Memphis, Tennessee. Rail cars are then transferred to another company for points further east. The main artery provides branch lines to Houston, Texas and New Orleans, Louisiana, which also serve major seaports. A northern line extends across the original transcontinental route from San Francisco, California, to as far as Chicago, Illinois. Like Memphis, additional railroad companies, trucking firms, and even merchant ships serving the Great Lakes are available to transport commodities further east. UPR lines extend north and south from Mexico to Canada. Its presence in over half of the fifty states covers a substantial portion of the continental United States. Strategic utility of cargo vessels is beyond question, as is linkage between sea-going craft and railroads. Where the water ends railroads become the most efficient system for continuing the journey:

> Only in the last century has land transport achieved anything approaching the ease of movement by sea, and in much of the Third World rivers are still the major highways; that is why most cities in the world are built either on the coast or on major rivers. Even where land transport has achieved maturity, it still depends on fixed highways or railroads, and so cannot easily shift to meet changing military situations. By way of contrast, although references to "sea lanes" are frequent, there is nothing in the sea which defines those paths, and they can be shifted without any particular effort.[41]

Norman Friedman defends maritime transport by comparing operating cost. Monetary value derived from merchant shipping guarantees it will remain an attractive transportation commodity:

> The Boeing 747, the largest commercial airliner, can carry 10 standard containers at a speed of 500 knots. Since a truck carries one container at about 50 knots, one might say that the 747 is equivalent, in load delivered over time, to 100 trucks traveling down a highway. This is quite apart from the fuel the 747 requires. By way of contrast, a modern container ship may transport 1500 or even 2000 containers at about 20 knots. At that speed a 2000 TEU ship is equivalent to eight 747s or 80 trucks on a highway, in terms of cargo moved over distance in unit time.[42]

Friedman's information reveals a significant relationship when joined by Union Pacific Railroad's service at intermodal port facilities. Discharging merchant ship cargo is critical to how well port facilities can handle traffic. Special trains are designated to transport flatbed cars carrying double-stacked shipping containers. UPR's intermodal terminal in Long Beach, California can build six or more of these trains each day.[43] Trains departing the intermodal facility at Long Beach may be over 8,000 feet in length, with well over 100 loaded cars. A huge 2000 container ship can be easily serviced by six trains or less leaving from this facility every day.

Financial benefits of train service over truck and air freight adds even greater value to merchant shipping. UPR is committed to maintaining and modernizing existing routes. High priority rail lines have been constructed with multiple main tracks. These allow several trains to operate simultaneously in both directions. Maximum authorized speeds of up to 80 mph for passenger service and 75 mph for priority freight is easily maintained. Major arteries with only single track service have computerized traffic control systems that dictate movement based on priority, commodities, and train length in relation to available siding.

Cargo moving on this transportation design is a staggering amount. Energy, such as coal, is the largest product with an annual growth rate averaging 8%. Coal fields in Wyoming, Utah, and Colorado generate over 130,000,000 tons annually. Product is transported by specially designated coal trains to electric generating plants in numerous states. Automobiles comprise 10% of business with approximately 150,000 transported each week. Many arrive from overseas through those critical seaports. Intermodal service has gained ground and is expected to eventually surpass coal as the largest commodity. Intermodal facilities also exist at key strategic locations within the US interior. This enables freight to be quickly separated from a train and either unloaded, or assigned to another heading a different direction. Since implementation of the North American Free Trade Agreement (NAFTA), UPR has expanded operations to include Mexico and Canada. Mexican and Canadian ports can now be used if US facilities are made inaccessible.[44]

This massive transportation operation remains in the hands of train dispatchers, a tradition that has not changed since the nineteenth century. Tools used today comprise sophisticated computer networks, including software co-engineered with the National Aeronautic and

Space Administration (NASA). UPR's brain trust for dispatching operations is located in Omaha, Nebraska. Omaha has become a major national communications hub for several corporations and government entities. Dispatchers direct UPR traffic from the Mississippi River to Pacific Ocean. Longitudinal domain covers Canada to the Gulf of Mexico. Regional control is maintained at select sites. These can assume command if Omaha's operational center is knocked out of service. Virtually any train in the country can be located twenty-four hours a day. Type of cargo carried, customer, weight, quantity, point of origin, departure date, and estimated time of delivery is instantaneously accessible. Sudden changes in operating conditions such as weather, accidents, or repair work are immediately responded to from Omaha. Dispatchers communicate with crews in over thirty states. Every possible contingency has been considered should any portion of the rail network or operations center become disabled. It is critical to UPR and America that operations continue unhindered in times of national crisis.

Primary criticism associated with rail service traditionally involves time transporting goods from point A to B. It was common for a shipment to take weeks getting from coast to coast. Issues over delivery time are a concern as Union Pacific pursues new and innovative ways to expedite service. Intermodal terminals, enhanced train dispatching technology, and more efficient rail and crew management has significantly reduced any time to customer factor. Rail's attraction has, as a saving grace, always been lower cost. Three times as much freight as over-the-road trucking can be transported by rail using the same amount of fuel. Cargo aircraft require eighty times the fuel to transport an equal quantity of goods. In comparison to trucking, manpower savings using rail transport runs as high as seven times the freight per employee. This figure jumps to over twenty times the amount with air cargo service.

Rail's future outlook is as strong as it appeared in the early twentieth century. Sir Halford Mackinder's view of this transportation mode warrants consideration. His geostrategic vision of railroads actually turned out to be a marriage with Mahan. Intermodal facilities accommodate merchant vessels at ports along America's coast for transcontinental distribution on land. Union Pacific elevates that to hot priority delivery for package shippers such as United Parcel Service. It is a testament of UPR's determination to fix discrepancies plaguing the industry since birth. Trains departing Los Angeles, California are now capable of arriving in Memphis, Tennessee in less than forty-eight hours. Successfully delivering commodities by rail as fast as the trucking industry is an event unimagined only a few decades ago. This is a masterstroke for railroads if it can be sustained. They have no choice, and neither does the United States. It would be a profound mistake to disregard the economic and national security advantages rail has to offer.

A Question of Efficiency

Right of way given toward transportation efficiency in the United States reflects a pro-business climate within government. An efficient network of road, rail, air, and waterways benefits economic growth. One of very few positive outcomes from the domestic attacks on 11 September 2001 came from a heightened awareness over exposure to terrorism. America has long suffered from a false sense of security. Several government agencies involved in public safety were found begging for scraps in the budgetary dungeon, while struggling to meet enormous responsibilities. These included Customs, US Border Patrol, and Coast Guard (USCG).

Merchant shipping comes with a host of management problems. The US Coast Guard is tasked with securing navigable waters within the national border and along the coastal periphery.[45] The enormous number of duties in relation to budgetary allocation has traditionally been an insurmountable challenge. Being locked inside the Department of Transportation's bureaucratic mill did not help matters. Since 9/11 budget-makers have assessed the full extent of Coast Guard utility in relation to funding and, as a result, operating capital is more in tune with operational burdens. Administratively, a wise move was made to the newly formed Department of Homeland Security. USCG responsibilities would put most frontline navies to shame:

- Search and Rescue
- Port security and force protection
- Protection of marine resources
- Humanitarian response to disasters
- Military environmental response
- Foreign vessel inspection
- International Ice Patrol
- Lightering zone enforcement
- US homeland defense
- General law enforcement
- Maritime pollution enforcement and response
- Alien migrant, drug, and maritime interdiction
- Forward-deployed support to regional military commanders-in-chief in peacetime engagement and crisis response joint/combined combat

operations in smaller-scale contingencies and major theatre war.
- Joint/combined combat operations in smaller-scale contingencies and major theatre war.[46]

     The US Coast Guard is in a league comprised of several agencies responsible for securing America's transportation infrastructure. It has also evolved into an essential maritime enforcer on the high seas, and is considered by many to be the world's fifth largest navy. Long overdue financial attention is resuscitating a very sick patient. The same applies to the Border Patrol, where personnel numbers are increasing after decades of poor and insufficient staffing.

     Skepticism about technological fashion deserves attention when applied to transportation efficiency. Highly sophisticated networks can become just as valuable to an invading army. Totalitarian states have no difficulty overcoming economic urges so that precedence is allocated to national security or regime survival. Economic delights of plasma televisions or amusement parks fall to the bottom of an oppressive government's strategic priority list. Germany's experience with all roads leading to Moscow during World War II became a devastating quagmire, only surpassed on the logistics agony meter by the Soviet rail system. Archer Jones graphically describes the madness:

> Before the army could resume its advance, the Germans had to restore railway service, a task complicated not just by having to rebuild bridges but also by the necessity of altering Russian railways to the narrower German gauge. This chore, and the operation of captured segments of Russian railroads, proved harder than anticipated. Their railway troops, inadequate in any case, encountered unexpected obstacles in such mundane matters as water tank locations and the need to change the gauges of sidings as well as the main lines. . . . Throughout the summer and fall the failure of rail traffic to approach needs halted and delayed the German advance.[47]

Oddly enough, it took the Russian winter's arrival to end road transport problems, but the weather caused even greater horror for rail:

> Until the freezing temperatures solidified the mud, motor transport encountered almost insuperable difficulties. And the frost, which came early in November and arrived in one area with a sudden drop to four degrees below zero Fahrenheit, compounded the problems of the still poorly functioning railways, freezing water pipes on at least two-thirds of the German locomotives.[48]

Stalin's trap, which surgically lured Hitler into the "Russian Tomb," developed into a more historically significant event than what Tsar Alexander did to Napoleon. Stalin's move ranks as a diplomatic and strategic masterpiece:

> Although Hitler recognized Russia's conquests and spheres of interest in the Middle East and in the Baltic countries to an extent which went far beyond all Russian aspirations since Peter the Great and up to Alexander Isvolski, Molotov curtly demanded further concessions in the Balkan area and the Dardanelles, fully knowing that this would enrage the Fuhrer and so lure him to declare war on Russia. The plan was a success and on 21 June 1941 Hitler started his fateful attack.[49]

How did the Germans last as long as they did? The USSR gained enormous military advantage by sucking in enough of the Wehrmacht to be decimated before mounting a full scale counteroffensive on Germany. All of Europe would soon follow.

The transportation and logistics web trapping the Wehrmacht had initially been spun by Soviet Commissariat for Foreign Affairs, Vyacheslav Molotov. Molotov insisted Germany recognize Soviet advantage over key strategic points around Europe's continental perimeter. If Hitler agreed, then Soviet influence would reign in the Balkans and Dardanelles. It was the maritime leverage needed to fulfill Soviet naval desires. Geography matters and Red Navy forces would gain access to the Mediterranean Sea, the Atlantic Ocean, and British Isles. The US could then be denied continental access, while Red Army divisions served as a spear into the gut of Europe's heartland. Stalin patiently waited for Hitler who, in a bizarre way, assisted the West by attacking when he did.

Confusion surrounding sea power exists because of an inability to place it on a proper policy-making track. Sea, land, air, and space power generate the sum of national power, which policy is entirely dependent on. Amos Jordan, William Taylor, and Michael Mazarr identify national power as "The general capability of a state to influence the behavior of others."[50] They then list many items this thesis identifies as power resources for national power in general, and power generators specifically.[51] Products noted by Jordan, Taylor, and Mazarr are either power resources or specific elements of those resources. These include: geography, national resources, industrial capacity, population, military strength, national character, and political cohesion.[52] Power generators draw their energy from these sources to carry out national grand strategy. National character could serve a willingness to fight. Willingness to fight is a sensitive issue with differences existing between whip-snapping dictatorships and constitutional democracies. Totalitarian regimes can easily implement ancient Chinese discipline to get everyone marching in lock-step: "If a brigade or column commander withdrew without orders, he lost his head."[53] Regime legitimacy may exist for various reasons.

Douglas Murray and Paul Viotti define national power as "The sum total of any nation's capabilities or potential derived from available political, economic, military, geographic, social, scientific, and technological resources. Leadership and national will are the unifying factors."[54] Policy-making emanates from strong leadership. Though science may have gained influence in making policy, ultimate responsibility, that final decision, still rests on shoulders belonging to a single individual. This is the purest form of art.[55] Murray and Viotti's explanation of national power is solid, with the exception of omitting reference to abilities. Leadership and national will, critical factors to getting all vehicles in motion, receive recognition. Sea power is derived from national power like the relationship between a parent and sibling:

- Sea power is the "sum total" of a nation's potential and ability to apply pressure directed from the sea.
- All political, social, economic, military, geographic, technological, and scientific resources provide a measurable contribution.
- It takes good political, military, and business leadership to make this complex mechanism perform to the utmost of its capability.
- A nation must be unified if it is to have a chance of succeeding. Embarking on a program to develop any power generator is a major endeavor.

Antonym of Mahan

Louis XIV's reign over France during the seventeenth and early eighteenth century serves as a stellar example of sea power incompetence. A massive French shipbuilding program had been underway; vastly outnumbering anything England could muster. Technology, weaponry, logistics support, and administration were far advanced. Upon taking the throne, Louis XIV's unstable character went to work on Jean Baptiste Corbett's plans; decimating all France accomplished. A grand strategy incorporating unmatched sea power got tossed in the gutter for a self-destructive land campaign. Linkage between grand strategy and strategy cannot withstand bad policy, or disoriented leadership. The War of the Spanish Succession is a classic example. Stability across Europe was achieved for a twenty-five year period following its end. Getting there involved profound challenges. England, once post-war finances were settled, developed at unprecedented rates, while enemies floundered. Reasons for English success happened decades earlier. Louis XIV's acerbic grasp of discipline building sea power contributed to the British Empire's rise:

> The sea power of England therefore was not merely in the great navy, with which we too commonly and exclusively associate it; France had had such a navy in 1688, and it shriveled away like a leaf in the fire. Neither was it in a prosperous commerce alone; a few years after the date at which we have arrived, the commerce of France took on fair proportions, but the first blast of war swept it off the seas as the navy of Cromwell had once swept that of Holland. It was in the union of the two, carefully fostered, that England made the gain of sea power over and beyond all other States; and this gain is distinctly associated with and dates from the War of the Spanish Succession. Before that war England was one of the sea powers; after it she was *the* sea power, without any second. This power also she held alone, unshared by friend and unchecked by foe.[56]

Louis XIV illustrates the ravages brought upon states by a cavalier approach toward sea power. He devastated Jean Baptiste Colbert's effort to mold France into a preeminent sea power. Colbert is arguably the greatest grand strategist France ever produced. Destruction of his work had a profound impact on Europe's political direction, and it served as a testament to the misery befalling those with no regard toward sea power value:

> Agriculture, which increases the products of the earth, and manufactures, which multiply the products of man's industry; internal trade routes and regulations, by which the exchange of products from the interior to the exterior is made easier; shipping and customs regulations tending to throw the carrying-trade into French hands, and so to encourage the building of French shipping, by which the home and colonial products should be carried back and forth; colonial administration and development, by which a far-off market might be

continually growing up to be monopolized by the home trade; treaties with foreign States favoring French trade, and imposts on foreign ships and products tending to break down that of rival nations, - all these means, embracing countless details, were employed to build up for France (1) Production, (2) Shipping, (3) Colonies and Markets - in a word, sea power. The study of such a work is simpler and easier when thus done by one man, sketched out by a kind of logical process, than when slowly wrought by conflicting interests in a more complex government. In a few years of Colbert's administration is seen the whole theory of sea power put into practice in the systematic, centralizing French way, while the illustration of the same theory in English and Dutch history is spread over generations. Such growth, however, was forced, and depended upon the endurance of the absolute power which watched over it, and as Colbert was not king, his control lasted only till he lost the king's favor.[57]

Those who learn from history take advantage of the knowledge gained: "The political prestige of having military control of Alsace-Lorraine has always been the bait which has lured the French out of their best strategic lines of defense. This took place in 1870 and again in 1914."[58] History is also a ruthless punisher of political leadership that ignores its warnings: "The same 'restrictive rules of engagement' decried by the Marines in Spanish East Florida in 1812 left Marines in the 1980s with the decidedly unhealthy regulation of not being able to shoot unless someone else shot them first."[59] Power resources arrayed by France against Britain were truly impressive. Even intelligence operations surpassed anything Britain could counter: "Again, the efficiency of the English navy, as has been said, was low, and its administration perhaps worse; while treason in England gave the French the advantage of better information."[60] Louis XIV's behavior and lack of knowledge is a template of what not to do, while fortunate timing, strategic prescience, and superior leadership skill helped Great Britain achieve the status of world's greatest sea power decades later:

> There were, indeed, consequences momentous and stupendous yet to flow from the decisive supremacy of Great Britain's sea-power, the establishment of which, beyond all question or competition, was Nelson's great achievement; but his part was done when Trafalgar was fought. The coincidence of his death with the moment of completed success has impressed upon that superb battle a stamp of finality, an immortality of fame, which even its own grandeur scarcely could have insured. He needed, and he left, no successor. To use again St. Vincent's words, "There is but one Nelson."[61]

Great Britain knew sea power success depended on numerous resources. In a manner reminiscent of Colbert, properly managed assets were combined to form a complete power package. Poor packaging by Napoleon would again lock France to Europe.

Wylie Fellow

Rear Admiral J. C. Wylie's keynote address at the Mahan Centennial Conference in Newport, Rhode Island emphasized moral, societal, political, economic, military, technological, financial, and psychological influences as essential to developing sea power.[62] These same elements apply to land, air, and space power. National grand strategy is unable to carry out policy designs if enough resources do not exist. Untrained eyes too often miss sea power's construction, capability, and force. It is a sum of gargantuan value and size. History has documented outcomes from unwilling participants. They failed to follow sea power's recipe, which feeds states a healthier line of communication, supply route, and defense parameter. Ignoring these benefits can financially drain a national economy:

> Lines of communication by sea, whatever their starting-point and their course, extend as far as ships can float and navigate. So far they exist independent of man's power, which does not determine their existence, but the use of them. In copiousness they exceed, irretrievably, the utmost possibilities of land travel. This is consequent, partly, upon the greater obstacles to transit imposed by the ground under its most favorable conditions, and partly upon the undue expense incurred, owing to the same obstacles, in attempting by increase of width, or by multiplication of tracks, to rival the expanses of water routes.[63]

Freedom of the seas requires a display of military might, backed up with a commitment to use it. This is an enforcement practice not uncommon to community crime prevention programs, which do not wait for criminal activity before hiring a contingent of police officers. Sufficient law enforcement must be present to prevent crime from happening. In the event of failure, resources are activated to stop criminal activity and prevent escalation. Deterrence from crime is more important than solving crime post-mortem and it requires sufficient means to restore peace when a show of force fails. Deterrence theory applies to nuclear weapons, forward naval presence, or a constable on patrol walking London streets. Policing the global community is applied in a similar manner. J. C. Wylie's three strategic theorems apply to this success. Neighborhood patrols are a show of strength and essential to maintaining good order. Who is in charge will always be an important consideration and this also applies at sea. It is prudent on the international stage to ensure military capability is ready and able to take action at all times: "Statistically, war has been more common than peace, and extended periods of peace have been rare in a world divided into multiple states."[64] Disarmament advocates forget military deterrence allows nations to remain free and secure:

> Nations, as a rule, do not move with the foresight and the fixed plan which distinguish a very few individuals of the human race. They do not practice on the pistol-range before sending a challenge; if they did, wars would be fewer, as is proved by the present long-continued armed peace in Europe.[65]

Jon Sumida's final chapter of *Inventing Grand Strategy and Teaching Command* opens with a quote by Mumon Okay, a thirteenth century Chinese master of Zen. It symbolizes the chaos which followed Mahan's effort: "He has made it all so clear. It takes a long time to catch the point."[66]

Chapter Six

Power Resources

"The circumstances that endanger the safety of nations are infinite; and for this reason no constitutional shackles can be wisely imposed on the power to which the care of it is committed."
- Alexander Hamilton

Cataloguing assets of national power is not an easy task. The most difficult challenge occurs while creating theoretic designs. Explaining the end result is the easy part: "The aim of any discussion as this should be to narrow down, by a gradual elimination, the various factors to be considered, in order that the decisive ones, remaining, may become conspicuously visible."[1] Sea, land, air, and space power draw their energy from national grand strategy's center of power. Fuel for this energy comes from various power resources. Two distinct categories are involved; fundamental and fluid power resources. Examples of fundamental resources include geography and time. Fluid resources comprise such things as intelligence and logistics. Power resources are accumulated by national grand strategy and discharged into power generators as needed to optimize their utility at the right time and place. Each power generator is affected in various degrees of impact by power resources.

Fundamental Power Resources

Fundamental power resources are generally not subject to pressures from change unless calamitous events force a transfiguration of that resource. Fate, fortune, or just plain bad or good luck determines fundamental power resource value within national grand strategy's theater. Every citizen and their leadership are permanently attached to fundamental power resources, whether they like it or not. A nation rich in fundamental resources can do a lot if it knows how to exploit advantages. A nation suffering from deficiencies cannot do much without great sacrifice. Topography may destine some to a life of subjugation. Mongolia is an example belonging to this category.

A number of overwhelming uncertainties can arise while carrying out policy. Therefore, a state benefits by having a high number and quality of fundamental power resources. If and when fluid resources run dry, then there are the fundamentals to fall back on. Tsar Alexander used this to his advantage against Napoleon Bonaparte. Joseph Stalin followed suit in his game of chess with Hitler. Those tasked with carrying out grand strategy based on national policy continually strive to minimize the unknown. Contingency planning for notorious "what ifs" is a complex process, especially when resources are limited. A long list of fundamental power resources not subject to change can lower strategic odds. There is no guarantee when pursuing state policy, but learning from the past as Stalin did and Hitler should have can curtail annoying perils.[2]

Fundamental power resources are comprised of elements that provide fixed energy derivatives to support power generators. These are linked to Mahan's six fundamental factors of sea power.[3] Each resource and element affects all four power generators to some degree:

Geography
Elements:
- Topography / Terrain
- Climate / Weather
- Location / Position

Natural Resources
Elements:
- Minerals
- Energy
- Agriculture

Willingness to Fight
Elements:
- War History
- Culture
- Solidarity

Time
Elements:
- Efficiency
- Management
- Exploitation

Regime Legitimacy
Elements:
- Form of Government
- Administration
- Support

Manpower
Elements:
- Population
- Education
- Health

Geography

Geography is the most important power resource. Along with time, it is also least likely to change. Geography acts as a primary motivator for pursuing political objectives: "From the shores of the

Pacific, and the heights of the Himalayas, Russia will not only dominate the affairs of Asia, but those of Europe also."[4] Barring a natural disaster of apocalyptic proportions, Earth's landscape is a fixed quantity. It is known where continents, islands, littorals, deserts, mountains, etc. are located. 75% of Earth's surface is covered in water, and yet less than 1% is fit for drinking in existing states. Polar icecaps are located north and south. Tropical climates and deserts permeate regions closest to the equator. This is basic information readily available to those possessing a desire to know.

Unexpected developments can shatter nerves, break unity, and cause chaos in an otherwise cohesive formation: "Ever since primitive man first lay in ambush for his enemy the importance of surprise in war has been fully admitted."[5] Known quantities are a saving grace of nations that understand geographic realities.[6] There is no substitute for possessing knowledge of geography, and no excuse for failing to capitalize on all it has to offer.[7] Geography is a mainstay not subject to change unless your research involves plate-tectonics, Noah's Ark, or the lost city of Atlantis. Geographic position on land is the foundation for deployment of sea, air, and space power. Land power is axiomatic to the success of all power generators. Several factors contribute to sea power's strength, but a nation's geographic association with land is the most fundamental necessity.

Nation-states take on profound differences when it comes to geographic destiny. Survival depends on an ability to use that position in maximizing sea, land, air, and space power: "Every danger of a military character to which the United States is exposed can be met best outside her own territory–at sea."[8] Contrasting two countries such as New Guinea and Paraguay requires no further explanation. A nation such as Nepal could build a fleet of ships, but what would this accomplish? Iceland could build an army of mercenaries, but what would be its purpose? Geography has advantages and disadvantages to a sea power effort. This depends on physical location and domestic environment. While geographic position is certainly important, several other power resources must fall in place.

An island nation such as Cyprus would normally be thought to possess maritime power in size and number to at least remind regional states they exist. Cyprus has much to offer as a geostrategic asset. It has served as a land platform for air operations throughout the eastern Mediterranean region on numerous occasions. It often acts as a logistics base and transit point for military and commercial enterprises in route to other locales. Cyprus does not have global security commitments like the United States. That degree of responsibility would be smothering. America must maintain a military presence in the Mediterranean by way of its Sixth Fleet. This is achieved because of other power resources. Cuba and Cyprus fit similar geographic criteria. Cuba's ability to harass the US is made possible by its relationship with Russia and the People's Republic of China. Mahan's view of Cuba and the Caribbean parallels Cyprus in relation to the Mediterranean Sea. The Panama Canal is equivalent to the Suez Canal, while Cyprus and Sinai are positioned quite similar to Cuba and Panama. This makes surrounding states susceptible to political instability if a decision is made to take dastardly measures.

Time

Application of time within grand strategy's jurisdiction is not pleasing for those accustomed to instantaneous success. Grand strategy can take a very long time to develop. This is incomprehensible for those lacking patience and self-discipline. Formulating sea power can take decades. Individuals possessing tactical minds frequently miss this excruciating requirement. A professional athlete must prepare for years to earn the worthy title of *grand* master. Rewards are bestowed upon those with patience and a willingness to use it wisely. Failing to consider the time involved in building national grand strategy will likely end in doom and gloom. Efficient and cautious planning is critical to formulating and placing in action national grand strategy. Analysis able to look for clues decades ahead may be required. This became the case as the United States watched Imperial Japan flourish in the Pacific before World War II. Great Britain observed the same in Germany's rearmament by the USSR.[9]

Nations with limited resources require precise planning and time management. They cannot afford to make mistakes. Too many states tactically blundered because of poor time management practices: "For there has never been a protracted war from which a country has benefited."[10] Sea power can exert "leverage by its ability to enlist time as a critical ally and by its invaluable capacity to shape the geostrategic terms of engagement in war."[11] Proper preparation of a maritime portfolio enables maritime capability to be unleashed when buying time. The alternative is saturation of goods and resources to sustain mistakes by a blithe nation until desired outcomes are achieved. The United States has historically possessed such a luxury, while others looked on with envy. However, heavy dependence on a large supply of resources against less endowed adversaries is a psychologically dangerous course of action: "When the army engages in protracted campaigns the resources of the state will not suffice."[12]

Time within a realm involving military contact (tactical situations) can be a trusted friend or formidable foe. Time can determine the outcome of high stakes global events. Though its influence is not as pronounced in planning stages of national policy and grand strategy, speed does become important once strategic and tactical phases are entered: "The need to fight quickly led man to invent appropriate devices to gain advantages in combat, and these brought about great changes in the forms of fighting."[13] Resulting physical clashes of opposites can now be measured in seconds and minutes rather than hours or days. This has nothing to do with decreasing value of national borders and geographic boundaries. Modern technology simply enables states to supply greater pressure with more resources and speed. Time's feature and impact on national grand strategy takes on an entirely different look:

> Preparation for war, rightly understood, falls under two heads, preparation and preparedness. The one is a question mainly of material, and is constant in its action. The second involves an idea of completeness. When, at a particular moment, preparations are completed, one is prepared – not otherwise. There may have been made a great deal of very necessary preparation for war without being prepared. Every constituent of preparation may be behindhand, or some elements may be perfectly ready, while others are not. In neither case can a state be said to be prepared.[14]

Application of time in grand strategy has not witnessed the velocity associated with tactical or even strategic encounters: "It is better to be frightened now, while we have time to prepare, than next summer, when the French fleet enters the Channel."[15]

The United States Marine Corps demonstrated time's value on tactical transition by advancing amphibious operational reach to greater than 200 miles inland from the coast. Beachhead boundaries of today drive USMC weapons research and development. New aircraft such as the V-22 Osprey is an effort motivated by needs for speed and coastal inland reach.[16] Establishing amphibious forces ashore traditionally involved gaining control of the immediate beach, lifeguard observation tower, and the fishing pier. This is no longer an option if amphibious operations are to remain a viable instrument of military force. Marines must now reach far inland to eliminate threats to their existence.

Amphibious operations are further complicated by a global population shift to coastal regions. USMC training and planning must consider action associated with urban warfare, which is an incredibly risky endeavor.[17] Time and speed, as in all Marine assault plans, will be critical in determining success or failure in densely populated regions. A tradition of laying siege does not easily fit Marine lexicons. In the modern era such luxuries may not be possible, making the only other option a dangerous undertaking: "The worst policy is to attack cities: Attack cities only when there is no alternative."[18] To the USMC's credit, it is not an institution known for an ability to stand around with hands in pockets. Its record of success is based on a talent to keep moving, and going over or through whatever attempts to get in the way. Cities must be considered on a case-by-case basis. Gaining control of a coastal city may offer advantages because of available port facilities.

Natural Resources

Price volatility of global oil markets exemplifies pressure from multi-national pursuit of natural resources. A commodities broker predicting oil futures of $100/barrel when the twenty-first century began would have been considered for a bad conduct discharge at almost any investment firm. Oil to developing countries in recent years rose at an unprecedented pace. Imports to the People's Republic of China alone increased 40% in the first half of 2004.[19] While politicians in multi-party democracies take pleasure using the majority party's Middle East policies as cannon fodder, blame squarely rests with rapid economic development of the PRC.

India, another "emerging" market, and the People's Republic of China are the world's most populated nations. Between them they contain 40% of global population. It should not surprise anyone that quickly developing economies strain natural resource markets. While India may deserve patience because of political similarities with democratic government, the Western elite's craving to develop Communist China into a superpower is irrational based on profound philosophical differences: "The struggle of the people the world over against U.S. imperialism and its running dogs will assuredly win still greater victories."[20] Assisting the PRC is on a scale equal to the rearming of Nazi Germany and Soviet Union.[21]

Communist China's economic growth matched with population is an extraordinary combination. In a single year (2004-2005) it went from the world's fourth to second largest Gross Domestic Product.[22] It finds itself aggressively competing against the West for access to global oil fields.[23] Western governments, their citizens, and multinational corporations have only themselves to blame for a total disregard of moral political principle. There was ample warning:

> . . . if the advantage to us is great of a China open to commerce, the danger to us and to her is infinitely greater of a China enriched and strengthened by the material advantages we have to offer, but uncontrolled in the use of them by any clear understanding, much less any full acceptance, of the mental and moral forces which have generated and in large measure govern our political and social action.[24]

The Western consumer hordes goods manufactured in the PRC by cheap, if not forced labor. Money saved at a mega "China-Mart" checkout gets returned at the petroleum pump. Small business merchants, who took pride in quality and service over a feeding-frenzy of bulk, are summarily marched off to bankruptcy court. No regard is given to long-range damage caused by modernizing the economic base of a dictatorship that publicly declares America its main enemy in the twenty-first century: "Seen from the changes in the world situation and the United States' hegemonic strategy for creating monopolarity, war is inevitable."[25] American consumers and venture capital firms provided financial support needed by this dictatorship to penetrate previously allied continents like South America.[26] Recent moves by Communist China to turn South America away from the United States has gained momentum that borders a point of no return.[27]

Regime Legitimacy

States seeking exploitation advantages of the sea must create policies attainable with available resources. Leadership is necessary to motivate both citizens and bureaucratic engine. Prince Henry of Portugal, while attempting to build constituent support for a conquest of Africa, argued that its purpose was to "serve God and grow rich."[28] Peter Paret's analogy of the French Revolution is reminiscent of what every government must avoid:

If the French Revolution had proved anything, it was that states wishing to preserve their independence must become more efficient in tapping the energies of their populations. Elites existed in every society, and were justified so long as they strengthened the community, remained open to talent, and rewarded merit. But nothing could justify the continuation of privilege that protected mediocrity while depriving the state of the abilities and enthusiasm of the common man.[29]

Some people might believe Paret is referring to the US Congress. Regime legitimacy is essential to fulfilling national policy objectives. Populations must be willing to fall in line behind the regime in power. If government does not have popular support, then it is government that must follow the people to ensure compliance:

I conclude, therefore, that a prince need trouble little about conspiracies when the people are well disposed, but when they are hostile and hold him in hatred, then he must fear everything and everybody. Well-ordered states and wise princes have studied diligently not to drive the nobles to desperation, and to satisfy the populace and keep it contented, for this is one of the most important matters that a prince has to deal with.[30]

Constitutional bonds that tied the United States together were cut so completely by the outbreak of civil war in 1861 that damage penetrated family ties. Mahan observed challenges to regime loyalty when opposing family members face each other on the field of battle. As a young lieutenant onboard USS *Pocahontas* he personally witnessed the anguish and trepidation of Captain Percival Drayton as the Union fleet destroyed Fort Walker in Port Royal, South Carolina. Not only did Port Royal serve as Drayton's hometown, but his brother commanded Fort Walker.[31] Drayton's ability to maintain his composure while giving orders to attack profoundly influenced Mahan's view of navy command, tradition, and the leadership traits required.

Dennis Mahan's influence emphasized the art of leadership that goes with holding military command. This is reflected in Alfred Mahan's biographical praise of Admiral David Farragut. Farragut's performance during the Civil War elevated him to America's equivalent of Lord Horatio Nelson, while New Orleans served as a counterpart to Trafalgar. Farragut's gamble to ignore his written orders of battle resembled leadership traits keenly practiced by Nelson. His decision to bypass Confederate fortifications on the Mississippi River during the conquest of New Orleans possibly saved the Union. Like Admiral Nelson's memorial service following Trafalgar, Farragut's unprecedented New York City funeral in September 1869 is only surpassed in dramatic impact by his success saving the United States: "In the procession was General Grant, then President of the United States, with the members of his Cabinet, many military and naval officers, ten thousand soldiers, and a large number of societies."[32] Such respect has rivaled that given to presidents, making it equivalent to Ronald Reagan's funeral in 2004.

As long as citizens support their government in power, whether by heritage, nationalism, or pride, then willingness to fight will naturally follow. Superior leadership, often by example, makes an important contribution to earning public loyalty:

> If we then ask what sort of mind is likeliest to display the qualities of military genius, experience and observation will both tell us that it is the inquiring rather than the creative mind, the comprehensive rather than the specialized approach, the calm rather than the excitable head to which in war we would choose to entrust the fate of our brothers and children, and the safety and honor of our country.[33]

Willingness to fight results from regime legitimacy, and it is not confined to a battlefield. Support must permeate society at large during times of national challenge: "The name of AMERICAN, which belongs to you in your National capacity, must always exalt the just pride of patriotism, more than any appellation derived from local discriminations."[34] Shipyard workers building an aircraft carrier must understand the importance of what they are constructing; a Union Pacific Railroad train dispatcher in Omaha, Nebraska must grasp the priority for getting a military train across Utah on schedule; and taxpayers filing their income tax return must know the cause for which it goes. This is not to say a totalitarian state is unable to succeed. Many manage quite well from using sheer terror. This form of governing can go either way for sea power: "The simplicity of form in an absolute monarchy thus brought out strongly how great the influence of government can be upon both the growth and decay of sea power."[35]

Willingness to Fight

Willingness to fight may result for various reasons. NKVD enforcers, ready to shoot any troops with a sudden urge to retreat, ensured Soviet Red Army forces would charge German positions at

Stalingrad during World War II.[36] Red Army soldiers were stuck with
the unpalatable predicament of deciding which side got to take their
life. A stark difference in allegiance and devotion is seen by US
Marines confronting Japanese fortifications at Tarawa during WWII.
Facing incredible obstacles, a stubborn defense, and a casualty rate of
30%, US Marines did not give an inch during their assault: "When it
shuddered to a halt, seventy-six hours after the initial landing, nearly
6,000 men lay dead in an area smaller than the space occupied by the
Pentagon and its parking lots."[37] Determination of this caliber did not
come from fear of their government. It happened because of a belief in
that government. This characteristic carried enormous weight in
Mahan's respect and admiration for British sailors. His view of
Admiral Nelson epitomizes that opinion:

> Genius is one thing, the acquirements of an accomplished – instructed
> – officer are another, yet there is between the two nothing
> incompatible, rather the reverse; and when to the former, which
> nature alone can give, and to Nelson did give, is added the conscious
> recognition of principles, the practised habit of viewing, under their
> clear light, all the circumstances of a situation, assigning to each its
> due weight and relative importance, then, and then only, is the highest
> plane of military greatness attained.[38]

Opening words by Harold Rood have an agonizing way of
reappearing. British willingness to fight, wrapped around skill, self-
discipline, and grit in battle were keys to national success at sea.

Once victory is achieved, much then depends on how success is
managed. Victorious occupiers must never forget the dependence on
those newly acquired subject people. Rome's campaign against Celtic
tribes exemplifies stiff resistance when your enemy has no alternative
for losing. Legions did not possess a stellar reputation of mercy toward
the vanquished. There is not much maneuvering when choices are
confined to either death or brutal slavery. This motivated natives to
withstand chariot charges at all cost. Celtic resistance became so stiff
that mothers were used to reinforce front lines. Such a practice
horrified Roman troops who believed harming a mother cursed you for
life.[39] Rome's political leadership used this behavior to justify labeling
northern tribes as barbarous heathens.[40] Success at pacifying Celtic
hoards did not come about until Tacitus offered great enticements of
pleasure. Unfortunately for Rome, this practice did not become
standard operating procedure around the continental periphery.[41]

Manpower

Historically, no nation has matched Great Britain's production of superior sailors in proportion to population: "The quality of the whole is a question of *personnel* even more than of material; and the quality of the *personnel* can be maintained only by high individual fitness in the force, undiluted by dependence upon a large, only partly efficient, reserve element."[42] Manning is critical to maritime power and it comes with added burdens associated with close-quarters living. This puts a premium on crew health. From fifteenth to eighteenth centuries the British Navy had strategic planning of entire fleets collapse over crew health. Yellow fever grew so prevalent in the Western Hemisphere that battle plans were drawn with crew illness factored in as a major consideration. An influenza outbreak, for example, prevented a massive route of French forces in July 1558, following a stunning victory at Dunkirk. Britain's entire fleet was forced to demobilize, preventing further military action from transpiring.[43] As a result, sophisticated naval support facilities were eventually built along the coast to curtail these potentially devastating emergencies.

Quality of manpower is mostly determined by leadership traits of those in charge. Admiral Nelson's fleet did not win their decisive battle at Trafalgar because of over-powering military might, or because of the British Bar Association's bureaucratic overkill efforts. Nelson's streak for risk-taking, as Robert Massie notes, allowed the Crown to achieve naval success through superior leadership, training, experience, and tactical genius:

> No matter that Nelson himself had repeatedly disobeyed orders, that one of the most glorious moments in British naval history had been when Nelson put his telescope to his blind eye at Copenhagen and claimed that he did not see the signal to withdraw.[44]

History may dwell on battle drill, rate of fire, and tactics. This is secondary to those individual qualities of every man fighting at Trafalgar. Nelson knew his greatest advantage lay within Britain's quality of sailor. He gave his men unrivalled independence to exploit their skills as they saw fit.[45] He trusted judgments made by those under his command. While Nelson's cunning maneuvers did indeed break the mold of naval tactics, it turned out to be his men's grit that enabled it to happen.[46] Mahan saw Nelson's leadership and seamanship qualities reflected up and down his chain-of-command. It was a culmination of education and training taking centuries to fulfill:

As a strategist and tactician, Nelson made full proof of high native endowments, of wisdom garnered through fruitful study and meditation, and of clear insight into the determining conditions of the various military situations with which he had to deal.[47]

Royal Navy success "lay not in the number of her ships, but in the wisdom, energy, and tenacity of her admirals and seamen."[48]

Human resources are essential near the water's edge if a nation desires to field and maintain sea power faculties. Demographic estimates place seventy to eighty percent of the world's population within 100 miles of coastline in another 20 years. This reflects a growing attraction and need for sea power. Obviously, geographic features and weather conditions will dictate and must be favorable. Greenland has remained sparsely populated for a reason. The Soviet Northern Fleet had the luxury of a single port during ice-bound winter months. A nation with an extensive shoreline and sparse population opens itself to exploitation by others. The Falkland Islands immediately comes to mind. These examples clarify questions of geography's role and stamina in an age of "cyber-mania."

Navies have always suffered from a need for more time. Amount of time involved training naval officers is consistently greater than other branches of military service. A longer training curve comes with a higher cost. This can create financial stress during peacetime. Command of nuclear-powered Trident submarines, with their array of sophisticated equipment and intercontinental ballistic missiles, is an intense and complex effort. Moral burdens associated with knowing you can be called upon, at a moments notice, to annihilate cities adds to the stress. It is impossible to find a comparable example in civilian circles that match responsibilities of commanding a fully-fitted, $10,000,000,000, Nimitz-class nuclear powered aircraft carrier. Not many possess command character for such a monster when deployed to the eastern Mediterranean Sea during times of political instability. Grooming this individual is an enormous investment and process taking 25 years. Nothing on land can compete.

Mahan spent a lot of ink writing about naval leadership. His admiration for Admiral John Jervis, Captain Nelson's superior officer in the Mediterranean, is partly based on the Admiral's appreciation for naval officers' knowing when to take risks against standing orders: "It rests on good authority, and is eminently characteristic of one who valued beyond most traits in an officer the power to assume responsibility."[49] A Chief Executive Officer (CEO) may have

administrative responsibility for a financial portfolio of higher net
worth, but it is highly unlikely that a wrong decision can cause defeat
of a nation, a loss of millions of lives, and scholars writing books about
your blunder for over 500 years: "Political courage in an officer abroad
is as highly necessary as military courage."[50] Setting a price-tag on this
type of individual is impossible.

Fluid Power Resources

Those accustomed to national blunders know how sensitive
fluid power resources are to rapid shifts in strategic and tactical events.
Fluid resources require an enormous national investment that may be
wiped out in short order. Research and development, for example, is a
necessary evil of expense in pursuit of technological advances. A key
to that success involves financial strength for capital investment:
"Money, credit, is the life of war; lessen it, and vigor flags; destroy it,
and resistance dies."[51] William Livezey and Jon Sumida list several
power resources crucial to sea power's success:

> Mahan's sea power doctrine polarized a set of historical data
> concerning the role of the sea in its relation to national well being. As
> he viewed the constituent elements affecting power on the sea, he
> discussed geographical position, physical conformation, extent of
> territory, number of population, character of people, and character of
> government. In the creation of national greatness as connected with
> sea power, he saw industry, markets, [merchant] marine, navy, and
> bases closely related and theoretically, at least, in that sequence.[52]

Sumida's quotation from Livezey's analysis is a simplistic
overview of the challenge and solution now addressed. Fluid power
resources are comprised of elements considered highly susceptible to
fluctuations and influence. Their value can rise and fall gradually or in
quick order. This "fluidity" is an enormous challenge when devising
and fulfilling policy:

Technological Development   Industrial Production
Elements: Elements:
- Technology   - Sophistication
- Science   - Sustenance
- Research & Development   - Competitiveness

Transportation
Elements:
- Land
- Sea
- Air

Military Might
Elements:
- Naval Forces
- Land Forces
- Air & Space Forces

Intelligence
Elements:
- Foreign
- Domestic
- Analysis

Logistics
Elements:
- Distribution
- Storage
- Management

Financial Strength
Elements:
- Private Sector
- Currency
- Government Finance

Technological Development

Development of technology is a highly controversial power resource. Bernard Brodie performs a public service by defending Mahan from criticism over his skepticism of technology, and aggressive attempts to blame him for Pearl Harbor:

> Unfortunately for Mahan's memory, he is much more often criticized than read. For on the second page of his most famous work he pointed out that 'the unresting progress of mankind causes a continual change in the weapons; and with that must come a continual change in the manner of fighting.' He [Mahan] would have been the first to welcome the modern airplane to the arsenal of naval weapons; and he would have been the first to reject doctrines which confuse the aims of military power with the tools for carrying them out.[53]

Brodie's remark epitomizes sea power's broad implication and Mahan's grand design. Mahan did not oppose technical advances used in conjunction with thought-out strategic concepts. His hesitation concerned uncontrolled optimism and a lack of healthy skepticism, which always seems to be in short supply. Michael Isenberg joins Brodie's defense team by correlating aircraft carriers with Mahanian doctrine. This followed a flamboyant and highly promoted test bombing of a German battleship by the US Army Air Corps in 1921:

Mahan was indicted unfairly for his lack of consideration of the
airplane (he died before the machine had proven its capabilities in
combat), and, indeed, Mahanian doctrine found a new home with the
carrier advocates. Admiral William Sims, who had commanded
American naval forces in Europe during World War I, made no bones
about his opinion: "The fast carrier is the capital ship of the future."
Where naval orthodoxy saw aviation as, at best, an "adjunct" of naval
power, and the Navy stubbornly relegated its growing squadrons of
aircraft to secondary roles in its general doctrine for fleet operations,
"neo-Mahanians" could argue that the master's gospel still held, only
Armageddon would take shape as an all-carrier battle.[54]

Research and development is a necessary evil of expense.
While doing his part to further atomic research, Vannevar Bush argued
toward the close of World War II that far more money would be needed
to pursue such endeavors: "There must be more–and more adequate–
military research in peacetime."[55] While in agreement, a follow-up
question is warranted: "For whom is the research being done?" Power
resources of technological development and intelligence can merge on
this issue. Alternatives to financing R & D include letting another state
spend its national treasure, such as the United States did throughout the
twentieth century. For a fraction of the cost, totalitarian regimes can run
circles around open societies by putting a sophisticated espionage
action in place to acquire the information.

Technology has been an instigator of debate over each power
generator's true value. The atom bomb caused enormous controversy
during the twentieth century. After correcting distortions by hindsight
critics over Mahan and aircraft carriers, Isenberg then compares his
theoretical applications to atomic weapons:

> The Atomic Age had not materially altered Mahan's concepts of
> seapower. Technology had changed, and tactics would have to
> change, but the essential strategic underpinnings of Mahanian
> doctrine were sound – with the not-so-minor caveat that there seemed
> to be no other *navies* around to fight.[56]

It is on these remarks that national grand strategy and Mahan's
sea power philosophy come together.

Industrial Production

The United States government has traditionally maintained
close relations with its business community. A free market system

serves as the backbone to America's economy and benefits both private and public sectors. European allies have not always been so fortunate. During the early nineteenth century, for example, Great Britain's economy grew steadily while France was subjected to a revolutionary hangover, followed by Napoleon's continental implosion.[57] Many problems faced by France can be seen looming in today's over-regulated US economy. Government micro-intervention grew to epidemic heights. It self-perpetuated growth of an enormous French bureaucracy, not unlike accusations now made toward all levels of American government. The historical lesson is clear:

> From the manufacturers of Candles, Tapers, Lanterns, Candlesticks, Street Lamps, Snuffers, and Extinguishers, and from the Producers of Oil, Tallow, Resin, Alcohol, and Generally of Everything Connected with Lighting To the Honorary Members of the Chamber of Deputies.
>
> Gentlemen:
> ...We are suffering from the ruinous competition of a foreign rival who apparently works under conditions so far superior to our own for the production of light, that he is *flooding* the *domestic market* with it at an incredibly low price. . . .This rival...is none other than the sun... We ask you to be so good as to pass a law requiring the closing of all windows, dormers, skylights, inside and outside shutters, curtains, casements, bull's-eyes, deadlights and blinds; in short, all openings, holes, chinks, and fissures.[58]

Frederic Bastiat went on to recommend France should double the need for jobs by chopping off each worker's right hand.[59] This is not a viable policy position for a democracy to take. It does illustrate rising frustration when a free market and institutions of government clash. Every member of society pays when a nation's economy is overburdened by government control and regulation. The United States, for example, currently has one lawyer for every 300 people; Japan has an attorney for every 10,000 citizens.[60] This helps explain why America's industrial sector cannot compete globally. An over-regulated society comprised of swarming tort attorneys is a threat to national survival because a "lawyer who has not studied economics . . . is very apt to become a public enemy."[61]

Intelligence

The USSR/Russia has a long history of maximizing intelligence capabilities. During the Cold War it made certain Western governments did not feel left out. Herb Romerstein and Eric Breindel's discovery of a letter from US Army Intelligence to the Federal Bureau of Investigation (FBI) is a classic example of Russian expertise:

> Prior to 1933, the Comintern, and other Soviet Apparats, were active in gathering intelligence information in the Far East. The agents who gathered this information sent it to agents in other countries in coded telegrams. These agents then recoded the telegrams and forwarded them to addresses in Berlin, one of which was the office of Albert Einstein. . . .Einstein's personal secretary turned the coded telegrams over to a special apparat man, whose duty it was to transmit them to Moscow by various means.... It was common knowledge, especially in Berlin, that Einstein sympathized with the Soviet Union to a great extent. Einstein's Berlin staff of typists and secretaries was made up of persons who were recommended to him (at his request) by people who were close to the Klub Der Geistesarbeiter (Club of Scientists), which was a Communist cover organization. Einstein was closely associated with this club and was very friendly with several members who later became Soviet agents. Klaus Fuchs, who was associated with the club as a student in the early 1930s, was jailed in England for giving atomic bomb information to the Soviets. Einstein was also very friendly with several members of the Soviet Embassy in Berlin, some of whom were later executed in Moscow in 1935 and 1937.[62]

This information does not provide much comfort to Albert Einstein's public relations machine.

Intelligence operations carried out by Communist Bloc regimes were so frequent that cataloging them would stretch the limits of an encyclopedia. Penetration by Soviet assets in the West, the counterintelligence web tightly spun in Moscow, Peking, and Warsaw Pact capitals, and incredible deception activities devastated allied efforts. Unsuspecting Westerners assigned to Communist Bloc cities were easy prey for sophisticated blackmail operations. A true damage assessment may never be fully completed, possibly out of fear for the unknown. The Walker family spy ring, for example, took place inside the US and is regarded as the most catastrophic in US Navy history. Revelation of that group's activity brought a damage assessment going back decades and, inadvertently, uncovered other espionage operations extending to World War II.[63]

In current times national security seems to be looked upon as a nuisance rather than a serious concern. Maintaining harmony with political oppressors in the East provides a worthwhile cash return for some. The PRC has logged a phenomenal espionage record. No finer display of human denial exists than the American public's attitude toward countries seeking their demise:

> The PRC subjects visiting scientists to a variety of techniques designed to elicit information from them. One technique may involve inviting scientists to make a presentation in an academic setting, where repeated and increasingly sensitive questions are asked. Another is to provide the visitor with sightseeing opportunities while PRC intelligence agents burglarize the visitor's hotel room for information. Still another technique involves subjecting the visitor to a gruelling itinerary and providing copious alcoholic beverages so as to wear the visitor down and lower resistance to questions.[64]

What it takes to educate a naïve population is unknown. Left-wing media organs, and a public education system fed by bureaucratic expansion, cannot be trusted. In a society transfixed with pop culture headlines involving such pressing affairs as a rock star exposing her crotch to paparazzi, an "aspiring" actress of purely hereditary fame arrested for drunk driving, or court hearings on where a former stripper's body should be planted, minor issues like global tyranny's advance and the survival of a constitutional republic must seem boring.

Logistics

Railroads offer a superior mode of transportation to meet logistics requirements on land, while serving maritime assets at sea through port facilities. The contribution and benefit to economic vitality, lifestyle of citizens, and advancement of civilization cannot be denied.[65] It is understandable that Mackinder would bet so heavily on technology, particularly land transportation. His argument that railroads would make maritime shipping obsolete did not materialize. Rail transport has, however, elevated both modes to an equal and cohabitating par. Land power adherents failed to consider rail's role to both maritime and land transport. Railroads are arteries over land just as rivers provide the same for marine transport. An example of dual-use technology is the steam-driven engine, which was successfully applied to both rail and maritime shipping. Steam revolutionized maritime vessels while profoundly impacting delivery of goods by rail:

> Lewis and Clark had led the way to the Pacific. They did so by foot, pole, paddle, sail, or on horseback, whatever worked and whatever

they had available. No progress had been made in transportation since ancient Greece or Rome, and none when they got back to civilization, in 1806. Steam power was first applied to boats the following year, and two decades later to the development of the steam-driven locomotive. George Washington could travel no faster than Julius Caesar, but Andrew Jackson could go upstream at a fair pace, and James K. Polk could travel twenty miles an hour or more overland. The harnessing of steam power brought greater change in how men lived and moved than had ever before been experienced, and thus changed almost everything, but it meant nothing outside the seaboard or away from a major river, or until a track had been laid connecting one point with another.[66]

The great achievement for the United States in connecting continental points east and west resulted from constructing the transcontinental rail line. Union Pacific Railroad served this purpose and it passed with flying colors.

UPR and other rail companies remain vital to America's economy and national security portfolio: "The freight industry is like the electrical industry. Nobody notices it until it inconveniences them."[67] Train service provides substantial cost savings, while helping to alleviate traffic flow on the nation's roads. Government transportation officials should take notice. The US government budgeted $286.4 billion for highway construction and maintenance in fiscal year 2006 alone.[68] This excludes taxpayer money at state and local levels. Modernizing America's rail system takes substantial pressure off existing roads at less cost per mile constructed. 42% of US freight transported on an annual basis already moves by rail.[69] A problem for railroads involves capital cost associated with building new routes. Adding a parallel line of over 1,000 miles to an already existing UPR main artery (Riverside, California to Memphis, Tennessee) would cost over two billion dollars.

Investment in UPR rail lines enhances West Coast port facilities, relieves truck traffic congesting roads, and serves a national security role. Construction prices are prohibitive for private investors, even though highways cannot be built for less than an additional rail line. There is a real benefit and return using funds for road construction to assist in expanding rail service. If Congress can stretch fiscal creativity to identify a connection between highway funds and bicycle paths, then it would seem logical this money could also be dedicated to enhancing rail. Most would argue that "linkage" of highway funds and rail transport is far more obvious than nature trails. Rail's main concern with such a financial arrangement involves giving an over-regulated government rights to intervene in operations. A guarantee not to interfere with normal business activities would alleviate that concern.

Merchant shipping benefits from the free and natural state of rivers, lakes, and oceans of the world. Lower cost and efficient administration enabled shipping to blossom in England during the era of Queen Elizabeth I. Skills required for long-range planning and management of sea power strength became profoundly apparent and appropriately addressed.[70] Elizabeth's success at sea had as much to do with what she implemented on land. Maritime technology made unprecedented advances in engineering, maintenance practices, and ship production.[71] Shipyards and docks became worker friendly, while administration achieved a phenomenal degree of efficiency and success. Logistics support gained by construction of warehouses along the pier.[72] These were kept stocked for immediate loading on vessels. No longer would the British fleet be forced to scavenge as a means of survival.

Though Mahan often expressed frustration on matters concerning bureaucratic overkill, Jon Sumida points out his grudging acceptance as a necessary evil:

> Mahan's fundamental complaint was not with administration as such, but with bureaucratization. And even bureaucracy, he recognized, was necessary because the multiplicity of complex tasks required a division of labor. The great drawback was that distributed work partitioned responsibility, a division that Mahan believed was antithetical to sound – that is, intelligent, rapid, and unequivocal – decision-making. He was nevertheless resigned to the fact that maintenance of a balance between the needs of administration and of warfare was unavoidable.[73]

Military Might

Military might is the big stick of each power generator: "I say only that the evidence is strong...that we cannot be certain of our security in the future any more than we can be certain of disaster.... If we are to err in an age of insecurity, I want us to err on the side of security."[74] The political landscape is littered with records showing a high price for neglect, yet military might remains difficult to hold in a peacetime democratic society. Today's naval capacity includes the nuclear option. Contemporary military power and preparedness can be found "greater than 400 feet" below the ocean's surface.[75] A single ballistic missile submarine (SSBN) is capable of destroying most nations. Fortunately for the world at large, no SSBN has been ordered to discharge its payload since the USS *Nautilus* submerged off Connecticut's coast in 1958. America's military is often a victim of its own success. Nuclear deterrence causes uninformed civilians to question its value. SSBN's are examples of naval assets serving land power by operating in passive states. Assignment of these platforms manages to keep the peace on land: "The enemy must be disturbed or he will succeed."[76] The devastating missiles and highly trained crews accomplish their mission upon returning to port with the ship's arsenal intact.

Since World War II, the US Navy has acted as intermediary and peacekeeper on the largest geographic portion of Earth's surface. This enabled oceans to remain neutral territory for over 60 years. US behavior is on par with Phoenicia, which looked upon sea lanes as essential to communications and commerce between nations. The world benefited from America's role just as civilizations did with Phoenicia in an earlier era. This course may have turned out far differently if naysayer critics of sea power had their way:

> Throughout history, powers that did not have a strong navy, even though they were impressive on land, usually failed in all-out war. For example, Sparta wins the Peloponnesian War only when it builds a navy through Persian subsidies. Rome wins the Punic War only when it builds a navy. Germany loses both world wars, in part because it doesn't have a navy that can challenge the Allies. Japan is a formidable power beyond its population and resources because of its navy. And when that is gone, it fails. The Soviet Union cannot win the Cold War because it never can really challenge the United States at sea.[77]

It is fortunate the US did not follow Halford Mackinder's suggestion. Proper application of sea power allows nations possessing it to prosper in times of war and peace. It served with distinction those who knew how to use it. Critics are mistaken to blindly blame sea power for causing such things as poor fiscal management or leadership indecision. Bad policy and poor national grand strategy planning cannot discredit or be used to slander sea power utility. This is an institutional deficiency relevant to all four power generators. The main culprit in past cases often involved a serious infestation of passivity:

There is one opinion, which it is, needless to say the writer does not share, that, because many years have gone by without armed collision with a great power, the teaching of the past is that none such can occur; and that, in fact, the weaker we are in organized military strength, the more easy it is for our opponents to yield our points. Closely associated with this view is the obstinate rejection of any political action which implicitly involves the projection of our physical power, if needed, beyond the waters that gird our shores.[78]

Financial Strength

George Washington again provides important advice and pragmatism to his American off-spring that, in recent times, seems to be of little concern for wayward masses drunk with hedonism:

> As a very important source of strength and security, cherish public credit. One method of preserving it is, to use it as sparingly as possible; avoiding occasions of expense by cultivating peace, but remembering also that timely disbursements to prepare for danger frequently prevent much greater disbursements to repel it; avoiding, likewise, the accumulation of debt, not only by shunning occasions of expense, but by vigorous exertions in time of peace to discharge the debts, which unavoidable wars may have occasioned, not ungenerously throwing upon posterity the burden, which we ourselves ought to bear.[79]

Arguments over wealth creation have been raging for centuries between two fundamentally opposed groups. The most radical and revolutionary in recent decades are claims wealthy individuals got that way by exploiting the working class.[80] The opposite position argues wealth is created through principles of Western culture and political social contract theories. These allow individuals to excel economically and politically on their own, which then benefits all society:

> Now we can understand better why the West was able, between the sixteenth century and the nineteenth century, to subdue the rest of the world and bend it to its will. Indian elephants and Zulu spears were no match for British jeeps and rifles. Colonialism and imperialism are not the *cause* of the West's success; they are the *result* of that success. The wealth and military power of the European nations made them arrogant and stimulated their appetite for global conquest: thus the British, the Dutch, and the French went abroad in search of countries to subdue and rule. These colonial possessions added to the prestige, and to a lesser degree to the wealth, of Europe. But the

primary cause of Western affluence and power is internal – the institutions of science, democracy, and capitalism acting in concert. Consequently it is simply wrong to maintain that the rest of the world is poor because the West is rich, or that the West grew rich off "stolen goods" from Asia, Africa, and Latin America, because the West created its own wealth, and still does.[81]

Financial strength and efficient revenue generating programs are paramount if government is to fulfill *obligations* of national defense. A significant obstacle to national security during the reign of England's Charles I, for example, did not involve foreign threats but rather a consistent revenue stream into the treasury.[82] Signs of creative government finance schemes used as models for the modern era were first developed during this period. England was an environment with tight money and natives who were just as tight with their nest egg. Revenue enhancement devised by Charles charged coastal counties for the cost of naval expenditures.[83] The practice succeeded because taxpayers could witness a return on their investment.[84] This program was later expanded to include inland counties and other forms of government service. Problems began to surface at this juncture.[85] People along the coast saw ships constructed with expertise, sailors professionally trained, and material wealth accumulated from overseas. Land-shires were not so convinced and believed they were unfairly charged for benefits going to sea-shires. Payments did voluntarily continue from taxpayers aware naval force successfully protected the merchant fleet. Coastal citizens knew the gangster mentality that once permeated surrounding waters. Utilizing the seas and port facilities without fear of rape and robbery made it all a worthwhile investment.

An imaginative mind must exist to argue Western ideals of individual freedom, constitutional government, and capitalism did not create the environment for wealth creation. European travels around the globe, population settlements on foreign lands, and establishing lifestyle changes in territories resulted from success at home. Sea power enabled this to happen. Europeans went east, west, north, and south because they could, not because they were broke and backward:

> The general considerations that have been advanced concern all the great European nations, in so far as they look outside their own continent, and to maritime expansion, for the extension of national influence and power; but the effect upon the action of each differs necessarily according to their several conditions.[86]

Financial strength existing at home enabled Europeans to invent, explore, and expand. Economic models created by the West are today enabling nations to develop and prosper in ways not otherwise possible.[87] Colonial states that won independence and quickly reverted back to ancestral ways failed to develop. Others became havens for dictatorship. A few flourished because they adopted Western political ideals.

Trust Reality

Geography is the reason for technological development. It is not an enemy technology must seek to slay. States that identify geography as an ally to research and development succeed in achieving policy objectives. Computer technology and "cyber-space" are new additions to continuously building excitement that technology will conquer geography. Software firms claiming to honor individual freedom and privacy seek greater background on human subjects to sustain profit and relevance.[88] "Cyber-space" suddenly appears as "cyber-spy." Privacy rights surrender to techno-stock performance in order to justify a fad industry's continuation. Toiling masses are expected to line up and accept free exploitation of their personal data.

Recent military technology trends are based on arguments that death can be implemented at a keyboard, rather than the end of a bayonet. True or false, it does not alter fundamental laws of conquest. Geostrategic advantage remains a motivator behind punching those keys. Benefits from exploiting geography are the incentive for technological innovation and computers simply enhance geography's value. Therefore, power generators actually become greater assets to national grand strategy's composition. L.W. Martin emphasized this development 40 years ago. He argued technology would make the world's oceans increasingly significant over time. More states would realize its enormous value and seek to join the maritime party. Technology supports Martin's comment as easily today as it would have five hundred years ago:

> The increasing use of the seas for transport, the rapidly improving prospects for exploiting the marine life within them and the physical elements both within and below them, and the expanding range of military devices that can be deployed at sea all combine to intensify social, economic, political and ultimately strategic relations in the areas of the globe covered by water.[89]

Axis Powers on the Eastern Front discovered that infrastructure can make life miserable without proper attention. President Dwight D. Eisenhower's administration had a national security purpose behind creating the interstate highway system. It allowed removal of millions from cities across America to civil defense shelters should nuclear war with the Soviet Union erupt. These networks provide important transportation features for economic pursuits. Unfortunately, it caused serious damage to railroad commerce as the trucking industry took advantage and grew at an enormous pace. The underlying importance of transport from a single geographic location to another did not change. Exploitation methods associated with that endeavor did alter future modes.

Nations that need not worry about their people can accomplish great things. American business has a long history of serving government, citizens, and investors simultaneously. It is an art not many get right. Calvin Coolidge, thirtieth President of the United States, summed up this linkage with his popular phrase, "the chief business of the American people is business."[90] The quote is epitomized by Union Pacific Railroad's own slogan which simply states, "Building America."

Part III

Historical Development

"The clash of interests, the angry feelings roused by conflicting attempts thus to appropriate the larger share, in not the whole, of the advantages of commerce, and of distant unsettled commercial regions, led to wars. On the other hand, wars arising from other causes have been greatly modified in their conduct and issue by the control of the sea. Therefore the history of sea power, while embracing in its broad sweep all that tends to make a people great upon the sea or by the sea, is largely a military history; and it is in this aspect that it will be mainly, though not exclusively, regarded in the following pages."

Alfred Thayer Mahan, *The Influence of Sea Power upon History, 1660 – 1783*, 5th ed. (Mineola, NY: Dover Publications, 1987).

Chapter Seven

Exploration and Discovery

"Nurse our sweet children tenderly, and rear them. Home with you now, and hold your tongue, and tell no one your lover's name-though I am yours, Poseidon, lord of surf that makes earth tremble."
- Homer, *Odyssey*

Mahan's theoretical principles in *The Influence of Sea Power upon History* are brought to life by France's difficult trials and tribulations. Analysis of his favorite nemesis, Louis XIV, reveals an inability to recognize one very important link:

> History has proved that such a purely military sea power can be built up by a despot, as was done by Louis XIV; but though so fair seeming, experience showed that his navy was like a growth which having no root soon withers away. But in a representative government any military expenditure must have a strongly represented interest behind it, convinced of its necessity.[1]

Mahan lays down a common theme found in several upcoming case studies. Historical surveillance in remaining chapters is established by first focusing on six key civilizations. Each is directly connected to national grand strategy and sea power in several ways. Examination begins with three civilizations that effectively exploited the Mediterranean Sea region. Chapter 8 continues with a study of East Asia's turbulent sea power evolution and the exchange cultivated with Western maritime powers. Great Britain's impact on the entire world provides a grand finale.

There is a long and devastating history naming policy planners who failed to appreciate linkage. Those who ignored blatantly obvious connections comprise a long and impressive list of names: "Oversimplification in the writing of history – as in the drawing of maps – is a necessary exercise: reality is always too complex to replicate."[2] The cunning use of linkage to attain strategic objectives can easily escape untrained eyes: "Pretend inferiority and encourage his arrogance."[3] Many individuals in the past failed to recognize traits associated with linkage. A "distinct difference," for example, exists between Mahan's use of "military sea power" versus general reference to sea power. Models explain sea power's reality on international outcomes: "From the days when we humans first began to use the seas, the great lesson of history is that the enemy who is confined to a land strategy is in the end defeated."[4] Mahan's "military sea power" remark is crafted to separate an important element from broader concepts of sea power. To make certain this is not a slip of the Mahanian tongue, a look elsewhere finds several repeats showing careful distinction:

> Their poverty and their lack of military sea power, with the exception of a few cruisers that preyed upon the enemy's commerce, necessarily confined their efforts to land warfare, which constituted indeed a powerful diversion in favor of the allies and an exhausting drain upon the resources of Great Britain, but which it was in the power of the latter to stop at once by abandoning the contest.[5]

Stimulus for linkage is pervasive throughout various historical examples. Cohabitation and interoperability exists with all instruments serving power generation. Phoenicia, Ancient Greece, Roman Republic and later Empire, Ancient China, Japan, and Great Britain are discussed in terms of specific time periods. Though particular problems may be unique, all examples have the common denominator of linkage associated with success or failure.

Chosen Ones

Phoenicia invented sea power and, as a result, it had to learn the hard way. No previous models existed to build on...Phoenicia was the precedent-setter. This has a unique relationship to Sir Julian Corbett's remark concerning connections between exploration and strategy. Phoenicia exploited sea power to the hilt and, in turn, great economic rewards were achieved. It showed the benefits derived from international trade and maritime commerce, but also exposed what can happen when a single power generator dominates national security's faculty. An unbalanced power generating system caused unrealistic confidence in a single source. This limited freedom of action in other areas. Sea power built an impressive territory, but did not cause the downfall; over-confidence in what could be achieved and sustained made the biggest contribution.

Greek civilization was first to realize benefits in a well-blended land and sea power mix. This building process evolved from Phoenicia's unfortunate experience. Phoenicia provided Athens with Corbett's precedent needed to exert regional power. Great rewards were achieved through a thriving democracy that reflected positive gains for the government. Individuals had a stake in personal liberties and seeing to it that democracy survived. The Greeks were not afraid to fight for freedom and sovereignty. Motivation and later Athenian gambling won against Persia at Salamis. Over-confidence, yet again, caused a strategic disaster on Sicilian shores which left a humiliating blemish on an otherwise stellar record.

Rome provides an example of dominant land power attempting to adapt and modify assets for sea control. Rome failed to fully exploit all that interoperability offered by not incorporating sea power into a greater geostrategic defense role. It became heavily reliant on land boundaries that triggered a susceptibility to deep enemy penetration. This geostrategic quagmire inspired the transition from a republican form of government to an empire mixed with extremes of hedonism and oppression. That elusive thin line separating freedom from subjugation for the sake of security can be difficult to locate. Too often states have crossed it before realizing what took place. In Rome's case the damage had been done; it was permanent self-infliction; and the decline would be a long, grueling ordeal.

Dynasties are only as good as the internal politics nourishing their development. Domestic pressure in China could not be kept in check long enough to build a sustainable sea power state. Radical frequency of regime change made sea power an unattractive pursuit. Stable leadership is an essential ingredient, and China's turbulent ordeal with regime legitimacy stands out as a perfect historical example. Consistency is a mainstay of states that developed global sea power portfolios. Political unrest is often behind a disregard toward oceanic expansion. Like providence, each time China pursued activities overseas, domestic politics rose to the occasion and forced a strategic retreat. The twenty-first century affords unprecedented opportunities to overcome this curse. The current communist government is trying every available act of oppression to avoid a repeat performance. If failure occurs, it will result from a loss of regime legitimacy and refusal to share power. The subsequent overthrow will be a rerun of history.

Japan's geographic destiny made sea power critical to national survival. The number of islands creates a challenging predicament.

Proximity to continental Asia became advantageous for natural resource acquisition, a critical need for an industrial economy. It also made Japan vulnerable to mainland power politics. Japan is an ideal centerpiece displaying international trade's value to states possessing public support, but lacking power resources in other areas. Since the World War II's end, Japan has skillfully managed foreign affairs, while meeting critical economic needs of an industrialized free market modeled after the United States.

Free trade rules and so does the Industrial Revolution. Great Britain's economic growth and maritime superiority built a global empire that became the envy of most and frustration for the rest. Britain achieved success because of a government that rewarded ingenuity and fostered individual freedom. Property rights and capital investment provided an economic model beneficial to all classes of society. There were plenty of jobs and opportunity to go around. Britain's security dilemma is an example of benefits gained by identifying the origin of threats early. Once focused, a consistent military policy can then be formulated. Britain's greatest danger emanated from the European continent and as a result, they diligently policed it with sound acumen.

Two dominant themes deal with prevailing theoretic discourse surrounding power generator commonality. These consist of the geography power resource and national grand strategy model. Both are tied together by all four power generators. Even though air and space power were not yet discovered in many historical models discussed, a key connecting link between geography and all four generator definitions still existed. Systems can be identified and unequivocally observed by the way each state follows specific patterns. Poor decision-making and subsequent disaster are apparent for parties that ignored sound models. Sir Julian Corbett's remark on the importance of following a strategic map is similar to that overworked quote: "Those who cannot remember the past are condemned to repeat it."[6] While important to remember history, knowledge is of little value if calculated lessons cannot be derived from previous mistakes: "History is always written wrong, and so always needs to be rewritten."[7]

Phoenicia

Sea power's history began with Phoenicia, widely recognized as the earliest seafaring state.[8] The Empire started using seagoing craft to conduct commerce among civilizations blanketing the Mediterranean

Sea's perimeter around 3,000 BC. Three developments transpired during this period which evolved into a standard fact of life for mankind's future, state legitimacy, and world politics. The first is the idea and effort behind exploiting waterways as a transport medium. The second became a natural outgrowth, which involved the notion of international trade. In proper order, number three became an outgrowth of the second, which is establishment of the world's first official navy to protect trade routes.

Phoenicia's colonies and customer base were incredibly vast. Initially it extended across the Mediterranean from Mesopotamia to Spain.[9] Phoenician sailors, realizing the huge economic advantage, soon directed their trading domain around Africa's rim, arriving at the Red Sea and Persian Gulf.[10] This is an astounding effort considering the primitive nature of craft in use. Admiration for gallantry comes easy when considering so many hostile elements of men and nature. A ship's crew achieved enormous status and respect with people of regions visited. Aware of sea power's value to the Empire, Phoenicians took several precautions to protect their maritime skill from copycats: "The secrets of their routes and their maritime knowledge were jealously guarded."[11]

Phoenicia's positive reputation helped maintain good relations. As a result, Phoenicia became first to use sea power as an enhancement for international prestige: "The Phacacians were the ideal seamen, men who, unlike the Greeks themselves, had no horror of the sea and no reason to dread it."[12] Transporting goods across great bodies of water, using the navigational aides available, earned these adventurers unrivalled respect.[13] Trade colonies were established at strategic locations throughout the business empire. These became the first known overseas bases supporting maritime operations.[14] Harbors remained secure as civilizations within those regions saw the worth of such ports-of-call. Phoenician ships arrived with commodities from afar. They replenished their vessels while trading for local products. Maritime reach, according to Gerhard Herm, enlarged Phoenicia's value by providing the Mediterranean community more diverse goods:

> Historians today are united that the Phoenicians were not only the best seafarers of early antiquity but were also among the most outstanding technicians of their day. They probably earned this reputation both because they were simply more gifted in a practical sense than many of their neighbors, and also because their special position and their permanently threatened existence forced them to

exert all their mental resources much more intensely in this respect than those who could allow themselves, in view of their large population and secure tenure of land, to be somewhat more indolent.[15]

Phoenicia found it easy to expand its trading domain. Everyone they came in contact with realized a benefit for their own communities. It seemed a natural thing to do as various civilizations willingly greeted a ship's crew in their travels around Africa and Europe's coastal rim. There was a need worth filling and all hands were buying. Defending trade assets seemed unnecessary and, therefore, very little attention was given. Sea-lanes stretched as far as Britain and grew too fast to protect with resources originally available.[16] Defense did not seem to be a priority with so many willing customers. Carthage's location along Africa's northern coast became the largest and most valuable port. It also had the greatest degree of independence.[17] All the essential ingredients to support maritime affairs existed, including an excellent harbor, defensible position with favorable geographic features, and agricultural production to support a large population.[18]

Creation of a professional maritime military (navy) caused hostile reactions against Phoenicia's otherwise peaceful reputation.[19] Phoenicia's naval might developed from discovering the art of war on land. Benefits were gained by incorporating those methods into a battle fleet with men possessing great sailing expertise.[20] Nations were driven to action upon witnessing the phenomenon of unusual seagoing craft and fighting forces. Phoenicia's dilemma with Lebanon's vast terrain border brought problems associated with national grand strategy to the forefront. Homeland defenses did not possess a luxuriously large army to man the line. Fear of a naval force possibly assaulting coastal cities drove states to rise against the monopoly. The weakest link, as a result, turned out to be Phoenicia's position on land.

Phoenicia's national security lesson for those who followed involves geographic destiny and power generators. Mahan's thoughts on the need for overseas facilities to service a fleet, the problems and benefits associated with island territories, and the danger of becoming over-stretched stand out in Phoenicia's case.[21] The Phoenicians, like Mahan, were aware geostrategic connections existed between land and sea. Mahan's concept of strategic lines, travel routes, and geographic position can be found in the organization of Phoenician trade centers.[22] Unlike Mahan, the Phoenicians failed to consider adequate defensive measures as territory expanded. In Phoenicia's defense, historical records did not exist to guide construction and administration of a maritime empire.[23] Mahan did not appear for another 2000 years. Phoenicia was put on display like a scout serving point and going where no man had gone before.

Conditions surrounding the demise are complex. Many difficulties experienced still apply today. There remain positive and negative lessons to learn. Geostrategically, in Phoenicia's case, negatives far outweigh the positive. As an instrument of military power, navies became a valuable asset not only for the sole provider, but enemies as well.[24] Phoenicia did not consider the message sent as its fleet transited to a weapon of mass destruction. Lack of land forces caused this professional naval force to become the kiss of death. Phoenicia did not appear hostile until arming the fleet for battle. Viewing Phoenicia as a threatening military power culminated in Persia's conquest around 600 BC. The conquerors then incorporated ships and sailors in their own mediocre fleet, which greatly enhanced performance.[25] Phoenicia did not realize there would be such hostility toward its naval force that it justified a pre-emptive strike at the weakest link, which was on land: "To be certain to take what you attack is to attack a place the enemy does not protect."[26]

Geographic position has not changed and remains a defense strategist's nightmare. Even today, Lebanon is bordered on three sides by potentially hostile neighbors. This originally consisted of Hittites to the north, Persians toward the east, and Egyptians to the south. Today it is the Syrians, Iranians (vis-à-vis Hezbollah), and Israelis jockeying for control. Only the Mediterranean Sea along the western border offered a means of escape by way of maritime assets. Greek developments as a naval power, complements of pirated Phoenician technology, created less of a monopoly and more of a threat.[27]

The rugged Carmel mountain range to the east aided in a simultaneous land attack from north and south. Phoenicia's position along the eastern Mediterranean shore served as a transit highway between Europe, Middle East, and Africa. Traffic routinely passed through, making the homeland more vulnerable. This should have served as a wakeup call. Unwillingness to build militarily on land left no other option; find a niche in maritime power. Autonomy became threatened without an adequate land force factored into the national security folder. Phoenicia may have benefited by minimizing over-dependence on a professional navy. Geography has always been Phoenicia's biggest enemy and, at least in the earlier years, people smartly focused on a business service that every ruler desired. This lasted only as long as the customer base would allow.

Though Carthage was as free as any state, Phoenicia's jewel left the dance early. Limited sovereignty could not pacify Carthaginians and eventually a rebellion achieved its objective. Phoenicia never fully recovered from the loss and it marked a steep decline ahead. Placing the bulk of resources on sea power worked for a while, but patent protection laws were nonexistent. Blind faith in a single power generator ultimately became a dangerous policy once nations imitated the craft of sailing. Though the defense portfolio's addiction to sea power is a gamble considered political suicide in modern times, Phoenician policy-makers are not to blame for their chosen course. They achieved phenomenal milestones that remain worthy of respect. This is a reflection of superior statecraft, business acumen, and ingenuity. Phoenicia invented sea power and, ironically, it did provide a period of freedom and prosperity longer than most states can imagine under more favorable circumstances.[28]

Greece

Witnessing Phoenicia's trading success gave the Greeks a brilliant idea. Greece's own geographic relationship to the Mediterranean Sea served as a motivator for pursuing maritime trade and Phoenician methods were incorporated primarily by Athens. Greece, geographically, can be considered the inverse of Phoenicia. Phoenicia is surrounded on three sides by land, while Greece is surrounded on three sides by water. Greece's primary land mass has its northern border connected to the European continent. The rest is coastline that includes over two thousand islands within easy sailing distance. Only Phoenicia's western border has access to the Mediterranean Sea. The Peloponnesus is tied to the mainland by an isthmus at Corinth. The Greek islands consist of a cumulative area larger in size than the mainland. This strand serves as a frontline barrier to the Mediterranean Sea. If Phoenicia is difficult to defend because of its land border, then a logical assumption is Greece should be secure. This is not a correct assumption because the coast comprised thousands of miles of uninhabited shoreline. Total population of independent states during the Peloponnesian War reached a figure of approximately 500,000 people. This made amphibious landings an attractive consideration for enemies.[29]

Defensive challenges faced by nations attempting to balance topography and population are profoundly revealed with Greece.[30] A lack of population in relation to coastline did not prevent periodic population control efforts, which usually occurred when government officials grew concerned over grain shipments flowing from the Black Sea region. Population, Mahan's fourth of six sea power elements, is portrayed by Greek difficulty defending a vast coastal territory. Linkage is apparent with territory, Mahan's third key ingredient for sea power success: "As to these it is to be said that, the geographical and physical conditions being the same, extent of sea-coast is a source of strength or weakness according as the population is large or small."[31] Agricultural resources were a constant concern that prevented a population explosion and any hope of relocation efforts to coastal locations. Adequate supplies of grain from the Black Sea were critical to the Athenian government: "When Sparta acquired a fairly robust superiority at sea, she endeavored successfully to impose a maritime supply blockade against the Athenian grain route from the Crimea."[32] Interceding and denying food supplies became a regular target for Persia. The Greek population could not grow without unchecked access to foreign resources. Halford Mackinder and Adolf Hitler would view Ukraine's strategic value in a similar way over 2,000 years later.

Amphibious landings were a constant security problem.[33] This threat provoked formation of independent Greek city-states, which were deemed militarily necessary to protect all communities. Society began to flourish under the application of democratic principles and private property rights. This resulted in greater demand for resources and development of a large maritime capability.[34] Historians traditionally regard Athens as the commercial empire, while Sparta is the military equivalent. Even today their relationship is used to compare diplomatic activities involving two or more nation-states.[35] Athens served as a great sea power, while Sparta acted as the superior land power. Athens remained open-minded, while Sparta ran a highly regimented society. It built and maintained a powerful land force, while Athens gained enormous prestige with maritime reach. When they were not butting heads, their united force passed the superpower muster with flying colors. Phoenicia sorely lacked this type of alliance.

Threats from Persia, beginning with Darius I in about 500 BC, brought Greek city-states into an alliance against a common enemy. Assaults on inhabitants of Ionia, Chios, Lesbos, and Tenedos left communities with no alternative but war. Phoenicians, acting on orders issued by their new Persian masters, committed various unsavory acts that included burning, enslavement, castration, and rape.[36] The Greek fleet took to the sea but got off to a slow start with losses at Lade in 494 BC, and Thermopylae and Artemisium in 480 BC. Revenge came later that year following mobilization of 350 combat-ready sailing vessels. While Persia's land forces pillaged Athens, the outnumbered Athenian fleet lured Persia's fleet into a narrow strait off Salamis. By taking advantage of that secret weapon known as weather, and employing it in conjunction with geostrategic position, the Athenian fleet successfully turned the tide of war in a single engagement. The Phoenicians found themselves pinned in by topography and strong winds and, having no place to go, the Greeks were able to systematically eliminate over 200 of Persia's original 1200 ships.[37] The carnage would have been far worse had the Phoenicians not withdrawn when they did. Successful application of weather and topography along the Salamis coast forced Persia's huge army, diligently at work inland, to disengage and carry out a strategic retreat.

A single naval action at Salamis destroyed Persia's overall plan for conquering the Greek states. Xerxes, after witnessing the embarrassing battle first hand, ordered several Phoenician sailors who survived beheaded. He failed to realize those sailors actually performed a great service by preventing annihilation of his entire fleet. This would have then resulted in the complete loss of his army. Colin Gray's assessment of the festivities accurately identifies Persia's failure. It got caught in a situation where the strategic "triad" of land army, merchant fleet, and war galleys were totally dependent upon each other for success. Persia's army needed the merchant fleet to keep it supplied in the field. Naval force needed to defend the merchant fleet. Merchant and naval fleets needed the army to secure beaches at night so that they could lay-up without fear of attack. Loss of a single link, which is what happened at Salamis, caused the whole campaign to collapse.[38]

A break in linkage between power resources and/or generators can devastate survival chances. This strategic disconnect forced Xerxes back to Asia with over half his original force. Gray's reference to Persia's military fracture is, on a smaller scale, explanatory of the broader national grand strategy theater previously explained. The ability to assist Persia's navy in fulfilling duties at sea categorized the army as a resource of sea power. Xerxes failed to recognize this key feature. The fleet could not have survived without the army's ability to secure ports at night. It is dangerous to consider Persia's situation at

Salamis unique in history. F. E. Adcock credits Mahan with enhancing strategic awareness of the historical significance behind Salamis:

> Finally, I should add a word about the interaction of sea and land in a wider setting. Since the work of Mahan on the influence of sea power on history, we have all been very conscious of the effect of naval strength on war by land. The Grand Army of Napoleon on the cliffs of Boulogne foiled by "the weather-beaten sails of distant ships on which their eyes never looked" is, to me at least, a grateful and comforting thought. But, for reasons I have already given, ancient fleets could not exert this distant pressure. The fleets of Greece and Macedon, as indeed those of Rome, could better secure the movement of their own armies than hinder the movement of the armies of others. Still, the pressure of sea power might isolate or immobilize an army, even in antiquity. When the Athenians before Syracuse lost the battle in the Great Harbour, their army was lost with it. When the Greeks won the battle of Salamis, it meant the enforced reduction of the Persian army to a strength which was no longer invincible.[39]

Mahan's position on the utility and defense of overseas bases holds as much value in the war between Greece and Persia as it does for Phoenicia in building a trading empire. This principle has applied to every century since 3,000 BC, and includes the year Xerxes failed to recognize value in keeping Phoenician sailors alive. Athenian prestige, as Donald Kagan notes, rose to new heights across the Greek Empire:

> Athens's imperial revenue was large enough to provide a considerable surplus beyond the needs of the Navy, and the Athenians used it for their own purposes, including the great building program that beautified and glorified their city and gave work to its people and the accumulation of a large reserve fund. The Navy protected the ships of their merchants in their prosperous trade all around the Mediterranean and beyond. It also gave the Athenians access to the wheat fields of Ukraine and the fish of the Black Sea with which they could supplement their inadequate home food supply and even replace it totally, with the use of imperial money, if forced to abandon their own fields by war. Once they completed the walls surrounding their city and connecting it by long walls to its fortified port at Piraeus, as they did in mid century, the Athenians could be invulnerable.[40]

The feud that eventually developed between Sparta and Athens is a Greek tragedy of high drama. Fear of a rising maritime power motivated allies to urge Sparta into war. Passion eventually overcame those who should have known better than to act prematurely:

> If the Corinthians were led astray by the passion for vengeance and the Spartans by jealousy and fear, the Athenians may have suffered from excess of reasoned calculation. Pericles's diplomacy counted on the Spartans to see Athenian actions as what he intended – moderate responses to provocations – responses meant not to bring on war or challenge Spartan leadership, but to deter war and preserve the status quo. He counted on equally cool calculation, first on the part of the Corinthians, then of the Spartans, but passion proved stronger.[41]

A Corinthian plea to the Spartans in 432 BC is symbolic of a trend. Poor judgment and timing are problems when states enter into war. Decisions are too hastily made under duress with fierce emotion exerted by less strategically oriented minds:

> They are bold beyond their strength, they run risks which prudence would condemn; and in the midst of misfortune they are full of hope. Whereas it is your nature, though strong, to act feebly; when your plans are most prudent, to distrust them; and when calamities come upon you, to think that you will never be delivered from them. They are impetuous, and you are dilatory; they are always abroad, and you are always at home.[42]

Such badgering is more than any Spartan ego could handle. A similar statement today would likely result in polite demands for a diplomatic apology at the next embassy cocktail party. Making such an argument in ancient times directly challenged Spartan manhood.

Sparta eventually succeeded in defeating the mighty sea power, but it did not come without a price and willing assistance from Persia's fleet. Sparta's leadership realized a decisive victory was improbable unless it neutralized the naval force of Athens. Even with Persian assistance, Athenian sea power remained impressive in size. This quickly changed when Athens made its decision to launch a campaign in Sicily. The pride of Athenian power disappeared on Sicilian shores: "The disaster at Syracuse swept away so many fine ships and crews that the unchallengeable supremacy of Athens at sea disappeared."[43] The Athenian Assembly's decision to launch an expedition ranks among the top ten most catastrophic political moves in military history.[44] The campaign's resource requirements were so large, no room remained for strategic failure. Disaster in Sicily, resulting plague and starvation in Athens, and Persia's fleet disrupting Black Sea operations forced Athens into submission. That dreaded "blow-back" from strategy to grand strategy arrived with devastating consequences.

Two primary factors caused Athenian collapse. The first involved a loss of sea power. The second comprised enemy acquisition of dominant sea power. It can be argued that each received a vital contribution from land forces. Sparta's land force took advantage of Persia's naval help when Athens found itself down and out:

> The Peloponnesian War was one of those classic confrontations between a great land power and a great naval power. Each entered the war hoping and expecting to keep to its own element and to win a victory in a way that conformed to its strength at a relatively low cost. Within a few years events showed that victory would not be possible that way for either side. To win, each had to acquire the capacity to fight and succeed on the other's favourite domain.[45]

Destruction of the Athenian fleet in Sicily and Sparta's own ability to project maritime power as far as the Black Sea region signaled the end. Not only would Athens pay dearly, but the entire Greek experiment would tumble and implode from long-range political mistrust laid down for future generations. It may have been a powerful land force wielding the Spartan sword over the Athenian population, but sea power is responsible for allowing those sabers inside the walls connecting Piraeus to Athens.

National grand strategy's model can be referenced for answers to the disaster between Athens and Sparta. Each needed to perform their respective sea and land power duties. Any break between them ensured neither would survive. Athenian gambling in Sicily destroyed an enormous number of maritime assets. This was naturally followed by an Athenian collapse of morale, which is an important power resource element. Athens and Sparta failed to realize they were critical links to continuation of Greek civilization. They found themselves distracted from looking outward at threats on the horizon. Preoccupation with domestic grudges ruled the day. Willingness to fight certainly existed, but its concentrated force ran off in a wrong direction. It would not be the last time internal squabbling caused nations to implode while enemies looked on in amusement.

The Peloponnesian War will always be remembered as an avoidable tragedy. Sparta did not realize it was making a long-range blunder leading to its own doom. Even a period of hope during

Alexander the Great's reign could not restore full trust among city-states. Alexander's success conquering Persia was a brief reprieve. Competition for power following his death in Babylon broke in pieces all that had been built. Loss of regime legitimacy started the plunge. The entire Greek experiment went into an uncontrolled crash within a century of Sparta's victory over Athens. Rome to the west was waiting for an opportunity. Once accounts were settled with Carthage, Roman eyes turned east.

Rome

Rome's sea power legacy involved modifying land power assets to meet requirements at sea. The Mediterranean Sea became a gigantic lake encased in a shoreline under Rome's complete control.[46] Greece and Rome are commonly portrayed as opposites. Greece is regarded as a sea power while Rome a land power. Common characterization of differences in power generator choices is deceptive. While military instruments associated with land and sea power maintained physical continuity, each was strategically and tactically adapted to support efforts in another geographic domain. This achievement occurred with great care and Roman leaders did an excellent job utilizing land forces to support operations at sea. *If a mechanism is used to apply pressure in a particular geographic region, then it is considered a product of that region for as long as it is providing utility.* Facial features, meaning ships, chariots, or gladiators at the coliseum, did not determine power classification. Norman Davies personifies a tendency to look at Rome strictly in terms of land forces:

> The key to the Greek world lay in its high-prowed ships, the key to Roman power lay in marching legions. The Greeks were wedded to the sea, the Romans to the land. The Greek was a sailor at heart, the Roman a landsman.[47]

Davies is correct to argue Rome's main consideration involved land power. While focusing on land forces, any analysis must also include recognition that Rome incorporated those assets into sea power capabilities. Roman sailors and the legionnaires battling Carthaginians around Sicily's rim would not have considered themselves landsmen at that particular time. On the other hand, many Spartans would find Davies calling them sailors' offensive. Fortunately for him, his comment is recorded in 1996 AD instead of 432 BC. It is correct to state land power built Rome's early republic. But later events forced a move onto the sea in order to defeat a maritime challenge threatening Rome's existence. Legionnaires and Carthage's own fundamental fighting skills were incorporated to defeat that archenemy.

Sea power's leverage gives a nation-state freedom to do many things, which includes making military victory on land possible. Rome's experience with sea power took an unconventional approach. While the Greeks used maritime power to build and maintain their sea power capability, Rome used land assets to support a conquest of the Mediterranean Sea. Greece, Carthage and early Rome saw the Mediterranean as essential to geopolitical designs and economic stamina. Integrating sea power into grand strategy's portfolio became a necessity to empire building efforts. While each state had specific security needs, all depended on sea power as a key factor. Geostrategic objectives require four power generators today. Two existed in Greek and Roman eras. Rome's position focused on land elements: "to the Romans the land was the place to win victories rather than the sea, and it is also true to say that the Romans sought to conquer the sea from the land rather than the land from the sea."[48]

Rome's own sea power encounter began with Carthaginian battles off Sicily's coast during the First Punic War. The Punic Wars may be considered a two-part act, with the first lasting from 264-241 BC. Rome's familiarity with maritime matters revealed such amazing neglect at the start that Carthaginian military leaders considered attempts to engage them as useless exercises in strategic ineptitude: "As long as Carthage had this naval access, the Romans could not turn battlefield victories into strategically decisive results."[49] Over-confidence in maritime abilities turned out to be a Carthaginian liability. This resulted from the First Punic War's start, which showed Roman ships barely fit to cross the Strait of Messina.[50] Rome, however, soon started an aggressive ship design and modernization program. It is to their benefit that the war became a long, drawn-out affair.

Rome's leaders wisely capitalized on their military strengths and avoided known weaknesses. A naval fleet was designed for the purpose of maximizing the utility of dedicated legions. Roman engineers designed an instrument known as a *Corvus*, which comprised a sharp spike attached at one end of a long plank. While Carthaginian sailors howled with laughter at the sight of these unusual looking ships approaching for battle, Roman sailors were able to drop the *Corvus* on Carthaginian ships and lock opposing vessels together. Legionnaires, which were riding along for a piece of the action, were then allowed to storm enemy ships and do what they did best. The Battle of Mylae in 260 BC ranked among the war's largest naval battles. The method of fighting at Mylae forever changed Carthaginian perception of their adversary's maritime acumen. Rome learned to efficiently apply their most vital asset, the legionnaire, and incorporate his skill at sea with surgical precision.

Though successful in many naval engagements, Rome's legion never achieved a victory at sea complete enough to force the enemy's subjugation. This is a strategic decision based on F. E. Adcock's reference that Rome believed decisive victories were won on land. Rome maintained this position even after fielding first-class warships eight years into the First Punic War. The new vessels were more than able to face Carthage's fleet head-on. Those deployed at Cape Economus could transport 300 legionnaires. Both sides in this battle had a combined total of 300,000 troops engaged. Out of 350 Carthaginian ships, 30 were destroyed and another 60 captured.

It can be argued Rome failed to capitalize on the rout by not staying in hot pursuit back to Carthage. Instead, a strategic decision involved consolidating positions around Sicily, Corsica, and Sardinia. Prudence in first securing Sicily before crossing the Mediterranean possessed characteristics exhibited by the US military's Pacific island hopping campaign during World War II. Geostrategic equivalence does exist between Rome's perspective toward the Mediterranean Sea and America's view of the Pacific Ocean 2000 years later. Resource needs made it a necessity for both Rome and the US to proceed with appropriate steps toward achieving their ultimate goal. Selective avoidance, as noted by Tojo's earlier discussion with MacArthur, holds enormous value in these circumstances. Picking and choosing your battles wisely is a process incorporated with precision by the US Pacific Fleet during World War II. Secure lines of communication were as vital to Rome as the US, something Phoenicia failed to realize in an earlier time.

The Second Punic War lasted from 218-201 BC and witnessed Hannibal's famous land campaign across the Iberian Peninsula. Italy's topography has many similarities to Greece. It is surrounded on three sides by water creating an over-extended coastline. Though the peninsula does not include as many islands as Greece, there are enough to warrant concern. These could have served as staging grounds by Hannibal's forces in preparation for a mainland amphibious landing.

Hannibal beat the odds by taking his chosen path into northern Italy. His army wreaked havoc up and down the Italian boot until forced to flee when war's tide changed direction.

A combination of issues led to Hannibal's defeat. Rome's citizens deserve credit for staying united in dire situations. Regime legitimacy remained in full bloom and the population quickly rallied around Rome's leadership in a coming storm.[51] This critical factor is too often overlooked. A national emergency only overcomes danger if people are willing to support their government. In the case of Rome, the political leadership did not hesitate to lead a charge and the masses were ready to follow (leadership by example).[52] Alvin Bernstein further argues that there are very few examples in history where a general populace appeared so willing to step forth, and then proceed to fight and die against a rampaging foreign power:

> The Roman state's ability to elicit this level of service from both citizens and allies in return for minimal compensation was a remarkable phenomenon. It reflected a value system entirely foreign to that of the liberal societies of the twentieth-century West. The difference between Rome's approach to things military, its view of what strategy comprised, and our own underlines a crucial fact of life: it is dangerous for the West in general, and for Americans in particular, to believe that others view strategy and the nature and uses of force through an Anglo-American lens.[53]

Rome concentrated military might on land forces, and those were the engagement terms mistakenly chosen by Hannibal. Carthage feigned ignorance at what it did best, which consisted of naval operations. As a result, Rome deployed its own fleet to keep Hannibal ill-supplied on the Italian heel where he eventually had to retreat from: "After Rome's triumph in the Second Punic War, no power ever again contested its advance on anything approaching an equal basis."[54]

Rome's contribution to military history continued with combat action at Actium in 31 BC. Actium showed how a combination of sea and land forces can determine events at sea. The legions of Octavianus overwhelmed Antony and Cleopatra, while the tactical genius of his fleet commander, Agrippa, put on a spectacular performance. The naval battle, for all practical purposes, was Antony's to lose. But the outcome at sea found its destiny determined by Octavianus and his legions ashore. Defeat of Antony's army prevented any hope of reinforcing and supplying naval forces off the coast. The psychological jolt on

Antony's men caused panic and chaos. His fleet soon lost formation and a rout ensued. Cleopatra and her reserve fleet of sixty ships were observing from a distance but refused to engage. Instead, she left for Egypt with Antony where Octavianus found her seven months later.

Colin Gray's "triad" linking Persia's sea and land power with logistics at Salamis got cut again at Actium with dramatic flair. An inability to keep overseas bases and facilities secure creates devastating consequences for the loser. Failure to maintain sufficient logistics support distracts military forces as members scavenge for survival. At Actium the application of pressure at sea was caused by elimination of support facilities on land. Antony's fleet responded by imploding in battle at sea.

Rome's decline left historians with much to write about. The most notable project is work by Edward Gibbon.[55] Several reasons for Rome's demise have been advanced. While each theory may be considered correct to a degree, all are derivatives of geostrategic circumstances and political legitimacy: "History has conclusively demonstrated the inability of a state with even a single continental frontier to compete in naval development with one that is insular, although of smaller population and resources."[56] Public participation in government waned during Rome's transition from a republic to a police state. A hedonistic view of individual freedom gained enthusiasm, making attainment of power by those unfit for such responsibility a distinct possibility:

> Bureaucratic omnipotence tends naturally to convert the holders of key positions in the vast administrative machine into a new variety of notables and nobles. So it happened in the late Roman Empire. The aristocratic families had been ground to powder by taxation. Those, on the other hand, often the freedmen of subject races, who occupied strategic positions in the wealth-absorbing machine, got from it immense fortunes not unmixed with personal regard.[57]

By the end of Augustus Caesar's reign, turmoil from within became as frequent as on the periphery. Marcus Aurelius and Constantine brought brief respites, but their effort at restoring unity came to no avail. Citizens began to question what they were fighting for as the slave population became as large as the legion army.

Rome's poor choice at setting empire boundaries caused over-dependence on land power: "If we consider the first cause of the collapse of the Roman Empire we shall find it merely due to the hiring of Goth mercenaries, for from that time we find the Roman strength begins to weaken."[58] The Mediterranean Sea appeared to be nothing more than a giant pond instead of a defensive boundary. This made national grand strategy's model one-sided with land power. Sea power, rather than acting as a "crucial enabler" meeting sustainability needs of the state, became relegated to a position of an alternative mode of cargo transport if and when needed. How states use geostrategic position is critical to economic and security needs. A massive boundary associated with the European border area has been a constant problem that imposes numerous concerns for states. Rome provided an example for those that followed:

- The size of Rome's land border rivaled that of the Soviet Union, which benefited from air and space power to support its security needs. German incursions were always a threat, and success was eventually achieved by taking full advantage of the frozen Rhine.[59]
- Campaigns to conquer the British Isles had no strategic value at the time. Fortifying existing territory should have been given priority, while incorporating the English Channel as a barrier.
- Solidifying territorial integrity never came to be an aspiration of ruling elites. A tendency to just keep going made more sense and is a consistent problem with empire building. An expansionist mindset caused those holding power to overlook advantages of maritime defense. A maritime barricade could have allowed patience while building a more secure political environment and cultivating better relations with natives.

Government must create an environment where citizens can develop and flourish. Denying motivational incentive forces political leaders to take punitive measures that ensure compliance. Those states required to do so must dedicate substantial resources toward domestic, rather than external security. This evolved over time as Rome made its transition to empire status. Attempting to pacify a populace with self-indulgent enticements served as a temporary fix for an inevitable future security crackdown that rattled tranquility. According to Michael Grant, a course was set for a permanent downward spiral:

> Even if there was a merciful inability to bring into effect every coercion and prohibition which the emperors and jurists had thought

out, this was a totalitarian state beyond anything which the ancient Assyrians or the Ptolemies of Egypt had contrived. The censor-ridden, standardizing police-administration advocated by Plato's *Laws* had arrived, and there seemed no possibility of its withering away. Aristotle regarded the state as originating in bare needs, and continuing in existence for the sake of the good life. But now, if the empire was to hang together, its bare needs were so great that the good life was enjoyed by very few. Even under earlier emperors, presiding over far more relaxed regimes, Tacitus had noted that liberty was the price that had to be paid for peace. But he could have had no conception of the third and fourth centuries in which almost every trace of personal freedom was sacrificed to national survival. By these grim means, the empire regained its position against all its enemies, and endured. Many of its inhabitants at the time must have wondered if it was worth saving at the price.[60]

Security issues along the periphery created insecurity in Rome's political elite. Elite insecurity is duplicated centuries later with Nazi Germany, the Soviet Union, and People's Republic of China. It would be wise for great democracies in the West to take Rome's problem under consideration.

Chapter Eight

East Meets West

"The weak fade and disappear, the strong multiply and triumph."
- Jean Raspail, *The Camp of the Saints*

      Historical analysis of sea power in the Far East focuses on China and Japan. Great Britain is incorporated because of the global reach from its own sea power voyage. Britain's contribution to bridging the great divide between Eastern and Western culture is substantial. Many similar features existed at various times between European and East Asia powers. Geographic position of Japan, for example, resembles Great Britain in many ways. China's power generator portfolio took an identity comparable to the Roman Empire. Problems associated with foreign and domestic security issues, government administration, and public support for various Chinese rulers were quite similar to Rome.[1] Emotions relating to authority and power were more graphically played out in China. Power generation developed for reasons identical to Rome's dependency on land forces. China's land border encompassed three sides, subjecting it to identical problems with bands of so-called barbarians. Sea power did not seem as critical because of geographic boundaries.

      Hsiungnu and Mongolia were always a threat for the northern perimeter, just as the German and Gaul tribes were to Rome's northern border.[2] While geographic comparison can be made between Japan's archipelago and Great Britain, so too can such similarities be made between Ancient China and the Roman Empire. Chinese territory grew in size equal to Rome and expansionist tendencies moved toward the west, while the Roman Empire took an easterly course. Both Rome and China approached each other across Central Asia. A clash between Europeans and Chinese would have occurred if military forces not retracted. Even Alexander the Great had once nearly touched the China hand.[3]

      China's natural tendency to concentrate on expansion across Asia minimized sea power desires. Attempts made would usually result in a quick rise, and then an even faster collapse. This often came on the heels of regime change. The Japanese were quite pleased witnessing such a consistent problem as they maintained a close eye on continental events. This practice is similar to England's manner policing Europe and, in particular, France and Germany. While China took pride in technological advances, Japan's warrior spirit and quality of manpower achieved a quality equal to their British counterpart on the other side of the Eurasian landmass.

Enter the Dragon

Dynastic reigns in China are best summarized as violent and chaotic. The Han Dynasty is considered by many to be the most famous. It grew as Rome was transiting to empire status, and then collapsed at approximately the time Marcus Aurelius died. Descent for each dynasty repeatedly plunged at a faster rate than anything Rome experienced. Leadership instability contributed to violent unrest and regime challenges profoundly increased in proportion to provincial numbers under rule. Assassination among the emperor elite grew to become as sophisticated as methods incorporated in Rome. It achieved particular regularity between 291-306 AD; a time that became known as the Wars between Eight Princes. Nobody ever claimed Chinese politics were boring, and David Gazer notes how tribal war over authority provided good training to deal with foreign entanglements:

> Because the emperor was considered to be the "son of heaven," early Chinese political theorists were challenged to justify how a new line could claim legitimacy in succeeding the previous dynasty. Their solution was the "Mandate of Heaven," which held that heaven blessed China's emperor only so long as he ruled in the interest of the nation. If he failed to do so, he was liable to be replaced.[4]

Another similarity shared by China and Rome involved ingenuity. Both were robust civilizations with many inventions. Meticulous Chinese recordkeeping dates as far back as 2,000 BC. This has provided many scholars with a treasure trove of documentation unlike most other civilizations. Creativity concentrated on scientific discovery, while Roman efforts were dedicated toward construction and war fighting. The Chinese did contribute to combat's cause by making great strides with theories on military strategy and tactics.

Four distinct periods of overseas maritime venture were developed. The first is commonly referred to as the Indo-Iranian era, which began during the second century AD. Influence was minimal because of the domestic turmoil surrounding Han's collapse. Limited amounts of trade did take place by seagoing craft between the Roman Empire's eastern border and the southern shore of China. Traffic routinely traveled along the Indian Ocean's northern perimeter; as a precaution, sailors seldom strayed from sight of land. Rome's political elite considered this practice unproductive and, as a result, government subsidies gradually subsided. Virtually all further seagoing trade continued entirely independent of official sanction. Commerce between East and West was considered by both parties to be far more feasible on land across the Silk Road.[5]

The Indo-Iranian period failed because of timing. China's first successful navy possessing any significance was later developed by the Wu Dynasty. It served with distinction against Taiwan between the second and fourth centuries. Commerce by merchant shipping during Sung, Chi, and Liang Dynasties did occur around Southeast Asia and along the Indian coast. Very limited trade and diplomatic intercourse took place with Japan. Contact which occurred primarily involved dealings over Korea.

Rivers are where the bulk of naval power deployed during China's early history. It provided maritime forces with unique characteristics. A tumultuous domestic environment significantly contributed to a strong focus on tributary activity and, in fact, may be considered the first application of a coast guard for purposes of patrolling inland navigable waters. The Yangtze River witnessed the largest amount of naval action, while the East China Sea and Sea of Japan were relatively active open water regions. However, border issues on land and simultaneous civil unrest prevented bolder moves in the Pacific. Additionally, Silk Road trade and its known quantity remained attractive and a continuous lure for the business oriented.

Sea power capacity involves an incredible amount of time to build and a short supply of dynastic patience prevented success. Internal politics during the first millennium became a serious detriment to sea power expansion. The Sui Dynasty in 581 AD temporarily reunited the Chinese nation after four centuries of chaos; but even that lasted only 37 years. The Sung Dynasty's political climate finally brought stability as the second millennium arrived. The Silk Road's permanent geographic fixture remained more attractive and seemed less costly. Maritime efforts to points west did not compute when objectives could be achieved over land.[6] Naval action continued to feed on the

Yangtze and Yellow Rivers. This generally consisted of simultaneous land and sea battles not unlike Greek and Roman events.[7] Greater contact with the outside world compounded domestic volatility which, at times, took on an extremely violent nature. China, like Rome, failed to achieve border stability by using advantages of topography. Indian and Pacific Oceans were ripe for taking had the nation succeeded in solidifying territorial positions on land.

The second millennium's start saw an unprecedented degree of energy toward overseas venture. In fact, sea power, for the first time, became elevated to a level that political elites considered it necessary for survival. Attempts at conquest by Mongols and other foreigners, which began as the thirteenth century unfolded, resulted in a loss of Silk Road trade. Rather than cause a retraction, as in earlier eras, this threat added fuel to sea power legitimacy. For the first time Chinese leadership realized strategic utility existed with a maritime shipping portfolio.[8] Unfortunately, efficiency in naval manpower management never received serious attention. Sporadic, half-baked attempts at developing sea power destroyed any possibility of creating a permanent foundation. The climate toward such things as seafaring education and training, for example, was not unlike that displayed by Louis XIV of France.

Enough naval power and professionalism existed to parry Genghis Khan with various degrees of success for forty-six years. The same force dispatched a mediocre fleet belonging to the Song Dynasty in 1275. Like clockwork, another era of unrest soon appeared and destroyed all that had been previously accomplished. Nothing of significance resurfaced for almost a century when the Ming Dynasty rose with unsurpassed vivacity to challenge Mongol rule. In the early fourteenth century, Yung-le-ti embarked on an aggressive sea power program unique by Chinese standards. His fleet and sea power reach eventually surpassed anything the West could muster. China's largest class of ship reached 400 feet in length, three times larger than the St. Maria, flagship of Christopher Columbus. This effort enabled Chinese sailors to dominate the Indian Ocean and, had such enthusiasm been sustained, the same could have been accomplished in the Pacific. Disapproving attitudes toward sea power returned among the ranks as all eyes were glued once again on territorial expansion. A notorious Mongol menace also arrived just in time to provide an encore performance.[9] Japanese pirates were the most significant threat at sea and ruling elites regarded that activity as a simple distraction.[10]

Dynastic patterns were consistent. On those occasions a strong and stable ruler got firmly established, Chinese sea power made great strides and maritime fleets would travel the seas in search of foreign lands. Rene Grousset provides a perfect survey of China's experience by referring specifically to Yung-le-ti's reign:

> What might have been the fate of Asia if, when they reached the Indies, the European navigators had found them ruled by Chinese sea power? But here again Yung-le-ti had a breadth of vision which was out of keeping with the temperament of his people, or rather, which went against the ideology of the mandarinate. The China which he was creating was on too large a scale for its own strength: the Chinese had no vocation for the sea; the climate of Tonkin was too hot and that of Mongolia too cold for their soldiers. The world of the literati remained consistently hostile to what it considered costly and useless foreign conquests. The *Welpolitik* of the emperor Yung-le-ti had no future. China withdrew within herself and allowed the hour of destiny, on land and at sea, to pass her by.[11]

Two significant events during the fifteenth century profoundly changed China's internal affairs. One involved Europe's realization that sea power offered substantial gains in world affairs. Discovery of the Western Hemisphere caused subsequent and unprecedented launches of European exploration. The second event involved signs of the coming Industrial Revolution, which served as a catalyst for mechanization of society. China began its own pursuit of both developments to compete with Europeans. This friction surfaced just as foreigners arrived in huge numbers by way of sailing vessels. The previously popular Silk Road began to appear outdated.

Unfortunately for China, sea power pursuits once again suffered at the hands of domestic instability. Timing could not have been better for the Europeans and they took full advantage. China's territorial foray had risen to impressive heights, but again fell in rapid succession as Europe stayed busy mopping up. During this period of oriental funk, Chinese sailors were assigned duties having nothing to do with keeping their skills sharpened. Ships constructed with great care rotted away at anchorage. Overnight sea power became viewed as simply a trading mechanism to points inaccessible by land. In the mind of Chinese people, Europeans and the rest of the world had little to offer. Why build ships when there is no desire to intermingle with inferior races? Chinese were, after all, the superior ethnic group:

Believing themselves to be the "Middle Kingdom," located below heaven but above other earthly nations, the Chinese were convinced of their cultural and intellectual superiority. Thus, it seemed only natural to have little interest in the outside world, and to expect those nations that contacted China to pay deference. From these beliefs arose the tribute system, China's preferred method of foreign relations. Leaders of adjacent countries periodically sent emissaries to the Chinese capital to present tribute and Kowtow to the emperor. In exchange they were lavishly entertained, given expensive gifts, granted lucrative trading privileges with an otherwise closed China, and assured of non-interference in their national affairs.[12]

By the middle of the fifteenth century, in keeping with past performance, taste for worldly delights turned bitter. This attitude continued for centuries: "We have never valued ingenious articles, nor do we have the slightest need of your country's manufactures."[13]

A constant border threat and challenges to regime leadership prevented further pursuit of overseas luxuries. Suspicion of outsiders has always been endemic and an excuse for domestic problems: "Westerners smell; Chinese don't. And westerners had–by Chinese standards–very big noses, which in China are the sign of Satan."[14] Foreigners were viewed with caution, including merchant traders. Their activity became controlled and taxed to a degree that trade was strictly considered in terms of loading China's treasury. Economic stability suffered as legitimate international commerce ceased to exist.[15] The stage took shape for an extended period of foreign influence in domestic affairs. Europe's culture, mixed with Chinese feelings of superiority, created a violent climate during the nineteenth century.[16]

Overseas expansion has returned since creation of the People's Republic of China in 1949. Forced annexation of Tibet, covert action against Nepal, demand for Taiwan's subjugation to dictatorship, and activities against regional states around the South China Sea exposes a disturbing trend. By some act of providence, the Communist Party has even compelled itself to claim the South China Sea its own.[17]

The Rising Sun

China held identical opinions of Japanese as it did Europeans. Unlike China, Japan grew to appreciate advantages associated with sea power. Geography is an obvious factor in that vision. Japan's archipelago is arguably the most difficult to defend, both militarily and by economic means. Lack of natural resources complicated this situation further with the beginning of industrialization. Trade is critical for a manufacturing-based economy and Japan's ranks among the largest in the world: "a Japanese factory is one of the most extraordinary phenomena on earth."[18]

Japan's concern over security comes from spending centuries under relentless fear of amphibious invasion from mainland Asia. Anxiety dominated the defense culture after witnessing sporadic rises and falls besetting various Chinese dynasties. Unification of Korea, Mongol hordes, and Russian/Soviet expansion enhanced volatility. Europeans entered the fray in the middle of the second millennium, just as China's Ming Dynasty began its sea power venture. Arrival of Europeans from across the continent enhanced defense concerns. Portuguese and Dutch sailors were first to come knocking on Tokyo's door, but they certainly were not the last to leave.

Like China, Japan experienced periods of disunion and tribal warfare. Carnage did not possess the high drama and degree of destruction found in China, but tempers did flare when issues concerned rule over the entire island chain. Factional squabbling and resulting assassination developed into an efficient political solution. Friction appeared to have no end until the eighth century AD when the first centralized government formed. Establishing a Chinese model of governing came in response to threatening moods from the mainland. Japan's security concerns focused on activities around Korea's peninsula. Geostrategic position of Korea has always been a sensitive issue due to China's military might and population advantage. Fear for regional stability surfaced whenever the peninsula unified. Pusan's proximity to Japan's main island of Honshu (200 miles) is not a reassuring distance, even in 700 AD.

Balancing power took center stage in the eighth century AD. For the first time Japan realized survival against a mass of mainland Chinese depended on unified government. Displaying a united front sent a message any assault would come at a high price. At the time of unification, China deployed a fleet capable of crossing the Sea of Japan. This included troop transport vessels in significant number to carry out an amphibious landing. Korea's unification in 676 AD further complicated security concerns. The Paekche region in southern Korea had a tradition of serving as a trusted ally. That changed when Chinese forces conquered the peninsula in 660. The province's reputation as a safe buffer between aggressive Tang and Sillan forces of China, and

Tsushima and Honshu islands of Japan, all but disappeared. With this area of demarcation gone, and China's naval force patrolling the Sea of Japan, unification quickly dominated domestic concerns. Establishment of the Fujiwara family rose during this period. China's leadership, witnessing these political developments, wisely decided to disengage. There were far bigger issues underway on the mainland without the added burden of a prolonged two-front war.

Japan remained stable until the twelfth century when warring factions disrupted domestic tranquility. This did not prevent national dealings with threats originating overseas. Japanese warriors were allowed to put their tradecraft in use against two attempted Mongol invasions in 1274 and 1281. Though weather played an important part, impressive victories established credibility because the same Mongol force had previously defeated the Song Dynasty. The immeasurable prestige suppressed further fears of invasion by mainland powers. Willingness to fight is a prevailing power resource that can keep belligerents sober. All factions eagerly put aside political strife to combat foreigners. The Japanese possessed uncommon character overcoming differences, while returning to sender neighborhood bullies. Upon successful completion, warring factions would simply resume pounding on each other.

Numerous shogunate regimes rose to take charge ruling Japan as an insurance policy against invasion. This form of security continued until 1868 when European and American pressure served as a catalyst into the arena of foreign affairs.[19] Though the Tokugawa shogunate provided 265 years of relative peace and prosperity, it could not withstand criticism from signing international treaties with American, British, Dutch, and Russian governments. These were considered insults to national sovereignty. Trade treaties were debatable, but agreements granting port access to foreign ships were over the top. The actions of the Tokugawa shogunate caused political chaos and the unified government finally collapsed. Imperial rule quickly ensued out of concern for national security and an inherent mistrust of foreigners.

The United States showed little interest in Pacific Ocean affairs during the first half of the nineteenth century. With the exception of a periodic whaling vessel, America did not pursue trans-Pacific ventures of substance until Commodore Matthew Perry's journey to Japan in 1853.[20] Perry became the opening act in a relationship that culminated in one of the most prosperous among two nations. World War II aside, diplomatic and business activities with Japan are only surpassed by

America's association with Great Britain. A broader relationship between all three, with the US acting as the triad's center of mercantilism, is unique for international relations. Attachment is furthered by each party's dependency on sea power. This thread is unrivalled in history, and makes a vital contribution to an economic climate dependent on trade.

Japan's resistance to foreigners goes back centuries and the diplomatic circuit found this lack of interest stifling to their efforts. Japan's experience around the Pacific Rim prior to 1853 was restricted to insignificant contact with Chinese merchants. An exception came from annual ship visits by Dutch traders. American attempts to open dialogue repeatedly went nowhere and created hostility in the Foreign Service. Frustration is revealed in Admiral Perry's instructions prior to his departure.[21] Perry's executive summary is a laundry list of past encounters and previous attempts at building relations. It included what the United States sought, and what it could give in return. The journey became a success and relations developed until the US annexed Hawaii and went to war with Spain. Admiral Perry's fleet, setting anchor in Manila Bay at the close of the nineteenth century, served notice a new power had arrived in East Asia. This did not sit well with Japanese leaders. Geostrategic position now forced Tokyo's defense planners to consider threats in every direction; Russians poised to the north; a mass of Chinese in the west; Europeans having a heyday in the south; now America could be seen on the Pacific horizon.

The Meiji emperor advocated industrialization as the security noose tightened. Alexander Kiralfy identifies this modernization program as a means to stay astride perceived foreign encroachment:

> Japan retired from international society at a time when galleys were plying the Mediterranean and before the clumsy galleon had developed into the ship-of-the-line and frigate that were to hold sway during the seventeenth, eighteenth and part of the nineteenth centuries. Japan awoke in the days of steam and of iron ships.[22]

The Meiji's program duplicated European and American models. Industrialization resulted in an enormous population growth rate, which further strained needs for raw materials and foreign markets. Japanese citizens scoured Europe and America, observing manufacturing processes. Several power resources appeared with technology and industrial production profoundly apparent. Lack of other resources created a dependency on acquisition. Natural resources and geographic destiny are crucial to sea power, which spelled trouble for Japan. Japan's leadership knew domestic stability and economic survival depended on unmolested access to the sea.

Sea power dependency brought national grand strategy to the forefront as Japan proceeded to launch foreign ventures. They developed a naval fleet during the early twentieth century that turned out as capable as any in Europe or the US. This caused competitor states to blink. Fear ratchets received additional torque when Japan's Imperial Navy stunned maritime powers at the Battle of Tsushima Straits in 1905. Implications were so profound that experts considered it bigger than Salamis, Actium, or even Trafalgar.[23] The Japanese victory is both a display of power resources operating as intended, and superior strategic and tactical action practically applied. Destruction of Russia's fleet and capture of Port Arthur marked a new era and level of confidence in Japanese foreign policy.[24] Port Arthur's acquisition exemplifies Mahan's emphasis on foreign bases.[25] East Asia's heat index rose dramatically during the twentieth century's start as several powers jockeyed for influence in Manchuria. Russia's Far East designs were similar to motives in Central Asia. Geostrategic desire to influence both regions is a centuries old Kremlin priority.[26]

Japan found itself in an extremely favorable position by 1918. Escaping World War I's devastation enabled government leaders to capitalize from Germany's removal in the western Pacific.[27] Matters regarding China and Manchuria continued to dominate foreign policy concerns. National threat assessments of the US and USSR began to appear in policy circles by 1920. Soviet attempts to gain influence in China and Korea set-off national security alarm bells. American and European occupation of territory Japan considered its sphere of influence added to defense fears. America's foreign policy objectives came under assault by accusations of challenging Japanese sovereignty.[28] After all, the Japanese argued, the US would reach a similar conclusion if tables were turned.

Japan's Imperial Army took drastic measures that included actions independent of Tokyo.[29] Government officials sought and complied with Army wishes out of fear for their lives. The Imperial Army dominated society as its information ministry saturated the country with glorious phrases: "Japan's army not only fights but writes."[30] Such content had an uncanny relationship to propaganda permeating Soviet society. In fact, some grew curious over the source behind the process, especially when advocating totalitarianism:

The principles of freedom which previously pervaded the entire world are dying out. The world war was caused by conflicts in imperialism which were the ultimate growth of this period of free enterprise . . . A clash now seems inevitable between free enterprise and government control, between individualism and collectivism.[31]

Non-discriminatory Soviet-style indoctrination included plugs on behalf of the Japanese Navy: "It is absolutely necessary for Japan to have a powerful navy sufficient to defeat any state which will attempt to frustrate Japan's noble effort of making the Far East a paradise of peace and prosperity."[32] Obvious reference, of course, is the United States. Regime legitimacy squarely rested in the Imperial Army's hands and nobody dared get in their way.

Factories began retooling for a war industry as Japan's sphere of influence enlarged and conquered territories were officially annexed. The Japanese Imperial Navy's pragmatic and cautious nature was based on concerns with geography and economies of scale. Japan is completely surrounded by water that, like Greece, results in an extensive shoreline virtually impossible to defend. Island numbers would challenge any navy's ability to establish a defense perimeter. While Japan's Imperial Army stayed busy conquering foreign territory, the Navy found itself occupied by strategic dilemmas facing the homeland. Imperial Army designs ultimately prevailed and the Navy was left to combat America's sea power might: "Considering the American states as members of the European family, as they are by traditions, institutions, and languages, it is in the Pacific, where the westward course of empire again meets the East, that their relations to the future of the world become most apparent."[33]

Vulnerability of the Philippines to invasion concerned US military planners in the decades leading up to World War II. The General Board of the Navy played eternal optimist by claiming Manila Bay could be defended and used to launch a naval campaign against Japan. US Naval War College (NWC) planning saw this threat differently. NWC analysis claimed Japan knew of America's inability to maintain a strong presence in the region.[34] Therefore, if war did erupt, Japan would quickly take advantage and deprive the US access to Manila. War Plan Orange existed for almost twenty years. It envisioned forces in the Philippines holding defensive lines for six months. This was the lead time believed necessary for adequate reinforcement. Japan showed agreement with NWC strategic thinking by launching an invasion on 12 December 1941, five days following

Pearl Harbor. Loss of the Philippines left US forces supplying and fighting a war across the vast Pacific.[35] Japan, fortunately, did not do to Hawaii what it achieved in the Philippines. If Hawaii fell, then the entire US Pacific Fleet would have been stuck on the West Coast, dodging submarines while attempting to get underway.

Invading the Philippines was not new science. Forces left to defend the archipelago fought gallantly, fulfilling their end of the bargain. General Jonathan Wainwright finally surrendered almost six months to the day hostilities commenced.[36] Cavalry reinforcements never showed up and this experience proved, once again, a plan is only as good as the willingness to carry it out. When military operations are involved, vacillation by political elites is a hallmark that can cost lives. Failure to capitalize on the geostrategic advantages offered by the Philippines limited the US Navy's freedom to conduct regional maritime operations. Mahan's emphasis on overseas bases raises its mast again. Connecting national policy and grand strategy in a constitutional democracy can be a nagging problem: "Guam and the Philippines never were, and never would be, adequately fortified by us in peace, as they might be by a more military government."[37] The US Navy lost a geostrategic asset in Southeast Asia, and then spent three years fighting to get it back. Deterrence by overwhelming force in the Philippines may have caused Japan to avoid a bold strike at Hawaii. Luzon is 750 miles from Okinawa, which is not a soothing distance to Japan's leadership. The US military withdrawal from the Philippines in the 1990s showed persistence and neglect toward history.

Aircraft carrier platforms and island bases were used effectively for bombing missions on Japanese territory. Strategically, island hopping by US Marines created unbearable pressure. As control of the Pacific contracted, attempts were made to supplement a ravaged mainland war industry with factories in China. Even this became counter-productive. Though the Sea of Japan provided safer shipping lanes, prisoner and local populations sabotaged production: "Not only do Chinese patriots set out to murder every prominent Chinese who consents to work for the Japanese; in some cases they have searched out and despoiled the graves of their ancestors, which to a good Chinese is worse than death."[38] The noose tightened until Japan's climatic surrender in Tokyo Bay, three years after the Philippines fell to Japanese forces. Ironically, General MacArthur honored General Wainwright by giving him the pen used to sign Japan's surrender document onboard the USS *Missouri*.

God Save the Queen

No nation's history is tied more to the sea than Great Britain: "That luxury belonged to the English alone."[39] Britain's success with sea power provided Mahan an endless bulk of material to defend his treatise. Internal wars on the British Isles during the formative years established a learning curve for later global challenges. Once these domestic disputes were put in order the sea became a natural destiny and made attainment of empire possible.[40] N.A.M. Rodger shows how Britain's maritime history is an ideal log to explain relationships between national prosperity, international relations, and sea command:

> In any case it is in the nature of the history of the sea that it links many nations, and there is no true naval or maritime history which is not an international history. Whether in peaceful trade or warlike attack, the sea unites more than it divides. Even if it were possible to treat England, or the British Isles, as a single, homogenous, united nation, it would still be impossible to write its naval history without reference to the histories of other nations, near and far, with which the sea has connected it.[41]

The English Channel and warring continental parties provided an early taste of naval might. Fear is a powerful motivator and British tribes provided invaders uncommonly stiff resistance. There is a long list of those who learned the hard way about British grit. Even Rome's legions were stunned at the ferocity of islanders to defend their territory. Viking hordes plundering their way around the periphery only toughened resolve. Persistent maritime threats brought England no alternative but to devise a defense policy formulated toward the sea. This resulted in some harrowing on-the-job training but, as a result, no foreign power ever conquered the British Isles.

Fortifications were initially used to address Scandinavian rampages that occurred around the seventh century. This is an expected reaction based on previous domestic tribal wars. Castles, which were effective defense barriers against land armies, were built on the coast with a belief they could withstand maritime forces. Amphibious mobility deceived King Edward I as invading marauders successfully used freedom of action to locate positions offering minimal resistance. Troops could then disembark unmolested and at a time of their choosing. This left castle inhabitants to either subject themselves to a long siege, or move out and do battle on terms set forth by an invasion force. Early disappointments were only overcome because of determination, strategic thinking, and acquisition of needed resources: "In building a navy to resist Viking raiders, the English had shown the value to operations on land of contesting mastery of the seas."[42]

British seagoing craft during and following the Viking era were designed for either carrying out peaceful trade or supplying military forces on land. Adversaries gained enormous tactical benefit from this vulnerability. Once located, auxiliary craft could be eliminated at the enemy's pleasure, while British land forces were left searching in desperation for supplies and an alternate mode of transport home. The concept of the sea as a battle space came at a price but, once realized, England anxiously capitalized on the geostrategic domain. Richard I first recognized this value, but his experience traveling the Mediterranean made him overly keen of Italian ships.[43] These were not, as Caesar's fleet discovered in the North Atlantic, satisfactory for rough waters surrounding the British Isles. Many of the Mediterranean craft succumbed to weather and ocean elements. Those intact were no better off when left at the mercy of a superior Scandinavian fleet.

Military failures at sea often resulted from a lack of naval strategic and tactical training. The sea involved relatively new territory at the time of the Viking terror. Maritime education consisted of observing an adversary's punishing techniques. There is no substitute for experience and a peculiar naval ranking structure exemplified the chaos. Admirals seldom fought at sea and, in fact, were primarily used for land battles, coastal defense, or administration. Captain held an unrecognizable rank until the fifteenth century, with the vast majority serving on shore duty. Mastering seamanship comprised a hard learning curve full of enormous agony and bloodshed.

Interaction between states and people at sea during this period is best described as "survival of the fittest." Anarchy became popular, with relationships cultivated between states and sea bandits. Piracy served as a means of furthering state policy. Even private individuals and firms were encouraged to commit acts considered high crimes today. Britain's investment in manpower and resources began showing measurable gains by the sixteenth century. Navigating the sea had been a momentous challenge and significant scientific discoveries overcame this problem. British shipyards also began producing well designed and durable classes of ships. Naval leadership stepped to the plate, earning its rightful place with such legendary figures as Sir Francis Drake. His appearance onstage made a lasting mark. While war fighting at sea still employed traditional methods associated with hand-to-hand combat, significant changes were underway with development of projectiles.

Personal problems associated with Henry VIII's taste for women caused setbacks which spilled over into international politics. His determination to pursue a European land campaign in the sixteenth century drained sea power's financial resources. By the time of Henry's death in 1547, financial and religious turmoil reached a point that civil war appeared to be a real possibility. Rapidly unfolding events to the north brought badly needed policy reappraisal for the Crown. Scottish relations with France cultivated in a direction that England feared a military alliance. Having a traditional sparring partner across the English Channel is entirely different from that antagonist also ensconced along your northern frontier.[44]

The Spanish fleet compounded England's geostrategic predicament with France. Spain developed into an active menace around European waters and the world's premier maritime power possessed a sphere of influence crossing the Atlantic. The Western Hemisphere served as its playground and Spanish convoys loaded with silver gracefully transited the Atlantic Ocean unmolested. The thought of ambushing such a wealth of riches enticed English sailors. Spanish power dominated concerns of far less endowed states. Should it achieve complete control of the world's oceans, Spain would then proceed to dictate terms for all. N.A.M. Rodger notes how this geostrategic environment made going to sea England's sole option:

> Only with naval power was it possible to keep the French and Spanish threat at arm's length. Only by control of the Narrow Seas could England apply pressure on Spain; only by restraining communications between France and Spain could she hinder Scotland's absorption into the realm of France. For the queen herself, her ships were her personal defence in a dangerous world which offered no other security.[45]

Birth of the British Empire occurred on 15 November 1577 in Plymouth, England. It is here that Sir Francis Drake departed on his legendary journey to circumnavigate the globe. Only Magellan had achieved such a *tour de force* and, unlike Drake, he did not survive. Drake's achievement had a profound psychological impact on England. Drake showed Spain and Portugal no longer held a monopoly on the world's oceans. England had been intimidated by the Spanish fleet's power for a considerable amount of time and Drake proved the emperor of the sea had no clothes: "The might of England was sufficient to keep alive the heart and the members; whereas the equally extensive colonial empire of Spain, through her maritime weakness, but offered so many points for insult and injury."[46]

Drake developed into such consequence that, by the end of his service, he managed to destroy Spain's image as a sea monster keeping everyone contained to coastal waters. The world turned out to be big enough for all and abundant resources were available for those willing to take a risk. England deserved as much access as any other state. Not only had the Western Hemisphere opened its doors for others, but the Far East offered similar swag. Drake proved Britain could equip naval forces for distant operations once thought impossible. National security priorities previously tooled for crossing the English Channel soon took on an international flavor.

Drake's success happened at a critical time. Queen Elizabeth I grew deeply concerned over Spanish moves to dominate the seas surrounding the British Isles. With Scotland and France talking, Drake became the single most valuable asset she had to rally a nation for war. Circumnavigating the globe brought enormous pride to an entire national population, including the man on the street:

> Whereas the French nobles got themselves known to the people as petty tyrants, often more unruly and exacting than a great one would be, the English nobles managed to convey to the yeoman class of free proprietors the feeling that they too were aristocrats on a small scale, with interests to defend in common with the nobles.[47]

King Philip of Spain, alarmed by Drake's success, decided to move against the upstart competitor. His assessment of rising English power was not misplaced. Elizabeth launched a foreign policy gamble by disengaging from her sister's previous deference toward Spain. This act of independence resulted in Philip sanctioning an assassination attempt on Elizabeth.[48] Though it failed, Drake grew enraged and decided to challenge Spain directly with maritime operations off the Iberian coast. Spain's fleet, in a completely confused state, failed to be drawn out for battle. Drake caused further embarrassment shortly after by conducting three specific operations which stunned Spain's elite.

His first occurred toward the closing months of 1585 when he led an expedition to the Caribbean Sea. The following year Drake's task force wreaked havoc on Spanish settlements throughout the region. This is unheard of for an empire thought to be invincible. Philip II and his court, convinced Spain's reputation and credibility were at stake, concluded no alternative existed but to mount a full-scale invasion of England. Drake had other plans, which included consistently pestering Philip. His second strike against the Spanish Crown came shortly after returning from the Caribbean. In the summer of 1586 he set sail again for an extended patrol off Portugal that lasted ninety days. A deployment this long and so close to Spanish home waters was a first for England. It tested extended operations in hostile enemy waters and advertised British seamanship's rising qualities to Europe's traditional powers. Many more than just Spain got caught by surprise.

Drake's third and final insult occurred in 1587 when he led a fleet of over twenty ships on a rampage of the Iberian shoreline. His flotilla remained undetected throughout the operation, even though two Spanish task forces of approximately fifty ships scoured the sea for three months. Spain's poor performance triggered a decision to delay invading England until the following year: "Everywhere in Europe Spain's enemies took heart, Spain's rivals took pleasure, and Spain's friends took fright."[49] English prestige, respect, and admiration rose to unprecedented heights in the international community. Morale at home had never been more positive. Drake's professionalism served as England's greatest asset against the Spanish Goliath and, as a result, public support for a permanent navy hit intoxicating levels. Enthusiasm went unchecked, while Spain's own service became rife with poor management. There was no sophisticated logistics support system, no maintenance program for her ships, and absolutely no semblance of administration. This is a disgraceful humiliation for the world's largest maritime power.

The contrast between England and Spain's maritime qualities reveals many benefits derived from efficient management. Less-endowed states must use care with limited assets, especially when deployed against a more fortunate adversary. Spain showed the danger of over-confidence. This got put on display in 1588 when a much smaller, but incredibly resourceful English fighting fleet ran circles around a disorganized behemoth. When Spain's armada headed home from the English Channel that August it was apparent Spanish maritime power might never recover.[50] Military engagements were not particularly intense during the campaign, but damage to the Spanish force from weather, marauders on land, illness, and lack of supplies destroyed nearly half the original number of ships: "The defeat of the Armada marked the end of the great days of Spain."[51]

Spain's experience became an embarrassment, while serving as a pronouncement of England's future. Drake's curse had run its course and Spain's price for attempting to assassinate his queen turned out brutal:

> Since the conquest of Granada in 1492, Spain had accomplished extraordinary things. Suddenly her sons had stretched out their hands and seized the limits of the known world. They conquered Mexico and Peru, planted colonies in southern, central, and northern America, spanned the Indian Ocean, and established the myth of their invincibility. They accomplished these marvelous things because they believed themselves to be the chosen instruments of God. The defeat of their Armada shattered this faith and destroyed the illusion that had fortified their fanaticism. Thirty years later Spain became decadent, not because the war with England had been long and exhausting, but because the loss of faith in her destiny was catastrophic.[52]

England grew into an impressive sea power state while Spain failed to learn those subtleties associated with mastering sea power. England, though much smaller, fully understood these technicalities:

> When Elizabeth I came to the throne in 1558, Spain and Portugal dominated the lands beyond the seas and blocked England's ambitions for maritime expansion. Thirty years later, when the shattered remains of Philip II's Armada limped home, the way was open for the spread of colonial activity in America and the Indies. That Armada fight, moreover, was a major turning point in naval warfare. Thanks to the work of Sir John Hawkins, the old close-range hand-to-hand fighting gave way to long-range gunnery and maneuvering which would last throughout the sailing ship era.[53]

Dispatching Spain's fleet from the Channel marked Great Britain's launch of sea power's second phase. This journey would be a hiatus lasting over three hundred years. The first three decades of the seventeenth century consisted of soul-searching, re-organization, and growing pains.[54] Domestic turmoil remained a concern. A fragile peace did hold with Spain and France, though both maintained grand visions of an amphibious invasion. England could not muster anything close to Spain and France's continental armies. This contributed to fears the two adversaries may eventually find a way to cross the English Channel unchecked. France and Spain's objective would remain a common goal of continental powers for centuries, and it defines the three primary objectives behind Britain's geostrategic relations with Europe since the War of the Spanish Succession:

-   Prevent invasion by maintaining control of the English Channel.
-   Protect England's overseas trade and encourage development of colonies.
-   Prevent any European power from achieving hegemony on the continent.[55]

The Peace of Utrecht resulted in Britain's recognition as a serious player in world politics. That status came with a price. At various times, up to 85% of the government's annual budget had to be dedicated to either the armed forces or servicing a bludgeoning war debt. This cost persisted during the eighteenth century, but economic security made it worthwhile.[56] National presence in the Western Hemisphere was fortified by acquisition of new colonies, which motivated further sea power expansion. European continental politics cost Spain dearly, forcing it to surrender a majority of territories.

Britain's favorable situation did not go unnoticed by adversaries as the War of the American Revolution approached. A threat of Russia joining continental enemies in an alliance with American rebels placed national grand strategy in serious danger. An anti-British cabal with Russia onboard would be unbearable.[57] France added spice to the anti-British feeding frenzy by embarrassing the Royal Navy at Yorktown. Wherever Britain turned during the years 1776-1781, it seemed vultures were standing by to take a hit. Solace arrived eight years later when the British Crown patiently witnessed the French Revolution: "As the French monarchy tottered to ruin, constitutional changes of greater historic significance occurred in North America."[58] France's Yorktown contribution came back to haunt her aristocracy and Napoleon turned out to be the end product.

The Battle of Trafalgar served as ultimate reparation for Yorktown. It marked the beginning of Britain's third and final stage of maritime supremacy. Nelson's victory unequivocally proved sea power's utility by forcing Napoleon to back his words with deeds:

> Do you suppose I want to risk my power and renown in a desperate struggle? If I have a war with Austria, I shall contrive to find my way to Vienna. If I have a war with you, I shall take from you every ally on the continent; I shall cut you off from all access to it, from the

Baltic to the Gulf of Taranto. You will blockade us, but I will blockade you in my turn.[59]

Napoleon's intimidation could not sway European geography or Britain's sea power might.[60] Dispatching Napoleon left Great Britain in an unprecedented situation. The sun truly did not set on the British Empire as territorial domain encompassed every continent but Antarctica. Economic might resulted from free enterprise, common law, and the Industrial Revolution. Within a few years Great Britain's industrial machine was producing twenty-five percent of the world's manufactured goods, while controlling a third of its international commerce. This is double the nearest competitor.

The Industrial Revolution raced ahead at full speed across Europe and America during the second half of the nineteenth century. Nations launched a feeding frenzy for market share. Britain continued to sustain an impressive growth rate, even compared to faster developing economies of Germany, France and the US. Germany's rate of industrialization was phenomenal, while its banking system became the most potent in the world. Imperialism grew in vogue and even previous skeptics, such as Otto von Bismark, rationalized conquests by arguing Germany stood to gain by acquiring territories. Occupation of foreign lands managed to be spun with compassion by his contention the result would be better educated natives.

Power politics went on display everywhere as states attempted to undermine stability in each other's overseas holdings. Britain's edge over traditional rivals continued with sea power supremacy. This fact escaped France when they built the Suez Canal. Threat of a traditional rival possessing a shortcut to India, while Britain's Royal Navy traveled around the Cape of Good Hope, was unacceptable.[61] Acquisition came from slick financial investing. Traditional military operations grew more costly as the century closed. As a substitute, missions were launched to agitate native discontent and unrest in rival territories: "Native agents are those of the enemy's country people whom we employ."[62] Observing European behavior in a fragile global environment gave America sound reason for pursuing maritime efforts.

Great Britain showed what can be achieved with sea power. This heightened awareness by European powers played out with amusing shenanigans at Suez. As "imperialism" debates raged in Europe, Mahan began his own campaign for maritime supremacy that even convinced the traditionally anti-British critic John Hobson.[63]

Paul Halpern notes how Germany's justification of imperialism fueled motivation for deposing the Royal Navy's supremacy once and for all:

> The Germans were in a position to dominate the Continent both militarily and economically, and their decision to challenge the British at sea created a new and revolutionary situation in international affairs. The Anglo-German naval race was one of the most important features of the prewar period, but it is important to remember that the powerful modern warships being built by other countries also did much to erode that perceived British supremacy.[64]

Germany achieved phenomenal growth with land power. With title of continental CEO firmly in hand, and Britain looking on with concern, military policy turned toward naval supremacy. Germany signaled its intent by building impressive docks at Emden, which were capable of embarking 300,000 troops. This, according to Arthur Marder, followed a two-year publishing marathon by German staff officers who described the ease launching an amphibious invasion of Britain.[65] London's press corps fanned the flames when a German flotilla comprised of eight battleships paid a port visit in May 1902:

> For the first time in our history, a foreign force, superior to any squadron which we have in commission in home waters has been at work upon our coasts, performing evolutions, learning the navigation of our harbours, and training for war. The force comes today as a friend, but in future it may come as an enemy – for Germans have openly avowed the purpose of building a fleet to destroy the British naval predominance.[66]

Developments in Germany were making it the continental danger British foreign policy experts had warned about: "The habit of mind is narrow which fails to see that a navy such as Germany is now building will be efficacious for other ends than those immediately proposed."[67] The British were troubled by a lack of allies willing to keep Germany boxed in. Though it had often assisted continental states in times of peril, no nation had gone to Britain's defense.[68] This changed with the outbreak of World War I.

Body Count

Some foreign policy experts have sought to blame WWI on Mahan. These accusations are based on Great Britain's global maritime strength and an unwillingness to allow the same in a competitor. Germany's effort to become a rival maritime power, so the argument goes, gained its inspiration from Mahan. Size and scope of events leading up to hostilities became more than Mahan could muster in print. Though his books on sea power and national grand strategy were popular, it is not a copy of *The Influence of Sea Power upon History* which struck down Franz and Sophie Ferdinand in Sarajevo. Assassination of a nation's political elite provides far greater stimulus. This same energy can be seen by Drake's response to Spain's murder attempt of Elizabeth.[69]

World War I's cost in finance, resources, and manpower devastated Great Britain, as it did the continental powers. By 1920 a vacancy had opened for another maritime power and, fortunately, the newly formed USSR or Germany did not occupy first position. Old-timers spent their stock on the battlefields of France. Japan and the United States were left unscathed by WWI's outcome. America's power resource base, unlike Europe, found itself in prime shape and, thanks in large part to Mahan, the throne was waiting:

> The great task now before the world of civilized Christianity, its great mission, which it must fulfil or perish, is to receive into its own bosom and raise to its own ideals those ancient and different civilizations by which it is surrounded and outnumbered, - the civilizations at the head of which stand China, India, and Japan.[70]

Six scenarios were covered and none dwelled in great detail. This compassion occurred for the sake of space and to avoid repetitive pronouncements of certain technical aspects. Discussion in each model provides a history enabling readers to understand power generator operations, national grand strategy, geostrategic advantage, and critical linkage between them all. Phoenicia's dependence on merchant fleets and trade cost it an empire; Athens and Sparta showed what happens by failing to marry unique contributions in a permanent force; and Rome attempted to do with legionnaires at sea what they achieved on land. Sea power is better understood by grasping the reasons behind each prototype's success and failure. Ancient China generally avoided open-water warfare. Ralph Sawyer notes how Chinese leaders instead chose to exploit amphibious operations to support engagements on land:

> Everyone knew how to exploit the current's strategic power and launch a downstream attack, as may be seen in the Spring and

Autumn conflict between Ch'u and Wu, which coincidentally witnessed the extensive use of ships to transport invasion-bound troops.[71]

Failure to keep a nation united caused problems for more states than just China.

A rare, non-violent power transition in the rise and fall of interstate competition may be found in Great Britain's peaceful exchange with the United States. This event not only benefited British and American governments, but the entire world as well. Though initially destroyed beyond recognition at the end of World War II, Japan for example, was able to rebuild and develop into the world's second largest economy. Thanks are owed to active and sincere help from the United States. Stalin would not have been so kind. US generosity became a win-win for all parties, including Great Britain. History is important to those responsible for national security. Grasping how history can support national security priorities is best understood by grasping grand strategy's resources and methods.

Chapter Nine

A Nation Like No Other

"Sell not virtue to purchase wealth, nor liberty to purchase power."
- Benjamin Franklin

America's sea power capacity in the earliest years can be described as hideously inadequate, but understood considering the state of affairs. A feeble stock of ships did not dampen maritime motivation within America's leadership circle: "In any operation, and under all circumstances, a decisive naval superiority is to be considered as a fundamental principle, and the basis upon which every hope of success must ultimately depend."[1] Westward expansion occupied primary national policy focus throughout most of the first century. While America's government kept busy acquiring land, the US Navy stayed busy just trying to justify its existence.[2] After all, the French fleet at Yorktown served as dispenser of misery, denying Cornwallis his badly needed reinforcement from Royal Navy ships. The French Alliance of 1778 gave Washington access to naval power sorely needed against a far superior British Royal Navy.[3] Though still inferior in size, the French offered enough leverage to sway key tactical events. The War of 1812 saw British naval might trying to find something in America's inventory worth engaging. Outside of inland lake confrontations, no action at sea involved operations against three or more American naval vessels.[4] Commodore Perry's diplomatic mission to Japan provided the biggest naval event until arrival of the Spanish-American War in 1898. The USN was not front page news.

Power generators and resources appear in profound ways throughout American history. While sea and land power dominate previous centuries, air power arrives as the US becomes global cop in the twentieth century. A common characteristic between the United States and earlier state actors involves stability of power resources. Their application remained the same through two centuries of America's development. Facial features evolved, but national grand strategy's basic structure remained unchanged. Power resources applied by those actors in 2000 BC are just as important in 2000 AD.

Air power became momentous as the twentieth century unfolded. Space made its presence known in the century's latter half. America's initial national grand strategy environment is obvious and depressing. Many power resources did eventually cultivate and manage to appear by the early nineteenth century. Vitality rose as the United States developed, expanded westward, secured its borders, and added two additional power generators. Prescience is noticeable in various phases of national expansion. America's political leadership took appropriate policy-making steps to ensure respect in the world arena. National grand strategy received careful nurturing in preparation for superpower status. There are three phases for implementing grand strategy; peaceful guardian, passive hostile, and active hostile. All can be identified at various times. The US routinely applied each by using a gradual approach when dispensing pressure.

Colonial Discontent

Some consider the American War of Independence a tragedy. There is plenty of blame to go around on both sides of the Atlantic. Mahan stated the obvious on behalf of those hoping for reconciliation:

> The war of the American Revolution was, it is true, a great mistake, looked at from the point of view of sea power; but the government was led into it insensibly by a series of natural blunders. Putting aside political and constitutional considerations, and looking at the question as purely military or naval, the case was this; The American colonies were large and growing communities at a great distance from England. So long as they remained attached to the mother-country, as they then were enthusiastically, they formed a solid base for her sea power in that part of the world; but their extent and population were too great, when coupled with the distance from England, to afford any hope of holding them by force, *if* any powerful nations were willing to help them.[5]

Primary cause points to poor communications. Depending on a sailing vessel to carry messages that took several weeks to transit the Atlantic Ocean is beyond comprehension today. In a modern world of electronic communications, revolution caused by slow correspondence is unlikely. Flying from the Pacific Ocean side of the United States to London can now be completed in ten hours. Tools used in support of government administration today were sorely missed in colonial times.

Ironically, the same nemesis that haunted British officials during the War of Independence caused identical problems for Abraham Lincoln during the Civil War. France, if ensconced in Mexico during the Civil War, was positioned to move on western US territories from the south. The threat to colonies during the French and Indian Wars, which lasted from 1756 to 1763, emanated from the northwest. The Seven Years' War had a lasting impression on Britain's arch rival, and Mahan keyed on this long-held grudge in their manifesto from the united Bourbon (Spanish and French) courts: "To avenge their respective injuries, and to put an end to that tyrannical empire which England has usurped, and claims to maintain upon the oceans."[6] France certainly did not fit the role as a haven of democracy and an example for the rest. In fact, it was only a few years later that "Emperor" Napoleon Bonaparte arrived to ravage all of Europe.

The Seven Years' War had long-range significance: "The one nation that gained in this war was that which used the sea in peace to earn its wealth, and ruled it in war by the extent of its navy, by the number of its subjects who lived on the sea or by the sea, and by its numerous bases of operations scattered over the globe."[7] The statement accurately describes action carried out between France and Great Britain. This particular war, however, developed unique characteristics thanks to rancorous colonists. The King's insistence on a state of emergency during the war provided an attractive reason to complain. Enforcement mechanisms employed to fulfill Crown dictates brought outrage, over-hyped to some extent, and often concerned perceived abusive demands to support an unpopular war. Fred Anderson further adds that Lord Loudoun, an over-bearing elitist representing the Crown, was regarded as a snob and thug. This did not help public relations:

> As a professional officer who had been granted extraordinary powers and as an aristocrat with scant sympathy for the cultural norms of the provinces, Loudoun interpreted any resistance to his authority as evidence of colonial inferiority, corruption, and rebelliousness. His virtually automatic response to opposition was to threaten to use force to compel submission. That tactic, while effective in the short term, tended over time to convince the colonists that Loudoun himself posed at least as grave a threat to their liberties as the French and Indians – and one much closer at hand.[8]

A culture of anger ripened with revolutionary zeal and France could not resist the opportunity:

The appearance of France and Spain as active supporters of the colonists' cause made no change in England's objects, whatever change of objective her military plans may, or should, have undergone. The danger of losing the continental colonies was vastly increased by these accessions to the ranks of her enemies, which brought with them also a threat of loss, soon to be realized in part, of other valuable foreign possessions. England, in short, as regards the objects of the war, was strictly on the defensive; she feared losing much, and at best only hoped to keep what she had.[9]

Had Britain been the least sagacious toward colonial complaining then an armed resurrection may have been avoided. London, and particularly its colonial governor, failed to consider negotiations. This friction turned combustible due to a lack of frank, honest, and serious trans-Atlantic communication. The tax argument justifying an uprising is, based on today's rate of taxation, laughable. Britain miscalculated by treating North American colonies in a manner very similar to other foreign territories possessing distinct native races. They tended to forget colonists comprised fellow British people and, to a lesser extent, other Europeans. It turned out to be a costly mistake.

Growing Pains

The Articles of Confederation were an impossible experiment. Devotion to central authority simply did not exist, and a weak national government could not build any structure resembling unity. Thirteen states acted independently in dealings with foreign powers and each other. The national government found it impossible to borrow money from Europe, collect taxes, duties, or fees for operations. Getting a quorum to conduct congressional business was a rare event. Financial straits forced the newly established nation to sell its last Continental Navy ship in 1785.[10] Mahan's summary of the Dutch Republic a century earlier parallels the ordeal of a young United States:

> Composed of seven provinces, with the political name of the United Provinces, the actual distribution of power may be roughly described to Americans as an exaggerated example of States Rights. Each of the maritime provinces had its own fleet and its own admiralty, with consequent jealousies. This disorganizing tendency was partly counteracted by the great preponderance of the Province of Holland, which alone contributed five sixths of the fleet and fifty-eight per cent

of the taxes, and consequently had a proportionate share in directing the national policy. Although intensely patriotic, and capable of making the last sacrifices for freedom, the commercial spirit of the people penetrated the government, which indeed might be called a commercial aristocracy, and made it averse to war, and to the expenditures which are necessary in preparing for war. As has before been said, it was not until danger stared them in the face that the burgomasters were willing to pay for their defences.[11]

The United Provinces developed independent maritime fleets out of a necessity to have something seaworthy. America's national government soon realized convincing states to finance even a token army was not much different than pulling teeth. Federal authority finally gained long awaited relevance with the Constitution's ratification. It still took until the early years of the nineteenth century before a unified foreign and military policy compass could be achieved.

Inland waterways played a significant maritime role in both the Revolutionary War and the War of 1812.[12] Navigable inland waters offer unique challenges to states and their perception of sea power.[13] Land, islands, coastline, as well as correlated waterways are puissant factors contributing to and benefiting from sea power faculties. Value of a geographic feature depends on particular states. The Panama Canal has greater geostrategic importance to the US than does the Magellan Strait. It is considered more useful to the United States than a country such as Somalia. Suez is more advantageous to Britain's Royal Navy than the Cape of Good Hope. It also supports British geostrategic designs far better than it does those of Mexico.

A problem with the definition by Admiral Ricketts in Chapter 2 becomes clear studying maritime action on Lake George and Lake Champlain during the latter half of the eighteenth century. France, Great Britain, and American settlers jockeyed for strategic advantage as they saw these waterways holding keys to the New World.[14] The most significant naval battle during the War of the Revolution occurred on Lake Champlain.[15] Lake Champlain's geographic position in upstate New York borders Canada. This region remains militarily important for its navigable water access to St. Lawrence and Richelieu rivers. These waterways during colonial times provided France and England access to the domain of American colonies. Dominating these lakes and rivers offered the controlling party efficient transport in a land of highly dense forest and few overland routes. Hostile environmental conditions existing on land made travel by ship a safe and attractive mode of transportation.[16] Military engagements that occurred along the waterways surrounding Lake Champlain, Lake George, and other lakes situated in the St. Lawrence region were considered essential to fulfilling grand strategic designs. The United States rediscovered this value thirty years following independence from Great Britain.

The War of 1812 resulted from differences over governing the sea in time of war. Not surprisingly, this involved yet another British-French fight. America believed cargo destined for a British adversary could only be taken at sea if directly related to war fighting. Crown interpretation saw maritime law in far broader terms, meaning any merchandise sustaining an opposing state. Additionally, former British sailors granted American citizenship for their sailing expertise found themselves forcibly removed from US flagged ships and placed back into naval service. Many who resisted were executed. Mahan defies mainstream American thinking by defending Great Britain's action. Without their most precious asset, the Crown stood a very real chance of losing its war with France:

> Her salvation depended upon her navy; and seamen were so scarce as seriously to injure its efficiency and threaten paralysis. This was naturally no concern of the United States, which set up its simple, undeniable right to the protection the neutral flag should give to all persons and goods under it, which were not involved in any infraction of belligerent rights. The straits of Great Britain, however, were too dire to allow the voice of justice to override that of expediency.[17]

Britain produced the highest quality, best trained cadre of sailor and they believed the United States was poaching.[18] Removal of men often left US cargo vessels undermanned following inspection. Britain ignored American insistence that ship documents be the sole source of scrutiny while underway. Instead, Royal Navy inspections comprised physical examination. President James Madison's request for war in June 1812 created consternation and dismay in London. Problems outlined in Madison's resolution occurred years earlier and most were thought to have been remedied. Most people believed good relations were cultivating on all fronts. In fact, Madison personally took charge of developing closer American-British ties during his service in the earlier administration of Thomas Jefferson.[19]

The War of 1812 ended up being another "family feud" among two parties having much in common. The formidable size of Britain's military left a far inferior United States with few options. France made a contribution by keeping many British assets busy in Europe. The only viable strategic option for the US appeared to be fighting a land war in Canada. This forced a British commitment of fleet assets spent transporting troops to Canadian soil. Waterways lining border regions between the US and Canada were important to transportation efforts on both sides.[20] There were five reasons favoring America's decision to take the fight north:

- The US could not effectively attack Great Britain at sea. The entire US Navy consisted of four frigates and eight sloops.
- The British possessed over 100 warships of her own and were in good position to conduct a maritime blockade of the eastern seaboard. The United States would be lucky just to get a squadron of frigates out to sea.
- Napoleon's European campaign had managed to deny the British access to the Baltic region's timber, forcing greater dependency on Canadian resources for ship construction.
- Canada was poorly defended. Only four British regiments were available to defend the 1700 mile border with the US.
- American land forces consisted of an impressive militia with ample military resources to launch a campaign into Canada.[21]

    J. F. C. Fuller's description corresponds to the young US Navy's state of affairs. Mahan links this predicament to what would have been possible with a financial commitment dedicated to creating naval force befitting national capabilities:

> The lesson to be deduced is not that the country at that time should have sought to maintain a navy approaching equality to the British. [Given] the state of national population and revenue, it was no more possible to attempt this than it would be expedient to do it now, under the present immense development of resources and available wealth. What had been possible during the decade preceding the war, - had the nation so willed, - was to place the navy on such a footing, in numbers and constitution, as would have made persistence in the course Great Britain was following impolitic to the verge of madness, because it would add to her war embarrassments the activity of an imposing maritime enemy, at the threshold of her most valuable markets, - the West Indies, - three thousand miles away from her own shores and from the seat of her principal and necessary warfare.[22]

Mahan's comment is a reference to power generator and resource value when combined and deployed by designs of national grand strategy. The US has consistently done a robust job balancing and exploiting power resources. They could have challenged the British at sea if America's inferior naval force utilized all means at its disposal. America's geostrategic position served as its most advantageous weapon. Paul Kennedy makes a case against his own thesis in *The Rise and Fall of British Naval Mastery* by arguing Britain stood a better chance winning the war if they denied US merchants access to foreign trade. A naval blockade of the eastern seaboard would achieve this objective, but this required maritime power which Kennedy so often criticizes.[23] Kennedy's position justified Mahan's naval analysis and expected gains by a United States Navy of sufficient force:

> The war of 1812 demonstrated the usefulness of a navy – not, indeed, by the admirable but utterly unavailing single-ship victories that illustrated its course, but by the prostration into which our seaboard and external communications fell, through the lack of a navy at all proportionate to the country's needs and exposure.[24]

J.F.C. Fuller describes the war as "unwanted as an illegitimate child."[25] The US and Great Britain had substantial economic interests at stake. American and British merchants were advocating expansion of these ties long before war erupted. Lack of enthusiasm caused several unexpected outcomes. The Royal British Army, against a far superior American force, successfully defended Canada. The US Navy, against a far superior Royal Navy, achieved some surprising victories with minimal resources.[26] Both sides had enough by December 1814. Realizing the stupidity of it all, they agreed to sign the Treaty of Ghent. The pre-war status quo was restored, with all territory taken returned to rightful ownership.[27] Many were left wondering what the fighting had been about. Cessation of hostilities gave Britain freedom of action in Europe so that the full might of its war machine could engage in final subjugation of Napoleon.

The French Connection

The greatest foreign threat faced by the United States between the War of 1812 and the outbreak of the Spanish-American War came from Napoleon III's desire to ensconce French control over Mexico. Conquering Mexico would plant a potentially hostile European power south of the Rio Grande. Maintaining a stable north-south land border is an ongoing national security priority for US defense experts. Stable borders provide the United States flexibility to dedicate resources toward sea power objectives. Napoleon III's letter to General Forey in 1863 described France's grand strategic vision, while revealing a persistent predicament faced by the US from points south:

> In the actual state of civilization of the world, the prosperity of America cannot be a matter of indifference to Europe.... We are desirous that the republic of the United States be powerful and prosperous, but we are not desirous that she should make herself mistress of the Gulf of Mexico, dominate the Antilles and South America, and be the sole dispenser of the products of the New World.... If, on the contrary, Mexico preserve her independence and maintain the integrity of her territory, if a government be established there with the assistance of France, we shall have rendered to the *Latin race* on the other side of the ocean its strength and its prestige; we shall have guaranteed security to our colonies and those of Spain; we shall have established our beneficent influence in the centre of America; and that influence, in creating immense outlets to our commerce, will procure for us the materials indispensable to our industry. To-day, our military honour, the exigencies of our politics, the interests of our industry and our commerce, demand that we march upon Mexico, plant boldly our flag, and establish there even a monarchy, if that be not incompatible with the national sentiment of the country, or at least a government that promises some stability.[28]

Rebellious southern states actively sought recognition and assistance from Europe during the early 1860s. France was in Mexico, Great Britain in Canada, and even Asian countries were getting in on the act. The West Coast would quickly become a valuable real estate acquisition for pan-Pacific strategic goals if death came to the Union.[29] Discreet hints of French meddling can be seen in Abraham Lincoln's address to Congress on 04 July 1861 (Independence Day). It is a depressing summary of America's international and military situation:

> The forts remaining in the possession of the Federal government in and near these States were either besieged or menaced by warlike preparations, and especially Fort Sumter. . . . A disproportionate share of the Federal muskets and rifles had somehow found their way into these States, and had been seized to be used against the Government. Accumulations of the public revenue, lying within them, had been seized for the same object. The Navy was scattered in distant seas,

leaving but a very small part of it within the immediate reach of the Government. Officers of the Federal Army and Navy had resigned in great numbers; and of those resigning, a large proportion had taken up arms against the Government. Simultaneously, and in connection with all this, the purpose to sever the Federal Union was openly avowed. In accordance with this purpose, an ordinance had been adopted in each of these States, declaring the States, respectively, to be separated from the National Union. A formula for instituting a combined government of these States had been promulgated; and this illegal organization in the character of confederate States, was already invoking recognition, aid, and intervention, from foreign powers.[30]

Timing of Napoleon III's letter to Forey indicates French enthusiasm for the Confederacy. Establishing support bases across the Rio Grande may have been the Civil War's most decisive event.

The United States has never been ignorant of Mexico's importance and neither was General Antonio de Santa Anna. Mahan's biography of Admiral Farragut notes Santa Anna's message during their meeting at Vera Cruz, Mexico, just prior to the French attack in 1838: "Tell President Van Buren that we are all one family, and must be united against Europeans obtaining a foothold on this continent."[31] European meddling might have been avoided if Santa Anna's remark been taken seriously. Mexico's loss of Texas in 1836, coupled with the very real threat of French occupation, influenced Santa Anna's view that Mexico's future depended on ties with the United States. This relationship for US policy planners, on the other hand, always involved consideration of Mexico's political stability and corruption. Napoleon III's geostrategic view of Mexico as a pivot-point between the US and Latin America made it imperative Mexico not become a French colony. The highly touted westward expansion would otherwise be in grave danger of coming to a screeching halt.

Admiral Farragut's action along the Mississippi River during the Civil War dictated the course of world history. His decision to run the fleet past Confederate fortifications at Fort Jackson and Fort St. Philip on the Mississippi River isolated and cut communications with New Orleans, the one city those installations were tasked to defend. Events may not appear monumental until national grand strategy implications are considered. This single military victory eliminated any chance that Britain and France would diplomatically recognize the Confederacy. Threat of European intervention had successfully been destroyed forever:

It was elsewhere, far and wide, that were felt the moral effects which echoed the sudden, unexpected crash with which the lower Mississippi fell – through the length and breadth of the South and in the cabinets of foreign statesmen, who had believed too readily, as did their officers on the spot, that the barrier was not to be passed – that the Queen City of the Confederacy was impregnable to attack from the sea. Whatever may have been the actual purposes of that mysterious and undecided personage, Napoleon III, the effect of military events, whether on sea or shore, upon the question of interference by foreign powers is sufficiently evident from the private correspondence which, a few months after New Orleans, passed between Lords Palmerston and Russell, then the leading members of the British Cabinet. Fortunately for the cause of the United States, France and Great Britain were not of a mind to combine their action at the propitious moment; and the moral effect of the victory at New Orleans was like a cold plunge bath to the French emperor, at the time when he was hesitating whether to act alone. It produced upon him even more impression than upon the British Government; because his ambitions for French control and for the extension of the Latin races on the American continent were especially directed toward Louisiana, the former colony of France, and toward its neighbors, Texas and Mexico.[32]

Napoleon III developed into such a threat that when Union Army units reached the Texas border with Mexico, General Sheridan began furnishing Mexican resistance fighters with all the weapons and ammunition needed to eradicate French forces. Sheridan took unprecedented measures by allowing immediate discharges to Union soldiers willing to join Mexican troops and fight the occupiers. This became extremely valuable because of combat experience brought to the battlefield by these men. Those who volunteered to proceed south across the Rio Grande were allowed to remain in the Union uniform and keep their US Army-issued weapons.[33]

Mahan prophetically combined each of Colin Gray's four geographic points into a single historical outcome. Commingling geography and military might is a valuable link providing benefits if properly exploited. Mahan closes his treatise on New Orleans by noting the European response or, at that point, lack of response:

In its moral effect, therefore, the fall of the river forts and of New Orleans, though not absolutely and finally decisive of the question of foreign intervention, corresponded to one of those telling blows, by which a general threatened by two foes meets and strikes down one

before the other comes up. Such a blow may be said to decide a campaign; not because no chance is left the enemy to redeem his misfortune, but because without the first success the weaker party would have been overwhelmed by the junction of his two opponents.
The heart-rending disasters to our armies during the following summer does but emphasize the immense value to the Union cause of the moral effect produced by Farragut's victory. Those disasters, as it was, prompted the leaders of the British ministry to exchange confidences in which they agreed on the expediency of mediation. They did not carry all their colleagues with them; but who can estimate the effect, when the scales were thus balancing, if the navy had been driven out of the Mississippi as the army was from Virginia?[34]

This is a triumphant outcome for national grand strategy. Designated power resources and their elements were put in play when and where needed. Grand strategy then deployed sea power to fulfill requirements of policy. This did not occur without the willingness of a great man to break procedure when necessary. Leadership of this type is rare and, fortunately for the Union, Farragut ensured a resolute message reached capitals across the Atlantic.

The Wild West and Gulf of Mexico

French attempts to exert control on Mexican soil during the Civil War were enough for US officials to take new, more aggressive action on policy related to national security. Western Hemisphere threats from Europe were real and just the right environment would entice trans-Atlantic powers. The Civil War brought the Monroe Doctrine of 1823 to America's border. Napoleon III proved there were those willing to take advantage of a United States preoccupied with internal affairs. It is not a coincidence that the Monroe Doctrine originated when France became executor of Spain's political situation following Ferdinand VII's removal from power.

The bulk of US naval activity during the Civil War took place along the Mississippi River. Primary purpose was to support Union Army land campaigns. Mahan's narration of general views toward naval affairs beyond the coast describes shallow national priorities:

Despite the extensive sea-coast of the United States and the large maritime commerce possessed by it at the opening of the war, the navy had never, except for short and passing intervals, been regarded with the interest its importance deserved. To this had doubtless contributed the fixed policy of the Government to concentrate its attention upon the internal development of the country, and to concern itself little with external interests, except so far as they promoted the views of that section which desired to give extension to slave holding territory. The avoidance of entangling alliances had become perverted to indifference to the means by which alone, in the last resort, the nation can assert and secure control in regions outside its borders, but vitally affecting its prosperity and safety. The power of navies was therefore, then as now, but little understood.[35]

Fortunately the Civil War did not involve fleet action of any substance. Northern naval forces were strong enough to constrain the Confederacy in a manner similar to that imposed on France by Great Britain.[36] Europe's preoccupation with continental balance of power issues ensured the Union's inadequate navy could not be exploited. This enabled America's post-Civil War domestic house to be put in order before taking on the rest of the world.[37]

Less than a year following Lincoln's Independence Day speech to Congress, the United States government, fearing for its life, concluded that it must commit to a transportation project that firmly established claim to the West. Prior to completing the transcontinental railroad, a journey to the West Coast involved incredible risk. Overland travel by covered wagon subjected passengers to marauding Indians, bandits, and roving gangs. Terrain was impassable in many places until scouting expeditions discovered suitable routes for wagon trails. Incredibly harsh weather shifted with dramatic change and little warning. Those same trails were susceptible to flash floods, tornadoes, and blizzards. Illness and death were daily events for the traveling public. Alternative modes of transport could not be considered much better. They involved departing the East Coast by ship, disembarking at Panama, traveling across the Panamanian jungle to the Pacific Ocean side, and then boarding another sailing vessel for a ride up the coast. The other seagoing route required six months travel passing around Cape Horn at the southern tip of South America. This is a fourteen thousand mile journey. Sailing to India from Boston is equal distance and less dangerous. Stephen Ambrose notes how communications was America's only hope for building a secure nation between two shores:

> Throughout the Pacific Coast, the territories from California north to Washington were like overseas colonies: immensely valuable, but so far away. They could be reached by sea – but the United States had

nothing like a two-ocean navy – or overland via carts drawn by horses and oxen. But it took seemingly forever. Americans knew how difficult or impossible it was to defend overseas colonies – even for Great Britain, with the mightiest fleet of all. The French could not hold on to Haiti, or Canada, or Louisiana, just as the British could not hold their North American colonies.[38]

Union Pacific Railroad provides a fine example showing the correlation of power resources and elements with sea power. When properly applied, achievement of great things becomes possible. Superior results occur when assets normally associated with a particular power generator can be incorporated to support an entirely different generator. An element (railroads on land) from a power resource (transportation) profoundly influenced America's land *and* sea power portfolio.

Union Pacific started with Abraham Lincoln signing the Pacific Railroad Act of 01 July 1862. It called for a rail line stretching from the Pacific Ocean in California, over the Rocky Mountains, and across the Great Plains of the Midwest. The route joined those already existing across the Missouri River at Council Bluffs, Iowa.[39] Union Pacific's instructions originated with Lincoln himself. They were to proceed from Omaha, across Nebraska, Wyoming, and on into Utah.[40] Westward and eastward rail gangs officially met at Promontory, Utah on 10 May 1869. This happened seven years ahead of schedule and, at the time, earned recognition as the greatest construction project in American history. Challenges confronting these men were daunting. Dangers are impossible to fathom in a modern workplace full of ergonomic chairs and "sensitivity training." The task is more admirable when realizing America's survival rested on the shoulders of these crusty railroad workers. They did not have lawyers or politicians standing by to "feel their pain."

In January 1889 Mahan and fellow members of a designated site commission boarded a train in New York and traveled the transcontinental route to Puget Sound, Washington. Their mission involved identifying a site for a naval yard north of the 42nd parallel. This journey happened at the time Mahan was writing his monumental work, *The Influence of Sea Power upon History*. Inquiries made to political and business leaders duplicate his research on sea power. A total of twenty questions were submitted requesting information on available natural resources, population, skilled labor supply, climate, standards of living (including wages, prices, and rents), birth and death rates, manufacturing facilities, communications, and cost of building materials.[41] Queries are documented in assets of sea power and properly categorized under power resources.

Geostrategic value of Union Pacific to America is apparent from its start and remains significant today. A major undertaking created to secure territory between two of the world's most vital oceans has become a transportation asset of international importance. Mahan's analysis in 1898 is consistent:

> The military needs of the Pacific States, as well as their supreme importance to the whole country, are yet a matter of the future, but of a future so near that provision should begin immediately. To weigh their importance, consider what influence in the Pacific would be attributed to a nation comprising only the States of Washington, Oregon, and California, when filled with such men as now people then and still are pouring in, and which controlled such maritime centres as San Francisco, Puget Sound, and the Columbia River. Can it be counted less because they are bound by the ties of blood and close political union to the great communities of the East?[42]

The Spanish-American War served as a wake-up call over realities of global politics. Naval policies pursued prior to the fighting enabled the US to compete with Old World leaders. Spain's steady rate of decline got its start with the curse of Sir Francis Drake. Losses in 1898 cost the Spaniards virtually all remaining colonial territory. American influence suddenly spanned the Pacific Ocean, the Caribbean Sea, and portions of South America. The US did not yet possess a fleet able to patrol these massive regions. Mahan's public appearance is well-timed. Policy recommendations made years earlier were implemented without delay: "For national security, the correlative of a national principle firmly held and distinctly avowed is, not only the will, but the power to enforce it."[43] Willingness to fight and regime legitimacy arrive with enormous relevancy.

War with Spain exposed several problems defending the Gulf of Mexico, and both Pacific and Atlantic coasts simultaneously. Mahan, while serving on the Naval War Board, witnessed the stupendous mediocrity of both the US Navy and Army manhandling a broken Spanish fleet and fortifications in Cuba, Puerto Rico, and the Philippines. Post-war assessments showed this largely resulted from indecisive acts by higher echelon military and political leaders. On the Spanish side Mahan identified a lack of qualified sailors by quoting a

Spanish naval officer: "The Americans keep their ships cruising constantly, in every sea, and therefore have a large and qualified engine-room force. We have but few machinists, and are almost destitute of firemen."[44] Neither side appeared capable of winning a war. This is not reassuring compared to naval might emanating from Europe. Even Admiral Dewey's success in Manila, from a geostrategic position, caused Mahan troubling unease:

> Personally, I have not yet become wholly adjusted to the new point of view opened to us by Dewey's victory at Manila. It has opened a vista of possibilities which were not by me in the least foreseen, though the intimate contact of the East with the West, and a probable imminent conflict (not necessarily war-like) between the two civilizations had long been a part of my thought. As it is, I look with a kind of awe upon the passage of events in which the will of man seems to count for little.[45]

Mahan ranked among a well-heeled circle concerned over profound security dilemmas facing the Philippines acquisition. Dewey himself noted the exposure shortly following Spain's surrender:

> I look forward some 40 or 50 years and foresee a Japanese naval squadron entering this harbour, as I have just done, and demanding surrender of Manila and the Philippines with the plan of making these islands a part of the great Pacific Japanese empire of the future.[46]

The territory involved a range of problems. For the first time in American history, foreign policy appeared to be moving the Monroe Doctrine into the Eastern Hemisphere. Proactively, this equation had merit. Pulling out of the Philippines would have left a vacuum for Germany, Great Britain, and Japan to fill.[47] Events in the Pacific, Atlantic, and Caribbean made construction of a canal through Central America critical. Naval forces were exposed if they did not have an expedient means to augment security responsibilities in both ocean regions. This turned out to be only a temporary problem.

President McKinley's assassination while touring Buffalo, New York in 1901 propelled McKinley's vice president, Theodore Roosevelt, into the hot seat as new president. He launched an aggressive shipbuilding program which reached unprecedented levels. Euphoria permeated society as people grew more optimistic about the future. This served as an ideal climate for Roosevelt and Mahan to exploit.[48] The European nations were embroiled in traditional rivalries that prevented a check on American expansion. Mahan became a global celebrity. Publication of *The Influence of Sea Power upon History* resulted in a widely read book by government officials around the world.[49] On the home front Mahan earned an impressive reputation as an outspoken critic of cultural and social hedonism permeating society at the expense of military readiness:

> But men do not covet less the prosperity which they themselves cannot or do not create, - a trait wherein lies the strength of communism as an aggressive social force. Communities which want and cannot have, except by force, will take by force, unless they are restrained by force; nor will it be unprecedented in the history of the world that the flood of numbers should pour over and sweep away the barriers which intelligent foresight, like Caesar's, may have erected against them. Still more will this be so if the barriers have ceased to be manned – forsaken or neglected by men in whom the proud combative spirit of their ancestors has given way to the cry for the abandonment of military preparation and to the decay of warlike habits.[50]

Mahan's staying power is again apparent by reflecting on what he foretold at the close of the nineteenth century materializing again at the close of the next.

Matters of Military Importance

Conclusion of World War I found traditional European powers buried in debt. Britain and France were in a fragile state. Germany wasted little time searching for ways to rebuild militarily. Japan leaped into a comfortable international position among world powers and, in Moscow, Lenin stayed gainfully employed solidifying his dictatorship by eliminating White Russians. The United States, like Japan, bypassed old hats and took on a greater international role. A sudden shift in players placed the two nations in competition for control of the Pacific. Japan's rise did not go unnoticed by the Naval War College or Mahan. His Strategic War Plan of 1911 provided guidance if a Pacific war erupted. The appropriately timed forecast surfaced six years before Japan's decision to triple naval expenditures, which rose to an eye-opening $245 million by 1921, three years following Europe's armistice and while those states were poised on bankruptcy. Japan's enormous investment made the entire Pacific region look unstable.

The Pacific's explosive situation is apparent by failure of naval treaties between Japan, United States, and Great Britain. The Lansing-Ishii Agreement of 1917, for example, is full of contradictions with secret agreements made between Britain and Japan. Woodrow Wilson's internationalist mood quickly faded.[51] Competition over Pacific islands, China's instability, and a Russian revolution concerned Japanese foreign policy experts just as instability in Mexico and Canada would for the US. Though Great Britain desired peace out of fear for its treasury, the US believed Japan and Great Britain could become mutual enemies. The General Board of the Navy feared a simultaneous two-ocean challenge based on agreements between London and Tokyo. George Baer notes advice to President Harding before the 1921 Washington conference: "So long as Britain was in alliance with Japan, or might ally with the Soviet Union or a revived Germany, security demanded a total force equal not just to that of the world's strongest navy but to the British and Japanese navies combined."[52] Matching British and Japanese navies would be a major endeavor.

Initial agreements did result between the three maritime powers, but lack of trust hindered a positive negotiating climate at future conference tables. Continuation of diplomatic intercourse between Britain and Japan justified American plans to build a two-ocean fleet. Behind the scenes, British and American governments were reaching consensus on controlling a naval arms race through capital ship restrictions. John Gunther notes how Japan, which was financially better off, saw American arms control efforts as an attempt to box it in:

> Japan wants to expand in order to be stronger vis-à-vis the Soviet Union, in order to squeeze Great Britain out of China, in order to extend its nationalist influence southward into Asia and the Pacific. It has never precisely defined what it means by "East Asia," but it regards large sections of Asia as we regarded the land west of the Mississippi in our own expansionist days. Questions of ultimate *power* move Japan. It wants political hegemony over what it calls its hinterland.[53]

Tokyo, believing it had every right to maritime supremacy, walked out of the London Naval Conference in 1935:

> The British and Americans refused to grant parity to Japan, which would have ended the idea of limitation. The British suggested the interchange of information, so that each country would at least be informed of the building programs of the others, since actual

limitation seemed impossible. The Japanese refused this, on the ground that they could find out about British and American building, but that the British and Americans could not find out what they were building. Japan traded on its ability to conceal its naval activity. As a price for exchange of information, the Japanese demanded parity.[54]

Japan's perceived appropriate response involved deploying a whole new class of battleship. Nothing like the 70,000 ton *Yamato*, with eighteen inch guns, had ever been built. This monster almost doubled capital ship sizes discussed at London or Washington conferences, and it served as a message of coming events.

America's destiny as world leader was carved in stone during World War II. Contrary to the NWC, WWII confirmed Mahan's sea power doctrine. America's industrial might turned in a star performance. It rapidly retooled for war and ran at unprecedented speed. Strategically positioned territories around the world supported operations. America's people, for the most part, remained positive knowing the great risk involved. Edward Beach describes the USN's unprecedented challenge, global implication, and urgency:

> There was a sense of Armageddon at sea in 1942, a feeling that the great test for which our navy had been created had at last arrived. Not merely the "greatest" of all tests, but the culmination of its entire history, of everything that had gone before. It was this for which all the wars, campaigns, battles, and, particularly, all the work it had done and all the development it had been but preliminaries.[55]

The US Navy had officially clocked a grand total of 56 hours combat experience prior to Pearl Harbor's attack. This included the Civil War, Spanish-American War, and World War I. Pearl Harbor began a four year non-stop run for sea control. On-the-job training took on new meaning for American sailors. Years spent perfecting aircraft carrier operations were paid back in full over a four hour period at Midway Island.[56] This is where the entrance door from strategy to tactics is passed and military action takes on unique features. Basil Hart explains this transition in terms of offense verses defense:

> The other form of surprise which may be attained to-day is by the time of the attack – mental unexpectedness. Defence is now so superior to attack that, unless the defence is caught unaware, the attack is likely to fail. The prospects of attack diminish once the initial surprise is over.[57]

Hart's "mental unexpectedness" gripped Admiral Yamamoto and his staff in June 1942, which enabled the war's entire course to change direction at *point of transition*. It is the pivot-point where a major historical event is about to unfold, just as strategy evolves into tactics. The victory over Japan by the US Navy at Midway set a course for blue-water domination. Though Japan remained powerful, the loss of four carriers, 2200 sailors, and 250 aircraft flown by some of the world's best pilots brought a devastating jolt to naval planners. Fatalities did not end when the shooting stopped as several senior officers, embarrassed and disgraced, committed seppuku.[58]

The US Navy's grand finale came at the Battle of Leyte Gulf on 25 October 1944. It developed into the largest display of Mahan's blue-water naval warfare since publication of *The Influence of Sea Power upon History*. Over 185,000 Japanese, American, and Australian naval personnel took part. The engagement covered an area so vast that those in combat, as well as Admiral Nimitz, Commander, United States Pacific Fleet (CINCPACFLT), did not know the status until Japanese forces departed in full retreat: "The Allied victory finally and thoroughly destroyed the offensive power of the Japanese navy and realized the sea-power goal of American naval planners of the previous 40 years."[59] Destroying four of Japan's few remaining carriers in a single day announced America's ascent to sea power's throne.[60]

The Atlantic theater during World War II comprised a war over logistics and convoy operations. Unfortunately, countering U-boat attacks did not achieve success until May 1943. Staggering losses of ships and men continued until concentration of force techniques were merged with anti-submarine close air support. Mixing air and sea assets achieved overnight success. Japan was not so fortunate in the Pacific. Convoy operations were attempted, but the Imperial Navy failed to incorporate anti-submarine air warfare methods equal to US and British efforts in the Atlantic. The Pacific Ocean offers "island hopping" opportunities unlike other oceans. American forces took advantage by using these parcels as logistics support bases for further advances.

Island hopping belonged to US Marines, and their crowning achievement took place on Iwo Jima in 1945. The USMC spent six months at Camp Pendleton, California formulating a fighting force of 21,000 men to lead the invasion. This later paid off when, for the first time in history, an invasion and conquest of Japanese soil succeeded. US military leaders wasted little time turning Iwo Jima into an 'aircraft carrier' supporting USA Air Corps bombing missions. This required removal of enemy forces so that construction battalions could build a runway and support facilities, while Air Corps personnel serviced and launched long-range bombers.

Ships transporting Iwo Jima Marines departed Honolulu, Hawaii in January 1945. The massive fleet stretched over 70 miles, making it the largest and most powerful naval operation in US history. James Bradley's description of this armada summarizes sea power and national grand strategy's close working relationship:

> The movement of over 100,000 men – Marines, Navy support personnel, Coast Guard units – across four thousand miles of ocean for three weeks is a triumph of American industry galvanizing itself in a time of great national peril. At the outset of the war, Japan's naval strength was more than double that of America's. . . And it has not been just a matter of hardware. The civilians of America have mobilized behind these fighting boys. Behind each man on board the ships are hundreds of workers: in factories, in the cities and towns, on the heartland farms. Rosie the Riveter. Boy Scouts collecting paper and metal. The young girl who will become Marilyn Monroe, sweating away in a defense plant.[61]

Invasion of Iwo Jima began on 19 February 1945 or, in actuality, on 04 June 1942 at the Battle of Midway. The psychological jolt of home territory being conquered by American forces devastated Japan's morale. A repeat performance came weeks later with Okinawa's invasion. Both invasion forces reached their objective because the US Navy achieved blue-water dominance in the Pacific.

A revolution in military affairs (RMA) occurred twenty years prior to World War II. It prepared America's maritime forces for expected obstacles if and when hostilities commenced. Iwo Jima's success advertised Marine Corps amphibious assault capabilities. Less obvious were aircraft carriers. Mahan would have been first to endorse each RMA pursuit. They were decisive instruments for winning control of the Pacific. When in search of history's greatest events, research identifies a pivot-point marking directional change. America's point for conquest of sovereign Japanese territory can be found at Midway.

History Lives

Japan's decision to seek peace with the United States is one of the wisest foreign policy moves of the twentieth century. Annihilation of Japan's Imperial Navy came at a high price. A leading global industrial engine found itself out of fuel, Japan's national economy laid in shambles, and Stalin licked his chops anticipating an opportunity to pounce.[62] Long-established economic relations with America helped in the decision. US grand strategy did not seek an empire or wish to conquer the planet. Okinawa's invasion showed humanitarian contradictions with Imperial Army horror propaganda that contributed to mass suicides by Japanese. Seeing this carnage, combined with evidence Japan intended to defend the mainland at all cost, convinced President Truman detonating an atomic bomb offered the most humanitarian ending. Hiroshima and Nagasaki eradicated remaining grand schemes of a fight to the finish.

Within six years America's occupation force officially ended its mission. Japan modeled a constitution based on representative democracy. Its economy rebounded and showed positive signs of an upswing. Culmination of direct US political involvement came with the peace treaty of 1951.[63] The United States continued defending the archipelago. This grew crucial as events in Asia unfolded. Cultural indifference is a tradition among America's population and includes many serving the political elite. A profound example occurred during an argument between Walt Rostow and Dean Acheson over the Vietnam War: "The only reason I told the President to fight in Korea was to validate NATO."[64] Acheson's view is telling by his famous speech in January 1950 at the National Press Club where he claimed Korea resided outside America's security sphere.[65]

The Philippines is strategically significant for America's operational dominance in the western Pacific. Its value was proven in every decade since the Spanish-American War. The Philippines serves as a classic example of the marriage between geostrategic positioning and power generators. It made facilities available for naval power projection. US Air Force B-52 bombers benefited by having bases to launch flying missions destined for parts unknown. The archipelago served American ground forces with logistics facilities in both Korean and Vietnam Wars. It remains vital to military forces from three power generators. Roosevelt's administration proved how crucial this real estate is to surrounding waters when it failed to build adequate defenses in preparation for WWII.

US history is perfect for explaining power generation and principles of national grand strategy. This comparison will continue in following chapters with analysis of US action during the Cold War.

Soviet efforts to penetrate the highest ranks of the US government prior to World War II continued paying dividends as Cold War events intensified. American complacency among political elites made Washington's back-scratching circuit a significant contributor to the coming storm. Warnings by hard-line hawks went unheeded as unsuspecting lemmings headed for the cliff. Frustration reached a point that anti-communist administration officials took their case to the press:

> I find that whenever any American suggests that we act in accordance with the needs of our own security he is apt to be called a god-damned fascist or imperialist, while if Uncle Joe [Stalin] suggests that he needs the Baltic Provinces, half of Poland, all of Bessarabia and access to the Mediterranean, all hands agree that he is a fine, frank, candid and generally delightful fellow who is very easy to deal with because he is so explicit in what he wants.[66]

The Soviets took full advantage of a naïve and penetrated American diplomatic corps:

> General Marshall feels that the inactivation of China Theater at an early date will greatly strengthen the Generalissimo's pressure for the removal of Russian forces from Manchuria. I concur in this idea, and we have been striving to evolve a *modus operandi* in order to submit appropriate suggestions to you and the Joint Chiefs of Staff. Since V-J Day, the Chinese Communists (with the support of Soviet Communists and fellow travelers in America) have been urging the removal of all Americans from China. The Generalissimo desires to retain U.S. forces, but agrees that their removal – that is, combat elements – might help his position vis-à-vis Russia. The present strength of our forces, air and ground, would preclude [an] effective fight against a determined Soviet Russian effort; however, the presence of the Marine Corps reinforced by an Air Wing has undoubtedly served as a deterrent to more aggressive steps by the Chinese Communists and even possibly the Soviet Communists. General Marshall feels that the presence of the Marines, in fact any American combat units in the area, is really an irritant and, inasmuch as we do not have sufficient strength to cope successfully with a serious Russian effort, he concludes that it would be better to remove the irritant.[67]

It is amazing Marshall believed standing down the USMC and pulling them from China would encourage a Soviet withdrawal from China, even with Chiang Kai-shek's warning. Viewing the US military as destabilizing, while Soviet Red Army forces are not, seems odd. Perhaps the Red Army is really the Red Cross in disguise. The message is historically disturbing because of Marshall's reference to "support of Soviet Communists and fellow travelers in America." Who were these fellow travelers in America? What were their numbers? Where could they be found? Were they so powerful to dictate American foreign and military policy? Where are these little rascals and their descendents today? There is no precedence supporting Marshall's position. It certainly could not have been based on Soviet congeniality in Europe. The political right's frustration is understandable.

Sea and land power's long arm are joined by air and space power as the West faced a global communist movement. World War II showed success in war depends on the quality of individual power generator tools organized for a great clash. These instruments were brought to the main stage in the decades that followed. A small group of men demonstrated that value years earlier by breaking the Japanese code name for Midway Island.

Part IV

The Modern Era

"The clear expression of national purpose, accompanied by evident and adequate means to carry it into effect, is the surest safeguard against war, provided always that the national contention is maintained with a candid and courteous consideration of the rights and susceptibilities of other states. On the other hand, no condition is more hazardous than that of a dormant popular feeling, liable to be roused into action by a moment of passion, such as that which swept over the North when the flag was fired upon at Sumter, but behind which lies no organized power for action. It is on the score of due preparation for such an ultimate contingency that nations, and especially free nations, are most often deficient."

Alfred Thayer Mahan, "The Future in Relation to American Naval Power," *Harper's New Monthly Magazine*, Vol. 140, no. 545 (October 1895).

Chapter Ten

Cold War Rising

"Nothing stands between Europe today and complete subjugation to Communist tyranny but the atomic bomb in American possession."
- Sir Winston Churchill

A unique feature of the Cold War involved aggressive deployment of power generator resources on a far greater scale than previously witnessed in the annals of warfare. Rather than military might serving as primary arbiter for achieving national objectives, the stable of remaining power resources and their instruments were brought to the forefront as weapons of choice. Military might often maintained a holding pattern waiting to pounce at those moments when pouncing was warranted. The title "Cold War," though deceiving, earned its reputation from hefty exploitation of power resources not commonly associated with the public's image of war. Ultimate contributor for this unusual arrangement came from the intelligence power resource.

Military power remained checked thanks to nuclear weapons and their deployment strategy. During the Korean War, for example, US President Harry Truman resisted pressure to activate America's atomic option on overwhelming Chinese forces challenging UN troops. This resulted from concern for Europe and Stalin's response with the newly acquired weapon in the Soviet arsenal. The intelligence power resource's impact rose to the occasion with revelation of the Soviet-controlled Rosenberg spy ring. Linkage provided by a network of agents enabled Stalin to restrain Truman. Nuclear strategy kept both sides contained as the USSR achieved parity years later. An added burden on Western defense planners, which did not concern their Soviet opponent, involved knowing that enemy did not need nuclear weapons: "Soviet military strength was ample enough in every way that the Soviets were unlikely to initiate the use of nuclear weapons; they could get what they wanted without them."[1] The stark advantage of Warsaw Pact conventional forces left the West in an unpalatable predicament of having to initiate the nuclear option. The Strategic Arms Limitation Talks (SALT) during the 1970s caused setbacks at the expense of lofty goals for compromise and peaceful coexistence. The

arsenal of weapons arrayed against Warsaw Pact forces did remain
sufficient to force the Soviets to blink: "These weapons *persuaded* the
Japanese to surrender and *persuaded* the Soviets not to exploit their
advantage in conventional forces in Europe; they did not cripple the
Japanese invasion defenses or the Warsaw Pact's arrays of tanks."[2]

The impact of nuclear weapons on maritime and naval strategy
did not compute in the decade leading up to Hiroshima. The historical
significance of the United States being first to develop atomic weapons
is that maintaining supremacy, and later parity, ensured America did
not lose its leverage with Mahanian doctrine. The West and other
sovereign states were fortunate to have US military forces at the
forefront of a global nuclear arms race. America did not harbor
expansionist tendencies, and the nuclear shield enabled European
governments to free ride in pursuit of their own self-interests: "For
example, does a containment policy require that more than 300,000
U.S. military personnel be retained on garrison duty in Western
Europe? Or, phrased in the political vernacular, should 249 million
Americans be obliged to generate the lion's share of security for 381
million Europeans *vis-à-vis* 288 million Soviets?"[3]

Can it be honestly stated the Soviet Union would have behaved
in an identical manner as the United States if nuclear fortunes were
reversed and Red Army forces held the upper hand? Would the Soviet
Union have tolerated development of a nuclear capability in their
adversary to a point of parity and eventual superiority? Not likely and,
outside of disinformation artisans, there are not many that would dare
to argue differently. This same line of reasoning applies to maritime
supremacy if advantage had belonged to the Soviet Union. Chances are
slim Moscow would have tolerated a move to surpass it in naval and
maritime power. A peacetime approach toward policing sea-lanes
which ensures unfettered access for those respecting maritime law is a
hallmark of US naval policy. This is not symbolic of past Soviet
behavior on related matters.

America's sea power portfolio enabled maritime and naval
strength to remain unrivalled because of its well-oiled power resource
machinery. Fortunately, as Colin Gray notes, this edge held tight in the
latter half of the twentieth century:

> In its grand strategy, a sea power competent in statecraft does not
> repose its security simply in the fact of a national geography which
> lends itself to maritime exploitation. The *final line* of national defense
> is provided by those military assets which directly protect the more or

less insular homeland. However, the *first line* of defense for a well-governed sea power is a bevy of land-oriented allies, or - strictly – the diplomacy which forges and then helps sustain a mixed maritime-continental alliance.[4]

Geostrategically, the Cold War involved a collective of sea power states against a land power alliance of unprecedented strength. A key ingredient to the West's national grand strategy model has been an ability to maintain firm presence on European and Asian continents, while providing a logistical train spanning both Pacific and Atlantic Oceans. NATO's ability to maximize the recently added utility of air power also aided in restraining Soviet action against inadequately manned ground forces defending Western Europe. Military might between superpowers stayed contained thanks to not knowing each party's response. This pulled the Soviet camp toward greater reliance on other means in waging war against the West:

> Plans and projects for harming the enemy are not confined to any one method. Sometimes entice his wise and virtuous men away so that he has no counsellors. Or send treacherous people to his country to wreck his administration. Sometimes use cunning deceptions to alienate his ministers from the sovereign. Or send skilled craftsmen to encourage his people to exhaust their wealth. Or present him with licentious musicians and dancers to change his customs. Or give him beautiful women to bewilder him.[5]

While the West continued giving primacy to traditional military methods, the Soviets and their partners-in-crime incorporated an impressive array of unconventional channels. These included aggressive penetration and manipulation of unsuspecting institutions throughout the West.[6] Influencing public opinion became second nature with a sophisticated propaganda operation.[7] Indoctrination succeeded via numerous publications full of dialectic half-truths and lies.[8] Blackmail took place using cash, women and drugs.[9] The People's Republic of China provides an impressive contemporary example. PRC agents now have access to endless amounts of cash as an added incentive that entices hungry targets. Though women remain an effective tool, James Adams shows they are not deployed to the same extent Russian swallows are released in pursuit of their prey:

> They [PRC] know that simple cash, and not very much of it, can buy access to the heart of power; that America may have more raw

military power at its fingertips than any nation on earth but that the will to use it is weak. Does America understand the way China works? Successive U.S. governments have maintained that China will eventually be tamed by the power of the marketplace, that Adam Smith, perhaps in cahoots with Mickey Mouse, will depose Karl Marx and set the people free; that it is wiser to do business with the dictators and treat issues like human rights violations, proliferation of weapons of mass destruction and trade piracy as completely separate.[10]

Drug smuggling occurred on a massive scale with control and coordination emanating from the Kremlin and Great Hall of the People.[11] Not only did it destroy an entire generation's willingness to fight, but also managed to provide an attractive resource for financing the war effort. Assassination was looked upon as just another asset for advancing state policy to the next level.[12] Formalities of diplomatic intercourse with civilized societies were but a nuisance and cover for greater tasks at hand. James Tyson argues that influencing opinion to achieve strategic advantage developed into an easy exercise for totalitarian regimes engaged in a war of words against open societies:

> A study by Accuracy in Media showed that throughout 1976 the *New York Times* and the *Washington Post* combined contained only 13 mentions of human rights violations in Cambodia compared to 124 for Chile and 85 for South Korea. The performance of the major networks was similar: 16 for Cambodia compared to 137 for Chile and 90 for South Korea.[13]

Citizens of free societies may associate with those they choose, including agents of foreign powers seeking to undermine their nation.[14] A Cold War advantage for tyrants of communism is that no formal declaration of war existed to constrain Western citizens going about their "personal" business. Domestic influence of open societies took but a few sympathetic journalists and members of the film industry.[15] Economic blackmail came about by enticing egotistical executives with succulent joys of life's great pleasures (all caught on camera), or a threat of withholding natural resources.[16] Operations grew massive in scale (national grand strategy), but remained local in practice (tactics). Communist regimes saw this as full-scale war on unsuspecting enemies: "War acknowledges principles, and even rules, but these are not so much fetters, or bars, which compel its movement aright, as guides which warn us when it is going wrong."[17]

The Soviet Hand

Formation of the Axis Powers leading up to World War II is a record full of missed opportunities for the US and Great Britain. Germany and Italy had organized a united front against the Soviet Union's Comintern operation (Anti-Comintern Pact of 1936). German and Italian governments uncovered a massive global communist intelligence and subversive operation underway against nations around the world:

> Here is what Krivitsky [Walter] wrote. In Great Britain, "anti-fascist slogans captured a substantial number of students, writers and trade union leaders. During the Spanish tragedy and the Munich days, many scions of the British aristocracy enlisted both in the International Brigade (the army of the Comintern in Spain) *and in our intelligence services.*"[18]

Moscow, as Stephen Koch proves, was aggressively waging global war against the world through some very unconventional means. Stalin, as Japan quickly discovered and the US should have, did not discriminate by stopping at the Atlantic or Pacific Ocean:

> Then came America: Bright young people from the Ivy League were the obvious targets. "With the thousands of recruits enlisted under the banner of democracy, the Communist Party OGPU espionage ring in the United States grew much larger and penetrated previously untouched territory. *By carefully concealing their identity, Communists found their way into hundreds of key positions.*" Finally, there was France, in many ways the most thoroughly penetrated of all...[19]

Shortly after walking out of the London Naval Conference, Japan, experiencing many of the same Soviet active-measures within its own borders, joined the Axis alliance.[20] Japan's Imperial Army believed simultaneous Soviet moves in Manchuria provided further justification for the Pact. The great unknown of history may be whether Tokyo could have been kept out of the Axis camp with more positive diplomatic efforts by America and Britain. Shut out of maritime relations with the world's dominant naval powers, Japan took the alternative course of alliance-seeking which, after all, made geostrategic sense as an East Asia counter to Soviet moves in Europe. Hitler and Mussolini welcomed the company.

Japan's observation of Soviet action in Mongolia became a determining factor in its 1937 decision to invade China. As a Pacific war drew closer for the United States, Franklin Roosevelt discovered his staff had independently implemented economic sanctions against Japan. Many injunctions involved badly needed natural resources. Soviet dominance in Mongolia combined with efforts to control Manchuria, threatened Japan's highly industrialized economy. Those turning economic screws in Washington had to know sanctions would force Japan's military hand:

> The consequences for Japan of the economic isolation which such a coalition [British, Dutch and American] would be able to enforce without the moving of a single warship or plane into Japanese-controlled waters would be devastating. The effects would not be immediate, but they would be inexorable. Japan is peculiarly dependent upon uninterrupted economic relations with areas outside the range of her own naval power for the materials necessary to sustain her military efforts and to maintain the living standards and the employment of her people. This is the result of her geographical situation and the nature of her economic life.[21]

An economic strangle-hold of this magnitude is not smart diplomacy unless done for ulterior motives, such as appeasing Stalin. Whitney Griswold explains how perceived mistreatment of Japanese immigrants on Hawaii and the West Coast became an invite for war:

> Complicating all of these problems, darkening the atmosphere in which they were studied, the issue of Japanese immigration hung like a cloud over the Pacific. Exigencies of race relationship and economic competition had made it necessary for the United States to curb the flow of oriental immigrants into its territories. But the methods it had employed in so doing had proved no exception to the law of diminishing returns. They had offended the one nation whose co-operation the success of American diplomacy in other spheres most urgently required. Thus they, too, had impaired the security of the Philippines, the defense of the open door and, for that matter, the preservation of China's territorial integrity – consequences which other no less effective methods might have avoided.[22]

Issues surrounding immigration have roots in the Japanese migration to Hawaii during most of the nineteenth century. By 1886, for example, their numbers comprised 40 percent of the island chain's total population. It is the basis for a letter between Theodore Roosevelt and Mahan in 1897 that describes action to take if confrontation came about over a mass migration of Japanese.[23]

Though relations continued to decline in the decades leading up to World War II, America remained Japan's single largest trade partner. The market provided enormous potential for Japanese business and, in turn, Japan absorbed fifty percent of US exports to the Far East. Economic relations continued unhindered until Franklin Roosevelt's administration. US foreign policy then started clashing with Japan over military behavior and regional expansion efforts. This contact became more aggressive following Japanese withdrawal from Washington and London naval treaties. It also happened to coincide with Roosevelt's cultivation of closer ties to the Soviet Union: "The United States continued to show support for the Soviet Union as pressure between Tokyo and Moscow grew."[24]

Throughout July 1937 the US embassy in Moscow diligently worked to renew a major commercial treaty. The signing ceremony occurred on 04 August.[25] This did not escape the watchful eye of Japanese intelligence. Relations with the USSR were so solid by 1938 that Roosevelt ordered his ambassador to Moscow, Joseph Davies to meet Stalin and devise a plan for military assistance should the Soviets find themselves in a war against Japan.[26] Backing away from Japan, while developing closer ties with Stalin, had been pushed by Harry Hopkins and Harold Ickes Sr., two high-level Roosevelt officials.

Evidence pointing to Soviet manipulation of US – Japan relations has surfaced with increasing frequency in recent years.[27] While US officials stayed busy believing they were helping the Soviets prepare for war with Japan, the Soviets were manipulating Japanese and US policy to ensure the two parties would fight each other on Moscow's terms. Soviet archives and testimony from witnesses confirm, for example, that Harry Bridges, head of the West Coast Longshoreman's Union throughout the 1930s, served as a fully controlled Soviet product. Bridges was tasked with locking down West Coast ports if the US carried out any Pacific naval action not meeting Stalin's approval.[28] The only American foreign policy in the Pacific acceptable to Moscow involved war with Japan, and Soviet-controlled assets within Roosevelt's administration made certain they got their wish. Extent of Soviet control over maritime ports is featured in an anonymous letter sent to J. Edgar Hoover in August 1943. It is highly indicative of the enormous operation underway:

Khejfets – vice-consul in San Francisco, deals with political and
military intelligence on the West Coast of the U.S....has a large
network of agents in the ports and war factories, collects very
valuable strategic material, which is sent by Zubilin to Japan.[29]

What happened with information sent to Japan? Its content
likely involved controlled information disseminated by Soviet
personnel in Tokyo, and designed to assist Japanese naval forces
engaged against the US Pacific Fleet. Soviet moves in China would
benefit by a prolonged conflict between Japan and America. The
contribution by Harry Bridges is clear in an intercepted message from
the Soviet Naval-GRU officer based in Washington, DC. It is a
summary of processes used to smuggle "illegals" off Soviet ships and
through ports at San Francisco and Portland, Oregon. The message
reveals procedures to follow assimilating individuals into society. This
includes passenger train operations, clothing to wear, identification
required, and where security can be expected. Active participation of
dockworkers can be derived from message content.[30] Robert Sherwood
ignites intrigue with a revelation in his publication of Harry Hopkins:

> During the latter part of October [1944], Hopkins heard from General
> Marshall the amazing story of how someone, apparently in the armed
> services, had imparted to Dewey the fact that the United States had
> broken the Japanese codes before Pearl Harbor, and of Marshall's
> urgent message to Dewey that the revelation of this fact would be
> calamitous.[31]

Hopkins proceeded to write a memo to himself concerning
Roosevelt's reaction that his political rival, Thomas Dewey, had been
informed of this potentially devastating information:

> Later that day I repeated this conversation to the President. The
> President was surprised at the action Marshall had taken but
> expressed no criticism of that action. He merely stated that he felt
> confident that Governor Dewey would not, for political purposes,
> give secret and vital information to the enemy. His only other further
> comments were: "My opponent must be pretty desperate if he is even
> thinking of using material like this which would be bound to react
> against him." The President wondered what officer or government
> official had been so faithless to his country as to give Governor
> Dewey the information. To the best of my knowledge the government
> never discovered who gave Governor Dewey this military
> information.[32]

Release of the Venona documents by America's National Security Agency in 1995 reinforces accusations among the political right that Hopkins and others in FDR's administration were active Soviet agents.[33] Hopkins became so influential he selectively spiked cables from Winston Churchill sent for FDR's immediate attention.[34]

Hopkins made a valuable contribution to Stalin's strategic designs in the Pacific. His significance to Soviet Red Army plans would come about in the creation of post-war Europe. Herbert Romerstein and Eric Breindel identify Hopkins in Venona signal traffic as agent "19." Degree of impact this revelation exposes can be found in a message from the Soviet mission in New York and concerns a private meeting between Churchill and Roosevelt to discuss opening a second front in Europe. Hopkins attended and he later forwarded the outcome to his handlers.[35] In his message Hopkins references Henry Wallace, Roosevelt's vice president. He notes Wallace was denied access to information of substantive military information. Suspicion of Wallace belonging to the same Soviet intelligence circle has not been settled.

Hopkins played an important role keeping America and Great Britain from forming a united front against Soviet geostrategic moves in Europe. His choreography is observed in notes taken by then Secretary of the Navy, James Forrestal:

> I met with Averell Harriman and Charles E. Bohlen of the State Department at Harry Hopkins' house. The latter told me he was going to Russia on behalf of the President to try to get some evaluation of the Russian attitude, and to develop their attitude on many questions which at this time it seems difficult to understand, and on which at the present time there seems a danger of a sharp and substantial division between the United States and Russia. Harry said that he was sceptical about Churchill, at least in the particular of Anglo-American-Russian relationship; that he thought it was of vital importance that we not be maneuvered into a position where Great Britain had us lined up with them as a bloc against Russia to implement England's European policy.[36]

The US and Great Britain should have formed a bloc against Stalin's assault on Europe. Distancing US foreign policy from Britain in favor of Soviet efforts would have caused an enormous uproar in any previous administration. It is a slap in the face of every American and British government official who advocated closer relations, most notably Admiral Mahan:

When we begin really to look abroad, and to busy ourselves with our duties to the world at large in our generation – and not before – we shall stretch out our hands to Great Britain, realizing that in unity of heart among the English-speaking races lies the best hope of humanity in the doubtful days ahead.[37]

Britain's long-held foreign policy position denying single state domination over Europe was in jeopardy.

Sea, land, air, and space power work to fulfill requirements demanded of national grand strategy. This is put in place by those creating national policy. It is every patriotic citizen's hope that leaders make proper decisions regarding national security. Colin Gray summarized Britain's foreign policy by noting "British Statesmen believed sea power tends to grow from unbalanced land power. In a sense they saw excessive land power as sea power delayed."[38] The British knew quite well dangers from European domination. Kaiser Wilhelm II provided proof of British concerns early in the twentieth century. Hitler again vindicated that philosophy, and the Soviet Union would have done so by the end of 1945 had allied forces not invaded France in June 1944. The policy decision and national grand strategy design for an amphibious invasion of German-occupied France is based on Gray's comment. That decision had nothing to do with "defeating" Hitler, but it did have everything to do with preventing Stalin and his Red Army machine from overrunning Europe. London's concern remained in existence throughout the twentieth century and on both sides of the Eurasian land mass:

China represents a bridge between East and West. Today, as the result of the emergence of a powerful Soviet Russia, China is also a political and economic arena of the world's two greatest powers, Soviet Russia and America. If China were to become a puppet of the Soviet, which is exactly what a Chinese Communist victory would mean, then Soviet Russia would practically control the continents of Europe and Asia. Domination of so great an expanse, particularly by a totalitarian power, would jeopardize world peace. We were determined to prevent Japan from making China a puppet power. It is believed even more important, if we are to realize our policies with reference to China, that Russia not be permitted to do so.[39]

Japan is the equivalent geostrategic platform toward East Asia as Britain is toward Europe. What would be the outcome had it allied with the United States and United Kingdom, keeping Hitler and Stalin boxed in? In a private conversation James Forrestal had with Joseph Kennedy, who began his tour as United States Ambassador to Great Britain in 1938, Kennedy expressed frustration over Washington's insistence the British get tough with Hitler:

> Kennedy's view: That Hitler would have fought Russia without any later conflict with England if it had not been for Bullitt's [William C. Bullitt, then Ambassador to France] urging on Roosevelt in the summer of 1939 that the German's must be faced down about Poland; neither the French nor the British would have made Poland a cause of war if it had not been for the constant needling from Washington. Bullitt, he said, kept telling Roosevelt that the Germans wouldn't fight, Kennedy that they would, and that they would overrun Europe. Chamberlain, he says, stated that America and the world Jews had forced England into the war. In his telephone conversations with Roosevelt in the summer of 1939 the President kept telling him to put some iron up Chamberlain's backside. Kennedy's response always was that putting iron up his backside did no good unless the British had some iron with which to fight, and they did not...[40]

Soviet penetration efforts throughout American society and government were paying big dividends. The most significant foreign policy act carried out by Roosevelt during his initial year in office involved granting formal diplomatic recognition to the USSR. America's first ambassador to Moscow, ironically, happened to be William Bullitt who, according to Charles E. Bohlan, went above and beyond the call of duty to cultivate US-Soviet relations:

> In those days the ballerinas were given free run of the diplomatic corps, and many temporary liasions were formed. One of the girls had an unrequited passion for Bullitt, and she spent hours talking of her undying love for the ambassador, describing him as her sun, her moon, and her stars."[41]

Maybe Bullitt's better judgment found itself overcome and consumed by blind lust for his ballerina in Moscow. Or, perhaps, it involved very clear NKVD film footage. It would rank among mankind's great tragedies if Bullitt's extracurricular activities played a part in World War II's development and resulting Cold War. The academic accolades heaped upon Roosevelt's "progressive" domestic and foreign policies should be suspect based on an inability to maintain control over those working under his tutelage.

By 1940 Japan believed it to be a victim of double standards. The USSR, which invaded Finland, forcibly annexed Latvia, Estonia, and Lithuania, while carving up Poland with Nazi Germany, suffered no repercussions from Chamberlain, de Gaulle, or Roosevelt. If Great Britain and France believed war worthy of declaring against Nazi Germany for invading Poland, then why was the same not done against the USSR? On the other side of the Asian continent the Soviets were regarded in Tokyo as great a rival as Great Britain, France, or America. Unfortunately, Roosevelt administration foreign policy seemed to be primarily focused on servicing Stalin's needs. World War II became the arena for settling an argument that had long passed that infamous diplomatic point of no return, and it set the course of international relations for over fifty years.

Get Ready

By the final days of World War II American military leaders realized they had been duped by the Soviets, and Great Britain, yet again, would be awarded the diplomatic shaft:

> It is abundantly clear that the Anglo-American coalition was mistaken in its higher strategy during the war toward Russia. That policy was based on two assumptions, both of which can now be proved false: (1) that there was grave danger that Stalin, if not sufficiently supported with materiel and appeased by political concessions, would conclude a separate peace with Germany, as Lenin had done in 1917, and leave the Western Allies holding the bag. (2) That if we treated Russia honourably and generously, Communist hostility to us would be assuaged and Russia would continue to be a dependable ally after victory was achieved. We now know that there was no chance – except in the case of an overwhelming German victory – of the U.S.S.R. concluding a separate peace; and we have bitterly learned that the long-range higher strategy of Communism, its determination to subvert and destroy all governments not dominated by Reds, was only temporarily suspended during the war.[42]

The United States blundered by giving Harry Hopkins free reign to appease Stalin while, at the same time, shunning Churchill's attempt to solidify a British-American alliance. A geostrategic vacuum quickly followed Japan's surrender and this left little breathing room for US Navy officials. The enemy this time included not only a rising Soviet threat, but military budget-chopping mania emanating from members of Congress. Elections were just around the corner and domestic pork was a means to winning. George Baer notes developments underway endangering Mahanian doctrine which was, contrary to some opinion, proven highly effective in World War II:

> The postwar Navy was not prepared for peacetime politics. In part, that was a consequence of Roosevelt's vague postwar policy. Roosevelt's wartime goals of unconditional surrender and alliance solidarity had taken the urgency out of postwar strategic planning. His hazy internationalism suggested order and cooperation, not a reversion to competition in a hostile, fragmented world in which the Navy would defend, as it had for 50 years, the interests of an insular America.[43]

The determined effort by a hard-charging group of naval and government officials saved sea power's position within national grand strategy. Several challenges arose, with budget constraints the most immediate. An isolationist mind-set resurfaced among many of the electorate and their political representatives were feeling heat. The Navy/Marine Corps future appeared dim and fading fast as technologies developed over the course of the war gained relevance. Baer explains how jet aircraft, rocket technology, and atomic bomb were exploited to promote discontinuing naval funding entirely:

> The need to justify itself came upon the Navy with unnerving suddenness and left the service confused. The Navy was hard put to counter the Air Force's appropriation of its most popular concepts. The Navy did not know what to do about its ships, its aircraft, or the atomic bomb, that wonder weapon that was gaining strategic primacy and budgetary advantage.[44]

The newly formed US Air Force eyed USN cash as naval advocates fought hard to incorporate technological assets into their strategic and tactical portfolio. Rather than decrease fleet utility, US Navy leadership successfully added newly acquired technologies to their own political firepower. This quickly paid dividends with the Korean War's start.[45] The survival plan was accomplished in a manner similar to aircraft carrier/naval air proposals decades earlier. Soviet action subconsciously contributed to the cause with extraordinary displays of self-serving behavior. It did not take long to discredit Harry Hopkins and his optimistic comment to Robert Sherwood following the Yalta agreements:

The Russians had proved that they could be reasonable and farseeing and there wasn't any doubt in the minds of the President or any of us that we could live with them and get along with them peacefully for as far into the future as any of us could imagine.[46]

Western attempts to negotiate with civility were met with pompous belligerence by many Soviet diplomats. America's political elite soon realized the only military option to mobile forward presence in times of high-stakes diplomacy came by way of a naval fleet.

Events developing during the closing months and immediately following Japan's surrender revealed the prophetic geostrategic forecasting qualities of Alexis de Tocqueville:

> There are at the present time two great nations in the world, which started from different points, but seem to tend towards the same end. I allude to the Russians and the Americans. Both of them have grown up unnoticed; and while the attention of mankind was directed elsewhere, they have suddenly placed themselves in the front rank among the nations, and the world learned their existence and their greatness at almost the same time.[47]

The idea of rolling back Soviet expansion actually developed before Germany's surrender in 1945. Unfortunately, it did not receive serious consideration until Chiang Kai-shek's eviction from China in 1949. Public anger rapidly ruffled political feathers and then boiled over when North Korea stormed across the 38th Parallel the following year. Plans related to "roll back" were quickly replaced by hope of "containment" as hawkish warnings over the past decade became reality. Policy-makers had contemplated post-war East Asia as early as 1943.[48] Of primary concern to American military planners was Mao Zedong and a large Soviet presence. Richard Aldrich notes the peculiar position of civilian officials and their opposition to military efforts:

> Throughout early 1944, Roosevelt appears to have become increasingly dependent upon OSS for clear intelligence about the situation in China as he pressured Chiang to fight the Japanese. OSS intelligence on Sino-Soviet border incidents in Sinkiang and Mongolia were especially important, suggesting that Chiang had provoked the Soviets and was becoming increasingly anti-Russian. OSS suggested that uncritical support for Chiang would look like backing for internal anti-communism and therefore threaten Soviet-American relations.[49]

The theater commander in China, General Albert Wedemeyer, saw things differently than the open-minded political class. Wedemeyer grew convinced, with plenty of evidence to back his assertion, that the Soviets were intent on a conquest of the entire East Asia region. Plans were drawn during World War II for Japan to act as an operational base to defend Manchuria and Korea from Chinese Communist and Soviet Red Army forces. With Truman's blessing, Wedemeyer created a proposal that envisioned using Kuomintang and Japanese troops to fight alongside American forces when peace terms could be concluded with Emperor Hirohito.[50] Japan's concern over Soviet expansion went back decades. Four possibilities exist for an administration decision not to pursue a united plan against Soviet military conquest of East Asia:

- Soviet supporters serving in the administration had a piece of the White House occupant's ear.
- Washington Europhiles, fearful of the Red Army's power, had an interest seeing the proposal buried in bureaucratic minutia.
- Domestic political support for fighting a war in China with Japan as an ally appeared politically shaky and hard to justify.
- Congressmen were anxious to get hold of the defense budget for pork projects in their districts.

Stalin's water carriers were sufficient to sway White House policy. Political pressure to placate Soviet designs rather than support anti-communist allies turned out to be a disaster. Some officials seemed obsessed with a different view of China's future from what US military leadership was attempting to achieve. Many of these confused souls were later identified in the Venona documents as Soviet-controlled assets.[51] The civilian apparatus in Washington not compromised by Soviet intelligence became more enthralled by European developments. As East Asia burned, Japan's geostrategic importance to mainland politics continued to occupy secondary importance in Washington. This is the mindset sought by Stalin since the dedicated work of Harry Bridges on the West Coast. Fortunately, fantasies of caving in to an oppressive regime did not infect the military leadership:

> The nagging fear was that perhaps the Communists had wormed their way so deeply into our government on both the working and planning levels that they were able to exercise an inordinate degree of power in shaping the course of America in the dangerous postwar era. I could not help wondering and worrying whether we were faced with open

enemies across the conference table and hidden enemies who sat with us in our most secret councils.[52]

A determined effort to deny China, Korea, and Japan the same outcome unfolding in Eastern Europe drove military policy in 1944-1946. China's priority in the diplomatic community lost its status at some point between 1946 and 1949. South Korea would have followed China into bondage if not for pressure on the political right.

US military officials were determined to support Emperor Hirohito in his effort to reform and rebuild Japan. This included defending the nation against Soviet encroachment. Korea is a significant part of that defense perimeter, just as it was for shogunate regimes in an earlier era. A continuous stream of intelligence revealing Soviet designs for the region extended far beyond the Chinese border. This justified preservation of hard fought force projection and logistical island train networks across the Pacific during World War II. The Philippines and Guam became frontline American military assets. Had this network not existed in 1945, Soviet and Communist Chinese forces would have stood a very good chance of overrunning the entire region five years later.

The Dilemma

No military service can provide the mobile forward presence found with naval power. It periodically required an international incident to remind budget-makers the price for not funding a blue-water navy was, politically, far more expensive. An aircraft carrier off the coast of a hostile far-off land is a beautiful thing for civilians barricaded in an embassy, or a politician subjected to public outrage at home. Diplomatic personnel and elected representatives came to appreciate this fact on numerous occasions.

Soviet behavior on land at the close of World War II gave supporting evidence to keep Mahanian doctrine in full operational mode. Ironically, it also justified continuation of Mackinder's geostrategic concepts related to his Midland Ocean theory:

> Western Europe and North America now constitute for many purposes a single community of nations. That fact was first fully revealed when American and Canadian armies crossed the Atlantic to fight in France during the Great War... In the United States the most abundant rainfall and the most productive coalfields are to be found

in the east, but in Europe they are in the west. Thus the west of Europe and the east of North America are physical complements to one another and are rapidly becoming the balanced halves of a single great community.[53]

The Soviet war machine clarified the connection between Mackinder and Mahan. Sea power would, once again, be called on in an effort to save the West from a Eurasian superpower. Doing so required domination and control of Mackinder's Midland Ocean. Regardless of the long-range air force capability hyped on Capital Hill, United States foreign policy required a military stick in the form of forward naval power projection. This made unrestricted access to the sea and overseas allies willing to stand with the US mandatory.

Dominating the sea offered a vital artery to the defense of East Asia and Europe. Colin Gray successfully argues that a forward naval and maritime presence, combined with multi-tasked military installations in strategic locations, guaranteed freedom of travel on the seas and the maintenance of peace through deterrence on land:

> The maritime theory of Western defense says: deter nuclear use by nuclear counterdeterrence; be prepared to fight hard for those continental holdings of the Western coalition that unfortunately are readily accessible to Soviet land power; but emphasize that the Soviet Union cannot necessarily win a war by winning a land campaign in the European region.[54]

Gray explained the problem faced by the Soviet Union during the Cold War when it attempted to devise grand strategy against a seafaring nation such as the United States:

- An inefficient economy.
- Unwilling allies.
- Problems of political legitimacy.
- Landlocked strategic condition.
- Geostrategic position flanked by potential super-states in West and East.
- Vanishing vitality of ideology.
- Safe-guarding society and bureaucracy.[55]

His analysis is accurate from a purely Clausewitzian paradigm. However, these points must not be viewed in the context of Western military strategic thinking. The Soviet paradigm is a complex dilemma that can counter each point. An inefficient economy is a problem for capitalist societies, but not where an iron fist rules. Unwilling allies cannot be considered from a perspective of Western democracy. The USSR had no problem policing satellites with the KGB entrenched throughout societies and governments of puppet regimes.[56] Short of arresting the homeless for vagrancy, few states could act without Soviet permission. The West, however, often preferred blaming these parties over an international incident to avoid directly offending the Soviets. Political legitimacy did not matter in communist society, and this is seen today in blatant totalitarian states such as Cuba and North Korea.

Revelations of operational coordination among nations allied with the Soviet Union is destroying opinion that those countries were uncontrolled loose cannons. Though it is convenient to blame rogue states for the sake of maintaining "superpower harmony," it is no coincidence that the level of activity against Western interests always increased over unfavorable policy implementation. President Reagan's "Star Wars" speech and the Pershing and Cruise missile deployments in December 1983 are perfect examples. A strategic analysis of violent acts instigated by Soviet puppets that year shows clear culpability and direction by the USSR. Examples include the well-timed Cuban-inspired regime change in Grenada with Syrian activity in Lebanon. America's invasion of Grenada and simultaneous Syria-sanctioned bombing of the US Marine barracks in Beirut must not be parceled as unrelated.[57] Both transpired just as US Navy officials prepared for a major Sixth Fleet aircraft carrier turnover in the Mediterranean Sea.

Libya, yet another Soviet client state fulfilling its master's desire, compounded the problem for the US Sixth Fleet throughout 1983. Libyan intervention in Chad provided a constant diversion during the summer and distracted assets away from more pressing matters, such as quickly unfolding events in Lebanon.[58] The Soviets, not to be outdone by minions, contributed by downing KAL 007 over the Sea of Japan in September, seven weeks prior to the Beirut bombing. An upswing in terror attacks against NATO countries came from state-sponsored/supported terror groups such as Islamic Jihad, German Red Army Faction, Italian Red Brigades, Irish Republican Army, and a host of Latin American and Palestinian groups.[59]

The crowning glory for Soviet Bloc coordination came in November when a North Korean assassination team murdered the bulk of South Korean government officials in Rangoon, Burma: "It is rare to find such a clear example of an act of state."[60] Arnold Beichman, considering the USSR's ability to operate on multiple fronts and in unconventional ways, accurately predicted Soviet bloc actions:

> Sometime this year, when the cruise and Pershing II missiles are due for deployment in Western Europe, the Soviet Union (with or without an ailing Yuri Andropov) will do something that will precipitate a confrontation between the two superpowers. The confrontation will be one for which American public opinion will be ill-prepared.[61]

Each event managed to divert US naval forces from other commitments in order to support rapidly unfolding operations.[62]

The USSR did a phenomenal job creating a buffer around its perimeter with satellite states. This included the People's Republic of China for those not accepting a "Sino-Soviet split," or the political maneuvering of a perceived Tito-Stalin/Khrushchev break:

> In general, the shifting of forces should be done secretly and swiftly. Ingenious devices such as making a noise in the east while attacking in the west, appearing now in the south and now in the north, hit-and-run and night action should be constantly employed to mislead, entice and confuse the enemy.[63]

The highly touted disengagement between the People's Republic of China and Soviet Union is based, in large part, on information fed to the West by those governments and their own propaganda organs. The West's ability to consume this line is a fantastic example of gullibility: "If circumstantial evidence for the direction of international policies among ruling and non-ruling communist parties by the Soviets has long been abundantly available, why has the opposite conclusion been so prevalent?"[64] John Lewis Gaddis, while following standard procedure of a Yugoslav break with the USSR, manages to make an interesting observation:

> Tito's complaints about the Soviet-Yugoslav relationship were no more serious than those that arose routinely between London, Paris, and Washington: the British and the French frequently challenged American priorities with respect to the treatment of Germany, the terms of economic assistance, and the need for military protection.[65]

Perception of a split created profound strategic opportunities for the USSR, Warsaw Pact, and Third World puppets.[66] Yugoslavia provided a channel for technological transfers to the communist alliance. Western governments furnished technology, trade, and economic aide to Tito under an optimistic mantra that it built a wedge against the Soviets. Economic vitality did not concern East Bloc leaders. Regimes could play loose with facts to deceive the West without worry of a popular uprising over inadequate supplies of goat's milk, designer jeans, or "male-enhancement drugs." Safeguarding society and the bureaucracy was as easy as executing troublemakers in the basement of Lubyanka.

Soviet sustainability would seem to be a truly daunting task considering its border perimeter. This problem existed for numerous powerful states throughout history. It would be foolish to believe Soviet strategic analysis never took this problem under consideration. They of all people are well aware of historical lessons.[67] Geostrategic destiny confounded Russian leaders since 1717 when Peter the Great sent 4,000 troops on a one-way journey to Turkmenistan. While searching for an overland military route to India, his entire expedition got chopped to pieces by the Khan of Khiva's army.[68] Identical geostrategic concerns faced by Russia on land apply to an island nation surrounded by the sea. The difference, of course, involves those instruments applied to deal with specific topography.

The advent of air power, followed by space power, brought about new methods for fulfilling national grand strategy. Border size suddenly began to appear less problematic as air and space power assets were incorporated into Soviet defenses.[69] A number of resources played supporting roles. This included a large KGB border guard element and a population aware of the price for ignoring territorial infringement. The USSR's talent at border security far surpasses the US at controlling its own southern border with Mexico. Evidence is readily available from witnessing an uncontrolled mass of humanity entering the United States, verses the number that attempted to leave the USSR or Warsaw Pact client states. The Berlin Wall's trigger-happy border guards were not shooting at people entering, but those trying to escape.

Human Resources

Unlike totalitarian regimes, political leaders in a constitutional republic are highly sensitive to casualties. This risk-averse mindset places them at a considerable disadvantage: "Half a million people can demonstrate in Central Park for a nuclear freeze, while eleven members of a week-old Soviet independent peace movement are harassed, arrested for 'hooliganism,' and have their leader dispatched to a psychiatric hospital."[70] The West has an added burden of a free press that can be used by an adversary to influence news reporting. Without a declaration of war, US government officials cannot prevent dissemination of information deemed harmful or designed to advance the enemy's strategic advantage. World War II is the last time media controls were enacted, and also the last time America won a war.

Minimizing casualties has been a driving force of recently developed military technology. During Hannibal's land campaign on the Italian peninsula Rome lost over 150,000 men in just three battles.[71] All three; Cannae, River Trebia, and Lake Thrasymene took place within weeks of each other. It is impossible to imagine the media frenzy and domestic political uproar had such figures occurred at any time during the Cold War. This sensitivity drove policy-makers to wonder if the West was willing to fight for their cause:

> Was it not conformable, you sr. with the laws of history that a great society, such as is the Western World of our day, forming in itself a slice of civilization, should become demilitarised as its development proceeded? Had not the phenomenon been seen to happen in the Roman world? The longer this civilization lasted, the less inclined did its members become to take up arms. The military calling, which had been in early days the natural vocation of every adult man – as among all the primitive peoples, such as the Iroquois, the Zulus, the Abyssinians, it is seen to be – became in the end a specialized and discredited profession.[72]

Problems associated with sustaining an all-volunteer force have dominated modernization programs in numerous ways. Concern over adequate manpower needs drives pursuit of such things as combat robots and drones. Willingness to fight is a power resource influential enough to undermine policy objectives. John Morgan and Anthony McIvor argue that it can be the reason why a decisive victory is achieved or lost:

> From the individual war fighter to the resolve of a nation, will is often the deciding factor in combat and war. The outnumbered Spartans who faced Xerxes at Thermopylae, the colonists who faced the might of the British Empire, and Admiral William F. "Bull" Halsey's forces at Guadalcanal all proved that victory often goes to the side with stronger will.[73]

The United States Navy has managed to maintain a global forward presence by dispatching fleets around the world. Allies assist the US in meeting numerous maritime responsibilities. America's military is able to go anywhere, at any time, from any place to accomplish their objective. This had vital importance throughout the Cold War. The US Navy is a major contributor with its fleet structure. The 3rd and 7th Fleets are assigned to serve in the Pacific Ocean. The 7th Fleet primarily covers the western Pacific region. It can also serve other parts of the Pacific or Indian Ocean if needed. The 3rd Fleet maintains a presence throughout the Pacific region, while the 2nd serves in the Atlantic. Since the 1979-80 forced confiscation of sovereign US territory and hostages in Iran, the 5th Fleet in the Persian Gulf has gradually assumed a greater role. The Mediterranean 6th Fleet was traditionally more active because of its proximity to flash-points. This made it a prime objective on Soviet target acquisition lists.

The popular argument against aircraft carriers involves cost verses life expectancy. This comparison is manifestly wrong in a context of all-out global war. With the exception of total war in the modern nuclear era, an aircraft carrier battle group is fully capable of defending itself. If superpower war on a worldwide scale did get unleashed, a battle group's primary mission is to send all aircraft off the carrier's flight deck. Then they are instructed to proceed toward a predetermined target as quick as possible (also known as an Alpha Strike). Once the carrier's mission is accomplished by discharging those aircraft, then what happens afterwards is not relevant in the grand scheme of a third world war.

Chapter Eleven

The Outer Limits

"We are taught nothing on this subject, by reflection, that is not entirely confirmed by observation."
- Jean-Jacques Rousseau

Western use of a containment policy against the Soviet Union resulted from a haughty idea that, by keeping the monster caged, it would eventually heel or die: "Dynamic containment is not cheap, but neither is running the Soviet empire."[1] While success can be debated, as it should considering the spotty record and current global political landscape, there were three regions where actions reflecting Mackinder's heartland theory maintained good relations with Mahan's doctrine of maritime supremacy. Unfortunately, as Everett Dolman alludes, victory for the West is never guaranteed:

> Mackinder's world view divided the globe into three primary regions: the heartland or pivot area; the *inner crescent* comprised of the marginal lands around the heartland's periphery (including Western Europe, the Middle East, Indian subcontinent, and China); and the *outer crescent*, the great islands and island continents separated from the heartland and inner crescent by water (including the entire Western Hemisphere, Britain, Japan, and Australia). Crucial to Mackinder's strategy for Britain was the notion that if a state desired control but could not physically occupy the critical keys to geodetermined power, *then it must deny control of those areas to its adversaries.* So long as the peoples of the outer crescent could prevent any one state from uniting the heartland, their independence was assured, but should they fail to do so, the military juggernaut of a united heartland would be destined to rule the Earth.[2]

It is this view that drove Cold War policy against Soviet and Communist Chinese expansion for fifty years. Danger for the West is found in a defense model that assumed the Sino-Soviet bloc would follow international laws of fair play. Without all parties agreeing to abide by identical rules, catchword phrases such as "containment," "détente," and "peaceful coexistence" simply become good political rhetoric for sedating the masses. Soviet and Communist Chinese government leaders must have looked on in amusement at such credulity. Winning in global politics to them involves whatever is necessary. The Soviet Union managed to geostrategically undermine the US vis-à-vis Cuba in similar fashion to the West using Great Britain's position facing Europe, and Japan's in relation to Asia. Cuba became a spear in the heart of the Monroe Doctrine, and its impact on US statecraft gradually worsened for various interests in the Western Hemisphere.[3] Ronald Reagan's doctrine of support to groups opposed to Soviet expansion was a noble cause but, as Robert Conquest notes, it found powerful political resistance among well financed left-wing individuals and movements inside both NATO countries and the US:

> We have spoken earlier of the mental quirks which led a section of those Westerners critical of their own society to temper the wind to the failings of that society's enemies. This applied, of course, not only to comparing Western social faults to the imaginary social triumphs of the Soviet Union but also to the Soviets' supposedly more acceptable foreign policies. A search of Nexus of the use in American newspapers of the word "bellicose" of various leaders in the post-1979 period gives: Reagan – 211 times, Thatcher – 41, Brezhnev -5; and this in a period covering the Afghan war. As to those still further out, I noted (a perfectly ordinary example) the Catholic bishop of Stockton, California, bad-mouthing his own government as totally untrustworthy, but urging as a solution to our international troubles the reposing of total trust in – the Soviet leaders![4]

Social pressure from Lenin's "useful idiots" had the potential of undermining efforts to roll-back Soviet and PRC expansion; hence the concept of containment serving as a last resort. John Koehler identifies events in Chile during the early 1970s as a classic example:

> Allende's Marxist fervor and the fact that Chile's Communist Party was the largest and best organized in South America made Chile a perfect target for expansion of the Soviet bloc in that part of the world. From a geopolitical view, the possible establishment of a Moscow-financed communist dictatorship presented a threat to the national security of the United States. Those who were reviled for their support of such Chilean political parties as the Christian Democrats were proved correct by subsequent events.
> Allende was elected president of Chile, and the East German regime was ready to lend him Stasi support. Within weeks, a dozen

specialists in covert operations and guerrilla warfare were dispatched to Santiago under diplomatic cover. They were joined by other Eastern-bloc trainers, including officers from Czechoslovakia, as they set up camp near Valparaiso. The Soviets furnished the weapons and prefabricated huts. The "pupils" were young Marxist radicals of the Manuel Rodriguez Revolutionary Front.[5]

It should not be a surprise to question which side did the containing; the West containing the East, or vice versa? The parade of Western leftists backing Allende and Soviet operations, for example, is impressive.[6] Several serving the communist operation thirty-five years ago were behind recent efforts to jail Augusto Pinochet who, many argue, saved Chile from Soviet bondage and a far greater massacre.

East Asia

A profoundly pivotal relationship between the United States and Japan during the transition between World War II and the Cold War served both nations well. This geostrategic shift in preparation for the Cold War is dramatic for numerous reasons. Both countries were strong competitors at various times during the first half of the twentieth century. They then became staunch allies and remain so today. Roots of their previous adversarial relationship originated, in part, from the Soviet Union. Causes for their close relationship since the end of World War II is also a contribution of the Soviet Union. Japan's archipelago is the geostrategic pivot-point between the Western Hemisphere and Asia. This served a critical role as a launch pad for power projection in East Asia throughout the Cold War.

Japan and the 7th Fleet have a distinction for possessing the only American aircraft carrier battle group home-ported on foreign soil. This is a direct reflection of priorities given to that region of the world. Recognition came about at a high price on Korea's peninsula. Three overriding conditions dominate all rationale for maintaining a forward naval presence in Japan. The treaty terminating World War II resulted in the United States assuming a significant part of Japan's defense posture.[7] America's disregard toward empire building is evident from Japanese insistence on ignoring US prodding to reconstruct a military.[8] This left the United States shouldering the brunt of Japan's military needs. Unfortunately, many shakers and movers in Truman's post-World War II administration seemed to give that responsibility little care. Virtually all of Japan's oil comes from overseas by way of ocean transport. Denying access to this resource would be catastrophic for Japan's economy. This alone rationalizes rebuilding a naval fleet. Instead, Japan insisted on a post-WWII constitution renouncing militarism and abstinence from an armed force with offensive capability. As a result, the US fills Japan's power projection needs.

The second reason for a US naval presence parallels the first. World events wasted no time testing US resolve in fulfilling its security commitment to Japan. Soviet passive-aggressive behavior in the north and west continuously challenged Japanese and American defense planners.[9] US officials began expressing unease during the closing months of World War II.[10] Accusations raged among Truman administration officials over a perceived disregard for Asia and preoccupation with Europe. Ironically, Douglas Macdonald argues it was America's allies in Europe that sounded the greatest alarm:

> British and other allied threat perceptions were often higher than U.S. fears prior to the Korean War, both in Europe and in the periphery. This phenomenon cannot be explained by reference to internal U.S. psychological or political processes. Indeed, in congruence with traditionalist interpretations, recent British historical works emphasize that prior to the Korean War, the Foreign Office saw the United States as too sanguine about the Soviet bloc threat and felt it necessary to prod the Americans into action in Asia and elsewhere. Fears of Soviet bloc expansion became widespread among the other Western powers also, especially following the Czech coup in February 1948, the onset of the Berlin Blockade in June, and the beginning of the collapse of the Chinese Nationalist armies in the fall of that year.[11]

America did have an inherent domestic problem with money, military manpower, and an isolationist mentality with links to Soviet agitation. All of this could have been overcome with stronger political leadership. These shortcomings furthered perceptions of ineptness inside Truman's administration as communist revolutionaries, with assistance from the Soviets, dispatched Chiang Kai-shek to Formosa:

> Events of the past two years demonstrate the futility of appeasement based on the hope that the strongly consolidated forces of the Soviet Union will adopt either a conciliatory or a compromising attitude, except as tactical expedients. Soviet practice in the countries already occupied or dominated completes the mosaic of aggressive expansion through ruthless secret police methods and through an increasing

political and economic enslavement of peoples. Soviet literature, confirmed repeatedly by Communist leaders, reveals a definite plan for expansion far exceeding that of Nazism in its ambitious scope and dangerous implications. Therefore in attempting a solution to the problem presented in the Far East, as well as in other troubled areas of the world, every possible opportunity must be used to seize the initiative in order to create and maintain bulwarks of freedom.[12]

US Secretary of Defense James Forrestal, General Douglas MacArthur, Commander, Far Eastern Command, and others firmly believed events unfolding in East Asia were a result of American bungling.[13] Forrestal, just before his unfortunate fall out a sixteenth-floor window at the Bethesda Naval Hospital in Maryland, proclaimed American troops would perish on Korean soil as a result of foreign policy neglect.[14] His prediction soon came true. Unease became so prevalent that many anti-communist hawks in Truman's administration were working behind the scenes to recruit challengers for the next election. General Wedemeyer, having personally witnessed the catastrophic events in China and subsequent disregard in Washington, reflected growing outrage in a personal letter to General MacArthur:

It is very significant that in a more recent Gallup Poll involving you and Truman (although you have not been back in the States for several years) you were accorded an almost even chance with the President. I predict that, should you return early next spring, you will be acclaimed by a vast majority as the logical man to be president in this critical period of our history. I have heard so many men whose judgment I value highly, and whose integrity I respect, state emphatically that the American people would enthusiastically rally behind your leadership.

Regardless of personal reaction, I believe that you should carefully weigh these developments from a sense of duty. I know Bob and Martha Taft quite well and I am quite certain that he would throw his support in your direction. Also ex-governor Martin, now senator from Pennsylvania, and speaker Joe Martin as well as ex-president Hoover are loyal and enthusiastic supporters. You enjoy the confidence of the American people and, although the task would be difficult, nevertheless if your health maintains, I hope that you will consider the post.[15]

As is often the case with matters of national security in multi-party democracies during times of peace, war on the Korean peninsula resulted from alarm bells setoff by military leaders and ignored by a political establishment preoccupied with more critical matters such as spending. The initial rout of US and South Korean troops exposed a need for rapid regional response forces, and the precarious situation with military preparedness. Korea quickly brought a sobering realization that the state of affairs in America's force structure was exactly what Forrestal had persistently warned about. Pork fever in Congress got immediately cured with a vaccine of realism and the burden of responsibilities going with global leadership.

War in Korea exposed complexities behind conducting rapid reaction operations, especially when the bulk of overseas forces are dedicated to defending Europe. A lack of readiness and weakness of South Korean defenses was viewed as an embarrassment by US hardliners. Vulnerability of the Japanese island chain exposed itself when attempts were made to rotate troops from bases in Japan to Korea. Concern the People's Republic of China would use war as a diversion to move the US Army out of Japan permeated strategic discussions. If Korea is a distraction for something bigger, as the theory went, then the archipelago, and possibly Formosa were likely targets. An invasion by Mao's so-called "volunteers" with, of course, active assistance from the Soviet Red Army could not be prevented.[16]

Charges against MacArthur's prosecution of the war center on his effort to remove enemy forces from the entire peninsula. This, as the argument goes, left Mao no alternative but to intervene militarily. United Nations Forces (UNF) holding a position on the Yalu River and Chinese border was unacceptable.[17] North Korea's geography, and the strategic location of Chinese troops left MacArthur little choice. Government officials, for the first time in American history, were proactively expressing understanding for acts by an enemy gainfully employed in battle killing American troops. This attitude became prevalent during the remainder of the twentieth century.

Administration officials refused MacArthur's plan to deny Chinese Communist Forces (CCF) access to the peninsula by destroying all the Yalu bridges crossing into Korea. If allowed, it would have seriously jeopardized Mao's massive counteroffensive. In a haunting forecast of things to come in Vietnam, MacArthur could not allow his pilots to pursue retreating enemy aircraft back across the Chinese border after engaging them in aerial combat over Korea:

> I realized for the first time that I had actually been denied the use of
> my full military power to safeguard the lives of my soldiers and the

safety of my army. To me, it clearly foreshadowed a future tragic situation in Korea, and left me with a sense of inexpressible shock.[18]

Nobody seemed to notice that containment policy failed quite early in the 1950s. Justifying and excusing acts by communist tyrants is bad enough; criticizing decisions by American military leaders who are attempting to liberate humans from bondage is, for lack of a better word, perplexing.

The counteroffensive excuse commonly given for Mao's decision to invade across the Yalu cannot explain the large mass of People's Liberation Army (PLA) forces already in North Korea prior to the war even starting. Recently declassified records from Soviet archives show both Soviet and PRC culpability behind the invasion of South Korea, and they were totally prepared to fight World War III:

> The USA cannot allow itself to be involved in a large-scale war. Consequently, China will be involved in conjunction with the USSR as we are tied together by our mutual assistance treaty. Shall we be afraid of this? To my mind we shall not, because together we will be stronger than the USA and England. Other capitalist states, except for Germany, which cannot provide any help to the USA, constitute no serious military force. If a war is inevitable, let it come now and not several years later when Japanese militarism is restored as an ally of the USA.[19]

America's military presence in Japan served as an insurance policy against a flourishing of revenge following World War II. Widespread anger in countries occupied by Japan's Imperial Army put the United States in an uncomfortable position of intermediary. Many of Japan's enemies later became adversaries of the US, further complicating arbitration efforts. This resulted in good communist propaganda for stirring up the masses. A show of force has been required to keep highly emotional parties in a pseudo-passive state.

Many East Asia governments support a US presence to provide that third party interference if and when needed. This was successfully done throughout the Cold War by the naval presence in Japan. As a consolation, the US did receive a military benefit by maintaining assets on Japanese soil. Geostrategically, Japan served as a deterrent and US offensive forces on the archipelago would benefit operationally if mainland action was required. This reasoning drove prudent application of X Corps and the Eighth Army during Korean War.[20]

East Asia's political environment following Japan's surrender illustrates the complexity of national grand strategy. National grand strategy's role in implementing policy involves identifying, developing, accumulating, and distributing all assets needed to fulfill policy goals. Liddell Hart provides a description of national grand strategy that helps explain many problems faced by the US following World War II:

> The role of grand strategy – higher strategy – is to coordinate and direct all the resources of a nation, or band of nations, towards the attainment of the political object of the war – the goal defined by fundamental policy.[21]

Hart's definition is a close comparison to Geoffrey Sloan's earlier explanation. Flexibility required for national grand strategy's success could be met if Hart used "objectives" rather than "object of the war." This provides a basis for extension of Clausewitz's axiom "Once the expenditure of effort exceeds the value of the political object, the object must be renounced and peace must follow."[22] Michael Howard's reference to General MacArthur's farewell address is a fine link connecting the comments by Hart and Clausewitz:

> A theater commander (he informed the Senate after his dismissal) is not merely limited to the handling of his troops; he commands the whole area, politically, economically and militarily. At that stage of the game when politics fails and the military takes over, you must trust the military. . . . I do unquestionably state that when men become locked in battle, that there should be no artifice under the name of politics which should handicap your own men, decrease their chances for winning, and increase their losses.[23]

Howard proceeds by noting how panic set in among political elites over MacArthur's blunt talk. Some claimed to detect a promotion of the atomic option.[24] Revisionist history is worth considering if US forces had used atomic weapons while holding a clear edge. Would mankind been spared the ravages of the following fifty years? Would the People's Republic of China been replaced by a multi-party democracy, saving over 75 million Chinese from Mao's Marxist schemes?

Howard notes a positive outcome from Korea may have been Clausewitz's reemergence following decades of Jominian dominance in US military academies.[25] Though a coordinated and gradual transformation had been in the works since World War I, events in

Korea expedited that change. Unfortunately for MacArthur, while the military stayed busy reorienting itself with Clausewitz, the Washington elite became totally disconnected from any comprehension of Chinese strategy: "To put a rein on an able general while at the same time asking him to suppress a cunning enemy is like tying up the Black Hound of Han and then ordering him to catch elusive hares."[26]

A powerful mixture of sea, land, and air power deployed with success during the Vietnam War. Military supremacy of a geographic region now involves doing the same in another. Sea and land domination, for example, often require securing the atmosphere above. Though it cannot be physically held, air and space are territories worth exerting control over. Holding the area above the physical element of land and water makes it possible to dictate a lot of what is going on below. Level of control may be total, while at other times just enough flexibility is allowed to achieve specific tactical objectives.

Vietnam became another proving ground showing how atmospheric domination assists in sea and land control. General William Westmoreland's description of the North Vietnamese Army's siege at Khe Sanh, South Vietnam in 1968 is telling of this new era:

> The thing that broke their back basically was the fire of the B-52s. Now yes, we did have additional firepower. We were putting in around 100 TAC air sorties a day. We had sixteen 175-mm guns of the US Army that were moved within range of Khe Sanh base and they fired a number of rounds each day and they did an excellent job but the big gun, the heavyweight of fire power, was the tremendous tonnage of bombs dropped by our B-52s. Without question the amount of fire power put on the piece of real estate exceeded anything that had ever been seen before in history by any foe and the enemy was hurt, his back was broken by air power.[27]

Control on the ground, compliments of the B-52 workhorse, resulted from US air superiority.[28] Those B-52s would have a more difficult time penetrating enemy air space and hitting their target area with a sky full of MiG- 25 aircraft.

More recent experiences in Afghanistan and Iraq showed the B-52 still capable of rattling enemy nerves. A note of caution is warranted for US military and strategic planners. The Royal Afghan Air Force (RAAF) and Mother of All Air Forces (MAAF) were not in operation. It is no guarantee that future conflicts will not involve formidable foes possessing enough assets to challenge air superiority:

"Air power had a field day: no air opposition, poor enemy anti-aircraft and poor radar. If we draw too-firm conclusions, based on these conditions, the boys may have very unpleasant surprises when heavy opposition comes along."[29]

The ability to quickly dispatch Taliban resistance in Afghanistan, and Saddam Hussein in Iraq, brings up questions concerning problems during the Vietnam War. South Vietnam involved a vastly intense effort to permanently discredit America's military institutions. Jeff Huber, in a manner akin to the American press corps, uses the Vietnam War as part of four examples showing why Carl von Clausewitz caused the bulk of military difficulties over the past 50 years.[30] The US military, however, was not the problem alluded to by Huber and other critics. US forces did their job. The great mistake of the conflict involved micro-managing a monumental effort from Washington, with a fair number of media elites keen on witnessing a policy failure.[31]

The Vietnam War's most important accomplishment is that it proved what results when bureaucrats and politicians carry out battle management from far away lands. This sorry practice evolved from concern over Soviet and PRC sensitivities. US infatuation with statistics and computer modeling came into existence during this time. The roots of dependency originated with Robert McNamara, then Secretary of Defense (SECDEF). John Tower argues that his insistence on quantifying military operations, while catching John Kennedy and Lyndon Johnson's admiration, was discouraging to the realist camp:

> McNamara thought he was smarter than all the generals and all the GIs. He attempted to quantify the unquantifiable, to fine-tune war, the crudest of all enterprises. McNamara thought like a technocrat and business executive. There were statistics and computer readouts to justify every move. Anecdotal evidence, like reports from the field that the rules of engagement were permitting the enemy to operate out of sanctuaries off-limits to U.S. bombers, was discounted as being without scientific merit.[32]

Attempting to "quantify the unquantifiable" is evident throughout government today. It has done an admirable job of boosting the careers of statisticians and political economists. Quantification methods are analytical tools worth considering to a degree but, in Clausewitzian fashion, they implode upon entering the arena of human culture and morality. John Lehman adds fuel to McNamara's fire:

Although Robert McNamara brought some much-needed budgetary discipline to the Pentagon process, he also brought one of the great heresies of our time, the cult of "systems analysis." Putting some tough restraints on the infinite desire of the uniformed services to develop quicker, slicker, and thicker weapons is one of the greatest management tasks of the civilian leadership of the Pentagon. The tools of empirical analysis can be very useful in providing a framework for making such judgments. Unfortunately, such useful tools once set in motion within the government bureaucracy are very often carried to absurd extremes, and this is exactly what happened to systems analysis in the 1960s and 1970s in the Pentagon. Instead of a tool, it *became* the decision process.[33]

McNamara's techniques would be better served in the Office of Management and Budget (OMB). Since President Carter's final budget of $600,000,000,000 in 1980, the amount has climbed 400% in twenty-five years. This is a 16% annual rate of growth. America's federal debt alone at the start of Fiscal Year 2008 surpassed $9,000,000,000,000. The rising red ink meter spins at a rate faster than the eye can see. 2008's figure is a 900% increase over 1980's total debt.[34]

Federal debt does not include state and local governments, which have similar strains on their budget. Adding personal debt by individual citizens paying the government's tab - which includes home mortgages, auto loans, education loans, and credit card debt - shows a nation entering bankruptcy. A family of four making $110,000/year in California witness 42% of income going to various forms of taxation.[35] This leaves a net sum of $65,000. This is not reassuring for a high cost-of-living state where housing alone can easily consume over $48,000 of annual income. Socialist cries for debt relief to Third World countries by wealthy rock stars leaves American taxpayers asking, "With what?"

An enormous number of US military successes took place during the Vietnam War. An equal number of times saw US forces pulled from the brink of victory for questionable political purposes. The Tet offensive in 1968 is an example of a mainstream media bent on manipulating public opinion. Contrary to reports by America's "most trusted news figure," Walter Cronkite, Tet was a smashing success for US and South Vietnamese forces. The Vietcong were annihilated and only managed to survive as a political entity because their ranks were rebuilt with North Vietnamese Army (NVA) troops. That is not the message beamed to the folks back home.

There were numerous occasions when North Vietnam came within days of unconditional surrender. Washington's political elite, in routine fashion, always forced a military pull-back at that "decisive" moment. The Phoenix program, which is today demonized as symbolic of gruesome American behavior, succeeded at eradicating Vietcong and undercover NVA political bullies busy intimidating South Vietnamese villagers. Those targeted by Phoenix personnel were not innocent villagers marked for cold-blooded execution by a supposedly out-of-control CIA. Targets were highly trained communist operatives. It is a tragic and uncomfortable reality that people do, unfortunately, die in war. This is something the press is incapable of grasping.

America's closing chapter of a presence in South Vietnam consisted of the political leadership folding its hand and going home. South Vietnam is yet another news flash for a growing list of historical examples where America's supposedly enormous power did not get its way in the world. A contemporary paradigm can be found with US frustration over the international community's support in Iraq. Lack of persistent US support for allies in various regions around the world leaves many wondering if that superpower reputation is a mischaracterization. Though it may have been decades ago, America's decision to abandon South Vietnam has not been forgotten by any of the few remaining democracies surrounding the "Socialist Republic of Vietnam." South Vietnam fell into a category of expendability. Asian allies were treated to an appalling opera of indifference and betrayal. Anton Nugroho gives evidence that a politically weak stomach and ability to turn on friends is not just an issue for the American public:

> U.S. neutrality in the South China Sea probably works in favor of China. The lack of U.S. reaction to Chinese provocations in Mischief Reef, for example – even though Washington has a defense pact with Manila – sent the wrong signal to Beijing. A similar message was sent in 1974, when another U.S. ally, the Republic of Vietnam, was overrun in the Paracels. It is equally unlikely that Washington would come to Indonesia's defense if the PRC made a move on the Natunas.[36]

Many of these regional states look at America's Cold War record and wonder if they are considered expendable by Washington's standard. Once Richard Nixon had been dispatched from the Oval Office over a purposely inflated, two-bit Watergate burglary, North Vietnam's government made its move on South Vietnam. The US

Congress assisted in this offensive by cutting off military aid to the South Vietnamese government. They also failed to support Nixon's agreement to return if South Vietnam were invaded. The communist dictatorship of North Vietnam, seeing this as a signal from their friends on Capital Hill, were able to reengage and take Saigon without concern for resumed bombing of Hanoi.

Events surrounding the Vietnam War were far outside limits of Clausewitzian doctrine. This included bombing missions with orders to avoid SAM sites because of their location; and a well-coordinated foreign inspired anti-war movement on the home front. Both were tragically destructive to the war effort but too often ignored as collateral damage serving the enemy. Sadly, the body count of lives lost from pursuing a communist utopia in Southeast Asia came in at around ten million thanks, in large measure, to the Western press and political left. The Cold War's passive nature continued.

Caribbean Sea

Each nation has unique geographic features impacting their policymaking decisions. These policy choices are then set forth in national grand strategy's operating arena where resources determine the strength and appropriate application of each power generator. Great Britain, based on its geographic destiny, became a maritime power in order to survive. Achieving this advantage, along with acquisition of technological advances (a fluid power resource), made Great Britain a powerful "aircraft carrier aimed at the heart of Europe." Britain's geographic position has prevented European domination by a single tyrant. The infuriated dictator honor roll is long thanks to that watchful eye off the northwestern shore.

Just as island nations of the United Kingdom and Japan provide leverage over their neighboring continent, the same applies to Cuba in relation to North and South America. Mahan's remarks over Cuba's geographic importance remains consistent, further indicating a far-sighted vision that America's Cold War adversary, the Soviet Union, took great care to understand:

> Cuba has no possible rival in her command of [the] Yucatan Passage just as she has no competitor in point of natural strength and resources, for control of the Florida Strait which connects the Gulf of Mexico with the Atlantic.[37]

This quote held its value throughout the Cold War and remains significant today, especially now that the People's Republic of China is positioned to influence transit through the Panama Canal:

> U.S. imperialism is the most ferocious enemy of the people of the entire world. It has not only committed grave acts of aggression against the Panamanian people, and painstakingly and stubbornly plotted against socialist Cuba, but has continuously been plundering and oppressing the people of the Latin American countries and suppressing the national-democratic revolutionary struggles there.[38]

Harold Rood reapplied Mahan's geostrategic view to the Cuban Missile Crisis of 1962 with some disturbing possibilities:

> It would be dangerous to suppose that the intrinsic importance of Cuba and the seas it helps contain would have escaped the consideration of those abroad who interest themselves in the strategic circumstances of the United States.[39]

What happened to geostrategic thinking inside John F. Kennedy's administration during this period of high-stakes confrontation? Did Soviet planners have bigger ideas for the island nation? Were those famous missiles simply decoys used in fulfilling other strategic designs? It is not luck that consistently allows Russian minds to rule in chess, the world's ultimate game of strategy.

Great Britain repeatedly showed geostrategic advantages that go with possessing an island base off a continental coast where threats consistently emerge. US military planners discovered during the twentieth century a multitude of opportunities available with this resource positioned in an adversary's backyard. Likewise, gaining a foothold in the underbelly of America offers many opportunities. A large Soviet presence in Cuba is an "aircraft carrier aimed at the heart of America." It is the Kremlin's ultimate fantasy for several reasons:

1. The Soviet Union is in position to potentially control access to and from the Caribbean Sea region.

Mahan warned of Cuba's value to foreign powers hostile to America. His map of the four shipping lanes existing between Panama, US Gulf ports, and the Atlantic Ocean is sobering in an era of precision-guided missiles.[40] Distance from Cuba to Mexico's Yucatan peninsula is less than 200 miles. The gap between Key West, Florida and Cuba is 90 miles. No vessel can depart from a US port along the Gulf without passing through these locations. Acquisition of another island takes care of all traffic destined to or from the Atlantic Ocean. Haiti, if it could be allied with Cuba, would be considered a ripe plum worth picking. It is 100 miles to the east of Cuba and less than 500 miles north of Venezuela. The Dominican Republic would be next to fall. Political control of Cuba, Haiti, and Venezuela provides an axis of evil spanning all sea lanes into and out of the Caribbean.

In June 1959, shortly after Castro toppled Batista's government and long before the Bay of Pigs, Castro had over 200 guerrilla troops transported by boat to the Dominican Republic in an attempt to overthrow Rafael Trujillo's government. Then in 1965, US military forces had to deploy and save the Dominican Republic from a Cuban-inspired Marxist revolution.[41] Success at installing a satellite in the Dominican Republic would have completed Soviet designs for a "gatekeeper" extending across the eastern Caribbean Sea. The public relations coup would have made them and Cuba's dictator regional rulers.[42] The Kremlin must have been full of joy when Kennedy's administration, at least officially and on the surface, committed the US to renouncing Cuba as a primary security interest.

> 2. Cuba becomes a base of operations and launching pad for exporting revolution throughout Latin America.

Once the United States made a commitment to not intervene in Cuba's so-called "domestic affairs," operations could be conducted without fear of molestation. Non-intervention did not, however, stop Kennedy from attempting to get rid of Castro. This is out of character with Soviet Chairman Nikita Khrushchev's belief that JFK was a weakling and easily manhandled:

> Look, we helped elect Kennedy last year. Then we met with him in Vienna, a meeting that could have been a turning point. But what does he say? "Don't ask for too much. Don't put me in a bind. If I make too many concessions, I'll be turned out of office." Quite a guy! He comes to a meeting but can't perform. What the hell do we need a guy like that for? Why waste time talking to him?[43]

Khrushchev's remark leaves an awful lot of unanswered questions that, to this day, are disturbing.

3. Geographic location is ideal for a communications monitoring station within close proximity to the US.

Capturing message traffic is possible throughout the eastern half of the United States thanks to a transmission intercept station that remains in full operation.[44] Robert Scheina notes how Cuba's close geographic proximity allows all forms of havoc to be waged:

> According to Eden Pastora Gomez, at the time a member of the Sandinista National Directorate, Fidel Castro decided to enter the narcotics business in 1982 with the objective of introducing drugs into the United States in order to undermine the social fabric.[45]

The US is far from unique to these types of operations:

> During the 1980s, Cuba continued to transport weapons to guerrillas via water routes. The Columbian Army captured a guerrilla, who a few months earlier had been granted asylum in Cuba. He testified that he had flown from Cuba to Panama and along with other guerrillas and arms had been landed from a boat named the Freddie on the coast of Columbia. As a result of this and other Cuban activity, the Columbian government suspended diplomatic relations with Cuba on 23 March 1981. On 14 November of the same year the Columbian Navy intercepted and sank the boat *El Karnia* attempting to land guerrillas and weapons on that nation's Pacific Coast.[46]

Seeking to overthrow the democratically elected government in Columbia has been ongoing for decades. Currently, financial support includes unsuspecting Americans filling their vehicles at Venezuela's state-owned Citgo petroleum stations.[47] Few countries would tolerate this type of financial support to Hugo Chavez, a sworn enemy, who is operating against an ally situated so close to a major shipping artery.[48]

4. Cuba provides military facilities for Soviet forces to operate from in order to fulfill regional objectives.

In addition to disrupting communications between the Mississippi River and Panama Canal, a hostile navy could support operations against the four transit routes for US shipping.[49] Cuba can provide logistics and maintenance support, enabling an enemy fleet to challenge shipping between the Panama Canal, Atlantic Ocean, and Mississippi River. These facilities could also be available to ballistic missile submarines. The result for Red Navy planners is a first-class fleet operation that includes nuclear missile capability in the seas close to the United States.[50] Therefore, Moscow's leadership still achieved strategic missile positioning close to America's shore.

The downing of Francis Gary Powers and his U-2 spy plane over the Soviet Union on 01 May 1960 turned out to be an intelligence success and publicity stunt. In typical East Bloc coincidental fashion, Powers mysteriously went down on the same day as the annual global celebration of socialist and communist parties. Workers of the world were clearly celebratory during their parades in Moscow, Peking, and Havana. Photographic equipment remained largely intact at the aircraft recovery site and even found its way to a Moscow museum. This technology transfer enabled Soviet leaders to discover US aerial reconnaissance capabilities. Possessing this information two years prior to the Cuban Missile Crisis makes it seem strange the Kremlin would allow nuclear missiles to be photographed on ships in transit to Cuba, as well as during installation on the island.

Is it possible the Cuban Missile Crisis was staged to help Kennedy's image? That would not seem far-fetched based on verbal exchanges with Khrushchev at Vienna. Or did the Cuban Missile Crisis have designs for future and more profound strategic gains? Could both questions explain Soviet action in Cuba? Russia and the PRC seldom make strategic or tactical moves unless for multiple reasons. This admirable trait has fooled the West on several occasions (watch this hand while I slap you with the other). Both are also quite gifted at dealing with those who double-cross them. So what did the Kremlin give up in its showdown with the Kennedy administration back in 1962? Euphoria and hype over America coming out a big winner is worthy of another look. US compromise caused several states in the Western Hemisphere to spend decades resisting Cuban-backed guerrilla forces and Soviet-inspired revolutions. JFK did not turn out so lucky. His part of the bargain may have come at a higher price.

Europe

Roots supporting US and NATO military policy toward Soviet moves in Europe can be found in their dealings with Nazi Germany during World War II. Germany's geostrategic location in Europe convinced Sir Halford Mackinder it could only be defeated with a two-front engagement:

The polluted channel might be swept clear very effectively if it were controlled by strong embankments of power on either hand – land power to the east, in the Heartland, and sea power to the west, in the North Atlantic basin. Face the German mind with an enduring that any war fought by Germany must be a war on two unshakable fronts and the Germans themselves will solve the problem. The other threat was the Soviet Union. If she was to emerge the conqueror of Germany, she would rank as the greatest land power in the world: the Heartland is the greatest natural fortress on earth. For the first time in history it is manned by a garrison sufficient both in number and quality.[51]

Mackinder's concern about Soviet power reinforced the Allies' rush to Berlin in order to face Red Army troops. Allied success at sea during World War II stimulated Mackinder into considering maritime power. In fairness to Mackinder, few people foresaw or imagined the incredible sea power projected by the United States. To muster such a force on a global scale is an impressive display of national power. It is at this point where Mackinder and Mahan become united and, in another sign of similarities, both find common ground distrusting the USSR/Russia. Mahan gained his initial suspicion when he served on a US delegation to the Hague Conference in 1899. The conference, called at the request of Czar Nicholas II, disappointed Mahan who saw it as an attempt by Russia to gain geostrategic advantage over Great Britain. This would be achieved by preventing a maritime alliance with the US. Doing so could help Russian efforts to reinforce their position in Asia:

My own persuasion is that the immediate cause of Russia calling for the Conference was the shock of our late war, resulting in the rapprochement of the US and Great Britain and our sudden appearance in Asia, as the result of a successful war. In peace, Russia's aggressive advance moves over the inert Asiatics like a steam-roller; but the prospect of America and England, side by side, demanding that China be left open for trade, means either a change in her policy, or war. Hence she wishes peace – by pledge. . . . [a nation] should never pledge itself, by treaty or otherwise, to arbitrate before it knows what the subject of dispute is. Needless to say, I have no sympathy with those who hold that war is never imperative.[52]

Commingling of sea, land, air, and space power rose to the occasion in Europe's theater during the last half of the twentieth century. The US Navy made a major contribution to Europe's defense portfolio with its "attack at the source" strategy. George Baer notes how this justified its continued existence in the face of budgetary challenges from a pork-infested Congress:

> The doctrine of "attack at the source" expressed a practice as old as naval warfare. Nonetheless, it reconceptualized naval strategy just when the Navy needed a contemporary categorization of its position. In its justification of existing offensive force, the doctrine was as brilliant as Mahan's had been 50 years earlier. Power projection in the name of sea control gave the Navy a role in the late 1940s, as it would also in the 1980s. The genius of the doctrine, Norman Friedman noted, was in its equating freedom of action at sea with freedom to strike at targets on land. Even the Air Force could not rebut the argument that deep land strikes served a sea-control function.[53]

Air Force admission of a land and sea power link is a major contribution to the definitions. A typical flaw in past descriptions of land power helps explain Europe and NATO's security dilemma at the time. *Webster's College Dictionary*, for example, defines land power as "A nation having an important and powerful army; Military power on land."[54] The description, like so many other attempts at defining power generators, is fixated on strictly military terminology. This would be armies on land as it relates to land power. *Webster's* explanation has better association as a definition for land "force" because of its connotation to "military power on land." This persistent problem in geographic spheres prevents flexibility for features associated with power generation. It also underestimates land power's actual value. Identical problems exist with labeling sea, air, and space power.

The Soviet Union has routinely been identified as a dominant "land power" based solely on Red Army size. This would be true as applied to land force power. Red Army strength remained a frequent NATO concern as members attempted to measure staying power before getting pushed into the sea by a full-blown Warsaw Pact invasion.[55] Warsaw Pact forces possessed the dominant land *force* power. It is also correct to consider the USSR a dominant land power, but for multiple other reasons. This involves consideration for the cumulative sum of power resources and elements associated with land power generation, which adds enormous energy to Red Army size.

NATO's key to withstanding an invasion of conventional forces depended on holding the line until reinforced by America's trans-Atlantic maritime logistics train. This logistics link is considered a land power asset for purposes just stated. Even with maritime supremacy and a monopoly on the atomic bomb, US military leaders believed as early as 1947 that allied forces could not survive a Red Army assault.[56] Plans were drawn for evacuating Europe and establishing a base of operations in the United Kingdom and North Africa. The US Navy took responsibility for securing the perimeter and keeping Soviet forces boxed in until an amphibious invasion could be mounted.[57] The USSR transportation and logistics link stretched thousands of miles, providing land-based reinforcement of army units in an identical manner as a logistics train across the Atlantic. Which would outlast the other never got put to the test.

The Vietnam War's aftermath and ending the draft created a number of manpower issues for military planners faced with an ever-increasing Soviet threat. An all-volunteer force burdened an already shaky defense portfolio. Retooling the US Navy from strike operations ashore during the Vietnam War took time and hampered USN effectiveness against Soviet aggression elsewhere. In assessing the October 1973 Arab-Israeli War, and stand-off between US and Soviet naval fleets in the Mediterranean Sea, Lyle Goldstein and Yuri Zhukov note a peculiar state of naval aviation:

> A third lesson is that a strategic focus on "strike" ashore versus "sea control" can result in doctrinal and tactical unpreparedness for interactions with "upstart" naval powers. One former US naval aviator who served in the Sixth Fleet during the crisis explains that for the seven years before the Mediterranean crisis, the strategic focus of the US Navy had been on supporting the bombing campaign in Vietnam. The priorities in that war, of course, had been carrier warfare and close air support for troops in combat. Antisurface ship tactics and surface-to-surface missiles, which were perhaps more appropriate for a close-proximity war-at-sea scenario than was naval aviation, were insufficiently developed at the time. It is apparent, then, that the mission of projecting force "from the sea" in Vietnam had a debilitating effect on the fundamental US Navy task of sea control.[58]

This should bring immediate concern for inherent dangers in "Forward . . . From the Sea," a naval doctrine promulgated by the Clinton administration in 1994. The Soviet Fifth Eskadra, though way behind US Sixth Fleet technology, successfully neutralized the US Navy's freedom of action to mount a response. This accomplishment occurred by incorporating basic strategic and tactical practices. Goldstein and Zhukov agree with Soviet and American military personnel interviewed that, had a full scale naval battle ensued in the eastern Mediterranean; the Fifth Eskadra would have eliminated Sixth Fleet abilities to be a factor in the Arab-Israeli fight.

Goldstein and Zhukov unsuspectingly identify a profound "coincidence" befalling Soviet naval success in Mediterranean Sea operations throughout the late 1960s and early 1970s. This included the phenomenal good fortune of staging a major naval warfare exercise, planned months in advance, at the same time Libyan Colonel Muammar al-Gadhafi overthrew King Idris. Goldstein and Zhukov suggest Soviet fleet action prevented British and US intervention.[59] If true, a significant Cold War event has dodged serious historical analysis. Why did US and UK government officials turn on King Idris? Were they threatened at the diplomatic level with Soviet action elsewhere? Gadhafi's coup d'état is still regarded as a joke. King Idris was out of the country at the time, Gadhafi's accomplices consisted of a small handful of fellow officers, and the lone casualty figure turned out to be a fellow plotter who accidentally shot himself in the leg.

The United Kingdom had a defense treaty with King Idris, but his request for assistance was denied. The United States had Wheelus Air Force Base east of Tripoli, which could have reinforced Libyan forces loyal to the King. Strategic planning following World War II involved NATO maintaining a perimeter around Europe in the event of a full-scale Red Army invasion. Wheelus served as a major part of that plan and, therefore, its loss became significant. Such inaction from supposed Western superpowers does not provide much comfort to allies. This incredible event led alleged Kremlin puppet, Armand Hammer, to sign a multi-year Occidental Petroleum contract with Gadhafi "whose terms were unlike any ever before agreed to by a Western oil company... With the stroke of a pen, Hammer had acknowledged the ultimate sovereignty of an oil-producing nation over its oil – and had forever changed the geopolitics of oil."[60]

The 1980s saw a resurgence of American naval might. In fairness to Ronald Reagan's predecessor, Jimmy Carter, it should be noted that advances in military technology deployed during Reagan's era resulted, in part, from Carter administration efforts to stay ahead of the Soviets in research and development. It is, after all, Carter who proposed the neutron bomb for use in Europe, which was later cancelled due to Soviet-inspired anti-nuclear protests.[61] What Carter could not provide is salesmanship qualities found in Ronald Reagan, who used his acting skill to get public support for a defense build-up.

NATO's inability to withstand a full scale conventional thrust by Warsaw Pact forces was corrected by not just maintaining, but enhancing nuclear options. This approach was also applied to improving NATO's logistical train across the Atlantic Ocean. Had NATO lost its ability to reinforce conventional forces on the continent, then unconventional options were the only alternative. This situation raises a common question not unique to Europe. It applied equally to such geostrategic points as South Korea: "If the conventional force strength was not adequate, then why sacrifice manpower at the hands of an over-powering invasion?" US Senator Henry "Scoop" Jackson's answer remained consistent policy throughout the Cold War:

> The main purpose of the U.S. troop commitment in Europe is to leave the Russians in no doubt that the United States would be involved if they attacked Western Europe – making it clear to the Russians that they would meet enough U.S. troops to make it a Soviet-American crisis, not just a European one.[62]

If the US Navy were allowed to die a slow death during the Cold War, as some advocated, then there remained few options for saving Europe short of going nuclear. The ability of US and NATO naval forces to reinforce Europe by sea, while preventing Warsaw Pact nations from achieving the same on land, presented Soviet strategists with a dilemma reminiscent of Britain's Royal Navy dealings with Napoleon's France. Colin Gray comments:

> The strategic geography of the East-West standoff of the Cold War had to give historians a pervasive sense of *déjà vu*. A maritime alliance denied a continental land power domination of Europe and Asia. That land power confronted strategic problems of awesome dimensions on at least two widely separated fronts (Europe and China). Moscow's ability in war to trouble the maritime alliance beyond the Eurasian landmass, or to outflank the operations of that alliance on that landmass could have been thwarted by the Eurasian rimland strategic geography on which the Western Alliance could anchor distant sea-air blockade.[63]

Soviet land power could not match NATO's sea power wherewithal, or come up with a conventional means on land for ending it. Maintaining nuclear parity with Warsaw Pact forces, while making it clear NATO would not hesitate to launch on demand, prevented the threat of having Soviet weapons used against Western maritime alliance assets. The cost for using such a device against naval forces would be a reciprocating loss of Red Army land forces.

The nuclear option against land forces protected NATO's maritime leverage. It is another example of sea power's grand strategic reach. Something not commonly considered an instrument of sea power is, in fact, a very important asset. It provided maritime forces a shield for freedom of action in the Atlantic. The ability to do unto others as they would unto NATO guaranteed that maritime forces, which were an essential link to the defense of Europe, would not be lost. As long as the alliance spanned Western Europe and North America, then the Atlantic (Mackinder's Midland Ocean) had to remain open. This is not negotiable. The same supply train that worked so effectively in two previous wars would be called on again in the event of a third.[64]

Chapter Twelve

To the Gay Nineties and Beyond

"It is the absolute right of the State to supervise the formation of public opinion."
- Joseph Goebbels

The 1990s unleashed a global-based economic model largely driven by quickly developing countries such as India and the People's Republic of China. Highly sophisticated technology, primarily driven by computer and software industries, advanced at a pace unseen in history. This economic storm motivated political elites to seek new ways of binding cultures into an organ of universal legal standards. It is not clear whether the process is carefully managed by powerful political forces, or simply driven by uncontrolled events. There are arguments on both sides of the issue, with Paul Busiek advancing the most disturbingly sinister possibility:

> It is germane to this hearing and to the present political warfare waged in our country that I mention a very important book which was leaked into the free world from Czechoslovakia after the overthrow of their free government. The book is titled, *How Parliament can Play a Revolutionary part in the Transition to Socialism, and the Role of the Popular Masses.* The Author was Jan Kozak, member of the Secretariat of the Communist Party of Czechoslovakia.
> Any person who is at all troubled by the behavior of our own Parliament (Congress) and recent trends in our legislative and electoral process, will do well to secure a copy of Kozak's book, see in it a near mirror image of the current troubled political scene in the USA, and realize that the 1988 elections are in reality political warfare with some very grim possibilities.[1]

In a quest to reduce the global masses into quantifiable economic rules of collective good, Thomas Sowell comments how affluent elites have failed to ponder the single most important fact of life which has driven states and individuals since man evolved from a roving hunter-gatherer:

History cannot solve today's problems, but it can expose fallacies which make matters worse, or which make resolutions harder to see or to achieve. Above all, history offers understanding – not in psychological sense of maudlin patronage, but in the sense of a clear-sighted view of reality, its limitations and its possibilities. Nowhere is such understanding more important than among peoples from different racial, ethnic, or cultural backgrounds.[2]

Contemporary political economists dominate the cheering section over globalization. Challenging this catalytic movement is a lack of popular support. Such political inconveniences are seldom an issue for dictatorships because discipline techniques are freely available. Unfortunately for the West, it is oppressive regimes that rule the majority of the planet's population. Free people in Western democracies will be hardest hit from developments driven by a very small minority of international elites holding glossy visions of global harmony. The price to be paid by average citizens of developed, multi-party democracies began to appear during the 1990s.

So-called "globalization" has made impressive gains, spanning virtually every institution and professional field in the West.[3] Enticement of quick financial gain and economic gratification is intoxicating otherwise rational minds. History and reality are thrown to trade winds as the electorate is blindly seduced by consumption and high-flying global mutual funds, which are addicted to the economies of oppressive governments. The emperors of Rome would be envious:

> Hobbes thought the fundamental struggle was over "men's persons, wives, children, and cattle." But the great struggles recorded in history do not tell a story of cattle thieves, kidnappers, and wife stealers. We have long ago learned that the Greeks did not sail to Troy simply to recapture Helen. Men fight over authority, for the control over men and wealth that authority achieves, for control over formal organizations and especially over the state's administrators and the military. It is only through organizations that men can raid, tax, irrigate the land, build roads or pyramids, keep the peace, and fight off invaders. Alexander, Xerxes, Caesar, Genghis Khan, and Napoleon struggled over authority, not over wives and cattle.[4]

Unsolved Mysteries

The "progressive" economist has roots in the philosophy of John Maynard Keynes: "*General Theory* caught most economists under the age of 35 with the unexpected virulence of a disease first attacking and decimating an isolated tribe of South Sea islanders. Economists beyond 50 turned out to be quite immune from the ailment."[5] Keynesian theories of government activism in private sector markets are propelling current international political economy schemes. It is a gamble to give such prototypes free reign when evidence remains inconclusive that the Keynesian model ended the Great Depression, its highly promoted qualifying hymn.

Data among traditional sources for the period 1932-1942 is conflicting and contradictory with recent discoveries. Evidence indicates powerful political forces were at play that had previously been discounted from most economic analysis. From June to September of 1932, for example, the US stock market staged an impressive recovery of 71%. Industrial production and farm prices were making similar gains.[6] Suddenly, only weeks before the presidential election, a negative correction occurred to propel Franklin Roosevelt in the White House. Economic misery continued for another seven years as government control increased: "In 1939 we had idle men, and idle technological ideas on an appalling scale. The war set them to work, but it took the war to do it."[7] Many liberal economists are now questioning New Deal designs. The war economy argument is reinforced by statistics showing minimal unemployment corrections.[8]

It was not until the outbreak of World War II that workers and factories came alive. It would be different if Keynes received credit for starting World War II, and war served as his basis for stimulating economic activity. Seventy years later his idea of government spending remains in question and yet, as Richard Pipes implies, loyal disciples continue to ramrod the program into virtually every facet of society:

> In 1900, the U.S. government owned 7 percent of the nation's capital assets and employed 4 percent of its labor force. During the next half century, these figures tripled: in 1950, the government owned 20 percent of the nation's assets and employed 12.5 percent of its labor force. Its share of the gross domestic product grew exponentially: from 3.9 percent in 1870 to 27 percent in 1970. This expansion occurred largely as the result of Roosevelt's New Deal and the welfare policies adopted during and immediately after World War II. But these figures grew still more dramatically in the second half of the twentieth century in the wake of vast increases in social services, especially those mandated by President Lyndon Johnson's "Great Society." In the 1990s, the share of government spending in the

United States climbed to one-third of the GDP. Approximately one-half of that money goes for social welfare – nearly triple what it was in 1960. By 1995, the number of American civilians directly employed by the government attained the figure of 19.5 million. Thus, whereas the population of the United States between 1900 and 1992 increased 3.3 times (from 76 million to 250 million), the number of government employees grew 18.7 times, or nearly six times as fast.[9]

This meat grinder is now advocated on a worldwide scale as a final solution to man's great problems in the twenty-first century. The disturbing figures noted by Richard Pipes reveal an out-of-control Keynesian model showing no sign of reversing itself, regardless of economic health. The amount of taxes now taken as a percent of US Gross Domestic Product (GDP) is greater than at any time during World War II.[10] Expansion of government today can be considered nothing more than a gasping attempt to keep the patient alive. Political elites appear to be holding on to power through an orgy of social programs, while forwarding the bill to the next generation:

> The king employs a considerable part of the tribute in grants of largesse, bestowed by way of banquets or presents, to those whose support consolidates his authority, whereas their defection would endanger it. Do we not see modern governments as well using the public funds to endow social groups or classes, whose votes they are anxious to secure? Today the name is different, and it is called the redistribution of incomes by taxation.[11]

Concern over disrupting globalization's development caused indecision following Iraq's invasion of Kuwait in 1990. The debate broke down to whether a passive hostile strategic channel should be pursued, or military force unleashed. Warnings of international and national doom were rampant. Claims that war against Iraq would be at a very high cost were common. History's database is full of those favoring passive hostile approaches. Seeking to implement active hostile channels against armed aggressors routinely faces loud opposition. According to Donald and Frederick Kagan, threats always worsen until strong political leadership frees active hostile channels:

> Like General Wilson and Milne when Kemal challenged the British at Chanak, but with infinitely less justification, they warned against taking military action. Before Congress, Powell's [Colin Powell] two

immediate predecessors as JCS Chairman, Admiral William Crowe and General David C. Jones, both called for the continuation of economic sanctions against Saddam instead of launching a war. Crowe said: "If, in fact, the sanctions will work in 12 to 18 months instead of six months, the trade-off of avoiding war with its attendant sacrifices and uncertainties, would, in my estimation, be worth it." Crowe could claim no expertise in the effects of economic sanctions, nor did he take note of the national coalition President Bush had cobbled together against Iraq.[12]

Kuwaiti citizens left to witness Saddam's military conducting combat maneuvers would not be pleased by a wait-and-see approach lasting 18 months, or fourteen years (2003). Even after removing Iraqi forces from Kuwait, followed by implementation of supposedly 'tough' UN sanctions, Saddam remained in power until US military forces returned to finish the job.[13] The attacks of 9/11 took place one year following publication of *While America Sleeps*. 9/11 resulted from an elevation of offensive action, motivated by failure to use active hostile strategic channels for similar, but less dramatic attacks during the 1990s. Saddam in fact, provided US Ambassador to Iraq, April Glaspie, a forewarning on the eve of his Kuwait invasion by informing her "we cannot come all the way to you in the United States but individual Arabs may reach you."[14]

Without the political willpower existing to take appropriate strategic channels when necessary, then grand strategy cannot operate and its instruments become useless. This distinguishes differences between capability and ability. Globalization's footprint is all over the lethargic national security policies of the Clinton administration in the 1990s. Oath of office and allegiance to the Constitution of the United States becomes a moral contradiction for political elites dedicated to internationalist ideals. A classic example would be the bombing of the USS *Cole* in Aden, Yemen, which got treated as a criminal act equal to Bonnie and Clyde.[15] Bombings of the US Embassy in Kenya and Tanzania, and military barracks in Saudi Arabia were acts of war which would have brought a profound military response in another era. Lack of reciprocity demonstrated weakness and only enticed further action.

It is politically deficient to label terrorism as criminal when such activity is targeted against military and government property of a sovereign state. These attacks have strategic purpose and value. Instead of an armada of naval power being unleashed on foreign shores, US officials sent FBI criminal detectives with paint brushes dusting for fingerprints. Contemporary America has a short attention span and easily forgets the United States fought a global war against Spain when one US Navy ship sank while at anchorage in Havana, Cuba.[16] Perhaps certain parties were banking on that short attention span running its course so greater political designs could resume without delay.

09+11+01 = The 21st Century

The horrific events of 9/11 bring back questions thought to have disappeared in 1992: Why is America persistently targeted by so-called "renegade groups" when, in fact, there are truly ruthless regimes worthy of exacting revenge on? Would it not be worth considering the possibility state-sanctioned warfare is still being waged against American interests? Or, is that too politically incorrect to imagine? Many terrorists are being tied to Osama bin Ladin, but nobody seems to consider who bin Ladin is tied to. James Angleton, legendary former head of counterintelligence (CI) at the Central Intelligence Agency, long suspected political elites refused to connect the USSR to "rogue elements" out of fear over the Soviet response.[17] Does this model also apply to Osama bin Ladin and Al-Qa'ida? Ray Cline, former Deputy Director of Intelligence and Angleton's colleague at the CIA, is far less optimistic of the global affection afflicting so many intellectuals today. His real-world experience should be taken into account considering the euphoria over international political economy (IPE) now rampaging through Western governments and institutions of higher learning:

> To those who would say that, given the cataclysmic upheavals of 1989 in the Soviet Bloc, this is all ancient history, I would respond: **Not so fast, do not be so sure**. Whatever the ultimate outcome of these upheavals, the fact remains that they have not reduced the military capability of the Soviet armed forces, but have actually improved and modernized the vast array of Soviet strategic intercontinental weapons. They have not yet diminished the levels of military assistance provided by Moscow to countries like Cuba, North Korea and Angola.[18]

Cline's expertise at analytical forecasting was put on display in September 2001. This followed a directly related statement in 1983: "We haven't kept our intelligence records on terrorists in this country for five years because we believe that it won't happen here as it has in other countries. But we are vulnerable to the same kind of campaign."[19]

The West has a long tradition of writing off attacks by fingering lowly figures. An unpalatable aftertaste from looking inside the abyss at the monster directing such action is too difficult for many to endure. Holding fully responsible those destitute minions who are drugged and fooled into conducting tactical action is a painless procedure. Projecting an image of terrorist group independence is tossed around in policy circles to a point that it blinds broader consideration. This only diverts attention away from a far nastier beast, while pacifying public interest with a satisfying product.[20] Yet another of Dr. Cline's colleagues refuses to close the door on state sanction:

> Mr. Chairman, while al-Qa'ida represents a broad-based Sunni worldwide extremist network, it would be a mistake to dismiss possible connections to either other groups or state sponsors – either Sunni or Shia [two different Muslim sects]. There is a convergence of common interest in hurting the US, its allies, and interests that make traditional thinking in this regard unacceptable.[21]

George Tenet's remark is a warning. He accurately points to "possible connections to either other groups or state sponsors." It is no secret to those willing to do the research that terror groups attacking Western interests during the supposedly peaceful Cold War often acted under direction and on behalf of the Soviet camp. It would be self-induced deception to assume such a successful method of statecraft somehow fizzled into oblivion during the 1990s.

Eloise Malone and Arthur Rachwald show how selling freedom can seem cheap for some. In contemporary times this involves sacrificing a way of life for low-priced manufactured toys from tyrants:

> The price of globalization ultimately may include a need to compromise some of our most sacred values, those that provide the very foundation of contemporary Western civilization. This begins with our notion of freedom. Freedom, while the main source of our strength, also makes us vulnerable. Americans and other citizens of the Western world may find it necessary to accept restrictions on their liberties to ensure protection from violence and fear. This begs the question of whether the concept of freedom as conceived by our founding fathers is applicable to today's borderless society.[22]

Today's borderless society became that way because political elites allowed it, often against protests by their constituents. Malone and Rachwald offer a chilling vision of globalization supposedly being embraced by the American people to a point that fundamental freedoms are willingly sacrificed for security. Surrendering liberty for the sake of feeling secure, while becoming addicted to a global economic buffet, should be rejected. It is hard to believe Americans would readily place their trust in dictators from other parts, while throwing away the nation's long-held constitutional framework. That is, of course, if they had a choice. Most would find sacrificing inconveniences of individual freedom, property rights, and a constitutional republic to be an unfair exchange for a feeding trough of cheap goodies from evil empires:

> Samuel Huntington, in *Clash of Civilizations*, mistakenly lumped Asia with Islam as "challenger civilizations." Nothing could be further form the truth. Developing Asia desperately needs two things in the coming years: energy from the Middle East and capital from the West. If either of these two global markets breaks down, Asia cannot move forward and instability will ensue.[23]

Thomas Barnett conveniently excludes Islam from Asia, even though Indonesia is the most populous Islamic state. He then buries the few democratic governments existing in Asia under Communist China's umbrella. Constitutional democracies and dictatorships possess fundamental differences, which must be made clear when attempting to discuss both in the same context.[24] America's allies in Asia do not deserve being ignored and written off under that PRC umbrella, even though Peking would gladly comply:

> Until September, the Bush administration clearly focused national security strategy on Asia in general and against China in particular. This was a huge mistake in the making, but the danger has not yet passed. As the United States pursues this war against international terrorism, we must be aware that the West and Asia can either come together or be driven apart by events in the Middle East. Remember this: as far as globalization is concerned, China is not the problem; it is the prize.[25]

An official PRC press spokesman could not have stated it better. Communist China does not represent the views of Asia any more than America represents the views of the Western Hemisphere. Attempting to argue that 9/11 proved the PRC is not a problem, based on Barnett's example, appears to instead provide motive for Communist Chinese sanctioning of the 9/11 attack:

> In a sign of Beijing's increasingly close ties with the Taleban regime in Afghanistan, China has signed a memorandum of understanding for economic and technical cooperation with Kabul, press reports from Afghanistan and Pakistan said.
>
> The agreement was reported Tuesday, the same day terrorists hijacked four planes in the United States and drove them into the World Trade Center and the Pentagon. A Chinese delegation signed the deal in Kabul with the Taleban's minister of mining, Mullah Mohammed Ishaq, the news reports said.
>
> China's agreement with the Taleban is the most substantial part of a series of contacts that Beijing has had with Afghanistan over the last two years. Of all non-Muslim countries, Beijing now has the best relationship with the isolated regime in Kabul in the world, a senior Western diplomat said.[26]

It appears PRC activity in Afghanistan has been ignored on the day of 9/11. In its place, US officials did the opposite and embarked on a diplomatic journey involving closer ties to the communist regime. Only a few months prior to 9/11 PRC officials embarrassed the United States after one of their People's Liberation Army interceptors collided into a US Navy P-3 reconnaissance aircraft over international waters. Against every treaty law governing aircraft in distress, PRC troops stormed the Orion upon making an emergency landing on Hainan. They then proceeded to gut and strip-search the equipment, while the crew was detained against their will. Some of America's most sensitive intelligence gathering technology wound up pirated in bandit fashion. PRC officials, after refusing to allow the plane to be flown on its own, required it be disassembled and transported on a "Russian" cargo plane.

In another era such acts of state would warrant an economic boycott, emergency session at the UN, recall of the diplomatic corps and, perhaps, military action. Thanks to the glories of globalization, Western governments are sending a message they are more concerned about maintaining trade deficits. A nation that willingly subjects itself to hostile acts that are in violation of international law invites a repeat performance. The Middle East did not gain by the events of 9/11. However, Communist China did. The incident on Hainan, just for starters, is quickly forgotten as a result of more pressing concerns.

Barnett's PRC does not appear to be much of a prize for America and that sucking sound of industrial production heading west across the Pacific should be an indicator. Communist China appears to be a big winner and the prize is actually America's pie.[27] Numerous oil producing nations seem to be helping this process along:

China's insatiable demand for energy is prompting fears of financial and diplomatic collisions around the globe as it seeks reliable supplies of oil from as far away as Brazil and Sudan. An intrusion into Japanese territorial waters by a Chinese nuclear submarine last week and a trade deal with Brazil are the latest apparently unconnected consequences of China's soaring economic growth. The connection, however, lies in an order issued last year by President Hu Jintao to seek secure oil supplies abroad – preferably ones which could not be stopped by America in case of conflict over Taiwan.[28]

If this is victory for America, then what does surrender look like? Fortunately, David Adams shows why there are many wearing the US Navy/Marine Corps uniform who maintain less rosy optimism:

Before the attacks of 11 September 2001, China was pursuing a strategic axis with the Middle East to bracket India and stretch U.S. resources. It is not surprising that a Chinese delegation was in Kabul on 10 September 2001 to negotiate a political-military agreement with the Taliban. By supplying weapons of mass destruction and missile technology to Iran, Pakistan, and other countries, China keeps the United States preoccupied with the Middle East, diminishing our military presence and power in the Western Pacific.[29]

The PRC has successfully diverted US military and diplomatic priorities away from East Asia toward the Middle East and North Africa. It stretches the imagination to believe the Taliban government would dupe a high level PRC delegation into signing a major treaty in Kabul on the very same day they were supporting the biggest attack in history on the US homeland. The post-treaty signing cake-cutting ceremony must have been a spectacular social event. What was the official PRC government response to the Taliban's action? Any other nation would regard such statecraft as a setup and insult worthy of war. Perhaps PRC delegates were simply overwhelmed by all the excitement simultaneously unfolding before their eyes.

Barnett brings forth a profound discovery that a threatening PRC is among the ten biggest Cold War myths. It is solely perpetrated by political-military analysts hungering for the good old Cold War days.[30] This is marvelous news. PRC espionage ransacking of US military and industrial research laboratories, which has been non-stop for the past thirty years, must have been a simple figment of the public's imagination.[31] The American people can now rest easier knowing Communist China is actually their strategic partner.

International Movements

Considerable motivation for global initiatives can be found in the political economy and peace studies movements. With the exception of a small element, the vast majority's focus is dedicated to three areas requiring greater government control of human activity:

- International trade: This argument states when trade among nations is cancelled, war erupts. When trade is allowed to flourish, then peace abounds.[32] As a result, government should do whatever is necessary to ensure free trade continues among all states. This is diametrically opposed to political realities that as long as man and the state exist, so too will war in various forms. Economic appeasement of Hitler and Stalin by the West is purposely avoided in this particular lexicon.
- Terrorism: The position claims events of 11 September 2001 uncovered a unique national security dynamic that transgresses sovereign boundaries. Redistributing wealth on a global scale, from the haves to have-nots, will prevent violent acts in the future. A free video game machine for all will stop terror. National security must adapt to realities of transnational intercourse.[33] Absorbing national institutions into global bodies should concern free societies, especially when observing oppressive regimes being selected to serve on UN panels.
- Decline of the USSR: This view states that collapse of East-West barriers affords an opportunity to bypass national politics and ideologies in order to concentrate on "world peace."[34] Based on an unusually high body count of deceased Moscow and Peking critics, skepticism is certainly warranted. Acts of state in the world arena today are not much different from past encounters. The same applies to similarities seen in current blueprints for future international governing bodies. While it is an honorable endeavor to seek peace and understanding, it is foolish to do so with identical methods that previously bombed so badly at the box office.

Western economic appeasement of authoritarian regimes is helping along current globalization and IPE lexicons. There is a small problem in that Vladimir Lenin and Joseph Stalin bear no political resemblance to George Washington and Thomas Jefferson:

> The American struggles against the obstacles that nature opposes to him; the adversaries of the Russian are men. The former combats the wilderness and savage life; the latter, civilisation with all its arms. The conquests of the American are therefore gained by the ploughshare; those of the Russian by the sword. The Anglo-American relies upon personal interest to accomplish his ends and gives free scope to the unguided strength and common sense of the people; the Russian centres all the authority of society in a single arm. The principal instrument of the former is freedom; of the latter, servitude. Their starting-point is different and their courses are not the same; yet each of them seems marked out by the will of Heaven to sway the destinies of half the globe.[35]

For those who believe history is not of great consequence, blindness denies them an ability to catch "distinguishing differences" between traditional rivals such as Great Britain and France, Japan and China, or Greece and Turkey. Most important of all, IPE fails to give serious thought to the profound *link* all have with geostrategic models formulated by Mahan (sea power) and Mackinder (land power). A common thread threatening to undermine globalization efforts may be found in the train wreck that could follow from succumbing national sovereignty to a global collectivist confab:

> The urge to international understanding is an admirable one. But it turns into problems when we look at the realities. The world that Americans, and other Westerners full of goodwill, want to mount and ride, feed and pat, is not a sweet-tempered pony but a huge, vile-tempered mule.[36]

In past times those who believe in individual liberty and true constitutional forms of government would turn away in disgust at the majority of countries running rampant in the United Nations. This stable of oppressive regimes, which comprises a majority voting bloc in the general assembly, does not represent Western principles of governing. Four questions are worth asking: Why should constitutional democracies, which possess profound political and philosophical differences with dictatorships, willingly surrender any of their political freedoms, including national economies? Is the UN all there is for free republics to work with in carrying out foreign affairs? Why must a culture that relishes individual liberty succumb to the wishes of dictatorship? Is sovereignty not worth protecting? Robert Conquest continues:

It [United Nations] is a "union," of course, not of nations but of states. And many U.N. states exist – even not counting ones recognized as "rogue" – that in no sense embody a civilized past, present, or future for the world or for themselves. Its members include governments largely or totally opposed to their own citizens' liberty and, of course, to Western culture in general. It lost some prestige when, for example, the U.N. Commission on Human Rights elected Libya as its chairman. Sudan is also a member, but the United States was dropped in 2001. Israel is in effect permanently barred.
Meanwhile, Syria was elected to the presidency of the Security Council.[37]

LOST Sovereignty

The United Nations and international nongovernmental organizations (NGOs) have pushed for legislative passage of a global Law of the Sea Treaty (LOST) governing the oceans. LOST presents those dependent on maritime power with troubling strategic dilemmas. US intervention efforts, such as its 1993 amphibious landing in Somalia, could be jeopardized if UN-backed international law gains authority to dictate rules governing the world's oceans. Enthusiasm surrounding LOST is misplaced from the perspective of nations that depend on sea power's contribution to national grand strategy. In their enthusiasm for international foreplay, supporters have miscalculated intricacies hidden in the agreement that can be used to legally constrain maritime states. A common defense of LOST argues that Article 51 "clearly recognizes the inherent right of self-defense."[38] Not answered is whether this outlaws the Bush doctrine of pre-emption. What is the UN's definition of self-defense? Do they now determine if sea power states can defend their own interests? Does LOST prevent offensive weapons on the seas? Is there a distinction between what constitutes offensive and defensive weapons? The treaty stipulates "the high seas shall be reserved for peaceful purposes."[39] This seems to eliminate the US Navy, USAF long-range bomber, US Coast Guard and, last but far from least, the US Marine Corps. What happened to self-defense?

Optimism for LOST exists among several civilian and military circles. Motivation appears to be purely financial. US Navy Captain George Galdorisi, for example, lists five reasons the United States should approve LOST.[40] Two are tied to the defense budget. His position places budgetary priorities over maritime strategic planning.

Concern for the taxpayer is certainly a noble cause. But it is a sorry state of affairs when national security must come in second behind critical federal funding priorities such as $800,000 to study atmospheric damage from methane gas in cows. LOST would be far less sensitive if, like landlocked Switzerland, power projection on the sea does not even register on the defense policy food chain.

Galdorisi's fifth reason why LOST should be supported is that failure to do so would prevent US officials from influencing the treaty's "further development and interpretation."[41] That reason by itself should scare any maritime power. It is indicative that further tightening of the screws can be expected. Using Galdorisi's own quote, he argues that the US must join LOST because it is "one of the most important agreements ever negotiated." Why is it important? International agreements get created for two simple reasons:

- There is a problem in existence that needs to be fixed.
- States are out to grab something they do not have.

The US and its maritime allies face no problem needing a fix. The only other explanation for LOST has to be a desire of certain parties to seek leverage over something they feel deprived of. In this case it would be control of the seas. Galdorisi's two remaining reasons justifying LOST involve global economics and freedom of the seas. Globalization is a domestic political minefield that should be avoided. There are countless American industries heading for bankruptcy court thanks to "global connectivity." The taxpayer from this group is not supportive of global initiatives that outsource their job.

Judicial globalization through such things as LOST is given a positive spin while chasing economic globalization. Idealistic views that judicial globalization makes tyrants follow international standards of law is without basis. The list of examples is incredibly short. A final reason given in support of LOST is freedom of the seas. The international community already enjoys this privilege. Nations are not harassing shipping thanks to the US Navy and Coast Guard. A US-led maritime alliance of states is not attacking and pillaging civilian vessels simply because it can. So what is the real reason behind LOST?

Sea power increased in value during the 1990s, while taking on a more deceiving look. This resulted from new technologies able to span geographic parameters with greater ease. The practice will not subside in the future and, instead, power generators will be enhancing each others' domains with greater intensity. The Law of the Sea Treaty has the potential to undermine that cohesion. Militarily, US efforts have concentrated on service integration with a bureaucratic program called "jointness." This is intended to amplify supporting roles military forces provide each other.[42] Historically, jointness is not new. It always existed, but without a flamboyant label. Forces representing different branches always assisted each other in time of need. Constrained by rules of LOST, however, threatens that intercourse between sea power and the other three power generators.

Possible loss of maritime projection became a concern during the 1990s. Having it occur under cover of international law did not previously register. LOST, while appearing quite innocent on the surface (as they all do), will be the opening volley to even more laws dictating terms of ocean access. The proposal is another example of "global connectivity" processes at work and, with 70% of Earth's surface falling within reach of LOST, the territorial jurisdiction acquired is unprecedented.[43] This opens doors for greater legal constraints down the road, such as the atmosphere over the seas.

Maritime states, whose history ties them to the sea, are pressured to surrender a vital operational domain. Would a large land power, such as the Soviet Union, willingly give up sovereignty on land for the sake of global brotherhood? It is naturally expected that land powers would gleefully support restrictions on those maritime powers that frustrated them in the past. J. C. Wylie once again saves the day:

> As long as the United States chooses to continue as the leader of the free world, sea power is the absolutely vital *basis* for United States policy, in peace or war, anywhere in the world. Without sea power as its tacit, but no less real, *basis*, no policy in the world wide interests of the United States would be fully viable. Such a policy would have little substance.[44]

Geographic realities associated with the US sitting in the Western Hemisphere makes freedom of action on the seas not negotiable if America is to fulfill foreign policy commitments. Israel, Kuwait, NATO, South Korea, and Japan are but a few sovereign nations existing because of the US global maritime commitment. Sea power is a dominant national grand strategy arm of this commitment. It has enabled America's allies to live in a more peaceful environment. The United Nations and sea power-deprived states are absolutely incapable of doing a better job, so why do they want it?

State of Military Affairs

Transformation from the Cold War to the popularly phrased "post-Cold War" era is often marked by the Persian Gulf War, Part I. The fact a two-part act applies indicates the unfinished business now underway in Iraq. Jeff Huber uses this event to further his criticism of Clausewitz.[45] It is obvious from reading *On War* that Clausewitz's decisive victory got stopped short on the "highway of death" leading to Baghdad. Charles Laingen contributes to Huber's cause by noting US combat missions over Iraq were flown for a longer period than the Vietnam War lasted. This is, Laingen states, because the modern world involves outside forces far above classic theories of war.[46] While correctly noting the CNN factor of simultaneous news broadcasting, Laingren is surrendering position to contemporary tangents influencing military action today. Impact of these matters has a lot to do with policy leadership and its ability to control political effects. The record is not encouraging. Failure to achieve Clausewitz's decisive victory in the first Persian Gulf war eventually fueled an attempted assassination of a former US president in Kuwait, numerous terrorist attacks during the 1990s, events of 11 September 2001, the death or displacement of over a million Kurds and Shiites, enforcement of a no-fly zone for air combat training, and a Persian Gulf War, Part II. Clausewitz is not to blame for those who choose to ignore his training manual.

Power generators connect with grand strategy according to Clausewitzian fundamentals. None can exist for long on their own, or survive if removed from national grand strategy. Japan's naval and merchant fleet discovered during World War II what can happen when strategy is detached from reality. Japan's failure involved the divorce of power from grand strategy. This result can occur in other areas where various elements must work as a team. Military branches, for example, routinely help each other overcome geographic obstacles:

> It used to be said that the British Army was simply a projectile to be fired ashore by the Royal Navy. In the future, that is still going to be a major naval role, to fire ashore Army special forces; or do what we did in Haiti – fire ashore the 10th Mountain Division, support them, and provide air cover and close air support.[47]

Military force is a distinct and profoundly important asset of each power generator. It would be a mistake to read John Lehman's description of Royal Army and Navy activities as two separate and parceled events. Britain's Royal Navy, in fulfilling a mission to fire ashore the British Army, acted in the capacity of a land power asset. Naval power offers many advantages when fulfilling foreign policy objectives. This is due to the vast geographic domain it can influence:

> Of these three major kinds of armed forces, only navies can have benign as well as an effective general employment in times of relative peace because, basically, they operate in the relatively neutral medium of the world's ocean waterways. Navies do not normally intrude upon the sovereignties of other and sometimes sensitive nations around the world.[48]

J. C. Wylie's medium of the seas has helped those possessing maritime power for centuries. Losing this domain as it is harnessed by international law threatens nations possessing sea power. LOST may be considered a logical strategic objective of those land powers incapable of maximizing sea power utility for themselves.[49]

Transformation and utilization of assets between power generators has positive and negative results. Success depends on those tasked with managing the process. Application of maritime advantage ashore is a perfect example of problems faced in the military arena. Power projection ashore received prominent attention during the 1990s. The US Department of Defense and NATO sought more efficient ways to apply existing assets. Motivation, once again, could be found in constricting budget limitations. The "Forward. . . .From the Sea" white paper, published by DOD, concentrated effort toward power projection ashore. Colin Gray noted that the US Navy was "shifting its principal focus from sea control to power projection against the shore and from the deep ocean to shallow water."[50] Disturbing thoughts of losing control of sea lanes come to mind.

Power projection from sea to shore has been a mainstay of US maritime force since Earl Ellis scouted the western Pacific on an intelligence gathering mission of Japanese fortifications. Then Marine Corps Commandant, John A. Lejeune, summed up USMC direction in the 1920s and it is not much different than what "Forward. . . .From the Sea" proclaimed to be doing in the 1990s:

> The primary war mission of the Marine Corps is to supply a mobile force to accompany the fleet for operations on shore in support of the fleet; this force should be of such size, organization, armament, and equipment as may be required by the plan of naval operations.[51]

General Lejeune's military arm he refers to is the expeditionary force now so widely used. Projecting power from the sea to land in such places as the Panama Canal has been a staple of maritime power for a long time. Could power projection be done better? Yes, but at what price? The danger of funds redirected from sustaining blue-water requirements to support a build-up of assets for coastal and littoral operations became a reality during the 1990s. Instead of making it a singular issue, spending priority should have been more funding of both programs.

DOD's white paper directive involved maximizing seagoing strike power to better influence hostile situations on land.[52] A "distinct difference" exists between better application of blue-water naval capabilities to support coastal operations and an uncontrolled urge to redesign the Department of the Navy into a riverboat patrol corps. Diversion away from blue-water dominance and concentrating on coastal objectives is itself a serious threat to influencing events in those same regions. The ability to dominate a geographic region (seas) in order to also dominate another (land) is critical for projecting power ashore. Sea control must exist in order to control events along the coastline with maritime force.

Ideas of a "peace dividend," widely stated in the US as grounds for cutting defense spending during the 1990s, developed from a *presumption* no superpower existed to challenge America.[53] This mind-set ignores an array of unconventional options available against a better endowed military adversary. It also ignores mankind's bloody history carrying out world politics. This is important when attempting to analyze future problems. Military power is an important issue that does not generate very active cries "against" demobilization efforts. Security-conscious Americans should be worried over a dramatic fall in numbers of naval vessels since World War II, when the USN had 5,000 ships in its inventory. George Baer notes how James Forrestal attempted to raise that figure even higher following Japan's surrender:

> Preparedness fell victim to the economizers. In 1946 Congress turned aside Secretary Forrestal's request to limit demobilization and keep an active and reserve fleet of over 6,000 ships. As far as Congress was concerned, the United States had command of the sea and was in no danger of losing it. Congress did not consider other uses of the Navy – power projection ashore, for instance, or intervention in limited wars. Predictable postwar retrenchment whittled the Navy down.[54]

Navy manpower plunged 90% from 3,380,817 in 1945 to 381,538 at the start of the Korean War.[55] Fleet size promoted by Forrestal is depressing compared to an inventory of approximately 300 ships US Navy officials are requesting in coming decades. The twenty-first century's first five years have not been favorable to the Department of the Navy, even in an era when its fleet, air-wing, and Marine Amphibious Group concept more than proved their utility operating from the Indian Ocean. They are finding unsolicited hostility toward a mediocre request for 375 ships.[56] This is not a maritime force associated with what people believe to be the world's pre-eminent superpower.

Over a century ago Mahan displayed his prophetic abilities by identifying a potential threat from an outward looking China. Mahan's disciples must wonder if he saw what was coming:

> It is a question for the whole civilized world and not for the United States only, whether the Sandwich Islands, with their other position in the North Pacific, shall in the future be an outpost of European civilization, or of the comparative barbarism of China. It is sufficiently known, but not, perhaps, generally noted in our country, that many military men abroad, familiar with Eastern conditions and character, look with apprehension toward the day when the vast mass of China – now inert – may yield to one of those impulses which have in past ages buried civilization under a wave of barbaric invasion.
>
> The great armies of Europe, whose existence is so frequently deplored, may be providentially intended as a barrier to that great movement, if it come. Certainly, while China remains as she is, nothing more disastrous for the future of the world can be imagined than that general disarmament of Europe which is the Utopian dream of the philanthropists.[57]

A look at defense budgets for Western democracies since 1990 shows Mahan's disarmament concern underway. The US defense budget in 1985 surpassed $385,000,000,000. Within a decade it declined 40% to $257,000,000,000. Force readiness analysis during the 1990s by Congressional Research Service staffers found that 66% of available Army divisions, 50% of existing carrier battle groups, 66% of deployable Air Force fighter-attack wings, and 66% of available Marine forces would be required to fight another Persian Gulf War.[58] And this is against a Third World despot. The current state of budget affairs with America's traditional allies is even worse. Canada spends just 1.1% of GDP, while Europeans allocate 2-2.3% for defense.[59]

Much of the military hardware used during the 1990s had been procured in previous decades.[60] This equipment turned out to be a savior for a declining defense budget. However, current and future procurement requirements are now in a bind that will require financial sacrifice.[61] Operating tempo of regional "peacekeeping" missions during the Clinton administration could only be reached because of existing inventory. That inventory is now tired and outdated: "We must replace Cold War-era systems with significantly more capable sensors, networks, weapons, and platforms if we are to increase our ability to deter and defeat enemies."[62] Alan Tonelson explains the thinking and outcome behind withholding financial resources during the 1990s:

> The Clinton administration's proposed fiscal 1994 defense budget makes it clear that, although the president may continue to affirm America's position as a superpower, he has denied the nation the military resources that role requires, even in a world with no Soviet rival. In other words, the "declinists" have won.[63]

Had 1985's defense figure just kept pace with a 4% annual inflation rate, then 1995's defense budget would have been at least $500,000,000,000, double the actual amount. The federal budget allocation for defense held at 29% in 1985, while entitlement spending consumed 42%.[64] By 2005, defense spending declined to 17%, while federal entitlement and domestic obligations rose to a whopping 65%.[65] The US defense budget is often attacked and compared to totalitarian states. Overhead costs from a free market system and all-volunteer force must be factored into that equation.[66] Omitting these key details is deceptive and designed to advance a political agenda.[67]

The argument is often made that current US government debt figures are a Cold War hangover.[68] This is not so much a result of military spending as it is political exploitation of domestic programs. Virtually every time a president found it necessary to increase defense spending, special interest groups and their allies in Congress would line up to demand likewise increases for pet social programs. Frank Moore, Jimmy Carter's congressional liaison, described this money grab as a "floating crap game" of competing interests: "One day we would be working with a coalition of conservative Democrats and Republicans trying to increase defense funding, and the next day we would be working with liberal Democrats and moderate Republicans trying to pass environmental legislation or kill the B-1 bomber."[69]

The move on Washington, DC by those lining up at the taxpayer trough during Carter and Reagan terms resulted in a growth from 4,000 to 20,000 lobbyists. All represent groups seeking to get their hands in the taxpayer's pocket. Between 1977 and 1982 alone, budget-makers witnessed a phenomenal 500% increase of professionals whose skill in life involves bribery and extortion.[70] Lowell Bryan and Diana Farrell's warning is amusing in light of America's financial situation. Though intended for developing countries, their message has greater application to the US government, business community, and individual consumer:

> A major challenge for individual countries and for the world as a whole will be to find a constructive framework for the resolution of social conflict that does not rely unduly on mortgaging and overleveraging countries by issuing unsustainable levels of debt.[71]

Projecting an image of "good times" to American citizens is psychologically beneficial and politically advantageous for elites:

> Above this race of men stands an immense and tutelary power, which takes upon itself alone to secure their gratifications and to watch over their fate. That power is absolute, minute, regular, provident, and mild. It would be like the authority of a parent if, like that authority, its object was to prepare men for manhood; but it seeks, on the contrary, to keep them in perpetual childhood, it is well content that the people should rejoice, provided they think of nothing but rejoicing. For their happiness such a government willingly labours, but it chooses to be the sole agent and the only arbiter of that happiness; it provides for their security, foresees and supplies their necessities, facilitates their pleasures, manages their principal concerns, directs their industry, regulates the decent of property, and subdivides their inheritances: what remains, but to spare them all the care of thinking and all the trouble of living.[72]

These observations are ahead of their time. In this case (1840), it seems to accurately describe launching of Franklin Roosevelt's New Deal in 1933. Government-directed economic theories, which are often based on printing presses continuously kicking out devalued dollars, has all the character traits of North Korea's counterfeiting effort. The scheme can only last so long before somebody must pay a price for such behavior.

Changing Course

The course taken during the 1990s by America and its allies is showing signs of a different direction. This started with launching of "Sea Power 21." It is a comprehensive doctrine based on three critical naval operational characteristics; sea shield, sea strike, and sea basing.[73] All three missions require nothing short of blue-water domination, and that vision takes a global instead of regional perspective. It would not be a surprise if "Sea Power 21" was an attempt to correct deficiencies previously set by "Forward....From the Sea." Sea, land, air, and space power definitions can be of enormous value if integrated into "Sea Power 21."

The various fleets of the United States have operational priorities based on a constantly changing global situation. They receive support from strategically positioned USAF bases around the world. Fleet priority fluctuates with current times. The Seventh Fleet could see itself surpassing the Persian Gulf's Fifth Fleet based on friction between the US and People's Republic of China.[74] The United States is committed to ensuring the security of numerous allies in the region. Drew Bennett explains why a failure to fulfill defense promises to a nation such as Japan would destroy American credibility for decades:

> The Asian region encompasses the world's largest geographic area, including ten strategic straits. It boasts the world's largest population. Economically, Asia has the largest amount of world trade – almost $2.5 trillion in imports and exports – and the largest holdings of foreign reserves, with China, Taiwan, Japan, and South Korea accounting for $700 billion. The Pacific region has the largest concentration of military power, emerging as the largest recipient of arms transfers since it doubled military spending in the 1990s; it is home to seven of the world's ten largest armies. To ignore Asia, or even to fail to make it a top priority, is to jeopardize U.S. national security.[75]

The spirit of James Forrestal seems to be crying out from the grave in an attempt to warn the US of a storm across the Pacific.

Part V

Back to the Future

"Finality, the close of a life, of a relationship, of an era, even though this be a purely artificial creation of human arrangement, in all cases appeals powerfully to the imagination, and especially to that of a generation self-conscious as our own, a generation which has coined for itself the phrase *fin de siecle* to express its own belief, however superficial and mistaken, that it knows its own exponents and its own tendencies; that, amid the din of its own progress sounding in its ears, it knows not only whence it come but whither it goes. The nineteenth century is about to die, only to rise again in the twentieth. Whence did it come? How far has it gone? Whither is it going?"

Alfred Thayer Mahan (Rear Adm., USN), "A Twentieth-Century Outlook," *Harper's New Monthly Magazine*, Vol. 95, no. 568 (September 1897).

Chapter Thirteen

Now and Forever

"When the right moment comes, the mask will be dropped and the Russians with Chinese help will seek to impose their system on the West..."
- Anatoliy Golitsyn

A number of issues will arise in the twenty-first century to challenge power generator sustainability and resource wherewithal. National success will depend on an ability to overcome greater international assaults on autonomy. This offensive will collide with efforts to deploy national grand strategy as needed to fulfill policy objectives established by political leaders. The United States remains the prototype of choice in this discussion because of its current power generator status, coupled to being the world's largest economy. Perilous times, however, are around the corner for continuation of American supremacy. There have always been surprises and attempts to circumvent national sovereignty in world politics. High and mighty goals of globalization are a future threat. Nations that remain standing will be those whose leadership avoided hazards disguised under a utopian ruse of globalization. This requires keen eyesight for dangerously deceptive intricacies that can undermine national grand strategy. Risk in various forms will dare American leadership. The price for ignorance will be a loss of freedom to act. Those in charge must remain alert for such enticements and hold a solid sovereign line.

Bondage under the guise of international law is going to be self-government's greatest menace in mankind's history. It threatens to depreciate power generator and resource value. America's financial strength, for example, has already been weakened. This is witnessed by pressures from rising debt during peacetime. Western governments are attempting to offset trade deficits and defend their way of life with patchwork social programs. Like an addiction, the easy political fix involves increasing government spending and social programs. This gamble is reflected by large foreign investments from some not-so-friendly parties. These regimes could not penetrate Western financial portfolios without the advantage of a trade surplus, which miraculously seems to be running on auto-pilot.

Few bothered to consider the price for surrendering their ability to act independently. Regulation burdens and growing government bureaucracy result from unbridled globalization. The United States, in particular, has experienced enormous economic pressure in recent years originating from overseas sources. These actions now test institutional sustainability, while tossing around newly printed greenbacks is viewed as a quick fix solution. Behavior is reminiscent of sailors on liberty after six months at sea. Federal, state, and local governments simply do what they do best; expand and spend money. This pace threatens to overwhelm a private sector economy's ability to pay the tab.

Technologically, there is a vast amount of published material supporting advances now occurring and those that are yet to materialize. It is important that fundamentals behind technology are not lost in research laboratories. This includes modes of future transport. Basics, anchored to strategic theory and geographic realities, are guaranteed to remain paramount fixtures. Willingness and ability of states to apply assets will be for identical reasons as past pursuits. Forward looking analysis must avoid seductive temptations associated with flamboyant technology. Expansion of space power will achieve exploitation levels similar to air power during the twentieth century. While addition and growth of this power generator warrants attention, it will not take away any utility from sea, land, or air power in the future. Those definitions created by this research ensure focus is not lost on geostrategic mainstays. Success of national grand strategy depends on all four power generators continuing to complement each other, regardless of technology or transportation wonders.

Globalization

A number of states, organizations, corporations, and prominent individuals from around the world are actively pursuing a globalization initiative. This stable of power is unparalleled, while the velocity is at a pace denying time for consideration of long-range consequences to national sovereignty. The two-pronged advance is composed of progressive social policy advocates and intellectuals on the left flank, while international economists guard the right. Those responsible for protecting a free nation find it difficult to challenge this degree of economic hedonism, especially when it is coupled to a global political movement. The two converge at the transnational level and, as a result, the security risk to national sovereignty is greatly enhanced.[1]

Unilateralism is on the verge of having its final sacrament administered. This sobering reality does not receive the attention it deserves by constitutional republics. Those who possess fundamental values associated with a free society are pushed into a marriage with governments and non-state actors having very little or no respect for the same political ideals.[2] Democracy's long historic record for pursuing such relationships is full of examples where a horrendous cost had to be paid on battlefields in exchange for earlier lustful cravings to practice economic intercourse with totalitarian states. Those who rule over toiling masses with an iron fist have a ledger showing them doing the same to governments assisting in their own development. Economic matrimony is a temporary luxury paid later in booty and blood as free societies must fight for their sovereignty.

The infusion of political economy into the national security structure, while an appropriate consideration for grand strategy, has become *the* prevalent theme in recent years. A troubling aspect of contemporary political economy is the drive to integrate Keynesian political and economic theories into a single global model. Politics is not economics and vice versa unless the goal is to practice some sort of quasi-Marxist philosophy. Traditional economists recognize a "distinct difference," as well as the stench of tyranny. They understand the importance of maintaining separate tracks in a free society. Thomas Barnett amusingly exemplifies a dedicated cadre IPE types who believe globalization will enable both to flourish on the same rail:

> To put it most simply, America's national interest in the era of globalization lies primarily in the extension of global economic connectivity. Global connectivity benefits America economically by increasing our access to the World's goods and services while promoting our exports of the same. With that growing connectivity around the planet, we see the rising need for political and security rule sets that define fair play among nations, firms, and even individuals, not just in trade but in terms of war, which – as we have seen with 9/11 and the resulting war on terrorism – is no longer restricted to just organized violence between nation-states. That global system of security rules is the most important peace dividend of the Cold War; these rule sets allow globalization to flourish and advance, and by doing so, they have effectively killed great-power war, a destructive force that haunted the international community for close to two centuries (dating all the way back to Europe's Napoleonic Wars of the early 1800s).[3]

Barnett's position must be analyzed outside the realm of theoretical bliss and observed through reality's harsh prism. It is a blind leap to assume no foreign government or entity was behind the events of 9/11. Additionally, trade deficits show this "global connectivity" utopia to be a one-sided event. An astute national security analyst views global trade with sworn adversaries as a different form of "waging war against your enemy." The United States consumer and capital investment firms make a substantial contribution to the modernization of Communist China. The enormous size and speed of this transition bankrolls the People's Liberation Army (PLA) into becoming a first-class global military fighting machine. America's industrial and manufacturing base is decapitated while capitalism's great engine rotates into a service economy of paperwork, tourism, and human body alterations. It has reached a point that Communist China is now bankrolling a large portion of US government debt.[4] Left out of the babble of collective consumption equations is any room for classics of political thought. John Ikenberry notes how these have inspired the human pursuit of freedom and self-government for thousands of years:

> Whatever the specific impact of British or American liberal ideas, it is probably also the case that the overall robustness of their economy and polity had a lot to do with the persuasiveness of their ideas. In effect, this is another aspect of hegemonic leadership – leadership by example. States are particularly willing to follow a state if that state is successful, that is, if it has developed a particularly appealing and prosperous domestic political order.[5]

Those who value freedom are best served by Great Britain and the United States acting as stewards of international power. Their historical contribution to global affairs is not based on an economic feeding frenzy, though that is a common battle-cry belching from the socialist camp. Prosperity occurred in Britain and America because of political ideals underlying philosophies of liberty and private property (social contract theories of John Locke).[6] Economic good times evolve from a belief in individual freedom, rather than a position that human masses are simple cogs of state production. John Ikenberry accurately noted that "German industrial and technological prowess in the mid-1930s impressed more than a few British and continental European elites, even to the point that it tempered their opposition to National Socialism."[7] The cost of overlooking Hitler's socialist experiment because of an economic orgy requires no further explanation.

The PRC has done a commendable job of constructing separate tracks for politics and economics which, sadly, the West seems to be losing the capability of maintaining. The PRC model is unique because it has been achieved while deploying the communist paddle on the governing rail. A similar practice can be found behind the rise of Nazi Germany. It is only made possible because the West, for whatever dysfunctional reason, allows Communist China to free-ride off Western markets, trade practices, regulation burdens, labor costs, currency fluctuations, and global capital investment. It is an incredible deal for the Peking oppressors. International trade with like-minded democratic states is entirely different from free trade with a dictatorship that annually ranks near the top of the world's most repressive regimes.

Average Americans working in the private sector have difficulty visualizing a positive connection between incredibly high numbers of manufactured goods coming in versus miniscule amounts leaving. Common sense is telling these people that the other side is gaining enormous leverage at their expense. This is something that seems to escape supposedly enlightened elites. Japan is a solid ally with a multi-party democracy. This is an entirely different model from what is now promoted as the Russian Federation.

While the US formats a budget for bankrupt social programs, and attempts to offset trade imbalances with soybeans from booming government-subsidized farm factories, American taxpayers proceed to modernize an industrial base of a nation that caused Mahan so much concern:

> China, however, may burst her barriers eastward as well as westward, toward the Pacific as well as toward the European Continent. In such a movement it would be impossible to exaggerate the momentous issues dependent upon a firm hold of the Sandwich Islands by a great, civilized, maritime power. By its nearness to the scene, and by the determined animosity to the Chinese movement which close contact seems to inspire, our own country, with its Pacific coast, is naturally indicated as the proper guardian for this most important position. To hold it, however, whether in the supposed case or in war with a European state, implies a great extension of our naval power. Are we ready to undertake this?[8]

During the twentieth century America answered Mahan's question with an unambiguous presence of sea power spanning the world. His query resurfaces at the dawn of the twenty-first century with a heightened degree of concern. There are critical questions concerning the direction America's political elites are taking the country.

National identity will be an enormous challenge as the human race, organizations, and institutions make global moves in larger numbers. Corrective action to reset traditional parameters of state identity becomes a daunting task as those numbers explode. The recently formed US Department of Homeland Security has spent its first five years in existence finding that out. Global governance, global connectivity, and a globally integrated economy steal the reins of national power from governing authority. James Rosenthau reveals how grand strategy's model loses relevancy and the policy-making process of sovereign states surrender any ability to determine their destiny:

> Stated differently, capital, production, labor, and markets have all been globalized to the point where financiers, entrepreneurs, workers, and consumers are now deeply enmeshed in networks of the world economy that have superseded the traditional political jurisdictions of national scope. Such a transformation was bound to impact upon the established parameters of world politics. Among other things, it served to loosen the ties of producers and workers to their states, to expand the horizons within which citizens pondered their self-interests, and to foster the formation of transnational organizations that could operate on a global scale to advance the interests of their members. The rapid growth and maturation of the multi-centric world can in good part be traced to the extraordinary dynamism and expansion of the global economy. And so can the weakening of the state, which is no longer the manager of the national economy and has become, instead, an instrument for adjusting the national economy to the exigencies of an expanding world economy. As one observer put it, "In effect, governments are acting as the midwives of globalization."[9]

It is an unprecedented event in the historical context of nation-state independence.

Economania

Emil Ludwig noted a profound relationship between the business practices of Phoenicians and rabid foreign investing by Western capital firms in recent times. His analogy is full of similarities with the globalization project underway. Unfortunately, the parallels

between ancient Phoenicia and contemporary America may proceed to
an identical ending:

> The Phoenicians were the first and for long centuries the wiliest race
> to shape the economic life of foreign nations as do the great banking
> houses in our own day, first as peddlers and swindlers, then as
> merchant princes and grandees. A lack of national sentiment helped
> them, as it does the banks."[10]

For the sake of their own health, financial portfolio managers
in the West should heed Mao's threat before providing the PRC further
war fighting capital: "I love Americans, but the Wall Street barons
must go."[11] Ludwig exposes a risky dilemma for those governments
and corporations in free societies who blindly chase after the markets of
repressive regimes:

-   To what extent does a financial portfolio influence loyalty to
    the state?
-   Do multi-national corporations lose sight of their national
    heritage?
-   Is there a threat of blackmailing executives of multi-national
    corporations (MNCs) for the purpose of getting them to serve
    the strategic objectives of the country their business operations
    are beholden to?

Global governance should concern all those with responsibility
for defending a multi-party democracy. The opportunity to influence
the politics of your chief adversary by gaining control over those sitting
on the corporate throne is a tyrant's fantasy. Counter-intelligence
experts know the opportunities available to hostile governments who
target influential people, regardless of profession:

> Among the official class there are worthy men who have been
> deprived of office; others who have committed errors and have been
> punished. There are sycophants and minions who are covetous of
> wealth. There are those who wrongly remain long in lowly office;
> those who have not obtained responsible positions, and those whose
> sole desire is to take advantage of times of trouble to extend the scope
> of their own abilities. There are those who are two-faced, changeable,
> and deceitful, and who are always sitting on the fence. As far as all
> such are concerned you can secretly inquire after their welfare,
> reward them liberally with gold and silk, and so tie them to you.[12]

The exploitable rewards are difficult to put a price tag on, especially when the object of so much affection is a venture capitalist with billions of dollars to manage. Thomas Barnett continues to justify globalization fever in the context of twentieth century events:

> When America turned its back on the world following World War I, the globalization it inevitably helped destroy was largely of Europe's creation. But the globalization of today is largely of America's creation. We set in motion following World War II, deliberately salvaging Western Europe and Japan when we could have just as easily walked away from these tasks. We protected these embryonic pillars of Globalization II through three and a half decades of Soviet military threat, and when that threat began to recede, we played bodyguard to Globalization III's inclusion of the emerging markets – more than half the world's population. We provided the security glue that let Developing Asia focus its resources on export-led growth despite remaining a powder keg of unresolved political-military disputes and rivalries. We stepped up to manage bad security situations in the Persian Gulf and the Balkans while Europe moved confidently toward economic union and simultaneously cut defence spending across the board. It was America that stood up as Gap Leviathan across the 1990s, after the Soviet bloc collapsed and ended its decades of malicious mischief there.[13]

Global Economy 101 would not have saved the world in any of the examples given. The problem with World War I is that the conflict was never clearly settled. The array of documents generated at its conclusion simply shrouded an unenforceable time-out. The violence of World War I resumed in 1939 with the intent of settling unfinished business.

Globalization efforts during the twenty-first century's first forty-five years had more to do with empire building, power-seeking, and socialist pursuits. Europe and Japan were rebuilt following WWII by the US as a necessity to prevent an active international communist movement from overthrowing free societies. This action is not economic but simple power politics. American military involvement during the first twenty years of the Cold War was centered on containment policy. Spreading economic benevolence to Third World nations was not intended for the purpose of furthering construction of hotel chains. The objective involved stopping a Soviet and PRC juggernaut (politics over economics). A review of many dictatorships aligned with the communist group shows their society not significantly more free today than fifty years ago, even with global trade. The PRC and Russia provide the West with contemporary proof that global free trade does not eliminate political repression. It does help ensure the continuation of corrupt regimes. Cries by "foreign policy experts" such as Bono to write-off Third World debt is a hopeless waste of taxpayer money if fundamental constitutional change does not also take place.

Proceeds from building a regimented industrial dictatorship provide the resources for a war machine able to challenge free societies that blindly assist in their development. Once parity is achieved, then a dictatorship has no further use for the provider. Western democracies, acting as initial vendor, witness other repressive regimes begin carrying on amongst each other. With over six billion people around the world, and 25% of that figure comprised of its own, the People's Republic of China does not need 300,000,000 US citizens. Once it has stolen all America has to offer and its own economy is fully developed, salvation from Western benevolence is redeemed by drawing the Third World's economic compass toward their Middle Kingdom. Kicking America to the curb then becomes an administrative exercise.[14] Meanwhile, Joseph Nye joins Barnett's euphoria over global collectivism:

> On balance, Americans have benefited from globalization. To the extent that we wish to continue to do so, we will need to deal with its discontents. This cannot be accomplished by resorting to slogans of sovereignty, unilateral policies, or drawing inward, as the unilateralists and sovereigntists suggest: "If we can't do it our way, then we just won't do it. But at least we the people, the American people, will remain masters of our ship." This prescription mistakes the abstractions of sovereignty for the realities of power. The result would be to undermine our soft power and America's ability to influence others' responses to globalization. Instead, the United States should use its current preeminence to help shape institutions that will benefit both Americans and the rest of the world as globalization evolves.[15]

There are no specifics explaining how the US benefits from trade deficits and, in fact, multi-billionaire investor, Warren Buffett (Oracle of Omaha), does not seem to agree with all this enthusiasm:

> The US trade deficit is a bigger threat to the domestic economy than either the federal budget deficit or consumer debt and could lead to political turmoil. Right now, the rest of the world owns $3 trillion more of us than we own of them. In my view, it will create political

turmoil at some point…Pretty soon I think there will be a big adjustment.[16]

It would be useful if suggestions for dealing with America's "globalization discontents" were available. Shades of authoritarianism come to mind. Perhaps a refresher course on the Constitution of the United States would help those confused over America's status as a federation of fifty sovereign states. A primary concern of the so-called, "globalization discontents," has to do with diametrically different founding principles and national charters. It cannot be reiterated enough that the Constitution of the United States is fundamentally at odds with the ideals of the vast majority of national governments and international organizations. This includes utopian-sounding NGOs acting as espionage fronts. How the problem of dealing with free people in a sovereign national government would be manhandled for the sake of global despotism is a major hurdle. Based on American judicial and legislative behavior in recent years, the national government does not seem capable of dealing with this matter either.

With the exception of a small handful of powerful opportunists, the total number of beneficiaries in a democracy who gain from unbridled trade with totalitarian regimes is miniscule. Democracies where free enterprise is allowed to flourish benefit more by using their economic power to maintain a policy of "free and fair" trade with like-minded national governments. Opening up the free market of a democratic society to oppressive regimes, in the great hope that change and civilized behavior will result, surrenders the single most important passive strategic asset that a multi-party republic possesses. The act is akin to an army handing over its order of battle prior to the fight. Dictatorships will, if allowed, take advantage of this opportunity to reinforce their authority and become more powerful. Rebuilding European and Japanese economies following World War II worked because the US had an industrial base unscathed by war, the market in place to support reconstruction and, most important, a group of recipients receptive towards a similar form of government. America supplied the goods and maintained a trade surplus that continued to fuel a huge post-war economy.[17]

Wily money managers, who scour the planet in search of great rewards, as Ludwig compared with the Phoenician experience, have sole allegiance to maximizing their financial portfolio.[18] Recent global oil market turbulence is a reflection of pressure caused by developing nations housing over 75% of the world's population.[19] As politicians point fingers everywhere but where the problem can be found, economies of those nations hostile to multi-party democracies persistently grow at the West's expense.

Communist China has witnessed a consistent annual growth rate averaging 9-10% since 1995. Its overall twenty-year rate has been at least 8%.[20] Since 1985 economic development has tripled thanks, in large part, to Western capital and market access. Paul Kennedy attempts to analyze what this means for the twenty-first century by looking at the previous one for guidance:

> Although nominally independent since decolonization, these countries are probably more dependent upon Europe and the United States than a century ago. Ironically, three or four decades of efforts by developing countries to gain control of their own destinies – by nationalizing Western companies, setting up commodity-exporting cartels, subsidizing indigenous manufacturing to achieve import substitution, campaigning for a new world order based upon redistribution of the existing imbalances of wealth – have all failed. The "market," backed by governments of the developed economies, has proved too strong, and the struggle against it has weakened developing economies still further – except those (like Korea and Taiwan) which decided to join.[21]

A problem with what Kennedy wrote in 1993 is that constitutional republics are now witnessing a colossal shift of their markets, or so-called "trump cards," to some very unsavory sharks. As factories close in the West, further eroding an ability to sustain manufacturing forces during times of national emergency, MNCs switch loyalties by building new facilities in places such as the PRC.[22] Natural resources needed for manufacturing have rotated their primary point of delivery from the West to the East.

Nations such as the PRC attract Western companies who then become dependent on a repressive regime for production. This requires companies to act as government agents on the global commodities market to divert greater numbers of natural resources for their host nation. Wily money managers, expecting double-digit returns on investments, are standing by to further this process along. Fear not, Western citizens are told, Gross Domestic Product continues to rise. Do you not understand rising GDP reflects the good times and highlife? The great unsaid is that GDP figures include such phenomenal

manufacturing facilities as daycare centers, fast-food restaurants, drug
rehab facilities and, last but not least, prisons.

While Western financial institutions readily provide capital for
developing the world's elite club of tyrants, Robert Art poses a
question the West must face as it looks to the twenty-first century:

> China has both the will and the potential resources to challenge
> America's military preeminence. The critical questions are whether
> China will overtake the United States in overall power and, if so,
> when. The Chinese themselves have given some answers to these
> questions. The China Institute for Contemporary International
> Relations (roughly equivalent to the analytical division of the U.S.
> Central Intelligence Agency) completed a study in the fall of 2000 on
> "comprehensive national power" (CNP). In China's lexicon,
> comprehensive national power is made up of economic, military,
> technological, scientific, educational, natural resource, and social
> stability components.[23]

It is entertaining to witness Sun Tzu Wu deception strategy at
work. The PRC uses consistent economic growth figures of 5-6% that
skew actual rates of expansion, while great Western democracies fail to
even care, or excuse the deception as a "misunderstanding." The
technique used is identical when publicizing military expenditures.

Continuation of globalization trends developed over the past
twenty years will result in growing subjugation of states to a global
governance authority, global connectivity, and global everything else.
Many individuals perceive this as a noble and so-called "progressive"
achievement. Humankind would witness an entirely new order for
policing mankind, done by a single entity whose territory encompasses
the entire planet. Instruments of enforcement are yet to be seen. If this
global "progressive" movement continues tearing down time-honored
borders of free nations, then national grand strategy's model will wither
into oblivion. This would cause a loss of virtually every power resource
and their supporting elements:

> Foreigners with fistfuls of devalued dollars now comb America for
> banks, businesses, factories, land, and securities. This shopping spree
> began in the 1970s, but its growing strength is a principal legacy of
> Reaganomics. As long as America consumes more than it produces,
> the imbalance must be made up with foreign money that purchases
> IOUs and equity. In the 1980s America began trading ownership of
> assets (and the future incomes they provide) for the privilege of living

beyond its means. The result is a continuing erosion of control over decision making and technologies that are crucial to the creation of national wealth and power.[24]

At the time of Thomas Omestad's report (1989), foreign ownership included 46% of the prime commercial property in Los Angeles, 39% in Houston, and even 33% in Washington, DC.[25] Figures were, in general, 20% higher by 2005. There is no reason to believe this expansion will not continue.

An ability of constitutional republics to exert independence becomes difficult when contract law is strictly enforced and property rights are a fundamental principle. Unlike Hugo Chavez's Venezuelan dictatorship, it is taboo in free and open societies for a government to flagrantly declare property contracts null and void. This is an attractive investment climate for not just foreign capitalists, but those regimes wishing to influence that government. Foreign parties operating in the US now hire lobbyists to scour the halls of Congress and various state legislative houses. They seek support for legislation favorable to their overseas client's interest, while using a wheel-barrel full of American dollars. This situation is dangerously close to the point where American citizens lose political influence to foreign parties. Regime legitimacy erodes and a willingness to fight no longer applies. People begin to consider for whom they are fighting as industrial might and financial strength "progressively" fall under greater control of foreign entities. In such a scenario even power resource elements such as intelligence become obedient to an internationalist status quo. Technological development, industrial production, manpower, time, and even geography no longer matter.

In the political environment just described, power resources are removed from contact with power generators. This cut is completed at national grand strategy's level. Sea, land, air, and space power become scattered outside national policy-making parameters. No longer will such issues concern sovereign states because leadership authority has voluntarily transferred its responsibility to a much larger political entity. That "average stiff" is getting taken, in several ways, toward a troubling destiny by those who believe they know what is best for everyone else. It is extremely likely this event will be put to a climatic test in the twenty-first century. The Oracle of Omaha raised a very sobering warning. It is a desire of sovereign people, comprising Barnett's globalization discontents, that failure be the outcome.

Where are the Aircraft Carriers?

This question, since the end of World War II, has been asked over three hundred times and by every president occupying the White House. It is more a statement than question but too many do not realize the value of that point. Presidential prerogative is the single greatest defense of forward power projection features provided by aircraft carriers. Though a variety of military assets have become available for strategic planning and enhancement of forward power projection, none can match an aircraft carrier's muscle. Saber-rattling despots understand the threat when seeing a real-life *Nimitz*-class carrier conducting combat "training" exercises on the horizon. Such statements have far greater impact than an embassy diplomat displaying images of a B-1 Bomber in the hanger at Ellsworth Air Force Base, South Dakota.

Anti-super aircraft carrier advocates consistently fail to consider the value of power packed in larger ships. New cutting-edge weapons readily provide fresh ammunition for this movement. The atomic bomb and advent of long-range bombers following World War II significantly challenged surface fleet utility. Satellite capabilities and precision guided weapons are contemporary equivalents.[26] Russia's *Shkval* torpedo, for example, is exploited by many anti-carrier advocates because of its 200 knot speed. The newest version, in fact, is expected to reach target speeds approaching 300 knots.[27] Naval research labs consider it an insult for people to believe countermeasures are not in the works. *Shkval* torpedoes are destined to be yet another technological marvel overcome with superior countermeasures. The super-carrier's greatest threat in the present century continues to be pessimistic views of its utility. An influential supporting cast remains those who enjoy sharpening the defense budget-cutting axe.

Recent advent of *Streetfighter*, a high-speed craft for naval coastal and littoral water combat, is another tool recently deployed against aircraft carriers.[28] *Streetfighter* is valuable to any navy's portfolio of combat vessels, but that is not the strategic and tactical problem. A grave error is its promotion as a vehicle for "smaller is better" arguments against large carriers.[29] Depending on the package inside, cost of a new, fully-modernized cruiser or destroyer easily surpasses $1,000,000,000. A *Nimitz*-class carrier exceeds ten times that amount. Size of both ships, however, enables them to possess an enormous portfolio of high-end offensive and defensive capabilities that cannot be crammed inside a *Streetfighter* hull.[30] Destroyers and carriers may show up as larger targets the closer they get to the coast but, because of the weapons package, each is able to remain far from that coast while delivering explosive misery upon an adversary.[31] It is a deceptive trade practice to draw comparison between smaller ships such as *Streetfighter* and blue-water fleet assets. Tactical and strategic roles of each are not in the same arena. A military jeep is not a suitable replacement for a tank, nor should patrol craft be considered an alternative to destroyers, cruisers, and aircraft carriers.

Exploitation of land assets by an adversary of the United States in a particular region of the world has been used several times to test the US Navy's ability to operate in multiple theaters. This is guaranteed not to change and, therefore, a president can be expected to continue asking for aircraft carriers. Cunning opponents, knowing this dependency, cleverly incorporate multiple power generators to destabilize America's maritime advantage. Depending on the scenario, USN assets could become over-stretched and unable to appropriately respond to a rapidly unfolding global security dynamic. Hostilities breaking out in various locations can deny forward presence in regions where the political environment is approaching critical mass. This puts enormous strain on policy-makers as their strategic options dry up and they must prioritize who gets saved and who dies. The possibility requires eternal vigilance by defense planners and, fortunately, the US possesses resources capable of supporting naval operations when pressure becomes overwhelming.[32]

This is the motive behind jockeying military roles during the 1990s as America's defense budget contracted. Land and air forces can be used against enemy maritime assets, just as they can also be used to free maritime assets for other priorities. US Navy and Marine Corps forces can deploy for purposes of immobilizing enemy land and air targets. They may also be put in service to free allied land and air resources for other ventures. This is a highly fluid and volatile event. Moving pieces involves a high degree of risk from not knowing the adversary's grand strategic designs or degree of talent possessed by their power portfolio.

America's relationship with Japan is well-suited for explaining this process. Distant allies help minimize US vulnerability to a global security commitment. An alliance of aggressor countries could create the environment on land that denies flexibility for naval forces at sea. A popular method is to incite chaos at geostrategically sensitive locations. Osama bin Laden and his business partners have been providing a taste of this practice since the 1990s.[33] Civil unrest can be easily whipped up by saber-rattling radical Islamists and anti-Israeli Arab masses. This pressures normally cautious Arab governments into taking an aggressive posture to maintain constituent legitimacy. Friction locks America's Sixth Fleet to the eastern Mediterranean Sea as insurance against a Suez Canal closure. Ongoing Balkans operations by NATO would require another carrier. Two more carriers must aid US Central Command in fulfilling Persian Gulf responsibilities. A single carrier battle group would engage hostile land forces in areas around Saudi Arabia, while the other ensured the Strait of Hormuz remained open.

Simultaneous revolution in Indonesia by anti-Western forces would jeopardize transit at the Strait of Malacca. Passage by merchant tanker is critical for the transport of oil from the Persian Gulf to Japan. The economies of several nation-states throughout Southeast Asia are dependent on this choke-point remaining open. Denying tanker access to Japan would force a response with an aircraft carrier battle group from the US Seventh Fleet. A simultaneous confrontation in the South China Sea over the Philippines claim to the Spratly Islands over-stretches Seventh Fleet assets. An additional aircraft carrier from California would be called to assist.

Threat of war in the Middle East and potential loss of three maritime chokepoints likely causes instability in global oil markets. Japan must have assistance from the US to meet its energy needs. This requires uncorking idle wells in the lower forty-eight United States, while diverting oil from Alaska's North Slope. Depending on threat levels, an aircraft carrier from Bremerton, Washington would be dispatched to provide tanker cover from Kodiak to Honshu. Chaos and anarchy throughout West Africa requires a commitment from the Second Fleet. A large number of US Marines would be required to protect Americans in the region. Overthrow of Panama's government then threatens another maritime chokepoint. An aircraft carrier from Jacksonville, Florida would enter the Caribbean, while a second from California deploys on the Pacific side of Central America. Global responsibilities have pushed America's maritime portfolio to the brink.

A solution to this predicament involves "jointness" on a massive scale. Land and air assets, as well as US Coast Guard and additional Marine Corps capabilities, are crucial to managing a geostrategic swamp. Allied forces provide additional support. US Army units from Fort Bragg, North Carolina, for example, could be rapidly deployed to replace a Marine Amphibious Group (MAG) operating in the West Africa region. Boeing C-17 cargo aircraft, with their huge 84 ton payload and 2700 mile range, provide logistics support to airborne units sent from Fort Bragg. Civilians can then be extracted on return flights out of the region. Releasing the MAG starts a phenomenal chain reaction of events spanning the globe. The contingent of troops, amphibious ships, and Harrier jet capabilities proceeds around the Cape of Good Hope toward the Persian Gulf in support of US Central Command. This releases an aircraft carrier battle group for service in Southeast Asia.

Army Rangers from Fort Benning, Georgia can be flown to the Panama Canal, which enables any Pacific-based carrier battle group operating off the coast to proceed toward Hawaii. It would join another carrier task force from San Diego. Jacksonville's carrier would remain in the Caribbean to support operations. A MAG from Camp Pendleton, California would meet the two carrier battle groups as they depart Hawaii for East Asia. Their purpose is to reinforce Marines already deployed, and to support the Republic of China, Japanese Defense Force (JDF), or US Army troops in South Korea.

US Air Force assets in Japan could provide cover over the Sea of Japan, freeing the aircraft carrier from Bremerton to support any action unfolding in Korea. In-flight refueling allows B-52 and B-1 bombers on Guam, Diego Garcia in the Indian Ocean, and the US to fly non-stop around the world in support of strategic or tactical needs. US tactical aircraft in Kuwait can support and help defend the Persian Gulf. A large logistics train springs into action linking the entire stable of land, sea, and air capabilities. This emanates from numerous locations, such as Diego Garcia, Guam, Cyprus, Puerto Rico, and Azores.

Shifting assets involves power resource elements able to transform their utility into each power generator's tool box. Transition is not permanent, but it is a fluid geostrategic alignment designed to fluctuate as events unfold. Flexibility of sea, land, and air elements transit into power that is vital for application of pressure at sea. While fluidity behind land and air instruments fulfill sea power requirements, the same applies for naval and marine forces that meet mission requirements beneficial to land and air objectives. USAF fighter aircraft provide security in seas around Japan. This enables underway naval forces to be used successfully on land throughout the Korean peninsula. Marine Amphibious Groups serve as land and sea assets around the Arabian Peninsula and East Asia. Army Rangers become instruments of sea power by reopening the Panama Canal. US Navy aircraft launched from carriers at sea are air assets providing fighter cover for long-range USAF bombers traveling over the oceans. Not to be left out, space power provides an elusive invisible hand for guidance, intelligence, and communications, which are vital to forces operating below. This entire process succeeds as a result of the solid professional relationship that exists between various military branches and national security agencies.

Numerous proposals have surfaced in recent years that could alter future mechanisms supporting forward presence. A public relations push, for example, has gradually evolved supporting development of sea-based military platforms.[34] Offshore engineering firms have designs and proposals for massive floating bases that are four times the length of a *Nimitz*-class aircraft carrier (4400 feet). This concept appears at a time when production of the Joint Strike Fighter (JSF) is ramping up. As the newest short take-off and vertical landing aircraft, JSF's arrival is adding momentum to sea basing.[35]

Sea basing has many advantages, as well as a fair number of disadvantages. Those disadvantages cannot be overcome entirely, but they can be minimized to a point that gains outweigh the risk. A problem involves mobility, both to the site and once in place. Exposure to hostile force is obvious. Designs exist for platforms able to move at roughly 15 knots and, unfortunately, faster on-site positioning may be required to sell the project.[36] Sea basing should not be confused with aircraft carriers. It is an entirely different strategic asset and issues involving speed should not be a factor. In fact, sea basing is a perfect example of how power generator definitions allow change to take place. Sea basing utility is found in its contribution as a substitute for land bases. Vulnerability warrants no greater degree of criticism than the exposure existing for land bases. Aircraft carriers, on the other hand, serve purposes of quick forward power projection that requires immediate response. It is critical to keep these differences in perspective because both possess profound relevance to Mahan:

> The flexibility offered by sea-to-objective maneuver underscores the time-honored strategic principle of position. In the early 1900s, Rear Admiral Alfred T. Mahan wrote of this concept, stating emphatically that mobile forces can determine a war's outcome through position, and that the sea itself becomes a central position – like a highway – where lines of communication are assured and forces are moved. During distant operations and maritime expeditions, Mahan noted, forces need to "establish a second base near the scene of operations." Although by "second base" Mahan meant a nearby port from which

to operate, the modern concept of Sea Basing provides a similar capability.[37]

John Klein and Rich Morales have described how sea bases do not replace waterborne craft, but they do replace land bases.[38] Similarities exist with naval assets responsible for tactical air power (aircraft carriers), strategic nuclear deterrence (ballistic missile submarines), and Marine amphibious operations (amphibious assault ships).[39] However, surface "fleet" assets possess unique qualities, and aircraft carriers are the best example. Sea bases support strategic objectives in a manner related to Mahan's view of overseas bases.

Armchair Admirals

Assertions that sea power has run its course are not in short supply. Every century has seen a cadre of individuals who argue against its utility. Mounting a defense only requires a look at history's ledger to prove otherwise. Sea power has consistently increased in value since the Phoenician Empire. If every century has in fact witnessed a growth in its utility, then what basis is there for stopping now? Attacks often come from narrow views focusing on physical objects. The sea power naysayer has been around as long as their target of criticism. Even 2,500 years ago, following the decisive Athenian naval victory at Salamis, Herodotus found himself having to defend the contribution of Athens:

> And here I feel constrained to deliver an opinion, which most men, I know, will dislike, but which, as it seems to me to be true, I am determined not to withhold. Had the Athenians, from fear of the approaching danger, quitted their country, or had they without quitting it submitted to the power of Xerxes, there would certainly have been no attempt to resist the Persians by sea; in which case, the course of events by land would have been the following. Though the Peloponnesians might have carried ever so many breastworks across the Isthmus, yet their allies would have fallen off from the Lacedaemonians, not by voluntary desertion, but because town after town must have been taken by the fleet of barbarians; and so the Lacedaemonians would at last have stood alone, and, standing alone, would have displayed prodigies of valour, and died nobly. Either they would have done thus, or else, before it came to that extremity, seeing one Greek state after another embrace the cause of Medes, they would have come to terms with King Xerxes; and thus, either way

> Greece would have been brought under Persia. For I cannot
> understand of what possible use the walls across the Isthmus could
> have been, if the King had had the mastery of the sea. If then a man
> should now say that the Athenians were the saviours of Greece, he
> would not exceed the truth.[40]

Many questions arise over how the political world of today
would look had those states that pursued sea power not done so. What
would be the appearance of nations, societies, political institutions, and
cultures had Great Britain not found their destiny at sea? How distant
would Napoleonic France, Nazi Germany, the Soviet Union, and
Communist China traveled had sea power not been there to check
tyranny's desire? Questions become more challenging as the future is
pondered. Even now, a pool of former sea power advocates exist to
argue that technology has caused sea power's loss in utility.
Ruminations of Halford Mackinder come to mind but, instead of land
transportation, modern Mackinder types base their position on such
things as missile technology:

> We have projected an evolution of the current primitive cruise missile
> into an instrument that can strike globally with centimeter precision,
> powered by scramjet engines, traveling so quickly that it can hit a
> ship in the center of the Atlantic Ocean from an East Coast base in
> under five minutes.[41]

Several facts surface to squash George and Meredith
Friedman's technology bug. Fundamental solutions involve coming to
grips with definitional clarity. Succumbing to gadgetry blurs clear view
of national grand strategy's blueprint. Something equivalent to a bottle-
rocket in expansive terms associated with sea power can cause
dangerously deceptive fixations. That same bottle rocket quickly
becomes nothing more than a puff of smoke if satellites in space used
to guide projectiles to their target are taken out.

Naval forces have historically incorporated weaponry similar to
what existed on land to fulfill roles at sea. The offensive utility
provided to forward power projection is, as a result, greatly enhanced.
In the military arena of naval force, integration of sophisticated warfare
assets is in constant evolution. In the near future a large naval armada,
for example, will possess abilities that enable domination of an entire
ocean region in which it sails.[42] That is an extraordinary amount of

territory. The same degree of technical initiative that enables achievement of this milestone will exist for all power generators.

The volume of Cold War and "post-Cold War" publications appearing in recent years is staggering. Numbers pertaining to the recent war on terror alone is unprecedented. This glut of literary performance will be more intense in years ahead; making criticism of those involved with decision-making processes a repetitive exercise. Jeff Huber provided an example emerging against US strategic and tactical decisions in the twentieth century's latter half. He is a member of a large fraternity targeting continued utility of Carl von Clausewitz's work. More will follow.

Those involved in important matters of state must take charge to ensure national grand strategy's process does not become buried in a barrage of fast publishing chatter. The United States could otherwise find itself stuck in a spiral decline not unlike Germany, Japan, and Italy during World War II. Legendary US Navy Captain John Paul Jones, who distinguished himself numerous times on both sides of the Atlantic, exemplifies strong devotion of a young but ill-equipped naval force determined to see the United States succeed at sea. His closing remarks to the Naval Committee of Congress, established to build a fleet in accordance with authority vested in Article I of the Constitution, was so instructional that it became a part of the introductory leaflet for entering midshipmen at the Naval Academy:

> You are called upon to found a new navy; to lay the foundations of new power afloat that must some time, in the course of human events, become formidable enough to dispute with England the mastery of the ocean. Neither you nor I may live to see such growth. But we are here at the planting of the tree, and maybe some of us must, in the course of destiny, water its feeble and struggling roots with our blood. If so, let it be so! We cannot help it. We must do the best we can with what we have at hand![43]

The course America takes in the present century is yet to be determined.

Chapter Fourteen

In the Year 2025

SINO-SOVIET PACT! RUSS, CHINESE SIGN FIVE-YEAR ACCORD "TO RESTORE SOCIALIST HARMONY AND REPEL IMPERIALIST AGGRESSORS." U.S. ISOLATED.
- Allen Drury, *The Hill of Summer* (1981).

CHINA, RUSSIA ISSUE JOINT STATEMENT ON NEW WORLD ORDER.
- *Xinhua, People's Daily* (14 July 2005).

      Conditions are already developing in the current century which could destroy the West's global leadership role. The climate that would allow an overthrow of this international tradition is beginning to favor tyrants in the East. Content covered previously makes it possible to game-play various possibilities in coming decades. One particular scenario is provided in this chapter. It directly or indirectly incorporates every subject discussed. A plausible and realistic event is formed that enables readers to note items covered earlier as they appear in precise sequence. Strategy, politics, theory, globalization, and history serve as seeds for a dynamic and destabilizing future. Geostrategic events described will consider unconventional, highly-coordinated attacks waged against the West during the Cold War. Methods used to undermine the social, political, and economic fabric were enormous and, to this day, nobody can prove their destruction. Contemporary events are a bridge between past and future possibilities. Readers contemplate possibilities, while material jumps out in various locations. A question will arise by the chapter's end: "Is it possible?"

Foundation for Defeat

      Ominous signs of a passive, highly-coordinated asymmetrical attack against the Western democracies by Moscow and Peking governments were obvious for several decades. Many political leaders in the West preferred living in denial. Their view resulted out of frustration with, and despair over the general public's declining regard on matters related to national security. A cult of the individual and, "My Rights!" developed into a contagious disease that caused any sense of unity or moral principle for the sake of a common good to completely disappear from society. Breakdown in national borders accelerated this process by creating cracks in the public's attachment toward their national heritage. What government can do for me became more important than saving that government from extermination. Such words as honor, courage, and commitment were confined to a minority who answered calls to military service.

Loyalty to country decayed to a point that many political and business leaders both consciously and subconsciously acted as servants of the PRC and Soviet Union (AKA, Russia). This particular cabal came primarily from hardcore ideologues of the baby boom generation. They were radicals of privilege who turned on all their parents had sacrificed and worked so hard to achieve. The "progressive" generation had no difficulty compromising principles to satisfy cravings for more, and the fortune sought could be found through economic prostitution with enemies now out to destroy the West. Otherwise patriotic leaders, who had become depressed to a point of denial, believed it was more convenient to pretend all is well. Facing the horror of an apocalyptic global war in which they would be held responsible did not create pleasing thoughts. Besides, the West would lose anyway and anger conveniently unleashed on them. In a modern era of media spin and state-controlled propaganda, tyrannical governments who were behind the violence would be promoted as saviors of the masses.

Determination within the Soviet/PRC effort had its roots in Vladimir Lenin's March 1919 launching of Comintern. That operation had been devised to create a worldwide communist revolutionary movement that would ultimately destroy long-held Western traditions of capitalism and multi-party democracy. World Wars I and II, global economic chaos during the 1930s, and Hitler's rise were exploited to extremes. It did not matter the USSR and its alliance of criminals were behind most events taking place. World War I launched Lenin's return to Russia from exile in Switzerland, enabling the overthrow of a legitimately installed Provisional Government. The anti-capitalism prescription came from the Great Depression, which caused people to believe in the weakness of free enterprise. Capitalism is a failure and socialism now the answer. Hitler became an invention and creature of Stalin. World War II was the instrument to justify a Soviet conquest of Europe. Stalin would be seen and anointed hero of the common man.

There were plenty taken in by such lies. Around the same time as Comintern's creation, Lenin and Felix Dzerzhynski, founder of the CHEKA (secret police), implemented the New Economic Policy (NEP). NEP served as a test laboratory to measure Bolshevik abilities at running scams focused on Western generosity. In fact, NEP's subterfuge, ironically titled "The Trust," acted as a bogus front to lure hundreds of thousands of anti-communist White Russians back to Moscow for execution. Ease at misleading the West was a cue for Communist Party strategic thinkers.

By May 1943 Soviet penetration of democratic countries is dug so deep that Joseph Stalin was able to officially disband Comintern as a publicity stunt. This falsely came across as a fair trade in return for Western concessions on Soviet spheres of influence. The list of those betrayed into bondage included parts of Finland, all of Lithuania, Latvia, and Estonia, Eastern Poland, Bessarabia, and Bukovina. More came later as recognition of Soviet interest in Central Europe, the Balkans, Far East, and Middle East were later granted by British and American foreign policy experts. Soviet planners took these gracious acts as a sign of weakness and it enticed further geopolitical moves.

Unofficially, Comintern is replaced by an operation simply called "The Plan" and, unlike Comintern, it would remain covert. The KGB began formulating Plan's long-range grand strategic design into a highly detailed template following Joseph Stalin's death. NEP and Comintern showed enough success to serve as a blueprint. The scheme's final stage is a multi-decade political program for global convergence. This was launched in 1990, thirty years following Plan's official birth and at the halfway point of the original sixty-year timeframe. Minor adjustments, resulting from unexpected events, had been made to allow for completion by 2030.

Plan was officially launched in 1960, just prior to Nikita Khrushchev's peculiar comment: "The American people will never accept communism. However, they will accept something called liberalism." Shortly afterwards the West's traditional understanding of liberalism began a metamorphosis. Determination by totalitarian regimes to destroy the West is seen as essential to survival. Dictators in the East realize ideals associated with individual freedom and self-government (classic liberalism) directly threaten their rule over controlled masses. Release of these teachings within their kingdoms would risk the power they had so ruthlessly acquired. Nothing short of a full court press is warranted.

On the foreign policy stage, Peking entered the game with its overture toward Richard Nixon's administration in the early 1970s. As Moscow and Peking expected and desired, Henry Kissinger launched his highly touted "triangulation" foreign policy. It became a tool benefiting the USSR and PRC. His so-called "China Card" is not in Western hands as believed, but instead serves as a crucial foreign policy maneuver promoted in public by the press. This maneuver allows for careful study of effectively manipulating Western masses.

The domestic matrix target included all social, cultural, political, and institutional domains, whether public or private. Discrimination did not exist. Plan would go to work in the early stages by using the West's own assets against itself. The initial phase involved discrediting and demonizing all who stood out and attempted to warn of the coming peril. Anti-communist hardliners and those resisting socialist encroachment were a threat and their warnings needed silencing at all cost. This is achieved by a public relations effort in the so-called "free and open" press that portrayed such individuals as unstable or deranged conspiracy theorists, unwilling to understand the other side for the sake of peace.

The public relations blitz on behalf of Mother Russia and People's Republic of China placed Western democracies on permanent defense. Allies began questioning motives of their partners. The public is subjected to a barrage of highly-coordinated and publicized actions designed to embarrass their government. As a result, faith in that government and its leadership is lost. Watergate served as the test case and it passed with flying colors, permanently changing the public's view of their elected representatives. Officials refusing to be quiet, or who continued their "counter-revolutionary" activities, were dealt with at the next higher level. The parade of enforcement mechanisms grows extensive and it no longer required high-powered rifles.

Western media organizations were penetrated at all levels and served as party organs for the toiling masses, without those masses even realizing a control process is underway. If a journalist or actor's inflated ego could not be massaged, then blackmail sufficed. Fame and fortune were the rewards for "talking heads" bloated with vanity. A willingness to keep the mob informed of "proper" news, spinning that which did not fit the mold, or avoiding events the public need not know about is a lone request in return for celebrity status. Before long the Western populace developed behaviors similar to fattening cattle for slaughter. Words, not corn, ensure their obedience. Political elites, in order to maintain contact with constituents, develop into controlled subjects of the propaganda machine. This media machine reached a point where it could dictate events and determine the survival of those seeking or holding public office.

Western democracy begins a steep decline by 2012. The public remain obtuse to conditioning processes at work. Cash then became king, while compassion was regarded as a disease. Bankrupt church buildings were turned into nightclubs. A legal system once groomed in common law evolves over time into a casino for winning at the expense of everyone else. A system once dedicated to seeking truth by "officers of the court" formed into a gang of card sharks feeding off private sector remains. Duty and self-sacrifice is overtaken by hedonism and self-absorption. Me-itis, cultivated by redefining liberalism within the 1960s counter-culture movement, spreads like a California fire.

Drugs became the cure, sobriety the illness. Western youth were targeted for purposes of ensuring their proper behavior as adults. Armies of nurses roam school halls passing out happy pills to calm and passive girls, while tranquilizers are fed to rough and tumble boys. Science textbooks, regardless of field, turned into political promotional pieces for radical environmentalism which, of course, served as another assault weapon firing away at capitalism. Social studies textbooks transformed definitions. Democracy is redefined to mean, "When everyone's economic condition is the same." Bombardment of so-called "pop culture" becomes hyper-inflated to make certain America's youth are properly indoctrinated with holistic group-think by the time they could be of productive value to society.

Moral values became viewed as psychological trash, eliminated by punishing moralists in a manner similar to handling anti-communist alarmists. Religious leaders are hunted until they get caught and exposed for some transgression which, in turn, manages to discredit the independent institution they represented. Rock stars and film actors became glorified idols and experts on foreign policy. Those who risk their lives for the defense of a nation and its constitution were looked upon as losers. A sense of duty toward righteousness is considered backward and replaced by intoxicating notions of no right or wrong.

Communist dialectic falsehoods appeared in full bloom as their ideological agents proceeded to destroy all that the West held dear. Foundations of law, cultural norms, societal standards, work ethic, respect for property, free enterprise, and the concept of family is undermined with precision. The assault gets led by politicians, lawyers, judges, educators, activists, and dictates of a power elite. Responsibility and respect disappear into oblivion. Common sense is supplanted by victimization: "People don't kill people, guns do." "Do as you wish, not as you should." The cult of Marx, Lenin, and Mao develop nicely.

Only when the West's belly had become fattened and its muscles softened would the dictatorships take military action. Success at an overthrow depended on using the West's own institutions, values, and assets against itself. Cuban dictator Fidel Castro knew the meaning behind his remark, "We will destroy you from within." With help of comrade Lenin's "useful idiots," the invisible hand of tyranny undermined as much as possible... laying the groundwork. Military force would deploy with near complete advantage and hopefully force the West into submission without any organized resistance.

Exhausted from what appeared to be inevitable subjugation, several business and political leaders succumbed to temptations of greed and compliance for the sake of maintaining stability. The uncomfortable realities of war could be simply avoided by compromising with the enemy. "Better red than dead" made more sense than "better dead than red." Thoughts of freedom and liberty were viewed as liabilities to a higher calling for "world peace."

Now, in the year 2025, the stage is set and gone from the United States is its position as the world's economic powerhouse. The People's Republic of China, with Russia/Soviet Union a close second, rules the roost. Conditioning processes implemented for controlling the West have succeeded. The reality of dethroning the US by Russia and the PRC is now viewed with indifference. Dismay and shock, an expected response as late as the 1980s, is replaced by "whatever." PRC ascension to superpower status results from the Communist Party's tight reigns on a regimented workforce. This keeps the country unified, something unheard of for centuries. The regime's technique for riding herd and policing laboring masses is rewarded by large sums of Western capital. Communist China becomes the most advanced nation on the planet thanks to Western technology, investment capital, and industry. Russia's treasure trove of natural resources in Siberia and its proximity to the PRC border made Moscow a huge beneficiary of this development. Both countries reach their levels of global supremacy thanks to Henry Kissinger's foreign policy initiative of "triangulation." This gave those regimes access to badly needed Western funds. The PRC is the world's factory and Russia fuel for her engine. Lenin's rope for the capitalist to hang himself had exceeded all expectations.

Forecasting a Final Phase

Overthrow of moderate Arab and Islamic governments by radicals throughout the Middle East and Africa over the previous five years has denied the West access to those oil markets. The writing is on the wall. With Communist China, India and the rest of the Third World starving for oil, old European and American dynasties are looking more like relics each day. Oil producing nations have plenty of customers waiting at the pump without having to deal with bankrupt nations and infidels from the West. The United States, in particular, does not possess material and financial fixes that once lured so many to its doorstep. Even America's dollar has been replaced as global currency of choice by strong Chinese paper.

The international community increasingly turned away from the US as it lost an ability to influence global events. Many of America's own multi-national corporations have shunned patriotic interest as they grow beholden to a Soviet/PRC cabal. Their enormous investment in Communist China's economy leaves them few options short of bankruptcy. America remains in stable domestic shape, but it does not possess that knowledge and leadership which once caused so many nations to seek its advice. Standards of living declined, quality of education fell, and crime turns into a major "cost of doing business" expense. Legal rulings and government regulation stifle what remains of incentive. Social welfare programs and deficit spending did enable consumption levels to rise at a respectable annual rate of 2.3% for over ten years. Unfortunately, this is not enough.

Though the US remains a decent market for foreign products, it does not generate investor enthusiasm. A federal government debt surpassing twenty-seven trillion dollars causes many to flee financial markets. Economic growth of Western states never came close to a 40-year 10% average annual rate in the PRC. Western Europeans watched in awe as France, Germany, and Britain got leapfrogged on the GDP scale. Communist China, with a population now close to two billion people, causes nations to increasingly notice where their future can be found, and they vote with their feet. PRC and Russian officials exert greater influence in various international organizations. States previously considered "developed" are pushed to the side.

Because of clearly blatant, politically-driven anti-Western sentiment, which has become more bellicose with strong arm tactics, American and British governments announce plans to disengage from any association with the International Monetary Fund, World Trade Organization, and United Nations. Timing is deemed proper as both nations, in a rare coincidence, have two heads of state that are not known for timidity. These men spent years observing a multi-pronged assault against their great nations and, refusing to sell out like so many others, they calmly waited for the exact moment to strike.

High-ranking defectors from Communist China and Russia warned the West decades in advance. It is not enough to generate public alarm. Overthrowing the West from within is easy using an enormous stable of resources available. An alphabet soup of national security agencies finds it virtually impossible to wage a response. Legal constraints imposed on their actions by lawmakers, bought and paid for with foreign largess, eliminated any chance of success from counter-intelligence operations. New political leaders in both countries, along with their faithful followers, devise a plan in great detail and far in advance. They have been patiently waiting and know it is now or never. Freedom would not get a second chance.

The US and UK formally announce plans to start fresh with new organizations that require political standards for membership. All states are invited to join as long as they support concepts of representative government, multi-party democracy, individual liberty, property rights, and free market economies. These precedent-setting criteria never existed before in formulating multi-national governing bodies. The US and UK leadership believe historically poor records of international solidarity could be tied to a lack of fundamental political standards existing among member countries. Respect for national sovereignty, human rights, and international law can finally be achieved with benchmarks for membership.

Each state requesting to join must go through a stringent examination prior to acceptance of their application. Monitoring their political situation by this newly formed United States of the Free World (USFW) will be an ongoing affair. It is virtually impossible for either candidates or existing members to get away with political shell games. Within forty-eight hours, Norway, Canada, Australia, Spain, Italy, Japan, Denmark, Poland, New Zealand, Portugal, Israel, Ireland, the Philippines, all of Central America, and half of South American states announce plans to apply as founding members. More express interest, but plan to wait and see the USFW's charter.

Political repercussions are immediate and profound. The foreign policy arena explodes with activity unseen since the 1950s.

Charges and counter-charges run rampant. A week after the USFW announcement, Communist China and Russian Federation announce plans to form separate international bodies but, supposedly, without interfering in the "internal affairs" of member states. Many Arab countries, most of Southeast Asia, half of Africa, and the remainder of South American states announce their intent to join. France, Germany and several European states do so while expressing hesitation.

Globalization's entire concept is beginning to look different. Financial turmoil forces markets in many countries to close until further notice. Those that choose to remain open witness record-setting declines in their currency. A run on banks is underway in several nations but, after revealing the USFW's well-devised plan for financial stability, things begin a turnaround among those states aligned with America and Great Britain. A massive PRC sell-off of Western debt is buffered by all USFW members agreeing to jointly absorb any financial shock. Enough assets exist in reserve to manage the blow. American, Australian, Norwegian, and Canadian governments simultaneously announce elimination of all previously imposed obstructions to oil exploration, extraction, and refinement. Many environmental restrictions are lifted by decree and corporations are lining up to restart dormant oil and mining industries. The United Kingdom and USFW-aligned Scandinavian countries announce plans for an unprecedented installation of offshore oil platforms in the North Atlantic. It appears the energy crisis from a loss of Middle East oil will be relatively short-lived. USFW members implement across-the-board conservation programs to help meet demand until production can be increased.

Britain and Norway are the first nations that raced to the South Pole over a century earlier in order to plant their national flags. As a result of that great achievement, they jointly announce claim to the Antarctic continent. Bids will be solicited from private sector companies for oil and mining operations. This does not sit well with the opposing faction of dictators who themselves had staked claims decades later. The United States fans the flames by announcing identical rights to Earth's moon. In a nationally televised address before the American people, the President of the United States makes an announcement: "Just as great sea power states throughout mankind's history have justly and rightfully laid claim to newly discovered territories on behalf of their great nation, then so too will the United States of America for achieving in July 1969 the dream of John F. Kennedy where, to this day, America's flag continues to fly."

Five days following the Antarctic proclamation, a group of Islamic states announce military mobilization orders over supposed Israeli military raids in East Jerusalem, capital of Palestine. Regional instability had been a problem for years even though, in a gesture of peace and good will, Israel surrendered control of the city in return for a declaration of its right to exist. Israel's military leadership categorically denies charges of armed action. A call-up is ordered for all reserve military personnel as a precautionary response. This is followed two days later by Egypt's announcement that ships of any state considered an ally of Israel face inspection before passage through the Suez Canal is permitted. It is done under an umbrella of self-defense and legitimate concern over cargo being transported. The US Sixth Fleet's Task Force 60 battle group, led by the aircraft carriers USS *Abraham Lincoln* and HMS *Queen Elizabeth* are put on alert and positioned in waters between the island of Cyprus and Alexandria, Egypt. At the same time, American and British intelligence receive evidence that a recent surge in Third World instability is not an act of spontaneous combustion. Corroboration from multiple sources exposes this chaos as being sanctioned by PRC and Russian governments. These events distract maritime operations from other pressing issues.

An Act of War

The owner of a Chinese restaurant outside the main gate at Fort Benning, a major US Army base in Georgia, overhears customers discuss a possible rapid deployment of Army Rangers to Panama. This is an effort to establish order following a successful coup. A group of military officers, hostile to the United States and closely allied with the PRC, overthrew the president three days after he announced Panama's intent to join the USFW. Diplomatic protests are ignored and CIA assets in Panama claim the PRC and Panama's new military junta are planning to shut down canal operations to all but PRC-allied traffic. The Rangers would be expected to secure and protect the Panama Canal for USFW shipping. Peking is updated by the restaurant owner.

Two days later the rapid deployment force departs Fort Benning on a fleet of C130 Hercules aircraft. PRC government officials are simultaneously notified by their agent-in-place. Within minutes of the message arriving in Peking, an array of explosive devices detonates at Hutchinson-Whampoa facilities located on both ends of the Canal and along the interior. Additional explosions completely destroy the gates and the artery's ability to function. Communist China's government immediately calls a press conference to express outrage and vow to track down all "criminal elements." This particular press conference, however, finds itself competing for air time with another underway at the White House, which comes about from tragic events unfolding in Barstow, California.

A separate "terrorist" attack has occurred, only this time it involved a significant nuclear detonation. The device had been staged inside a COSCO shipping container and off-loaded at the Long Beach, California terminal exactly seven days following the UK-US announcement to leave the United Nations. The container-carrying truck was left abandoned at a truck stop in Barstow. The blast resulted in total annihilation of everything within a ten mile radius, including any evidence and witnesses. Two of the most important trans-continental freeways are taken out of commission. The junction of Interstate Highways 15 and 40 meet at the weapon's point of detonation. These arteries serve as a lifeline for road freight into America's heartland from Pacific ports throughout southern California. Additionally, a major railroad line connecting Los Angeles to Salt Lake City and points east is destroyed. This includes the railroad yard in Barstow. Within a fifty mile radius is Twenty-nine Palms Marine Corps Base, Edwards Air Force Base, the Pacific Marine Corps Logistics Depot, and US Army National Training Center. All are shut down with varying degrees of collateral damage. The USMC Logistics Depot, Barstow, served as a major supply center for Fleet Marine Force (FMF), Pacific. A large Marine Amphibious Group (MAG) departed Camp Pendleton for East Asia five days earlier. They and Marines already deployed in the western Pacific are in jeopardy of losing their supply chain.

The nuclear device at Barstow was detonated via satellite transmission. A powerful Santa Ana windstorm from the Mojave Desert east of Barstow happened to be blowing toward Los Angeles and the rest of southern California. It reached speeds of 100 miles/hour when the explosion occurred. Radiation monitors in Los Angeles, Orange County, and San Diego begin reading dangerous levels of radioactive airborne particulate. Contamination intensifies as fallout scatters across the region. Decommissioning I-15 and 40, and discovery that both Interstates 5 and 10 are dangerously laced with contamination, leaves only two major road arteries out of the area, I-8 proceeding east from San Diego and the 101 Freeway north from Los Angeles.

Panic sets in as people attempt to flee. Fear factors are assisted by quickly spreading rumors of a surprise nuclear attack and enemy submarines sitting off the coast, ready to launch a salvo of cruise missiles. No commercial flights are allowed in or out of the region. A last resort involves taking waterborne craft out into the Pacific and an out-of-control mob is pirating whatever floats. Ports at Long Beach, Los Angeles, San Pedro, San Diego, and Port Hueneme are closed on national security grounds. Communication and power grid networks become over-loaded or knocked out entirely. Emergency services get tested beyond measure. Anarchy on a scale far surpassing anything seen in US history overtakes one of the world's largest metropolitan regions. The Los Angeles riots of 1992 begin looking like fan activity at a World Cup soccer match compared to the death, destruction, and criminal activity now underway. Twenty million people are left to their own devices, and the President of the United States declares a state of emergency. He orders US Army Rangers destined for Panama to change course and, for the first time in their long and storied history, they are instructed to be air-dropped directly over the city of Los Angeles. Orders seem simple: "To take any action necessary to re-establish civil conditions. Rules of engagement no longer apply."

While the Rangers are preparing to fulfill their unprecedented instructions, US Marines are deployed out of Camp Pendleton and sent to either southern California ports for security detail or Marimar Marine Corps Air Station for rapid transport to Guam in support of USMC operations underway around the East Asia region. Commander-in-Chief, Pacific Fleet (CINCPACFLT), grows concerned over PACFLT ships tied to piers in their homeport of San Diego. He contemplates the exposure from submarines and sabotage agents. Such enemy assets could disable a number of ships critical to the formulation of aircraft carrier battle groups at sea. This would over-stretch an already depleted fleet inventory now scattered around the world.

The PRC and Russian Federation express outrage, while extending condolences over the tragic events taking place in California. They announce that, regardless of a diplomatic break in relations instigated by US-UK imperialistic tendencies, cooperation and humanitarian assistance will be offered as a gesture of friendship. The PRC even suggests that the same group responsible for the Panama Canal's destruction may be behind Barstow's detonation. They are correct, but only a seasoned Foreign Service officer (FSO) would catch this discreet connotation of culpability. Out of deep concern for the safety of their citizens residing in southern California, the PRC and Russia state they are willing to extract those individuals as their status becomes known to proper authorities. They announce that both states, coincidentally, have submarines patrolling in international waters just off the coast to assist. This discreet message sends CINCPACFLT in orbit. He orders ships capable of doing so to get underway, regardless of manning. Crewmembers caught in the chaos will be ferried by helicopter to their commands upon reporting for duty. Fast attack submarines at Point Loma Submarine Base are put to sea with a simple mission, which is to hunt down the location, and prepare to destroy any submarine acting in an aggressive manner.

Policy Assessment

The US Navy Communications Center in Japan and another in Puerto Rico had intercepted peculiar communications up until the day of Barstow's catastrophic event. Coded messages, sent via satellite, would not normally attract special attention, except for the route taken. The crypto antenna was raised by a consistent pattern these particular messages formed. Originating in Peking, the initial course traveled to the PRC embassy in Panama. From there the identical message was sent to the PRC embassy in Havana, Cuba. The passage always seemed to end until hours later when it would then reappear. This time, however, transmission would dispatch from Russia's communications monitoring station in Cuba and travel via satellite to Moscow.

Though every message is coded, parts could still be deciphered. Once decoded, the word "Towbars" consistently stood out. When a message originating from Peking included "Towbars," then it would always travel along the same Panama-Cuba-Moscow data line. "Towbars" traffic began to appear in sparse bursts the day after Panama's military junta took power. These transmissions continued with increasing frequency up until the day of the Barstow detonation. "Towbars" traffic ended suddenly and intelligence analysts are convinced it is the scrambled word for Barstow.

Federal Bureau of Investigation (FBI) agents had been observing the owner of the Chinese restaurant outside Ft. Benning for months and, thanks to "unofficial" sharing of National Security Agency eavesdropping technology, Bureau personnel are able to intercept messages transmitted from the building. Going on a hunch, they pursued the possibility that identical operations were underway at other strategically important military and port facilities around the nation. That hunch turned out to be correct but, unfortunately, to a degree far greater than imagined.

The Bureau discovered that a Chinese restaurant, operated by PRC agents, would open in locations serving as an easy draw for lunchtime visitors from targeted military installations, government agencies, and high-technology defense firms. Each restaurant is wired for sound and the intelligence take develops into a goldmine of information. Those restaurants deemed the most valuable were provided with all necessary equipment to transmit data by satellite to Peking. Others had a cadre of PRC students from various American universities assigned as runners. These mules picked up tapes on a weekly basis and delivered their cargo to either consulates or People's Liberation Army front companies serving as import-export firms. Not to be left out, the practice is discovered underway in several other USFW countries.

Outsourcing data collection and file management got its start by American companies seeking lower labor costs. Lawyer- inspired worker lawsuits and "feel-good" legislation by politicians out to curry favor with a gullible electorate drives companies into PRC territory. This data door was gleefully opened during the Clinton administration in exchange for PRC campaign cash. By 2025 over 60% of global data storage is carried out by People's Liberation Army personnel disguised as civilian data-entry clerks. A massive database comprised of British, American, and USFW citizens is a mother lode of personal information, which includes government identification numbers, credit card purchase history, medical history, family information, and an endless array of other exploitable intelligence data.

Those overheard in a restaurant discussing information of value have a background check done of their personal data in PLA mainframe computers. This is made possible by cross-referencing information whenever credit cards are used to pay a meal ticket. Incriminating files show evidence of gambling problems, medical treatment for social diseases, trips to the no-tell motel, and undisclosed arrests for lewd and uninhibited behavior. All such digressive acts ripen individuals for recruiting. Blackmailing possibilities are staggering. Corporate executives, politicians, military personnel, and government officials at the highest levels are potential targets. Discrimination did not apply. A trash collector, with access to VIP waste, could be of value.

USFW intelligence has determined that destabilization efforts at geostrategic locations around the Third World were at the direction of the PRC and Russia. The conclusion is made that both countries believed it imperative to gain geostrategic leverage at key chokepoints. This would damage a US-led maritime force's ability to operate at will. Naval force is the greatest military threat to achieving Plan's grand strategic design. When the time came to announce an ultimatum, the West's maritime power had to be in such a negative geostrategic position that any response would be futile. Forcing US and allied compliance to Soviet/PRC diplomatic demands can be enhanced by placing puppet regimes at locations capable of denying maritime freedom of transit. Strategic planners in Moscow and Peking believed a Third World political realignment needed to start ten years ahead of their ultimatum. An incremental approach to installing client states offered the best chance of bushwhacking the West at a precise moment.

Time had come for concluding Plan's long-range grand strategic design. PRC and Russian officials miscalculated, however, by failing to consider the new UK-US leadership. Both men were military veterans who dedicated their lives in service to their country, constitution, and people. Neither was a hustler or political opportunist thirsting for power, ego, or taxpayer cash. Answering calls of service was done out of pure dedication. Fate placed both leaders in position at just the right moment. They took seriously stern warnings from Soviet and Chinese defectors, and spent years studying Plan's grand strategic design. They cross-checked material and gleaned valuable intelligence information from sources often ignored by others.

The new UK-US leadership had become astute philosophers of the East. They diligently studied the cunning teachings of Lenin and Mao. History uncovered a rank tyrannical smell that covered domestic and international disasters suffered by the West for over a century. It is time to act or go down trying. As a result of uncharacteristic resistance by Western leaders, a hastily thought out plan involving an act of physical destruction was decided by Communist China and Russian. Odds were, based on traditional Western apathy and weakness, that Barstow would get the West back on a proper path. USFW intelligence discovered this reasoning in various message intercepts between economic and diplomatic stations belonging to the PRC and Russia.

Communist China, in particular, grew nervous about losing access to USFW markets. Not only would a significant source of revenue be gone, but PLA intelligence would be deprived of a very lucrative military and commercial collection operation. If relations were completely broken off, then the PRC Communist Party could lose control of their economy and populace. China's mainland, as it had done so many times in the past, would again turn on itself. Concern grew sufficient enough for the Politburo to declare a controlled nuclear option worthy of risk. If all went well, some argued, Plan could actually be achieved sooner and, perhaps, by the time Barstow's mushroom cloud dissipated. Russian and Chinese officials mistakenly believed the calamitous event would force USFW nations back in the fold and under terms put down by them. Suing for peace would be the only alternative. USFW political analysts concluded, however, that in light of the detonation's location and existing evidence, even a Los Angeles jury would vote to convict. USFW governments saw enough and believed popular support would back a decision advocating military action.

There is a distinction that becomes the saving grace for this British – American alliance of states. A profound difference exists between competing parties that escaped both Communist China and Russia. The PRC-Russia alliance is primarily a land power, locked to the shoreline. USFW nations are primarily dedicated to sea power. This distinct dissimilarity between adversarial forces will be put to the test. USFW assets are soon in action, showing their talent on a global scale. Their leverage can only be achieved by a maritime alliance.

Appropriate Response

Five days following the tragic events in California, leaders from each USFW nation sign a document of solidarity and mutual defense in a treaty that surpasses even the North Atlantic Treaty Organization (NATO). NATO itself had been disbanded ten years earlier with official establishment of a European Defense Force (EDF). Those nations belonging to EDF and now with the newly formed USFW maritime alliance resign their membership from any EDF affiliation. France and Germany waste no time going into panic mode, while Communist China and Russian officials commence wondering what USFW governments may be up to. Things are already not going as originally planned. Russian and Chinese leaders begin contemplating what USFW governments might know about Barstow's operation. Nothing, as yet, had been formally announced in public or through diplomatic channels. Their fear of the unknown is short-lived when, two days later, USFW forces swing into action.

Upon raiding the Chinese restaurant outside Ft. Benning, Georgia, FBI agents arrest the owner for espionage. By employing convincing measures of persuasion, they instruct him to send a coded two-word message to Peking which simply states, "Watch this." At the exact moment, on the same day, one week from the satellite transmitted nuclear detonation in Barstow, each PRC and Russian satellite used in any way to transmit "Towbars" lose contact with Moscow and Peking. USFW government officials simultaneously announce formal banning of all PRC trading firms and ships from contact with any USFW member nation. Additionally, all PLA front-companies are raided at the same time in "Operation Peking Duck," the largest international dragnet of law enforcement agencies in history. Over 20,000 PLA firms are stormed at locations spanning the globe.

Though the Panama Canal remains a valuable maritime asset, there is a back up for America's predicament. Union Pacific Railroad had expanded North American operations to a point that rail lines stretched from Alaska to Panama. The entire system is as new and modern as any transportation operation could get. Railroad lines were connected to virtually every port along Pacific and Gulf of Mexico coastlines. Trains are able to route cargo in mass from port terminals on either coast to the other within 96 hours. Not to be outperformed, railroads that included those in Canada and Mexico had also dedicated substantial sums to upgrading North America's entire network.

The service called into action at this time of great national challenge is on a gigantic scale and, regardless of sporadic setbacks; this would become the railroad industry's finest hour. Train and work crews were on constant standby readiness to handle the volume and immediately jump on any problem that developed. Thousands of retired personnel voluntarily returned to help absorb demand shock. The ability of each company to handle such an enormous amount of traffic being generated is unprecedented. Nothing had ever come close.

American and Canadian Coast Guards announce operations to clear the old Northwest Passage and provide escort service for merchant shipping through the sea lane. In many ways, depending on port of origin, destination, time of year, and weather, this route was closer and faster than passing through the Panama Canal. Merchant ships departing from the United Kingdom or Norway could transit directly to Japan in less time. Additionally, every measure possible is taken to help expand capacity and operations on the St. Lawrence Seaway. Pacific cargo could be off-loaded at the port in Seattle, Washington, and then routed by Union Pacific or Burlington Northern-Sante Fe (BNSF) trains to UPR's giant intermodal facility outside

Chicago, Illinois. Within a day freight could then be re-loaded onto ships bound for the Atlantic Ocean. BNSF's own northern line enables cargo from Seattle to be transported along its Dakota route and offloaded in St. Paul, Minnesota. From there it can be reassigned to barges traveling down the Mississippi to the Gulf of Mexico.

The United States and Canada had devised a major financing program thirteen years earlier that provided the railroad industry no interest loans to rebuild existing rail routes. Additionally, matching funds were made available to any company willing to add entirely new lines between locations of economic benefit to both those companies and the public. The result made virtually every railroad on North America's continent a global showpiece. Modernization efforts enabled several alternative and backup operations to take place similar to the linkage between Seattle and Chicago. High speed train traffic between seaport terminals and any continental city became as common and efficient as truck traffic on interstate highways. In exchange for government financial assistance for this monumental rebuilding effort, companies were only asked to support their nation in a time of great peril. This is about to pay-off in dividends that taxpayers and even many skeptical government officials could not imagine. The US government had another purpose for modernizing the nation's rail network and it can light-up the night sky with great splendor.

One day after "Operation Peking Duck," entire squadrons of USN *Streetfighter* combat patrol craft suddenly appear from several island locations belonging to the Philippines archipelago. Accompanied by the bulk of the Philippines Navy, they then proceed to seize the Spratly Islands and establish control of the South China Sea. Two aircraft carrier battle groups, supported by ships belonging to the old Australia-New Zealand-United States (ANZUS) alliance, launch military operations in Southeast Asian waters. The USS *Ronald Reagan* battle group is strategically positioned off the coast of Jakarta, Indonesia, and provides air support for operations underway in the South China Sea. Within hours the skies are cleared and air support of *Streetfighter* operations are successful. The South China Sea is now under complete control of the maritime alliance.

A battle group led by the USS *Harry Truman* commences to bust open and secure the Strait of Malacca, which was shut down by Burmese, Malay, and Indonesian forces backed by the PLA Navy (PLAN). Burma had become a PRC puppet to a point that many considered it another province. A major overland transportation artery between Communist China's border and Gulf of Martaban was constructed years earlier to provide logistics support for PLAN ships based out of Burmese ports. When the Panama Canal was lost, Burmese forces seized the Isthmus of Kra from Thailand. This connected Burma directly to Malaysia. Little could be done initially to support Thai allies. The US found itself preoccupied with events elsewhere, especially in southern California. That would soon change.

At a London press conference British government officials announce that, in keeping with Egypt's spirit of inspecting merchant vessels destined for Israel, the same would be done throughout the world to those destined for Arab states. A possibility existed that Arab-allied ships were transporting war material for use against Israel. White House officials follow by announcing US intent to inspect all merchant shipping suspected of containing military equipment that is transiting between the Middle East and East Asia.

The two USFW battle groups strategically poised around Indonesian waters are joined by the aircraft carrier USS *George W. Bush* for commencement of "Operation Dragon Slayer." As these events are unfolding, two squadrons of long-range B-1 bombers are flown to Okinawa, Japan, while three squadrons of B-52s arrive in Guam. Their particular design enables them to launch newly designed nuclear-tipped cruise missiles from a range 1,000 miles off East Asia's coast to any location inside the PRC or Russia east of the Urals. In yet another bizarre space event, those PRC and Russian satellites monitoring USFW military activity throughout East Asia suddenly disappear and cease data transmission. This happens just as B-52 and B-1 bomber squadrons arrive at their respective locations.

In an unusual display of modern-day political backbone, the Marine Amphibious Group which had been crossing the Pacific Ocean for several days and which was now to the west of Guam receives orders to establish a defense position on Taiwan. This is done by formal invitation of the Republic of China government. The MAG is simultaneously supported by arrival in Taipai of five squadrons of F-22 Raptor fighter aircraft. US Marines based on Okinawa departed four days earlier and are already augmenting Filipino and Thai forces in those countries. Fighting to retake Thai territory from PRC regional allies is showing success. Joining those Marines in Thailand are Australian and New Zealand infantry units specially trained for jungle warfare. Additionally, the US Army flies infantry units to Korea in order to shore up forces manning the Demilitarized Zone (DMZ).

While Pyongyang's dictatorship is diplomatically informed of its life expectancy should any North Korean troops touch DMZ boundaries, the US Army's 82nd Airborne Division suddenly appears on Cyprus which, according to the press release, is in preparation for joint "training" exercises with the Israeli Defense Force (IDF).

To the disappointment of Arab states, Russia, and Communist China, a threat of losing access to the Suez Canal did not produce any desired results. Nor did the Panama Canal's loss force USFW nations into submission as Union Pacific and other North American railroads took over a majority of transportation duties. What escaped Sino-Russian strategic analysis is that Suez had limited value to USFW members as long as trade relations did not exist with land power states now confronting USFW forces. In other words, they shot themselves in the foot. Suez's value depleted further when USFW nations ramped up drilling operations of their own oil reserves. Denial of Middle East oil no longer mattered. USFW's maritime alliance has a well-stocked portfolio of options, which they are able to implement with precision.

Making matters worse for Communist China is the fact USFW forces gained decisive control in waters surrounding East Asia. Egyptian action at Suez provided diplomatic justification to intervene and dominate those sea lanes. With sea access gone, Communist China's hands are tied. Even the old Silk Road, meticulously rebuilt with PRC help and completed five years earlier, cannot handle more than a fraction of cargo traffic. Smaller European states not belonging to USFW's maritime alliance begin contemplating their options, which are quickly drying up. USFW's charter begins looking better as each hour passes by. Russia and PRC diplomats launch protests, but these are of little value since traditional international organizations no longer matter. They are left with a sympathetic press to vent their frustration, but even this is a worthless exercise. Public opinion changed when USFW governments exposed press and media personnel serving as controlled assets for a PRC and Russian propaganda machine.

Diplomatic relations disintegrated at Barstow and USFW business and government officials are pulling out all stops. Economic ramifications are starting to show. Exclusion of PRC merchant ships from USFW ports leaves cargo stuck on board those vessels with few places to go. Factory goods are left sitting in Chinese ports, while factory floors are idled. PRC officials start putting pressure on Russia to do something in Europe, but not much can be achieved without suffering geostrategic consequences of its own.

Following a rebuilding and manning effort that took ten years, the United Kingdom's land forces can now spring into action. Capabilities were restored to levels not seen since World War II. Though this expenditure came at a high price for Britain's Royal Navy, US naval forces willingly took up any slack left behind. British and Canadian Royal Marines are dispatched to Norway, where they reinforce the US Army's 10th Mountain Division already in position. An entire Royal British Army infantry division was deployed to Poland three days earlier, and joined later by the US Army's 4th Infantry Division. Norwegian and Polish contingents are backed up with three aircraft carrier battle groups. These consist of the USS *Dwight D. Eisenhower* and HMS *Prince of* Wales operating in the Norwegian Sea. In yet another incredible display of uncommon political courage, the USS *John Stennis* is ordered into the Baltic Sea.

Russian hands are tied in Europe and finally, over 100 years later, Kremlin officials start wondering if they spent the twentieth century on the wrong side of the fence. There is no doubt Russian forces can hit hard, and with a fair chance of some success. A problem still haunting Moscow and Peking, however, is the mystery behind so many satellites disappearing. That morning's conference call between Russian and Chinese leaders concludes no major counter-offensive should be launched until they figure out what is knocking out space assets. That graceful passage, "Watch this," sent by FBI agents from the restaurant outside Fort Benning, is not reassuring.

Their desperately sought after answer comes later that day at a formal Pentagon press conference held by the US Secretary of Defense. To the surprise of an entire Pentagon press pool, he announces that the United States possesses a weapon system able to locate and eliminate any "asteroid" in space that threatens peace and stability on Earth. This new weapon had been deployed two years earlier and was strategically installed on trains at undisclosed locations around America's heartland. The device remained on the move because, as SECDEF stated, "You never know when a pesky asteroid might appear." Weapon agility made it mobile enough to target "asteroids" from any angle. It was concealed and disguised as a normal box car when not actually being fired.

A decision to install the system on trains rather than space platforms was done to avoid galactic protests surrounding militarization of space. Department of Defense officials had contracted years earlier with several railroads, and the US government is now willing to provide this service, free of charge, to all mankind. Union Pacific, in a manner reminiscent of its achievement building the transcontinental railroad, acted as contract oversight specialist for this new "anti-asteroid" defense mechanism. It is also announced that an identical system was constructed on rail lines in Great Britain, Australia, and Canada six months earlier. "Global strategic planning, combined with extreme mobility, makes the entire space arena free from any hostile asteroid threatening the sovereignty of USFW members," commented the Secretary of Defense with a wink.

Communist China and Russia had some ability to destroy satellites from unofficial space platforms with minor success. They also had capabilities on land but these were stationary platforms, more inaccurate than their space platforms, extremely primitive in technology, and highly vulnerable to attack. Rapid surface mobility and accuracy is an unprecedented feature impossible to overcome. Every detail of weapon operation and firepower had been protected to a level that not even PRC/Soviet agents-in-place knew it existed. While enemies looked to the skies for signs of US military capabilities in space, those systems had been deployed on land. Based on events at Fort Benning, Peking and Moscow certainly did not doubt such a fast-moving platform existed. It now made what little satellite killing assets they possessed wide open for attack from locations that could not be pinpointed on Earth's surface. USFW nations could destroy their entire fleet of military satellites within hours. This would leave an increasingly fragile Sino-Russian alliance wide open to annihilation.

An inability to track USFW naval operations at sea, which is already reality in East Asia, could be eliminated elsewhere if USFW forces chose to do so. PLA naval forces were successfully pinned to the coastline after being pushed from Southeast Asia's blue- water regions. Spain and Portugal would not allow Russia's Black Sea Fleet access through the Strait of Gibraltar. Both USS *Carl Vincent* and *Chester Nimitz* aircraft carrier battle groups were standing by in case the Russians did not understand Spanish or Portuguese. Russia's fleet assets are boxed in between Gibraltar and those two carrier groups operating off Crete in the eastern Mediterranean Sea. Russia's Northern Fleet is at the mercy of *Eisenhower*, *Stennis*, and *Prince of Wales* battle groups. Simply put, Atlantic Ocean access is not allowed.

Communist China ignored Sun Tzu Wu. It panicked and overreacted by taking military action against the United States. Soviet/PRC diplomacy was poorly timed in carrying out Plan's final phase. Both nations became overconfident and failed to take serious note of Washington and London's new leadership. Though both Peking and Moscow dictatorships were ensconced as global economic superpowers, they failed to transpose that newly acquired wealth into a well-balanced stable of power generators and supporting resource elements. Their destiny was, as it had always been throughout history, chained to land power. This allowed USFW's maritime alliance to mount a challenge and respond with offensive measures. Sea power, yet again, prevailed over land power threats. The Sino-Russian alliance is left with a full-blown nuclear option, which is not an option at all:

> It appears to him that in the ebb and flow of human affairs, under those mysterious impulses the origin of which is sought by some in a personal Providence, by some in laws not yet fully understood, we stand at the opening of a period when the question is to be settled decisively, though the issue may be long delayed, whether Eastern or Western civilization is to dominate throughout the earth and to control its future.[1]

The Russian King knew fully well when the board was stacked against him. Time had come to assume the horizontal position. . . Checkmate.

Chapter Fifteen

Where to from Here

"It is not a defect to pray for peace and to hope there will be no war. But those who predict war have statistics on their side; those who predict peace everlasting are always wrong."
- Harold W. Rood, *Kingdoms of the Blind*

The number of situations that can arise which propel nations into pursuing grand strategy is vast. Likewise, motivation and justification behind development of sea power remains as important as those reasons for pursuing land power. This also applies to air and space power generators. Geography has always been the single greatest mainstay for power generation. It will continue to be an essential motivator behind application of all four power generators. Countries which were not covered in great detail, though they contributed to sea power in a number of ways, include Denmark, Portugal, Venice, and Spain. Each had colorful experiences because of their particular geographic destiny. Historical records are as valuable in contemporary times as in more halcyon days. Discoveries of Christopher Columbus and Ferdinand Magellan, as well as the quality of Scandinavian and Dutch ships, are significant to sea power's cause in unique ways. Other states are certain to pursue sea power in the future and their contribution will some day be recognized in similar fashion.

A single major event at sea can dictate history's course on land for decades: "Such is the profound influence on strategy of a fleet action lasting only a few hours."[1] The Battle of Midway is an example that reverberates throughout the tumultuous twentieth century's latter half. Events at Actium in an afternoon permanently altered the course of Rome's future. An identical result came about for Greece as a result of Athenian success at Salamis. Japan's shellacking of Russia's fleet in the Strait of Tsushima helped to create an environment which eventually allowed a few Bolsheviks to seize power from the Kerensky Provisional Government.[2] Many states underestimated sea power's importance and long arm in world affairs. Napoleon is far from being alone and the twenty-first century will continue to reveal numerous ways this problem endures.

Return of the Power Generators

The products of this venture, which are definitions for sea, land, air, and space power, were first explained in Chapter Two. They are worth taking into consideration in context with future expectations. Conclusions drawn in the following pages may be open to cosmetic change. Theoretic foundations supporting national grand strategy are not. Geography provides a "distinct difference" separating each power generator, while remaining characteristics are quite similar.

Fourteen facts of life are permanently anchored to power generators. Each of these enhances national power's relationship with grand strategy:

1. Geography will always dictate and rule. Geography does not change and neither does its importance as a foundation for political association.
2. A nation must possess sizeable amounts of power resources and management skills for sea, land, air, and space power to develop, exist, and thrive. Power resources and elements must be in good working order to have any chance of servicing each power generator and designs laid out by grand strategy.
3. Creating, building, and then maintaining sea power takes a long time to formulate. Certain criteria will remain permanently fixed to a specific timeframe. The environment may become more efficient, but mechanisms involved in sea power's creation will take just as long to culminate.
4. Though decades may be involved in sea power's development, its tools can be destroyed in hours. If time can impact success or failure, then it will be here. In certain circumstances sea power, which took so long to build, will be lost forever.
5. Physical features of sea power may appear deceiving, nonexistent, and sometimes not apparent until it is too late. This will increase as space takes on a greater role.
6. Resources normally acquainted with land, air, and space power electrify sea power when they support its mission and value. At that point those assets rotate into becoming a part of sea power. This remains for as long as service is provided.
7. The sea will be a significant factor over who wins, who loses, and how it comes about militarily. Global implications will have a connection to the sea.

8. When the world is stable, then so too will be the sea. When the world is at war, then the sea will explode. War involving multiple states, and sometimes just two, will have a decisive outcome on land influenced by what happened at sea.
9. Natural resources, either rich from within or accessible through other means, are essential to power generator survival and growth. States will accomplish many things with abundant resources. What is not possessed but desired must be acquired by other means, such as international trade or conquest.
10. Sea power is measured by degrees of influence brought upon the seas or other navigable waters. This amount determines a nation's sea power capacity.
11. Sea power is described in context of pressure applied for purposes of allowing states, organizations, or individuals to do as they please. Sea power is not physical. It is the outcome of intentions bestowed on geographic regions of the sea or other navigable waters.
12. A dominant sea power nation will maintain its position as long as other states accept that arrangement. A rising sea power indicates dissatisfaction with the existing order. Discontent may be justified, or simply a result of seeking power for power's sake. Either way, a great clash is likely.
13. He who controls and dominates the sea can do many things and has his way in the international order.
14. The seas have consistently increased in importance for over 5,000 years. There is no indication this course will change direction in the present century.

These fourteen facts of life, though primarily focused on sea power, have similar consequences for the other three power generators. Each power generator can be supplanted in place of sea power, as is true with identifying specific geographic domains in each definition. Additionally, sea power's definition and the facts of life provide a framework of general expectations for future planning:

1. Sea power assets of a military nature will be more technical. Defense experts and engineers will employ their ingenuity in a quest to provide sea power with new technology. Principles dictating technology's use will remain unchanged.

2. Sea power instruments will be located in greater numbers within geographically diverse regions. In other words, land, air, and space become more valuable points of origin.

3. Sea power will continue to dictate terms of foreign policy. Its value as an instrument of foreign policy will remain important to states with global responsibilities.

4. Those states who do not control the sea will survive as long as they accept the status quo. Those who resist and fight will die.

As with any forecast, caveats apply. The facts of life and future expectations are based on historical trends that have not changed for thousands of years. Developments since 1988, for example, threaten to shake the centuries old nation-state concept off its foundation. Success will mean destruction of national grand strategy's operating frame.[3] Foremost among recent dangers are concepts associated with "globalization" and "global governance." Construction of this entity and its objective remains vague. There is little doubt, however, that it would cause a colossal historical shift in world politics.

Forward...From the Land

Technology will continue to provide instruments for more focused exploitation of geography. It is geography that drives technological pursuits associated with each power generator. Otherwise, there is no real purpose for technology to evolve as a power resource. Technological advances will cause world politics to accelerate at an unprecedented pace in the current century. Challenges faced by nations seeking to acquire sea power will not change and, instead, continue with greater relevance. Thomas Sowell explains how inland waterways of North America and Africa are examples of stability and continuity behind the geographic power resource:

> The development of large, ocean-going commerce was physically obstructed in Africa by an absence of waterways capable of carrying such ships and bringing such commerce to the interior of the continent or, in many places, even to the shores, given the shallowness of some African coastal waters and the scarcity of natural harbors. In North America there were ample waterways capable of floating large vessels from the ocean to deep inside the continent.[4]

Mainstays of sea power such as strategic choke points, navigable tributaries, oil reserves, geostrategic islands, and issues dealing with international trade remain important as long as nation-states continue to exist. N.A.M. Rodger once wrote that England's war with Wales in the thirteenth century "demonstrated the successful, if unimaginative, application of overwhelming force; logistics were key to the victory, and ships were the key to logistics."[5] This simple remark about an event 800 years ago correlates to consistencies between power generators and their power resource base.

As long as nations continue to seek competitive advantage, then future geostrategic events will be no different than past encounters. An accurate explanation of sea power makes it possible to contemplate this future in context with historical reality. While looking into the current century's crystal ball, it is important to not lose focus on fundamentals. Forward looking initiatives should not dwell in techno-wizardry, classes of ships, or academic papers for brain-storming conferences and legislative hearings. A foundation simply considers itself a crutch for those more sympathetic to details and fancy gadgets. A firm foundation is crucial to identifying future trends from afar that may rise to threaten national sovereignty. Policy planning is intended to provide direction for national grand strategy, while those who specialize in specifics can tool and apply their craft as needed.

Within the military realm of sea power, "Forward . . . From the Sea" served a valuable purpose that singled out the importance of greater littoral and coastal military capabilities. This is a worthy endeavor for a civilian policy-making culture that finds maritime power projection to be a repetitive and mind-boggling quagmire. The document's tone, however, has left an impression that Mahanian fundamentals of sea control are worth sacrificing. Geography has consistently served as *the* constitutional principle upon which nations survive, compete, thrive, and perish. Consistency makes legends out of those strategic thinkers who attach their theoretical basis to geography's foundation. There will, of course, be a rumble and stirring of public masses as military techno-magic gets played out on 24-hour news channels. Such "shock and awe" should not get any further:

> Those who subscribe to the notion of a revolution in military affairs often expect that it will transform not only defense technology, tactics, and operations, but also broader matters of national strategy. For example, many are wont to claim that overseas military bases will become far less important in the future. Finally, some claim that the

advent of better verification technologies, as well as increasingly
lethal and accurate conventional military munitions, will make it
possible to eliminate nuclear weapons from the face of the earth
within the next few decades.[6]

Michael O'Hanlon correctly wraps his comment of arms
control and development within a context of reality. Based on history's
record, the best form of arms control is to be the most armed.

New spatial domains must be considered to exploit all national
grand strategy has to offer. Space is currently a highly under-utilized
region. Historically, every geographic domain was exploited to
maximum effect as soon as instruments were made available to take
advantage. This has not been the case with space. There are regular
satellite deployments and an occasional manned orbital mission to
determine survival rates of such things as bacteria, cockroaches, and
monkeys. The "space pace" accelerated dramatically during the 1960s
when America realized a danger from allowing totalitarian regimes to
gain control of the high ground. The US flag would have already been
planted on Mars had that motivation been sustained. America must
climb out of a financial funk that has burdened forward thinking
initiatives for over thirty-five years, especially since Communist China
has done a commendable job letting the world know its position on
issues surrounding space exploitation.

Mankind's need for room and a natural desire for exploration
will allow space to become the twenty-first century's historic claim to
fame. Seafarers from the past are no different than space explorers of
the future. Rand Fisher and Kent Pelot describe an identical reason:

> Space, like the high seas, is a medium over which nations inevitably
> will attempt to assert their authority. The United States needs to
> ensure free access to space in furtherance of its national interests, and
> to be capable of denying others the use of space against the interests
> of the United States and its allies. "Space control" is the term used to
> describe the functions of assurance and denial.[7]

There are many similarities with maritime power's growth over
the past 500 years. Technology will ensure it does not take as long to
master space as it did the seas. Satellite service is an example of this
dimension's evolution. Satellites provide instantaneous up-link service
for navigation, communications, weather, and intelligence collection in
both military and civilian maritime application. A lot of what goes on

way up high is not visible from below. A lot of what goes on down below cannot escape watchful eyes from above.[8]

Debate is underway over government's future in space. A lot deals with a new strategic arena for military application. Libertarians go so far as to ask, "What business does government have telling private individuals what they can or cannot do in space?" Space as a competing venue among nations is quickly unfolding. The US and allies should not delay pursuing every opportunity. Space is a geographic parameter for domination, just as seas became primary battle-spaces deciding victors and losers of violent wars on land. Space will provide freedom of action in the future. All four power generators gain from exploiting space. Assets operating in space can help dictate events on Earth. Failure to take advantage of a space lead, while the West still has it, may provide an opening for future adversaries.

Several influential groups oppose space for military purposes. Free and open societies bear the brunt of arguments against military use. Tyrants need not worry about such vocal behavior from counter-revolutionary ruffians. US Navy Captain David Hardesty, for example, lists four primary points argued on behalf of US superiority in space:

- U.S. Space Hegemony: We currently have it so let's hold on to what we got.
- Space Weaponization is Inevitable: It is going to happen sooner or later, so we might as well get started.
- The Space "Centre of Gravity" must be Protected: Space is already such a critical element to both the U.S. military and the national economy that it has to be protected at all costs. A successful surprise attack in space against U.S. space assets (the equivalent of a Pearl Harbor) could quite likely be decisive because of the magnitude of the loss.
- The U.S. economy is already highly dependent on space to the tune of hundreds of billions of dollars.[9]

Hardesty's bullets provide reasons for a massive space defense budget. Each factor is valid and significant. However, these are used to then frame an argument against militarization. The US, in his words, should agree to a freeze now while it still leads in space.

Hardesty's noble rationale seems to be a haunting prediction that America will lose superiority in that theater if an international agreement is not signed. Unfortunately, arms control efforts to stop

Soviet development of nuclear, biological, and chemical (NBC) weapons proves the fallacy behind space treaty enforcement. Those opposing militarization of space arrive late to the game, and this includes the United Nations. In an organization consisting of approximately 200 countries, there are perhaps 20 with space exploitation potential. It is only logical to expect approximately 180 others would vote against militarization of space. Space, for all practical purposes, is already militarized. Cruise missile and Global Positioning Satellite (GPS) abilities are nonexistent without space. It is naïve to believe a space document and treaty signing ceremony will work. No historical evidence exists to prove otherwise.

Interaction between power generators will become more connected in the twenty-first century. An example is the US Navy's Sea Shield program. It is designed to enhance contact between sea, land, air, and space power resources. Militarily, Sea Shield will project a strike capacity capable of reaching far deeper inland than ever before. It will be adept at taking offensive action against cruise and ballistic missiles while positioned thousands of miles off a coast.[10] Naval power and Sea Shield will create greater fluidity for use as an asset of land, air, and space forces. Fundamentals do not change, but technological advances enhance abilities to transcend geographic boundaries. Military power resources will provide greater service to power generators. Navy ships, using Sea Shield, will overcome and dominate hostile threats at enormous distances. Fleets will provide geographic regions with greater offensive *pressure* to meet policy demands.

Reflection

Sea power's elusive nature was captured in this research with creation of a solid definition. Confusion surrounding its meaning has been exposed. Corrections were made to existing material where an adjustment was believed to be necessary. This was accomplished by using those standards established in the opening chapters. Theoretical and empirical analysis provided firm guardianship of the research argument and product:

- History was incorporated to support the record where accurate, while challenging what is believed to be a misunderstanding.
- Documentation of past, present and future sea power motives were provided.

- Strategic demands were presented comprehensively in a manner showing a relationship that crosses geographic theaters.
- Ever-present dynamics of a changing world were incorporated to reveal technology's impact on sea power.
- Geography and time were brought forth as dominant power generator resources, critical to national grand strategy's needs.
- Contribution by all power resources to sea power success exposed interdependencies similar to power generator relations.
- Various theaters of operation were explored with components of sea power to show their complementary functions.

This inquiry succeeded because of contributions from so many producers of contradictory material. These primarily surfaced in an earlier era. Their assistance turned out to be as significant as the supporting cast. Strategic analysis of Mahan falls into two competing camps and the gap separating them is broad. Allies attempt to build on his existing work because they see unrelenting utility. Opponents seek to discredit Mahan with alternative methods and/or data newly available but not necessarily relevant. Both sides were premature in their effort, but a meticulous definition for sea power now exists to bridge the great divide.

Sir Julian Corbett's position as a die-hard supporter of maritime strength in support of land operations is well known. He is commonly used to show contradictions with Mahan's own theories of sea power. This is an incorrect approach. His maritime theories are - in relation to definitions from this research - closer to a concept of land power. Sir Halford Mackinder originally argued that the future of great nations belonged on land and not at sea. Sea power evolved into an archaic concept whose ending had arrived. Fortunately for maritime states, Mahan provided an intellectual buffer from this assault. World War II gave Mackinder an opportunity to reassess his own position.

Several objectives were laid out in opening chapters and completion of that task is worth revisiting:

- Primary reasons for defining sea power were achieved while, at the same time, excess verbal clutter was discarded.
- Related definitions for land, air, and space power were created using identical parameters.
- Development of a general classification process for fulfilling policy-implementation practices resulted.

- Greater understanding of national grand strategy's model dovetailed formulation of definitions for each power generator.
- An explanation of previously vague details associated with national power and grand strategy is now clear.
- Grasp of intricate differences existing between sea, maritime, and naval power broke the oneness habit.
- Accurate labels for military forces of various geographic regions were devised to reveal their complementary roles.

The US served as primary prototype because it possesses virtually every resource used to measure sea power. This includes just enough history to provide a track record. Great Britain's domination in eighteenth and nineteenth centuries provided support during that era. The love-hate relationship between the United States and Great Britain is unique. Rarely do two nations permit a passing of power transition without friction associated with war. Alfred Thayer Mahan and John Laughton helped this along by cultivating a trans-Atlantic relationship.

World War I devastated Britain's ability to sustain a global empire for much longer. The British deserve every nation's respect for paying such a high price to defend freedom. Civility was maintained during a shift in geopolitical status quo. Denmark is another example of many who considered a powerful United States beneficial to international stability. Willingness to sell America their stake in the Virgin Islands is a testament to that approval. A consensus by many Europeans to pass the superpower torch is also a sign of American generosity in return. This was repeatedly displayed by US entry into two world wars, and its effort to rebuild Europe following both. American support continued throughout the Cold War.

Exhilarating ideas of EU integration should be viewed with caution. Mahan would argue that Britain and many other European maritime states are better served turning their heads toward the western horizon. It is from that direction cavalry charges came during the twentieth century when those states found themselves under duress. Twentieth century history reveals that those who stood with Britain in time of need persistently arrived from locations outside Europe. Continental politics has, on the other hand, consistently been a point of origin for those in search of conquest. American involvement in this activity continues to be a subject of frequent discussion: "We wisely quote Washington's warning against entangling alliances, but too readily forget his teaching about preparation for war."[11]

Facial features of sea power may change, but the depths upon which it is anchored will ensure continued value. An exception involves powerful international political forces organized to gain the upper hand. Arguments on behalf of sea power's demise are but smoke and mirrors which are always proven baseless. Change will always occur by way of cosmetic features. This evolves with increasing velocity as technology advances. Sea power's influence is vast, its impact discreet, and contributions to global events precise. More contact between national economies will create added pressure, greater dangers, and opportunities for exploiting the sea. A persistent need for open sea lanes to carry out trade requires innovative ways to protect all parties. Ancient Greece was dependent on a free flow of grain from the Black Sea in a manner not unlike oil departing the Gulf of Oman. Potential hazards that have squeezed nations before will remain in dark shadows as threats to economic intercourse.

Research completed in previous chapters showed sea power's significant contribution to America's success. Geographic position and stable north-south borders ensured resources could be dedicated to maritime reach. Features provide freedom of action to build relations with diverse groups around the world. Most people realize US foreign policy threatens only those bullying thy neighbor. Determination to travel far and assist allies in need is not taken lightly. America's military and economic position following World War II showed respect for sovereign nations. A few tried to prove otherwise, but their bellicosity generally fell on deaf ears. A stale cry of imperialism ignores what America could have done if the political leadership desired. American lives were sacrificed and/or put at risk to help less fortunate fend off and then rebuild from evil clutches of dictatorship. Most nations are in broad agreement that if a maritime enforcer must police the seas, then let it be America. The fact that no current challenger exists reveals acceptance of this order. That will change in the future as certain tyrannical regimes grow insecure over individual liberty and democracy possibly spreading to their shores.

The Navy League

Mahan's classic works provided national direction based on offensive forward naval presence. It is arguably the most influential enterprise behind US foreign and military policy in the twentieth century. George Baer summarizes this contribution best:

Mahan sought to change the way Americans thought about their security. He declared that Americans must see themselves as inhabitants of a maritime state in a world of strong opposing navies. He proclaimed a new strategy for the US Navy – offensive sea control. He also prescribed a new force structure – the battle fleet. He said that the United States must, contrary to earlier practice, ready such a fleet in peacetime. Mahan's writings put the Navy at the center of national policy and provided rationale that would be used in the service's appeal for broad public support.[12]

Based on the US Navy white paper "Forward. . . .From the Sea," Baer puts forth an alarmingly bold statement:

After one hundred years, the Navy retired Mahan's doctrine that defeat of the enemy's battle fleet was the Navy's primary objective. Sea-power theory, and Navy practice, had again taken a new form.[13]

Baer's concluding paragraph in his introduction is a warning. The center of gravity driving change feeds from the same trough as misdirected comprehension of "limited" sea power parameters. Baer's use of sea power theory and Navy practice in a single sentence needs modifying if based on power generator definitions. The white paper referenced by Baer deserves a Mahanian statement reflecting generator definitions: "The entire might of US military force will be unleashed to destroy an enemy fleet in keeping with the principles established by Rear Admiral Mahan over a century ago." It is difficult to comprehend, reiterating a fact of life, how a flotilla mustered for purposes of going ashore in some far-off land, can get there without blue-water dominance. There is a glimmer of hope from contradictions found in "Forward. . . From the Sea":

Because we are a maritime nation, our security strategy is necessarily a transoceanic one. Our vital interests – those interests for which the United States is willing to fight – are at the endpoint of "highways of the seas" or lines of strategic approach that stretch from the United States to the farthest point on the globe. Not surprisingly, these strategic lines and their endpoints coincide with the places to which we routinely deploy naval expeditionary forces: the Atlantic, Mediterranean, Pacific, Indian Ocean, Red Sea, Persian Gulf, and Caribbean Sea.[14]

John Dalton appears to be showing geographic grasp of the landscape beyond America's shores. Every major body of water is well represented in his report. This should cause awareness of both a need and mandate that those seas be controlled in times of crisis. Dalton's paper mistakenly digresses into explanations that leave keen readers with a chilling realization that pork-barrel projects rule the cloakroom:

> Reductions in fiscal resources, however, dictate that we must refocus our more limited naval assets on the highest priorities and the most immediate challenges, even within these areas of historic and vital interest to the United States.[15]

Financial management of a nation's budget should be scrutinized whenever money is the primary determining factor for direction of national security policy. Health of the United States Navy and Marine Corps is too important. Sacrificing defense so that taxpayer dollars can instead build a $250,000,000 "bridge to nowhere" in Alaska is not a wise expenditure in a dangerous world. Tentacles of this addiction are tied to globalization and Keynesian economic theories. Rising social and entitlement spending deprives America the freedom to act in areas that matter most (defense). What would those men who risked their lives signing the Declaration of Independence think if their America of today has national security taking a bow so senior citizens can get pumped up on free Viagra? This will be a temporary indulgence if the nation cannot protect itself.

Political elites have relegated their job to pacifying an increasingly dependent electorate, while defense shoulders the brunt of a wildly swinging budget axe. Similarities exist with an earlier period:

> But underneath the wealth and growth, things were beginning to change for the worse. The expansion of Rome put a strain on old agricultural methods. Individual peasants, with a few acres of farmland and a few slaves and oxen, could not handle the enormous demands of the city. Rich men were buying up these inefficient small farms and creating huge ones which they operated with hundreds of slaves from Rome's conquests abroad. As slaves flooded the labor market, many citizen-farmers were put out of business and migrated in increasing numbers to the city, joined there by other immigrant workers and discharged soldiers who had developed indolent habits in the East. This new proletariat was unlike the responsible, property-owning voters of the early republic. Reforms were needed to stop the steady flow to the city of peasants who had once cultivated their own fields and fought in Rome's legions, but the senators' sense of civic duty receded as their greed increased. The dogged persistence which

had served them so well against Hannibal was now expressed, as a later Roman wrote, in a "lust for domination." Believing that their government was the finest in the world, they felt it was their duty to impose it on other less fortunate states. Some of them, as magistrates and army commanders overseas, became arrogant and harsh.[16]

Those determined to see America fall may simply have to wait and watch. The budget message surrounding "Forward. . . .From the Sea" is an indicator of a weaker US that will catch many eyes of up and coming challengers. There are two troubling questions concerning America's military might and its ability to serve as guardian of the sea. These stand out when measured with George Baer's reference to Mahan's retirement ceremony:

- If the US Navy is not going to take care of an enemy battle fleet at sea, then who is, where at, and how?
- If the US Navy is primarily focused on littoral action, then how will those assets get there without blue-water domination?

These two questions bring forth three historical realities working in a transitory manner. Unfortunately, they escape the minds of many who mistakenly believe they are preparing for the future:

- If America does not control the seas, then someone else will.
- If America does not police the seas to protect the interest of free nations, which it has done in good faith for over 60 years, then someone else will and they may not be so even-handed.
- The chance of losing is real if you do not have sea control in times of international conflict and high-stakes diplomacy.

The Navy League of the United States was launched in 1902, shortly following the Spanish-American War's conclusion. The League seeks to educate and foster support among a public unfamiliar with maritime power. It is not a coincidence the organization formed as Mahan was hitting full stride. His influence on maritime education carried over to the Navy League and this effect continues to ripple through that institution.

The Navy League is a persistent supporter of American sea power. It carries Mahan's torch by speaking before lawmakers and general public audiences. The League's statement of policy provides very good linkage to this book and each definition created:

- We of the Navy League of the United States stand for a strong America – a nation morally, economically and internally strong.
- We believe that the security of our nation and of the people of the world demands a well balanced, integrated, mobile American defense team, of which a strong Navy, Marine Corps, Coast Guard, and Merchant marine are indispensable parts.
- We support all Armed Services to the end that each may make its appropriate contribution to the national security.
- We know that in a free nation an informed public is indispensable to national security and, therefore, we will strive to keep the nation alert to dangers which threaten – both from without and within.
- We favor appropriations for each of the Armed Services, adequate for national security, economically administered.
- We oppose any usurpation of the Congress's constitutional authority over the Armed Services.
- We urge that our country maintain world leadership in scientific research and development.
- We support industrial preparedness, planning, production.
- We support efforts of our government to achieve worldwide peace through international cooperation.
- We advocate a foreign policy which will avoid wars – if possible: if not, win them.[17]

The Navy League's flagship publication is appropriately titled *Sea Power*. Their policy statement is in keeping with power generator definitions. Nations must be able to formulate and exploit power generation if they wish to dictate their own destiny. The Navy League's statement covers many power resources that make that effort possible. It will remain an accurate statement throughout the twenty-first century, just as Mahan's warning of China a century ago remains true today:

> It is enough to recall here, in summary, that the chief centre of interest, because of its extent and present unsettled state, is China, around which, however, are grouped the other wealthy districts, continental and insular, which constitute eastern Asia, from Java to Japan. These markets of the future are the near objectives of the political and military discussions which now attract attention; but beyond them, in any statesmanlike view, lies the remote future result upon Asiatics of the impressions they may receive in absorbing and assimilating European civilization. Will they, from the effects thus wrought upon them, enter its community, spiritually, as equals, as inferiors, or as superiors? politically, as absorbing, or absorbed?[18]

Scholarly endeavors often result in development of more questions than those that are answered. Rather than a detriment, such outcomes are considered a positive reflection. This research has generated new subject matter, inquiries, and energetic pursuits that cannot be addressed within the confines of this project. While none regard definitions, to the relief of all those reaching this point, several initiatives materialize:

- Contradictory issues involving international relations and politics should be reconsidered based on the power generator definitions and their place in national grand strategy's design.
- Unless an earth-shattering revelation suddenly appears out of a tomb in Transylvania, then debate over Clausewitz, Jomini, Mahan, and Corbett should come to a final closure.
- Definitions provide new approaches for measuring and comparing the utility of new technology. This deserves a look.
- An opening has been revealed that allows for unconventional ways to apply pressure on various geographic domains.
- Jointness should be reassessed for performance opportunities that may have been previously missed.
- Closer examination of the influence various power resource elements have on sea, land, air, and space power must be done.
- Space must receive more attention and analysis concerning its future influence over the other power generators.
- Reassessment of twentieth century events should be conducted that takes into consideration national grand strategic implications and *all* power resource elements in the context of asymmetric warfare. Did the West miss something?
- Globalization needs to be lassoed before it is too late. The entire concept of national sovereignty, multi-party democracy, capitalism and individual freedom depends on it.

Clarification brought about will provide a starting point for related research projects in the future. Definitions fill a void which previously hindered that vital link between sea, land, air, and space power. This problem has now been put to rest and neither Mahan nor Clausewitz would allow any other approach:

> The rule then that we have tried to develop is this: all forces intended and available for a strategic purpose should be applied

simultaneously, their employment will be the more effective the more everything can be concentrated a single action at a single moment.[19]

Explanations for each power generator will reduce future attempts to challenge the value of a definition by exploiting another, or by over-inflating the value of a definition at expense of another. The intensity of generator competition will be far less than previously seen. Sea power's meaning is settled and does not need revisiting in the present century. This also applies to land, air, and space power. Alfred Thayer Mahan would approve. *Where to from Here* will end where it began by reaffirming Harold Rood's statement that "there is a distinct difference." For the concept of power generation, that distinct difference can be found with geography.

Notes

Chapter 1: *Introduction*

[1] Holsti, K.J., *International Politics: A Framework for Analysis*, 4th ed. (Englewood Cliffs, NJ: Prentice-Hall, 1983), p. 19

[2] Kennan, George, *Memoirs, 1925-1950* (Boston, MA: Little, Brown, and Company, 1967), p. 233.

[3] Immerman, Richard H., *John Foster Dulles and the Diplomacy of the Cold War*, (Princeton, NJ: Princeton University Press, 1990), p. 271.

[4] Isaacson, Walter & Evan Thomas, *The Wise Men: Six Friends and the World They Made* (New York, NY: Touchstone, 1986), p. 477. The praise often attached to Soviet "containment" policy is questionable.

[5] Mahan, Alfred Thayer (Capt., USN), *The Influence of Sea Power upon History, 1660-1783*, orig. pub. 1890 (Mineola, NY: Dover Publishing, 1987), pp. 25-89.

[6] Ibid., pp. 1-89.

[7] Ibid., pp. 90-541.

[8] Jusell, Judson J. (Maj., USAF), "Space Power Theory: A Rising Star," *Research Document AU/ACSC/144/1998-04* (Maxwell AFB, AL: Air University Air Command & Staff College, April 1998), p. 7.

[9] Johnsen, William T., "Redefining Land Power for the 21st Century," *Strategic Studies Institute Research Document* (Carlisle, PA: US Army War College, May 1998), p. 6.

[10] Ibid., p. 7.

[11] Kennedy, Paul, *The Rise and Fall of British Naval Mastery*, 2nd ed. (London, UK: Ashfield Press, 1987), p. 1.

[12] Alfred Thayer Mahan, *The Influence of Sea Power upon History, 1660-1783*, pp. 29-58.

[13] Sprout, Margaret Tuttle, "Mahan: Evangelist of Sea Power," in Edward Mead Earle, ed., *Makers of Modern Strategy*, pp. 418-421.

[14] Mahan, Alfred Thayer (Capt., USN), "Subordination in Historical Treatment," *Annual Report of the American Historical Association*, 1902, pp. 49-63.

[15] Fisher, Dan, "Polish News Agency Surprisingly Helpful," *Los Angeles Times* (09 December 1982).

[16] Radio Free Europe, "Policeman Admits to faking Student's Death in 1989," *Weekly Record of Events* (06 December 1991). Czech Commander Ludvig Ziveak admits he penetrated the student protest movement and faked his own injuries as well as a student's death at the hands of police.

[17] Rohnka, Dariusz, "The Communist Threat," *Another Fine Specimen* (15 May 2003), p. 3.

[18] Radio Free Europe, "KGB Supported Perestroika in GDR," *RFE/RL Daily Report*, No. 17 (17 September 1993). A KGB operation was secretly established in East Germany during the mid-1980s to supervise planned political changes on a national scale and the program continued to exist in the 1990s.

[19] Lomborg, Bjorn, *The Skeptical Environmentalist: Measuring the Real State of the World* (Cambridge, UK: Cambridge University Press, 2001). Lomborg, a former member of Greenpeace, challenges inaccuracies secreting from politically-motivated radical environmental movements. His effort to bring scientific reality to the anti-capitalist cause has made him a recipient of many pie-throwing protestors.

[20] Riebling, Mark, *Wedge: The Secret War between the FBI and CIA* (New York, NY: Alfred A. Knopf, 1994), p. 200.

[21] Ibid.

[22] Ignatius, David, "A Ghost of the Cold War," *Washington Post* (20 April 2007).

[23] Dunn, James R. & John E. Kinney, *Conservative Environmentalism: Reassessing the Means, Redefining the Ends* (Westport, CT: Greenwood Publishing Group, 1996). Dunn and Kinney challenge the politically charged book by Rachel Carson, *Silent Spring* (New York, NY: Houghton, 1962).They note between 1941 and 1963, when DDT was widely used in the United States, the Robin population increased 1,138%. This is according to the National Audubon Society's own bird count figures (p. 170). The authors argue banning DDT, a primary target of Carson, kills 14 million people annually from diseases spread by insects. Figures based on World Health Organization estimates (p. 193).

[24] Horowitz, David, *The Politics of Bad Faith: The Radical Assault on America's Future* (New York, NY: Simon & Schuster, 1998), p. 32.

[25] Lewy, Guenter, *The Cause that Failed: Communism in American Political Life* (New York, NY: Oxford University Press, 1990), pp. ix-x.

[26] Clausewitz, Carl von, *On War*, Michael Howard & Peter Paret trans. (Princeton, NJ: Princeton University Press, 1989), p. 148. Clausewitz distinguishes art when, in fact, politics should be his discriminating reference. This dovetails often cited commentary that 'political science' is a contradiction of words.

[27] Kors, Alan Charles & Harvey A. Silvergate, *The Shadow University: The Betrayal of Liberty on America's Campuses* (New York, NY: Free Press, 1998), p. 252.

[28] The movie industry, operating under the guise of "art," is notorious for producing political film that is very loosely "based on a true story," or "inspired by historical events."

[29] Steele, Shelby, *A Dream Deferred: The Second Betrayal of Black Freedom in America* (New York, NY: HarperCollins, 1994), pp. 94-95.

[30] Sowell, Thomas, *The Quest for Cosmic Justice* (New York, NY: Simon & Schuster, 1999), p. 171.

[31] Shelby Steele, *A Dream Deferred*, pp. 79-80.

[32] Sommers, Christine Hoff, *Who Stole Feminism: How Women Have Betrayed Women* (New York, NY: Touchstone, 1995), pp. 106-117.

[33] Alan Kors & Harvey Silverglate, *The Shadow University*, pp. 122-124.

[34] Story, Joseph, *A Familiar Exposition of The Constitution of the United States*, orig. pub. 1845 (Lake Bluff, IL: Regnery Publishing, 1986), p. 368. Quotation by George Washington, *Farewell Address to the People of the United States* (17 September 1796).

Chapter 2: *Fundamentals*

[1] Sumida, Jon, "Alfred Thayer Mahan, Geopolitician," *Geopolitics: Geography and Strategy*, Colin Gray & Geoffrey Sloan eds. (London, UK: Frank Cass, 1999), pp. 45-46.

[2] Murray, Williamson & Mark Grimsley, "Introduction: On Strategy," Williamson Murray, MacGregor Knox & Alvin Bernstein ed., *The Making of Strategy: Rulers, States, and War* (Cambridge, UK: Cambridge University Press, 1994), p. 1.

[3] Abu-Nasr, Donna, "Danish cartoons ignite Islamic anger," *Houston Chronicle* (31 January 2006).

[4] Friedrich, Carl, *Man and His Government* (New York, NY: Wiley, 1965), p. 79.

[5] This is similar to balance of power theory between dominant state actors. The behavior between competing special interest groups is commonly called disturbance theory.

[6] O'Connor, Karen, Larry J. Sabato, Stefan D. Haag & Gary A. Keith, *American Government: Continuity and Change*, 2006 Texas edition (New York, NY: Pearson Education, 2005), p. 367. A public poll in 2002 of members on the U.S. Supreme Court revealed 11% of respondents could identify William Rehnquist as Chief Justice, while 24% knew Sandra Day O'Connor, first female appointee in the Court's history. 2% correctly named John Paul Stevens. On the other hand, 67% of those responding knew Snap, Crackle, and Pop were the characters for Rice Krispies Cereal. This is a stunning revelation considering the Court's influence over American society.

[7] Earle, Edward Mead, ed., *Makers of Modern Strategy: Military Thought from Machiavelli to Hitler* (New York, NY: Atheneum, 1966), p. viii.

[8] Ibid.

[9] Sloan, Geoffrey, *The Geopolitics of Anglo-Irish Relations in the 20th Century* (London, UK: Leicester University Press, 1997), p. 8.

[10] Buchan, Alastair, *War in Modern Society: An Introduction*, Colophon ed. (New York, NY: Harper & Row, 1968), pp. 81-82. Quotation from Russell F. Weigley, *The American Way of War: A History of United States Military Strategy and Policy* (Bloomington, IN: Indiana University Press, 1973), p. xvii.

[11] Corbett, Julian S., *Some Principles of Maritime Strategy*, B.McL. Ranft., ed. (Annapolis, MD: Naval Institute Press, 1972), p. 13.

[12] Alfred Thayer Mahan, *The Influence of Sea Power upon History, 1660-1783*, p. 331.

[13] Hart, B.H. Liddell, *The Revolution in Warfare* (New Haven, CT: Yale University Press, 1947), pp. 18-19.

[14] Luttwak, Edward & Stuart L. Koehl, *The Dictionary of Modern War* (New York, NY: HarperCollins, 1991), p. 569.

[15] Ibid. Quoted from *Dictionary of United States Military Terms for Joint Usage* (1964), p. 135.

[16] Ibid. Quoted from *Lexicon of Military Terms* (1960), p. 14.

[17] Carl von Clausewitz, *On War*, Michael Howard & Peter Paret trans., pp. 17-18.

[18] Ibid., p. 128.

[19] Wylie, J.C. (Rear Adm.), "Mahan: Then and Now," *The Influence of History on Mahan*, (Newport, RI: Naval War College Press, 1991), p. 44.

[20] Ibid., p. 42.

[21] Soukhanov, Anne H., ed., *The American Heritage Dictionary of the English Language*, 3rd ed. (Boston, MA: Houghton Miffin, 1996), p. 1627.

[22] Lenfestey, Thompson, *Dictionary of Nautical Terms* (New York, NY: Facts on File, 1994), p. 294.

[23] Sumida, Jon, *Inventing Grand Strategy and Teaching Command: The Classic Works of Alfred Thayer Mahan Reconsidered* (Baltimore, MD: Johns Hopkins University Press, 1997), p. 102.

[24] Ibid.

[25] Mahan, Alfred Thayer (Capt., USN), *Retrospect and Prospect: Studies in International Relations Naval and Political* (Boston, MA: Little, Brown, and Company, 1902), p. 39.

[26] Ricketts, Claude (Adm., USN), "Naval Power – Present and Future," *U.S. Naval Institute Proceedings*, Vol. 89, no. 1 (January 1963), p. 34.

[27] Amme, Carl H. (Capt., USN), "The Changing Nature of Power," *U.S. Naval Institute Proceedings*, Vol. 89, no. 3 (March 1963), pp. 27-28.

[28] McLean, Iain, ed., *The Concise Oxford Dictionary of Politics* (Oxford, UK: Oxford University Press, 1996), p. 396.

[29] Noel, John V., Jr. (Capt., USN), *Naval Terms Dictionary* (Annapolis, MD: United States Naval Institute Press, 1952), p. 291.

[30] Alfred Thayer Mahan, *The Influence of Sea Power upon History, 1660 – 1783*, p. 138.

[31] Carl von Clausewitz, *On War*, Michael Howard and Peter Paret trans., p. 95.

[32] Mahan, Alfred Thayer (Rear Adm., USN), Allan Westcott, ed., *Mahan on Naval Warfare: Selections from the Writings of Rear Admiral Alfred T. Mahan* (Mineola, NY: Dover Publications, 1999), p. 4.

[33] Wylie, J.C. (Capt., USN), "Why a Sailor Thinks Like a Sailor," *US Naval Institute Proceedings*, Vol. 83, no. 8 (August 1957), pp. 813-814.

[34] Carl von Clausewitz, *On War*, Michael Howard and Peter Paret trans., p. 128.

[35] Clausewitz, Carl von, *On War*, Anatol Rapoport, ed. (Harmondsworth, UK: Penguin Books Ltd., 1986), p. 241.

[36] Sun Tzu Wu, *The Art of War*, Samuel B. Griffin trans. (New York, NY: Oxford University Press, 1971), p. 77.

[37] Ibid., p. 97. Quotation by Ho Yen-his.

[38] Rickover, Hyman (Adm., USN), *United States Senate Committee on Defense Preparedness* (06 January 1958). Quotation in Paul B. Ryan, *First Line of Defense: The U.S. Navy Since 1945* (Stanford, CA: Hoover Institute Press, 1981), p. 153.

[39] Sledes George, ed., *The Great Thoughts* (New York, NY: Ballantine Books, 1985), p. 402.

[40] Wright, Quincy, *A Study of War*, 2nd ed. (Chicago, IL: University of Chicago Press, 1969), p. 6.

[41] Ibid., p. 7.

[42] Carl von Clausewitz, *On War*, Michael Howard and Peter Paret, trans., p. 149.

[43] Sun Tzu Wu, *The Art of War*, p. 40.

[44] Carl von Clausewitz, *On War*, Michael Howard and Peter Paret, trans., p. 605.

[45] Taylor, S.J., *Stalin's Apologist: Walter Duranty, The New York Times's Man in Moscow* (New York, NY: Oxford University Press, 1990).

[46] Brzezinski, Zbigniew, *Out of Control: Global Turmoil on the Eve of the 21st Century* (New York, NY: Macmillan Publishing, 1993), p. 12.

[47] It is possible to board a ship inside the interior at Pittsburgh, Pennsylvania, travel down the Ohio and Mississippi Rivers, circumnavigate the globe without disembarking, then end up in Minneapolis, Minnesota, 200 miles from the Canadian border.

[48] J.C. Wylie, "Mahan: Then and Now," *The Influence of History on Mahan*, pp. 43-44.

[49] Word of choice for the United States is "national," while "grand" is favored by the United Kingdom. Neither is correct without the other. "National" identifies the entity involved (national government), while 'Grand' identifies the strategic level. In a corporate environment, the word 'corporate' would be used in place of 'national.

[50] Mahan, Alfred Thayer (Capt., USN), *The Interest of America in Sea Power, Present and Future* (Boston, MA: Little, Brown, and Company, 1898), pp. 120-121.

Chapter 3: *Alfred Thayer Mahan*

[1] Alfred Thayer Mahan, *The Interest of America in Sea Power, Present and Future*, pp. 245-246.

Notes   333

[2] Mahan, Alfred Thayer (Capt., USN), "A Twentieth-Century Outlook," *Harper's New Monthly Magazine*, Vol. 95, no. 568 (September 1897).p. 533.

[3] McCullough, David, *The Path Between the Seas: The Creation of the Panama Canal, 1870 – 1914* (New York, NY: Simon and Schuster, 1977), p. 251.

[4] Seager, Robert, "Alfred Thayer Mahan: Christian Expansionist, Navalist, and Historian," in James C. Bradford, ed., *Admirals of the New Steel Navy: Makers of the American Naval Tradition, 1880 – 1930* (Annapolis, MD: Naval Institute Press, 1990), pp. 30-31.

[5] Sullivan, Brian, "Mahan's Blindness and Brilliance," *Joint Forces Quarterly* (Spring 1999), p. 115.

[6] Jon Sumida, *Inventing Grand Strategy and Teaching Command*, p. 110.

[7] Carl von Clausewitz, *On War*, Michael Howard & Peter Paret trans., p. 100.

[8] Moffat, Ian (Lt. Cdr., CRN), "Corbett: A Man before His Time," *Journal of Military and Strategic Studies*, Electronic Journal of the Centre for Military and Strategic Studies, University of Calgary (Winter 2000/Spring 2001).

[9] Ibid.

[10] Robert Seager, *Alfred Thayer Mahan*, p. 215.

[11] Brian Sullivan, "Mahan's Blindness and Brilliance," *Joint Forces Quarterly* (Spring 1999), p. 115.

[12] Ibid.

[13] Robert Seager, *Alfred Thayer Mahan*, p. 282.

[14] Jon Sumida, *Inventing Grand Strategy and Teaching Command*, p. 45.

[15] Sumida, Jon, "New Insights From Old Books: The Case of Alfred Thayer Mahan," *Naval War College Review*, Vol. LIV, no. 3 (Summer 2001), p. 102.

[16] Jon Sumida, *Inventing Grand Strategy and Teaching Command*, p. 45.

[17] Jon Sumida, "New Insights from Old Books," *Naval War College Review*, Vol. LIV, no. 3 (Summer 2001), p. 102.

[18] Alfred Thayer Mahan, *The Influence of Sea Power upon History*, p. 87.

[19] US Marine Corps, The Basic School, "Principles of Amphibious Operations," *Basic Officer Course* (Quantico, VA: USMC Combat Development Command).

[20] Ibid.

[21] Robert Seager, *Alfred Thayer Mahan*, pp. 378-379.

[22] Sloan, Geoffrey, "Sir Halford Mackinder: The Heartland Theory Then and Now," Gray & Sloan ed., *Geopolitics: Geography and Strategy* (London, UK: Frank Cass, 1999), p. 34.

[23] Jon Sumida, "Alfred Thayer Mahan, Geopolitician," Colin Gray & Geoffrey Sloan, ed., *Geopolitics*, pp. 58-59.

[24] Margaret Tuttle Sprout, "Mahan: Evangelist of Sea Power," Edward Mead Earle, ed., *Makers of Modern Strategy*, p. 445.

[25] Earle, Edward Mead, "Hitler: The Nazi Concept of War," Edward Mead Earle, ed., *Makers of Modern Strategy*, p. 515.

[26] Gray, Colin, *War, Peace, and Victory: Strategy and Statecraft for the Next Century* (New York, NY: Simon & Schuster, 1990), p. 60.

[27] Alfred Thayer Mahan, *The Influence of Sea Power upon History*, pp. 7-8.

[28] Ibid., pp. 11-12.

[29] Mahan, Alfred Thayer (Capt., USN), *The Life of Nelson: The Embodiment of the Sea Power of Great Britain*, orig. pub. Little Brown, and Company, 1899 (Annapolis, MD: Naval Institute Press, 2001), p. 71.

[30] Mahan, Alfred Thayer (Capt., USN), *Admiral Farragut*, orig. pub. D. Appleton and Company, 1892 (St. Clair Shores, MI: Scholarly Press, 1970), pp. 33-37.

[31] Ibid., pp. 37-44.

[32] Sun Tzu Wu, *The Art of War*, Samuel B. Griffith trans., p. 140.

[33] Jon Sumida, *Inventing Grand Strategy and Teaching* Command, p. 56. Quotation from Alfred Thayer Mahan, *The Influence of Sea Power upon the French Revolution and Empire*, p. 102.

[34] Ibid., pp. 107-134.

[35] A contemporary idea advocates a joint maritime alliance serving to protect the interest of Free World states in the twenty-first century. Democratic forms of government would be anchored to a common bond. See John G. Morgan, Jr. (Vice Adm., USN) & Charles W. Martgolio (Rear Adm., USN), "The 1,000 Ship Navy: Global Maritime Network," *Naval Institute Proceedings*, Vol. 132, no. 11 (November 2005).

[36] Alfred Thayer Mahan, *The Influence of Sea Power upon History*, p. 115.

[37] Alfred Thayer Mahan, *The Problem of Asia*, pp. 66-67.

[38] Lehman, John, *Command of the Seas: Building the 600 Ship Navy* (New York, NY: Macmillan Publishing Company, 1988), pp. 1-10.

[39] Ibid., p. 9.

[40] Ibid., p. 1.

[41] Jon Sumida, *Inventing Grand Strategy and Teaching Command*, p. 110. Sumida's revelation of D.H. and A.T. Mahan's emphasis on Clausewitz explains Admiral Mahan's trust in strategy.

[42] Hurt, Charles, "Congressional junkets picking up steam," *The Examiner* (15 April 2007).

[43] George Baer, *One Hundred Years of Sea Power*, p. 21.

[44] Alfred Thayer Mahan, *The Interest of America in Sea Power, Present and Future*, p. 26.

[45] Mahan, Alfred Thayer (Rear Adm.), *Lessons of the War with Spain and Other Articles* (Boston, MA: Little, Brown, and Company, 1918), pp. 232-233. Quotation in Reo Leslie, "Religion and Mahan," John Hattendorf, ed., *The Influence of History on Mahan* (Newport, RI: Naval War College Press, 1991), p. 135.

[46] Griswold, Whitney A., *The Far Eastern Policy of the United States* (New York, NY: Harcourt, Brace and Company, 1939), p. 11. Letter from Roosevelt to Mahan (21 March 1898).

[47] Hendrix, Henry J. (Lt. Cdr., USN), "Fulcrum of Greatness," *U.S. Naval Institute Naval History*, Vol. 16, no. 6 (December 2002), pp. 26-44.

[48] Mahan, Alfred Thayer (Capt., USN), *The Problem of Asia* (Boston, MA: Little, Brown, and Company, 1900), pp. 124-125.

[49] Lambert, Andrew, "The Principle Source of Understanding: Navies and the Educational Role of the Past," Peter Hore, ed., *Hudson Papers*, Vol. I (London, UK: Royal Navy Defence Studies, 2001), p. 55.

[50] David McCullough, *The Path Between the Seas*, pp. 254-255.

[51] Baer, George, *One Hundred Years of Sea Power: The U.S. Navy, 1890-1990* (Stanford, CA: Stanford University Press, 1994), pp. 35-36.

[52] Mahan, Alfred Thayer (Rear Adm., USN), "Admiral Mahan Asserts Its Ultimate Dependence on a Navy," *The New York Times* (12 April 1912).

[53] George Baer, *One Hundred Years of Sea Power*, p. 36.

[54] Alfred Thayer Mahan, "Admiral Mahan Asserts Its Ultimate Dependence on a Navy," *The New York Times* (12 April 1912).

[55] Ibid.

[56] Carl von Clausewitz, *On War*, Michael Howard & Peter Paret trans., p. 111.

[57] Gertz, Bill, *The China Threat: How the People's Republic Targets America* (Washington, DC: Regnery Publishing, 2000), p. 85. Testimony by General Charles E. Wilhelm, USMC, commander in chief of U.S. Southern Command before the Senate Armed Services Committee (October 1999). Wilhelm was sent after William Cohen, Secretary of Defense, failed to appear. The purpose, according to Gertz, was to gloss over PRC strategic gains in the region during the Clinton administration's watch.

[58] Schram, Stuart R., *The Political Thought of Mao Tse-tung* (New York, NY: Praeger Publishers, 1976), p. 413.

[59] New York Times Wire Service, "Peking's Plan to 'Encircle' the West," *San Francisco Chronicle* (03 September 1965), Associated Press Wire Service, "Chavez fuels trade relations with Beijing," *Houston Chronicle* (25 December 2004).

[60] Bill Gertz, *The China Threat*, p. 79. Two American companies, Bechtel and Stevedoring, had actually outbid Hutchinson-Whampoa (p. 81).

[61] Huck, Arthur, trans., "Map of the Excellent World Situation," *People's Daily* (26 September 1968).

[62] Taft, William H., *Inaugural Addresses of the Presidents of the United States from George Washington to John F. Kennedy* (Washington, DC: U.S. Government Printing Office, 1961), p. 191.

[63] Jon Sumida, *Inventing Grand Strategy and Teaching Command*, p. 35.

[64] Ibid., p. 34. Quotation from Alfred Thayer Mahan, *The Influence of Sea Power upon the French Revolution and Empire, 1793-1812*, 2 vols. (Boston, MA: Little, Brown, and Company, 1892), p. 327.

[65] Gray, Colin, *The Geopolitics of Superpower* (Lexington, KY: University of Kentucky Press, 1988), p. 126.

[66] Murray, Williamson, "Corbett, Julian: 1854-1922, British Naval Historian," Robert Cowley & Geoffrey Parker, ed., *The Reader's Companion to Military History* (New York, NY: Houghton Mifflin, 1996), pp. 108-109.

[67] George Baer, *One Hundred Years of Sea Power*, p. 82.

Chapter 4: *Critical Mass*

[1] Gray, Colin, "The Geopolitics of European Defence in 2020," Michael Duffy, Theo Farrell & Geoffrey Sloan, eds., *European Defence in 2020*, no. 2 (Exeter, UK: Britannia Royal Naval College, 1998), p. 13.

[2] Robert Seager, *Alfred Thayer Mahan: The Man and His Letters*, p. 432.

[3] Gray, Colin, *Explorations in Strategy* (Westport, CT: Praeger Publishers, 1998), p. 62.

[4] Earle, Edward Mead, "Adam Smith, Alexander Hamilton, Friedrich List: The Economic Foundations of Military Power," Edward Mead Earle, ed., *Makers of Modern Strategy*, p. 148.

[5] Paul Kennedy, *The Rise and Fall of British Naval Mastery*, pp. 184-185.

[6] Ibid., p. 183.

[7] Edgerton, Robert B., *Warriors of the Rising Sun: A History of the Japanese Military* (Boulder, CO: Westview Press, 1997) p. 210. Quotation by Theodore Roosevelt in J.A. White, *The Diplomacy of the Russo-Japanese War* (Princeton, NJ: Princeton University Press, 1964).

[8] Mackinder, Halford, *Democratic Ideals and Reality: A Study in the Politics of Reconstruction* (Suffolk, UK: Penguin Books, 1944), p. 86. Quotation in Geoffrey Sloan "Sir Halford Mackinder: The Heartland Theory Then and Now," Gray & Sloan ed., *Geopolitics*, p. 25.

[9] Friedman, Norman, "Fighting Far from the Sea," *U.S. Naval Institute Proceedings,* Vol. 127, no. 12 (December 2001), p. 6.

[10] Halford Mackinder, *Democratic Ideals and Reality: A Study in the Politics of Reconstruction*, p. 86. Quotation in Geoffrey Sloan, "Sir Halford Mackinder: The Heartland Theory Then and Now," Colin Gray & Geoffrey Sloan eds., *Geopolitics*, p. 25.

[11] Fettweis, Christopher, "Sir Halford Mackinder, Geopolitics, and Policymaking in the Century," *US Army War College: Parameters* (Summer 2000), pp. 58-71.

[12] Geoffrey Sloan, "Sir Halford Mackinder: The Heartland Theory Then and Now," Colin Gray & Geoffrey Sloan ed., *Geopolitics*, p. 35.

[13] Ibid.

[14] Paul Kennedy, *The Rise and Fall of British Mastery*, p. 87.

[15] Maltby, William S., "The origins of a global strategy: England from 1558 to 1713," *The Making of Strategy*, Williamson Murray, MacGregor Knox, & Alvin Bernstein, ed., pp. 161-162.

[16] This type of analysis is noticed in scientific data associated with global warming. See Wendy Reeves, "Scientist: Warming not caused by humans," *The Huntsville Times* (19 April 2007). Also see Senator James Inhofe, "Global Warming: The Worst of All Environmental Scares," *Human Events* (06 August 2003). Skeptics are questioning the starting point of scientific research used to argue Western economic behavior (meaning capitalism) is causing catastrophic climatic change.

[17] Paul Kennedy, *The Rise and Fall of British Naval Mastery*, p. 43. Ironically, Kennedy argues Mahan used the identical statistical maneuver to defend and support sea power.

[18] Alfred Thayer Mahan, *The Influence of Sea Power upon History*, pp. 322-323.

[19] Ibid., pp. 197-198.

[20] Ibid., p. 25.

[21] Kennedy, Paul, *The Rise and Fall of the Great Powers: Economic Change and Military Conflict from 1500 to 2000* (New York, NY: Random House, 1987), p. 198.

[22] Carl von Clausewitz, *On War*, Michael Howard & Peter Paret, trans., p. 136.

[23] Shulman, Mark Russell, *Navalism and the Emergence of American Sea Power: 1882-1893* (Annapolis, MD: Naval Institute Press, 1995), p. 5.

[24] Morris, Edmund, "A Matter of Extreme Urgency," *Naval War College Review*, Vol. 55, no. 2 (Spring 2002), pp. 73-85.

[25] Mark Shulman, *Navalism and the Emergence of American Sea Power,*. pp. 151-158.

[26] Ibid., pp. 142-150.

[27] Alfred Thayer Mahan, *The Influence of Sea Power upon History*, pp. 1-2.

[28] Macdonald, Douglas J., "Communist Bloc Expansion in the Early Cold War: Challenging Realism, Refuting Revisionism," *International Security*, Vol. 20, no. 3 (Winter 1995), pp. 152-188.

[29] Brian Sullivan, "Mahan's Blindness and Brilliance," *Joint Forces Quarterly*, p. 117.

[30] Van Creveld, Martin, *Technology and War* (New York, NY: Free Press, 1989), p. 210.

[31] Maslowski, Peter, "To the Edge of Greatness: The United States, 1783-1865," Williamson Murray, MacGregor Knox and Alvin Bernstein, ed., *The Making of Strategy*, p. 234.

[32] Weigley, Russell F., *The American Way of War: A History of United States Military Strategy and Policy* (Bloomington, IN: Indiana University Press, 1977), pp. 173-178.

[33] Brian Sullivan, "Mahan's Blindness and Brilliance," *Joint Forces Quarterly*, pp. 117-118.

[34] Colin Gray, *War, Peace, and Victory: Strategy and Statecraft for the Next Century*, p. 74.

[35] Werner, Max, *Military Strength of the Powers: A Soldier's Forecast for Citizens* (New York, NY: Modern Age Books, 1939), pp. 142-147, 213-214, 280-283.

[36] Duncan, Francis, "Mahan – Historian with a Purpose," *U.S. Naval Institute Proceedings*, Vol. 83, no. 5 (May 1957), p. 501.

[37] Russell Weigley, *The American Way of War*, p. 169.

[38] Ibid., pp. 190-191.

[39] Ibid., p. 180.

[40] Jon Sumida, "New Insights from Old Books," *Naval War College Review*, Vol. LIV, no. 3, p. 101.

[41] Ibid., p. 13.

[42] Jon Sumida, *Inventing Grand Strategy and Teaching Command*, pp. 68-69.

[43] Jomini, Antoine-Henri, *The Art of War*, G.H. Mendell (Capt., USA) & W.P. Craighill (Lt., USA) trans. (Westport, CT: Greenwood Press, orig. pub. 1862), p. 62.

[44] Ibid., p. 63.

[45] Brodie, Bernard, *A Layman's Guide to Naval Strategy* (Princeton, NJ: Princeton University Press, 1944), p. 4.

[46] Drew, Donald (Col., USAF) & Donald Snow, *Making Strategy: An Introduction to National Security Processes and Problems* (Maxwell AFB, AL: Air University Press, 1988), p.169.

[47] Brodie, Bernard, *Strategy in the Missile Age* (Princeton, NJ: Princeton University Press, 1959), p. 20.

[48] Ibid.

[49] Dennis Drew & Donald Snow, *Making Strategy*, pp. 154-156.

[50] Alfred Thayer Mahan, *The Influence of Sea Power upon History*, pp. 22-23.

[51] Bratton, Patrick C., "When is Coercion Successful? And Why Can't We Agree on It?" *Naval War College Review*, Vol. 58, no. 3 (Summer 2005), pp. 99-120.

[52] Bernard Brodie, *A Layman's Guide to Naval Strategy*, pp. 4-5.

[53] DeYoung, Don, "Strategic Vision Can Be Powerful," *US Naval Institute Proceedings*, Vol. 126, no. 11 (November 2000), pp. 53-55.

[54] Alfred Thayer Mahan, *The Influence of Sea Power upon History*, p. 88.

[55] Colin Gray, *War, Peace, and Victory*, p. 55.

[56] O'Neil, William D., "Transformation Billy Mitchell Style," *U.S. Naval Institute Proceedings*, Vol. 128, no. 3 (March 2002), p. 104.

[57] Quester, George, "Mahan and American Naval Thought since 1914," *The Influence of History on Mahan*, John Hattendorf, ed. (Newport, RI: U.S. Naval War College Press, 1991), p. 189.

[58] Harris, Brayton, *The Navy Times Book of Submarines: A Political, Social, and Military History* (New York, NY: Berkley Publishing, 1997), p. 120.

[59] Russell Weigley, *The American Way of War*, p. 181.

[60] Morison, Samuel Eliot, *Strategy and Compromise* (Boston, MA: Little, Brown and Company, 1958), p. 93.

[61] Machiavelli, Niccolo, *The Prince*, Luigi Ricci trans. (New York, NY: New American Library, 1959), p. 37.

[62] Ibid., p.63.

[63] Clark, Vern (Adm., USN), "Midway: Service and Sacrifice," *U.S. Naval Institute Proceedings*, Vol. 128, no. 6 (June 2002), p. 63.

[64] Kiesling, Eugenia, ed., *Strategic Theories: The Essays of Admiral Raoul Castex* (Annapolis, MD: Naval Institute Press, 1994), p. 27.

[65] Padfield, Peter, *Maritime Supremacy and the Opening of the Western Mind: Naval Campaigns that Shaped the Modern World, 1588-1782* (London, UK: Pimlico, 2000), p. 2.

Chapter 5: *National Power*

[1] Colin Gray, *Explorations in Strategy*, p. 114. Gray displays a related process in schematic form for policy guidance in the military realm of air power.

[2] Ibid., p. 119. Gray incorporates a similar decision-making paradigm for military use of air power based on different strategic demand environments.

[3] Associated Press Wire Service, "Chinese to ally with opponents of their enemies," *Progress Bulletin* (08 November 1977).

[4] A more open and democratic society would naturally be willing to compromise with those it has an affinity to. Qualitatively, South Africa, Chile, and Indonesia are more considerate of international pressure from the West. Iran, Libya, and Zimbabwe could care less. It can be safely stated that passive hostile action is only as good as the company you keep.

[5] Safire, William, "Selling the Rope," *New York Times* (09 October 1983).

[6] By a fantastic coincidence, Congressman Lawrence McDonald (D-GA), then president of America's most hard-line anti-communist organization, the John Birch Society, was traveling on the doomed KAL flight. Shortly following the attack, Henry "Scoop" Jackson (D-WA), one of the most anti- Soviet US Senators on Capital Hill, dropped dead of a heart attack shortly after announcing his intent to push legislation for trade sanctions against the USSR.

[7] John Scharfen, *The Dismal Battlefield*, p. 151.

[8] Colin Gray, *Explorations in Strategy*, pp. 17-18.

[9] Ibid., p. 8.

[10] Scharfen, John C., *The Dismal Battlefield: Mobilizing for Economic Conflict* (Annapolis, MD: Naval Institute Press, 1995), pp. 127-138.

[11] Wylie, J.C. (Rear Adm., USN), *Military Strategy: A General Theory of Power Control* (Brunswick, N.J.: Rutgers University Press, 1967), p. 80.

[12] Sun Tzu Wu, *The Art of War*, Samuel Griffith trans., p. 137.

[13] Alfred Thayer Mahan, *Mahan on Naval Warfare*, Allan Westcott, ed., pp. 21-22.

[14] Alfred Thayer Mahan, *The Interest of America in Sea Power, Present and Future*, p. 33.

[15] Bowen, Catherine Drinker, *Miracle at Philadelphia: The Story of the Constitutional Convention*, orig. pub. 1966 (Boston, MA: Little, Brown and Company, 1986), p. xvii.

[16] Alfred Thayer Mahan, *The Interest of America in Sea Power, Present and Future*, p. 39.

[17] Alfred Thayer Mahan, *The Influence of Sea Power upon History*, p. 328.

[18] Ferguson, Niall, *Empire: The Rise and Demise of the British World Order and the Lessons for Global Power* (New York, NY: Basic Books, 2003), pp. 347-348.

[19] Alfred Thayer Mahan, *The Life of Nelson*, p. 334.

[20] Niall Ferguson, *Empire*, p. 347.

[21] Alfred Thayer Mahan, *The Influence of Sea Power upon History,* p. 94.

[22] Ibid., p. 209.

[23] Carl von Clausewitz, *On War*, Michael Howard & Peter Paret trans., pp. 119-121.

[24] Ibid., p. 117.

[25] Donald Drew & Donald Snow, *Making Strategy*, p. 27.

[26] Gray, Colin S., "Inescapable Geography," Colin Gray & Geoffrey Sloan, ed., *Geopolitics: Geography and Strategy* (London, UK: Frank Cass, 1999), p. 163.

[27] Echevarria, Antulio J. II (Lt. Col., USA), "Clausewitz's Center of Gravity: It's Not What We Thought," *Naval War College Review*, Vol. 56, no. 1 (Winter 2003), p. 118.

[28] Colin Gray, *Explorations in Strategy*, p. 94.

[29] Gray, Colin, *The Leverage of Sea Power: The Strategic Advantages of Navies in War* (New York, NY: Free Press, 1992). Gray's thesis is that sea power acts as a great "enabler" giving nations strategic advantage to influence events on land. Sea power position within the realm of national grand strategy 'enables' this to happen and, therefore, national grand strategy is a great "enabler" between policy and strategy.

[30] Sun Tzu Wu, *The Art of War*, Samuel B. Griffith trans., p. 53. Quotation by Mao Tse-tung.

[31] Carl von Clausewitz, *On War*, Michael Howard & Peter Paret trans., pp. 100-112.

[32] Ibid., p. 183.

[33] Ibid., 119-121.

[34] Ibid., p. 137.

[35] Roskill, S.W. (Capt., BRN), *The Strategy of Sea Power* (London, UK: Collins, 1962), pp. 95-96. Though referring primarily to the British, Roskill accurately describes the problem Italy, Germany, and Japan had comprehending Mahan.

[36] Carl von Clausewitz, *On War*, Michael Howard & Peter Paret trans., p. 131.

[37] Ibid., p. 107.

[38] Ibid., p. 86.

[39] Alfred Thayer Mahan, "Subordination in Historical Treatment," *Annual Report of the American Historical Association, 1902*, pp. 49-63.

[40] Chronicle News Services, "Rails to increase Asia trade capacity," *Houston Chronicle* (25 March 2006).

[41] Friedman, Norman, *The US Maritime Strategy* (Annapolis, MD: Naval Institute Press, 1988), p. 63.

[42] Ibid., p. 64.

[43] The ports of Long Beach and Los Angeles, California combined handled over 50% of the nation's container cargo traffic in 2002. See Robert H. Pouch, "The U.S. Merchant Marine and Maritime Industry in Review," *U.S. Naval Institute Proceedings*, Vol. 128, no. 5 (May 2002), p. 110.

[44] Weissert, Will, "Mexico plans backup ports," *Associated Press Wire Service* (24 March 2006).

[45] Stubbs, Bruce (Capt., USCG), "We Are Lifesavers, Guardians, and Warriors," *U.S. Naval Institute Proceedings*, Vol. 128, no. 4 (April 2002), pp. 50-53.

[46] Stubbs, Bruce (Capt., USCG) & Scott C. Truver, *America's Coast Guard: Safeguarding US Maritime Safety and Security in the 21ˢᵗ Century* (Annapolis, MD: Tullier Marketing Communications, 2000), pp. 5-6.

[47] Jones, Archer, *The Art of War in the Western World* (New York, NY: Oxford University Press, 1989), p. 553.

[48] Ibid., p. 554.

[49] Hughes, e., *Churchill – Ein Mann in Widerspruch* (Tubingen, GM, 1959), p. 182. Quotation in Ernst Topitsch, *Stalin's War: A Radical New Theory of the Origins of the Second World War*, Arthur Taylor trans. (New York, NY: St. Martin's Press, 1987), p. 88.

[50] Jordan, Amos, William J. Taylor, Jr. & Michael J. Mazarr, *American National Security*, 5ᵗʰ ed. (Baltimore, MD: Johns Hopkins University Press, 1999), p. 26.

[51] Ibid.

[52] Ibid.

[53] Sun Tzu Wu, *The Art of War*, Samuel Griffith, ed., p. 35.

[54] Murray, Douglas & Paul Viotti, ed., *The Defense Policies of Nations: A Comparative Study*, 3ʳᵈ ed. (Baltimore, MD: Johns Hopkins University Press, 1994), p. 594.

[55] Carl von Clausewitz, *On War*, Michael Howard & Peter Paret trans., pp. 148-150.

[56] Alfred Thayer Mahan, *The Influence of Sea Power upon History*, p. 225.

[57] Ibid., p. 71-72.

[58] Kennan, George (AKA, X), "German Strategy: 1914 and 1940," *Foreign Affairs*, Vol. 19, no. 3 (April 1941), p. 505.

[59] Alexander, Joseph H., (Col., USMC), *A Fellowship of Valor: The Battle History of the United States Marines* (New York, NY: HarperCollins Publishers, 1997), p. 364.

[60] Alfred Thayer Mahan, *The Influence of Sea Power upon History*, p. 194.

[61] Alfred Thayer Mahan, *The Life of Nelson*, p. 742.

[62] J.C. Wylie, "Mahan: Then and Now," *The Influence of History on Mahan*, p. 45.

[63] Alfred Thayer Mahan, *The Problem of Asia*, pp. 37-38.

[64] Kagan, Donald, *On the Origins of War and the Preservation of Peace* (New York, NY: Anchor Books, 1995), p. 570.

[65] Ibid. p. 159

[66] Jon Sumida, *Inventing Grand Strategy and Teaching Command*, p. 99.

Chapter 6: *Power Resources*

[1] Mahan, Alfred Thayer (Capt., USN), "The Strategic Features of the Gulf of Mexico and the Caribbean Sea," *Harper's New Monthly Magazine*, Vol. XCV, no. DLXIX (October 1897), p. 690.

[2] Gray, Colin S., *Modern Strategy* (New York, NY: Oxford University Press, 1999) pp. 40-41.

[3] Alfred Thayer Mahan, *The Influence of Sea Power upon History*, pp. 29-59.

[4] Hopkirk, Peter, *The Great Game: The Struggle for Empire in Central Asia* (New York, NY: Kodansha International, 1992), p. 502. Quotation by Count Witte, Finance Minister to Tsar Nicholas II.

[5] Creswell, John (Cdr., BRN), *Naval Warfare: An Introductory Study*, 2ⁿᵈ ed. (London, UK: Sampson, Low, Marston & Company, 1942), p. 251.

[6] Archer Jones, *The Art of War in the Western World*, pp. 602-612.

[7] John Creswell, *Naval Warfare*, p. 224.

[8] Alfred Thayer Mahan, *The Interest of America in Sea Power, Present and Future*, p. 214.

[9] Philbin, Tobias R. III, *The Lure of Neptune: German – Soviet Naval Collaboration and Ambitions, 1919-1941* (Columbia, SC: University of South Carolina Press, 1994).

[10] Sun Tzu Wu, *The Art of War*, Samuel Griffith trans., p. 73.

[11] Colin Gray, *The Leverage of Sea Power*, p. 289.

[12] Sun Tzu Wu, *The Art of War*, Samuel Griffith trans., p. 73.

[13] Carl von Clausewitz, *On War*, Michael Howard & Peter Paret trans., p. 127.

[14] Alfred Thayer Mahan, *Mahan on Naval Warfare*, Allan Westcott, ed., p. 128.

[15] Alfred Thayer Mahan, *Naval Strategy*, p. 151. Mahan notes quotation by a British admiral "of long ago."

[16] Smith, Keith (Lt. Gen., USMC), "V-22 Is Right for War on Terrorism," *U.S. Naval Institute Proceedings*, Vol. 128, no. 1 (January 2002), pp. 42-44. The Osprey has a cruising speed of 250 knots and a tactical range of over 1100 nautical miles.

[17] Glenn, Russell W., "Urban Combat Is Complex," *U.S. Naval Institute Proceedings*, Vol. 128, no. 2 (February 2002), pp. 62-65.

[18] Sun Tzu Wu, *The Art of War*, p. 78.

[19] East Asia Intel.com, "China's huge footprint being felt with the rising cost of oil," *World Tribune* (22 October 2004).

[20] Stuart Schram, *The Political Thought of Mao Tse-tung*, p. 414.

[21] Walter Issacson & Evan Thomas, *The Wise Men*, pp. 98-118.

[22] Source: United States Central Intelligence Agency.

[23] Mbachu, Dulue, "China scores gains in Africa," *Houston Chronicle* (10 February 2006).

[24] Alfred Thayer Mahan, *The Problem of Asia*, pp. 166-167.

[25] Bill Gertz, *The China Threat*, p. 12. Quotation by PRC General Chi Haotian, Vice Chairman, Communist Party Central Military Commission (December 1999).

[26] Johnson, Tim, "China, Latin America getting into rhythm of good relations," *Houston Chronicle* (17 July 2005).

[27] Bridges, Tyler, "Latin states digging into Chinese," *Houston Chronicle* (28 July 2005)

[28] North, Douglass C., *Structure and Change in Economic History* (New York, NY: W.W. Norton, 1981), p. 144.

[29] Carl von Clausewitz, *On War*, Michael Howard & Peter Paret trans., p. 9.

[30] Niccolo Machiavelli, *The Prince*, p. 97.

[31] Hubbard, Charles, "Alfred Thayer Mahan: The Reluctant Seaman," *American History* (August 1998).

[32] Alfred Thayer Mahan, *Admiral Farragut*, p. 306.

[33] Carl von Clausewitz, *On War*, Michael Howard & Peter Paret trans., p. 112.

[34] Joseph Story, *A Familiar Exposition of The Constitution of the United States*, p. 364. Quotation by George Washington, *Farewell Address to the People of the United States* (17 September 1796).

[35] Alfred Thayer Mahan, *The Influence of Sea Power upon the French Revolution and Empire*, p. 74.

[36] Beevor, Antony, *Stalingrad* (London, UK: Penguin Books, 1999), pp. 84-101.

[37] Joseph Alexander, *A Fellowship of Valor*, pp. 137-138.

[38] Alfred Thayer Mahan, *The Life of Nelson*, p. 200.

[39] Herm, Gerhard, *The Celts: The People Who Came Out of the Darkness* (New York, NY: St. Martin's Press, 1975), p. 214.

[40] Antony Beevor, *Stalingrad*, pp. 106-107. The German Army was similarly appalled over the same Soviet willingness to force women in combat.

[41] Perowne, Stewart, *Death of the Roman Republic: From 146 B.C. to the Birth of the Roman Empire* (Garden City, NJ: Doubleday & Company, 1968).

[42] Alfred Thayer Mahan, *The Interest of America in Sea Power, Present and Future*, pp. 213-214.

[43] Rodger, N.A.M., *The Safeguard of the Sea: A Naval History of Britain, 660-1649*, Vol. I ((London, UK: HarperCollins Publishers, 1997), pp. 193-194.

[44] Massie, Robert, *Dreadnought: Britain, Germany and the Coming of the Great War* (London, UK: Pimlico, 1998), p. 393.

[45] Roskill, S.W. (Capt., BRN), *The Strategy of Sea Power: Its Development and Application* (London, UK: Collins, 1962), p. 80.

[46] Fuller, J.F.C. (Gen., BRA), *A Military History of the Western World: From the Defeat of the Spanish Armada to the Battle of Waterloo*, Vol. II (New York, NY: Plenum Publishing, 1955), pp. 376-404.

[47] Alfred Thayer Mahan, *The Life of Nelson*, p. 71.

[48] Alfred Thayer Mahan, *The Influence of Sea Power upon the French Revolution and Empire*, p. 141. Quotation in Jon Sumida, *Inventing Grand Strategy and Teaching Command*, p. 56.

[49] Alfred Thayer Mahan, *The Life of Nelson*, p. 241.

[50] Jon Sumida, *Inventing Grand Strategy and Teaching Command*, p. 53. Direct quote made by Nelson and documented by Mahan in *The Life of Nelson*.

[51] Mahan, Alfred Thayer (Capt., USN), *Sea Power in Its Relations to the War of 1812* (Boston, MA: Little, Brown, and Company, 1905), p. v.

[52] Livezey, William, *Mahan on Sea Power*, rev. ed. (Norman, OK: University of Oklahoma Press, 1981), p. 316. Quotation in Jon Sumida, "Alfred Thayer Mahan, Geopolitics," Gray & Sloan ed., *Geopolitics*, p. 41.

[53] Bernard Brodie, *A Layman's Guide to Naval Strategy*, p. 4.

[54] Isenberg, Michael, *Shield of the Republic: The United States Navy In an Era of Cold War and Violent Peace*, Vol. I, 1945-1962 (New York, NY: St. Martin's Press, 1993), pp. 37-38.

[55] Zachary, G. Pascal, *Endless Frontier: Vannevar Bush, Engineer of the American Century* (New York, NY: Free Press, 1997), p. 240.

[56] Michael Isenberg, *Shield of the Republic*, p. 334.

[57] Bethel, Tom, *The Noblest Triumph: Property and Prosperity Through the Ages* (New York, NY: St. Martin's Press, 1998), pp. 75-79.

[58] Bastiat, Frederic, *Economic Sophisms* (Princeton, NJ: D. Van Nostrand, 1964), pp. 56-57. Quotation in Todd G. Buchholz, *New Ideas from Dead Economists* (New York, NY: Penguin Books, 1990), p. 71.

[59] Ibid.

[60] In 2004 1,084,504 attorneys were actively practicing law in the United States (American Bar Association).

[61] Todd Buchholz, *New Ideas from Dead Economists*, p. 186. Quotation by Louis Brandeis, "The Living Law," Vol. 10, *Illinois Law Review* (1916).

[62] FBI report on Albert Einstein, File 61-7089-25 (13 February 1950). Quotation in Herbert Romerstein & Eric Breindel, *The Venona Secrets* (Washington, DC: Regnery Publishing, 2000), p. 279.

[63] Blum, Howard, *I Pledge Allegiance... The True Story of the Walkers: An American Spy Family* (New York, NY: Simon & Schuster, 1987), pp. 407-409.

[64] de Greaffenreid, Kenneth E., ed., *The Cox Report: The Unanimous and Bipartisan Report of the House Select Committee on U.S. National Security and Military Commercial Concerns with the People's Republic of China* (Washington, DC: Regnery Publishing, 1999), p. 74.

[65] Cameron, Rondo, *A Concise Economic History of the World: From Paleolithic Times to the Present*, 2nd ed. (New York, NY: Oxford University Press, 1993), pp. 204-209.

[66] Ambrose, Stephen E., *Nothing Like It in the World: The Men Who Built the Transcontinental Railroad, 1863-1869* (New York, NY: Simon & Schuster, 2000), p. 42.

[67] Dean, Josh, "The Rebirth of Rail," *Popular Mechanics* (January 2006), p. 59. Quotation by Rob Hoffman, World Business Chicago.

[68] Carpenter, Amanda B., "Highway Bill Spends $255 million on Bike Paths," *Human Events* (12 August 2005).

[69] Josh Dean, "The Rebirth of Rail," *Popular Mechanics* (January 2006), p. 58.

[70] N.A.M. Rodger, *The Safeguard of the Sea*, p. 327.

[71] Ibid., pp. 329-334.

[72] Ibid.

[73] Jon Sumida, *Inventing Grand Strategy and Teaching Command*, p. 65.

[74] Russell Weigley, *The American Way of War*, p. 438. Quotation by John F. Kennedy in a Senate speech titled, *The Missile Gap* (14 August 1958). Panic and fear over a missile gap favoring the Soviets was proven unfounded shortly after Kennedy was elected in 1960. It made good campaign politics, however, and Eisenhower administration officials knew his accusation was untrue. Richard Nixon, Kennedy's opponent, was refrained from stating so in public because of secrecy surrounding U-2 reconnaissance missions over the USSR. The damage, as far as Republican Party leaders were concerned, had already been done in losing control of the White House. Promoters of missile gap hysteria included Henry Kissinger and Lyndon Johnson.

[75] Actual submarine depth wisely remains classified.

[76] Alfred Thayer Mahan, *Naval Strategy*, p. 142.

[77] Hanson, Victor David, "We're Removing Saddam Hussein," *US Naval Institute Proceedings*, Vol. 129, no. 3 (March 2003), p. 98.

[78] Mahan, Alfred Thayer (Capt., USN), "The Isthmus and Sea Power," *The Atlantic Monthly*, Vol. 72, no. 432 (October 1893), p. 470.

[79] Joseph Story, *A Familiar Exposititon of The Constitution of the United States*, pp. 371-372. Quotation by George Washington, *Farewell Address to the People of the United States* (17 September 1796).

[80] Trotsky, Leon, "The Death Agony of Capitalism and the Tasks of the Fourth International," *The Transitional Program for Socialist Revolution*, George Breitman & Fred Stanton, ed. (New York, NY: Pathfinder Press, 1977), pp. 119-135.

[81] D'Souza, Dinesh, *What's So Great About America* (New York, NY: Penguin Books, 2002), pp. 66-67.

[82] N.A.M. Rodger, *The Safeguard of the Sea*, p. 433.

[83] Ibid., pp. 381-382. The payment scheme was called "Ship Money" and devised by Charles I to circumvent resistance in Parliament.

[84] Ibid.

[85] Lewis, Michael, *The History of the British Navy* (Harmondsworth, UK: Penguin Books, 1957), p. 77.

[86] Alfred Thayer Mahan, *Mahan on Naval Warfare*, Allan Westcott, ed., p. 312.

[87] The wise entrepreneur observes their competitor and emulates what they do right. Competition helps a market achieve greatness, just as it can for competing states. It does reveal the truth behind a dictatorship unwilling to relinquish power for the good of a nation and freedom of its people.

[88] Daniel, Caroline & Maija Palmer, "Google's goal to organize your daily life," *Financial Times* (22 May 2007). Has anyone considered the political blackmailing opportunities here (*The Prometheus Deception*)?

[89] Martin, L.W., *The Seas in Modern Strategy* (New York, NY: Frederick Praeger, 1967), p. 175.

[90] Sobel, Robert, *Coolidge: An American Enigma* (Washington, DC: Regnery Publishing, 1998), p. 313.

Chapter 7: *Exploration and Discovery*

[1] Alfred Thayer Mahan, *The Influence of Sea Power upon History, 1660 -1783*, p. 88.

[2] Gaddis, John Lewis, "The Unexpected John Foster Dulles: Nuclear Weapons, Communism, and the Russians," *John Foster Dulles and the Diplomacy of the Cold War*, Richard Immerman, ed., p. 77.

[3] Sun Tzu Wu, *The Art of War*, Samuel Griffith trans., p. 67.

[4] Colin Gray, *War, Peace, and Victory*, p. 67. Quotation credited to British Field Marshall Sir Bernard Montgomery.

[5] Alfred Thayer Mahan, *The Influence of Sea Power upon History, 1660-1783*. pp. 507-508.

[6] George Seldes, *The Great Thoughts*, p. 367. Quotation from George Santayana, *The Life of Reason, 1905-1906*.

[7] Ibid.

[8] Rondo Cameron, *A Concise Economic History of the World*, p. 33.

[9] Whitfield, Peter, *Mapping the World: A History of Exploration*, 2nd ed. (London, UK: Folio Society, 2000), pp. 15-16.

[10] Alexander, Fran, ed., *The Oxford Encyclopaedia of World History* (New York, NY: Oxford University Press, 1998), p. 524.

[11] Peter Whitfield, *Mapping the World*, p. 16.

[12] Finley, M.I., *The World of Odysseus*, orig. pub. 1954 (London, UK: Folio Society, 2002), p. 93.

[13] Rondo Cameron, *A Concise Economic History of the World*, p. 33.

[14] Ibid.

[15] Herm, Gerhard, *The Phoenicians: The Purple Empire of the Ancient World* (New York, NY: William Morrow, 1975), p. 69.

[16] N.C. Flemming, "Sunken Cities and Forgotten Wrecks," *Seas, Maps, and Men: An Atlas-History of Man's Exploration of the Oceans*, G.E.R. Deacon, ed., pp. 130-131.

[17] Hornblower, Simon & Antony Spawforth, ed., *The Oxford Companion to Classical Civilization* (Oxford, UK: Oxford University Press, 1998), p. 141.

[18] Flemming, N.C., "Sunken Cities and Forgotten Wrecks," *Seas, Maps, and Men: An Atlas-History of Man's Exploration of the Oceans*, G.E.R. Deacon, ed. (Garden City, NJ: Doubleday & Company, 1962), p. 153.

[19] Chambers, Mortimer, Raymond Grew, David Herlihy, Theodore Rabb & Isser Woloch, *The Western Experience: To 1715* (New York, NY: Alfred A. Knopf, 1974), p. 25.

[20] Ibid.

[21] Alfred Thayer Mahan, *The Influence of Sea Power upon History*, p. 43.

[22] Mahan, Alfred Thayer (Rear Adm., USN), *Naval Strategy: Compared and Contrasted with the Principles and Practice of Military Operations on Land* (London, UK: Sampson Low, Marston & Company, 1911), pp. 132-199.

[23] Peter Whitfield, *Mapping the World*, p. 16. Whitfield argues that the Phoenicians, unlike the ancient Chinese, may have actually preferred a lack of documentation to protect their skills from competitor states.

[24] Simon Hornblower & Antony Spawforth, ed., *The Oxford Companion to Classical Civilization*, p. 532.

[25] Ibid.

[26] Sun Tzu Wu, *The Art of War*, Samuel B. Griffith, trans., pp. 96-101.

[27] N.C. Flemming, "Sunken Cities and Forgotten Wrecks," *Seas, Maps, and Men: An Atlas-History of Man's Exploration of the Oceans*, G.E.R. Deacon, ed., p. 132.

[28] Gray, John, *The Canaanites* (New York, NY: Frederick A. Praeger, 1964), pp. 49-52.

[29] Population figures are difficult to identify, though many scholars have concluded Athens alone consisted of approximately 250-300,000 people by 400 BC. Figure from POL: 200, Ancient Athens I, Purdue University (Course Syllabus).

[30] Alfred Thayer Mahan, *The Influence of Sea Power upon History*, pp. 44-45.

[31] Ibid., p. 43.

[32] Colin Gray, *The Leverage of Sea Power*, p. 95.

[33] Archer Jones, *The Art of War in the Western World*, p. 90.

[34] Douglass North, *Structure and Change in Economic History*, pp. 102-112.

[35] Zumwalt, Elmo R. (Adm., USN), *On Watch: A Memoir* (New York, NY: Quadrangle, 1976), pp. xiv-xv, 319-320. Zumwalt claims then National Security Advisor, Henry Kissinger, used the Athens-Sparta model to compare the United States and Soviet Union. Kissinger, according to Zumwalt's notes, justified negotiating a favorable deal for the Soviets because he believed America no longer possessed the stomach to fight. Kissinger saw it as his job to get the best terms possible while the US was still in a negotiating position, and without public knowledge of what was taking place. He went on to argue, according to Zumwalt, that history and the American people would someday blame him for selling out, even though Kissinger believed it was their own fault. What he sold is yet to be determined.

[36] Herodotus, *Erato*, George Rawlings, trans., Fracis Godolphin, ed., *Greek Historians*, Vol. I (New York, NY: Random House, 1942), pp. 340-388.

[37] Haywood, Richard Mansfield, *Ancient Greece and the Near East* (New York, NY: David McKay, 1964), pp. 314-315.

[38] Colin S. Gray, *The Leverage of Sea Power*, p. 97.

[39] Adcock, F.E., *The Greek and Macedonian Art of War* (Berkeley, CA: University of California Press, 1957), p. 46.

[40] Donald Kagan, *On the Origins of War and the Preservation of Peace*, p. 25.

[41] Ibid., p. 73.

[42] Thucydides, "History of the Peloponnesian War," Maynard Mack, gen. ed., *The Norton Anthology of World Masterpieces*, Vol. I, 4th ed. (New York, NY: W.W. Norton & Company, 1979), p. 341.

[43] F.E. Adcock, *The Greek and Macedonian Art of War*, p. 36.

[44] Green, Peter, *Armada from Athens* (Garden City, NJ: Doubleday & Company, 1970). Green provides a colorful narrative of the human drama that unfolded over the entire campaign. This includes everyone from women in Athens to the men who fought and died on Sicilian soil.

[45] Kagan, Donald, *The Fall of the Athenian Empire* (Ithaca, NY: Cornell University Press, 1987), p. 423.

[46] Overy, Richard, ed., *The Times History of the World*, 5th ed. (London, UK: HarperCollins, 1999), p. 91 (Map).

[47] Davies, Norman, *Europe* (New York, NY: Oxford University Press, 1996), p. 149.

[48] Adcock, F.E., *The Roman Art of War Under the Republic* (New York, NY: Barnes & Noble, 1995), p. 31.

[49] Bernstein, Alvin H., "The strategy of a warrior-state: Rome and the wars against Carthage, 264-201 B.C." *The Making of Strategy*, Williamson Murray, MacGregor Knox, and Alvin Bernstein ed., p. 71.

[50] Antoine Jomini, *The Art of War*, G.H. Mendill & W.P. Craighill trans., p. 329.

[51] de Jouvenel, Bertrand, *On Power: The Natural History of Its Growth*, orig. pub. 1945 (Indianapolis, IN: Liberty Press, 1993), pp. 356-357.

[52] Alvin Bernstein, "The strategy of a warrior-state: Rome and the wars against Carthage, 264-201 B.C." *The Making of Strategy*, Williamson Murray, MacGregor Knox, and Alvin Bernstein ed., pp. 62-65.

[53] Ibid., p. 61.

[54] Ibid., p. 57.

[55] Gibbon, Edward, *The History of the Decline and Fall of the Roman Empire*, Vol. I–VIII, orig. pub. 1788 (London, UK: Folio Society, 1997).

[56] Alfred Thayer Mahan, *Retrospect and Progress: Studies in International Relations, Naval and Political*, p. 169.

[57] Bertrand de Jouvenel, *On Power*, p. 190.

[58] Niccolo Machiavelli, *The Prince*, p. 79.

[59] Archer Jones, *The Art of War in the Western World*, pp. 92-95.

[60] Grant, Michael, *The Climax of Rome* (Boston, MA: Little, Brown, and Company), pp. 64-65.

Chapter 8: *East Meets West*

[1] Even practices of "extraterritoriality" had similarities to Roman law. It concerned application of native laws for Chinese citizens while foreigners who broke the law in China were tried under judicial practices of their native country. This carried many similarities to Roman principles of "personal law."

[2] Alfred Thayer Mahan, *The Interest of America in Sea Power, Present and Future*, pp. 248-249.

[3] Ibid.

[4] Glazer, David W. (Cdr., USN), "Breaching the Great Wall," *U.S. Naval Institute Proceedings*, Vol. 126, no. 3 (March 2000), p. 70.

[5] Richard Overy, ed., *The Times History of the World*, p. 81.

[6] Gernet, Jacques, *A History of Chinese Civilization* (New York, NY: Cambridge University Press, 1982).

[7] Wright, Arthur F., *The Sui Dynasty: The Unification of China, A.D. 581-617* (New York, NY: Alfred A. Knopf, 1978), pp. 55-60.

[8] Richard Overy, *The Times History of the World*, p. 127.

[9] Waldron, Arthur, "Chinese strategy from the fourteenth to the seventeenth centuries," Williamson Murray, MacGregor Knox and Alvin Bernstein, ed., *The Making of Strategy*, pp. 97-107.

[10] Ibid., p. 108.

[11] Grousset, Rene, *The Rise of Splendour of the Chinese Empire* (Berkeley, CA: University of California Press, 1965), p. 264.

[12] David Glazier, "Breaching the Great Wall," *U.S. Naval Institute Proceedings*, Vol. 126, no. 3 (March 2000), p. 70.

[13] Meyer, Karl E. & Shareen Blair Brysac, *Tournament of Shadows: The Great Game and the Race for Empire in Central Asia* (Washington, DC: Counterpoint, 1999), p. 404. Quotation by Emperor Ch'ien-lung to King George III in a 1793 message, hand-carried by Lord George Macartney returning from Peking. During the period of Ch'ien-lung's rule (1736-1796), China briefly became the world's largest state but, like all other periods, it quickly retracted.

[14] Gunther, John, *Inside Asia* (New York, NY: Harper and Brothers, 1939), p. 148.

[15] Ibid., pp. 177-178.

[16] David Glazier, "Breaching the Great Wall," *U.S. Naval Institute Proceedings*, Vol. 126, no. 3 (March 2000), p. 71.

[17] Nugroho, Anton (Capt., IAF), "The Dragon Looks South," *U.S. Naval Institute Proceedings*, Vol. 126, no. 3 (March 2000), pp. 74-76.

[18] John Gunther, *Inside Asia*, p. 38.

[19] Alfred Thayer Mahan, *The Interest of America in Sea Power, Present and Future*, pp. 221-222.

[20] Doenhoff, Richard A., "Biddle, Perry, and Japan," *U.S. Naval Institute Proceedings*, Vol. 92, no. 11 (November 1966), pp. 78-87.

[21] "Instructions from the State Department (to the Navy Department) for the Expedition to Japan," in Arthur Walworth, *Black Ships off Japan: The Story of Commodore Perry's Expedition* (New York, NY: Alfred A. Knopf, 1946), pp. 240-246.

[22] Kiralfy, Alexander, "Japanese Naval Strategy," Edward Mead Earle, ed., *Makers of Modern Strategy*, p. 467.

[23] Quotation from Eric Grove, *Big Fleet Actions* (London, UK: Arms and Armour Press, 1991), p. 45.

[24] Hough, Richard, *The Fleet that had to Die* (New York, NY: Viking Press, 1958).

[25] Alfred Thayer Mahan, *Mahan on Naval Warfare*, Allan Westcott, ed., pp. 276-282.

[26] Kennan, George F., *Soviet Foreign Policy, 1917-1941* (Princeton, NJ: D. Van Nostrand Company, 1960), pp. 64-77.

[27] Alexander Kiralfy, "Japanese Naval Strategy," Edward Mead Earle, ed., *Makers of Modern Strategy*, p.479.

[28] Ikeda, Sogo, Kokushikan University, "American Attitude around the Ishii-Lansing Agreement," Conference Paper, *International Studies Association, West* (Claremont, CA: Claremont Graduate University, October 1998).

[29] Samuel Eliot Morison, *Strategy and Compromise*, pp. 10-11.

[30] John Gunther, *Inside Asia*, p. 48.

[31] Ibid., p. 50.

[32] Ibid.

[33] Alfred Thayer Mahan, *The Interest of America in Sea Power, Present and Future*, p. 259.

[34] Murray, Williamson, "Thinking about Innovation," *Naval War College Review*, Vol. 54, no.2 (Spring 2001), p. 121.

[35] Tuleja, Thaddeus, *Statesmen and Admirals: Quest for a Far Eastern Naval Policy* (New York, NY: W.W. Norton & Company, 1963), pp. 21-29.

[36] Wainwright, Jonathan (Gen., USA), *General Wainwright's Story: The Account of Four Years of Humiliating Defeat, Surrender, and Captivity* (Garden City, NJ: Doubleday & Company, 1946).

[37] Ballendorf, Dirk A. & Merrill L. Bartlett, *Pete Ellis: An Amphibious Warfare Prophet, 1880-1923* (Annapolis, MD: Naval Institute Press, 1997), p. 112. Quotation by Navy Captain William Pratt.

[38] John Gunther, *Inside Asia*, p. 282.

[39] William Maltby, "The Origins of a Global Strategy," Williamson Murray, MacGregor Knox & Alvin Bernstein, eds., *The Making of Strategy*, p. 151.

[40] The issue of empire, or imperialism as good or evil has more to do with who has the empire and power, verses those who don't. Had England not created the British Empire, then some other state certainly would have rose and filled that void.

[41] N.A.M. Rodger, *The Safeguard of the Sea*, Vol. I, p. xxvii.

[42] Archer Jones, *The Art of War in the Western World*, p. 617.

[43] Rodgers, William L. (Vice Adm., USN), *Naval Warfare under Oars: 4th to 16th Centuries* (Annapolis, MD: Naval Institute Press, 1996), pp. 110-113.

[44] William Maltby, "The origins of a global strategy," *The Making of Strategy*, Williamson Murray, MacGregor Knox & Alvin Bernstein, ed., pp. 151-152.

[45] N.A.M. Rodger, *The Safeguard of the Sea*, Vol. I, p. 196.

[46] Alfred Thayer Mahan, *Mahan on Naval Warfare*, Allan Westcott, ed., p. 22.

[47] Bertrand de Jouvenel, *On Power*, p. 208.

[48] William Rodgers, *Naval Warfare under Oars*, p. 241.

[49] N.A.M. Rodger, *The Safeguard of the Sea*, p. 253. Quotation in letter from Nicholas Oseley (aboard the *Revenge*) to Sir F. Walsingham, 23 July 1588, in DSA Vol. I, p. 302.

[50] N.A.M. Rodger, *The Safeguard of the Sea*, p. 271.

[51] William Rodgers, *Naval Warfare under Oars*, p. 328.

[52] J.F.C. Fuller, *A Military History of the Western World*, Vol. II, p. 37.

[53] Albion, Robert G., "The British Lion Afloat," *New York Times Book Review* (08 March 1959).

[54] N.A.M. Rodger, *The Safeguard of the Sea*, pp. 364-378.

[55] William Maltby, "The Origins of a Global Strategy," Williamson Murray, MacGregor Knox & Alvin Bernstein, eds., *The Making of Strategy*, p. 151.

[56] Peter Padfield, *Maritime Supremacy and the Opening of the Western Mind*, p. 187.

[57] Ibid., p. 257.

[58] Ibid., p. 282.

[59] Quotation from J.F.C. Fuller, *A Military History of the Western World* Vol. II, p. 406.

[60] Paul Kennedy argues that Napoleon's continental system would have worked with more time and he believes it was capable of bringing Great Britain to her knees. See, *The Rise and Fall of British Naval Mastery*, p. 143.

[61] Rondo Cameron, *A Concise Economic History of the World*, pp. 295-296.

[62] Sun Tzu Wu, *The Art of War*, Samuel Griffith trans., p. 145.

[63] Rondo Cameron, *A Concise Economic History of the World*, pp. 300-301.

[64] Halpern, Paul G., *A Naval History of World War I* (Annapolis, MD: Naval Institute Press, 1994), p. 2.

[65] Marder, Arthur J., The Anatomy of British Sea Power: A History of British Naval Policy in the Pre-Dreadnought Era, 1880-1905 (New York, NY: Alfred A. Knopf, 1940), p. 461.

[66] Ibid., p. 462. Quotation from *National Review* (May, June 1902).

[67] Alfred Thayer Mahan, *Mahan on Naval Warfare*, Allan Westcott, ed., p. 319.

[68] Robert Massie, *Dreadnought*, p.240.

[69] Gough, Barry, "The Influence of History on Mahan," *The Influence of History on Mahan* (Newport, RI: Naval War College Press, 1991), p. 8. Gough notes Sir Charles Webster telling students Mahan was a primary cause of World War I. Woodrow Wilson also believed the war's cause was "navalism," which justified his insisting on its elimination in the Points of Peace. Prior to his death, Mahan argued WWI was yet another unleashing of traditional rivalries that so frequently tore apart Europe's continent. In other words, if sea power never existed at all, there would still be war.

[70] Alfred Thayer Mahan, *The Interest of America in Sea Power, Present and Future*, p. 243.

[71] Sawyer, Ralph, trans., *Unorthodox Strategies: 100 Lessons in the Art of War* (New York, NY: Barnes & Noble, 1996), p.36.

Chapter 9: *Early America*

[1] Alfred Thayer Mahan, *Mahan on Naval Warfare*, Allan Westcott, ed., pp. 169-170. Quotation by George Washington, *Memorandum for concerting a plan of operations with the French army* (15 July 1780).

[2] Smelser, Marshall, "Whether to Provide and Maintain a Navy (1787-1788)," *US Naval Institute Proceedings*, Vol. 83, no. 9 (September 1957), pp. 944-953.

[3] Alfred Thayer Mahan, *Mahan on Naval Warfare*, Allan Westcott, ed., pp. 164-168.

[4] Alfred Thayer Mahan, *The Influence of Sea Power upon History*, p. 137.

[5] Ibid., p. 65.

[6] Ibid., p. 510.

[7] Ibid., pp. 328-329.

[8] Anderson, Fred, *Crucible of War: The Seven Years' War and the Fate of Empire in British North America, 1754-1766* (London, UK: Faber and Faber, 2000), p. 167.

[9] Alfred Thayer Mahan, *The Influence of Sea Power upon History*, p. 508.

[10] Peter Maslowski, "To the edge of greatness: The United States, 1783-1865," *The Making of Strategy*, Williamson Murray, MacGregor Knox, and Alvin Bernstein, ed., p. 208.

[11] Ibid., pp. 67-68.

[12] Callwell, C.E., *Military Operations and Maritime Preponderance: Their Relations and Interdependence*, orig. pub. 1905 (Annapolis, MD: Naval Institute Press, 1996), pp. 394-400.

[13] Ibid., pp. 391-393.

[14] Bird, Harrison, *Navies in the Mountains: The Battles on the Waters of Lake Champlain and Lake George, 1609-1814* (New York, NY: Oxford University Press, 1962).

[15] Wambold, Don Jr., "Sailing Through the Mountains," *US Naval Institute Naval History*, Vol. 15, no. 5 (October 2001), p. 38.

[16] Fred Anderson, *Crucible of War*, pp. 22-32.

[17] Alfred Thayer Mahan, *Admiral Farragut*, p. 7.

[18] S.W. Roskill, *The Strategy of Sea Power*, p. 86.

[19] Horsman, Reginald, *The Causes of the War of 1812* (New York, NY: A.S. Barnes & Company, 1962), pp. 45-59.

[20] Alfred Thayer Mahan, *Mahan on Naval Warfare*, Allan Westcott, ed., pp. 229-235.

[21] Fuller, J.F.C. (Maj. Gen., RBA), *Decisive Battles of the USA* (New York, NY: Harper & Brothers, 1942), pp. 102-104.

[22] Alfred Thayer Mahan, *Sea Power in Its Relations to the War of 1812*, pp. 208-209. Quotation in Jon Sumida, *Inventing Grand Strategy and Teaching Command*, p. 41.

[23] Paul Kennedy, *The Rise and Fall of British Naval Mastery*, pp. 138-139.

[24] Alfred Thayer Mahan, "The Future in Relation to American Naval Power," *Harper's New Monthly Magazine*, Vol. XCL, no. DXLV (October 1895), p. 770.

[25] J.F.C. Fuller, *Decisive Battles of the USA*, p. 102.

[26] S.W. Roskill, *The Strategy of Sea Power*, pp. 86-87.

[27] Peter Maslowski, "To the edge of greatness: The United States, 1783-1865," *The Making of Strategy*, Williamson Murray, MacGregor Knox, and Alvin Bernstein, ed., p. 224.

[28] Andrews, Charles M., *The Historical Development of Modern Europe: From the Congress of Vienna to the Present Time, 1815-1897* Vol. II (New York, NY: G.P. Putnam's Sons, 1910), pp. 175-176.

[29] Donald, David Herbert, *Lincoln* (London, UK: Random House, 1995), pp. 412-416.

[30] Jaffa, Harry V., *A New Birth of Freedom: Abraham Lincoln and the Coming of the Civil War* (Lanham, MD: Rowman & Littlefield, 2000), p. 359.

[31] Alfred Thayer Mahan, *Admiral Farragut*, p. 81.

[32] Ibid., pp. 173-174.

[33] Cinco de Mayo (5th of May), is an annual celebration honoring the 1862 defeat of French forces at Pueblo, Mexico. Though not immediately expelling the French, it did inspire Mexicans to arms. Ironically, Cinco de Mayo has become a bigger event in the US and it should be considering geostrategic ramifications during the Civil War.

[34] Alfred Thayer Mahan, *Admiral Farragut*, p. 176.

[35] Ibid., pp. 116-117.

[36] Alfred Thayer Mahan, *The Influence of Sea Power upon History*, p. 138.

[37] Gildea, Robert, *Barricades and Borders: Europe 1800-1914*, 2nd ed. (Oxford, UK: Oxford University Press, 1996). Gildea's thesis of continental power politics explains how World War I developed over a very long period of time. As a result, he unknowingly and indirectly defends Mahan from critics claiming he was the cause.

[38] Stephen Ambrose, *Nothing Like It in the World*, pp. 42-43.

[39] Tayler, Arthur, *Illustrated History of North American Railroads* (London, UK: Quintet Publishing, 1996), pp. 32-37.

[40] Wheeler, Keith, ed., *The Railroaders* (New York, NY: Time-Life Books, 1973), pp. 36-37.

[41] Robert Seager, *Alfred Thayer Mahan*, p. 193.

[42] Alfred Thayer Mahan, *The Interest of America in Sea Power, Present and Future*, p. 25.

[43] Ibid., p. 157.

[44] Alfred Thayer Mahan, *Mahan on Naval Warfare*, Allan Westcott, ed., p. 245.

[45] Robert Seager, *Alfred Thayer Mahan*, p. 392.

[46] Eyre, James K., Jr., "Early Japanese Imperialism and the Philippines," *U.S. Naval Institute Proceedings*, Vol.75, no. 11 (November 1949).

[47] Whitney Griswold, *The Far Eastern Policy of the United States*, pp. 22-23.

[48] O'Connor, Richard, *Pacific Destiny: An Informal History of the US in the Far East* (Boston, MA: Little, Brown, and Company, 1969), p. 237. Even pacifist communities supported an international role for America. O'Connor quotes John Lafarge, artist and friend of Henry Cabot Lodge, stating "the Pacific should be ours, and it must." Lodge, considered a pacifist, became one of Mahan's biggest allies in the US Senate.

[49] Robert Massie, *Dreadnought*, pp. xxiii-xxiv. Kaiser Wilhelm II insisted Mahan's book be read by all naval officers, and that a copy be kept onboard every ship. This is often used as evidence to accuse Mahan of being the cause for World War I. See Charles Glass, "The First Lies Club: How the Imperial Eagle Got Its Wings," *Harper's Magazine* (January 2003). The same magazine that once promoted Mahan's theories is being deployed to attack those same theories a century later.

[50] Alfred Thayer Mahan, *The Interest of America in Sea Power, Present and Future*, pp. 252-253.

[51] Whitney Griswold, *The Far Eastern Policy of the United States*, pp. 216-220. Griswold states Woodrow Wilson and Robert Lansing, Secretary of State, were aware of contradictions between their agreement with Japan and the one Japan signed with Britain. Griswold argues that Wilson simply used the Ishii – Lansing Agreement to buy time while he dedicated resources to dispatching Germany in Europe.

[52] George Baer, *One Hundred Years of Sea Power*, p. 95.

[53] John Gunther, *Inside Asia*, p. 104.

[54] Ibid., p. 59.

[55] Beach, Edward L. (Capt., USN), *The United States Navy* (New York, NY: Henry Holt, 1986), p. xv.

[56] Friedman, Norman, "The Future of Shipboard Aircraft," *Maritime Security: Light and Medium Aircraft Carriers into the Twenty-First Century* (Hull, UK: University of Hull Press, 1999), pp. 117-125.

[57] Hart, Basil L., "Sanctions and Measures of Mutual Assistance," Panel Discussion, Allen Dulles, Chair, *Collective Security: A Record of the Seventh & Eighth International Studies Conference* (Brussels, BG: Maison Vaillant-Carmanne, S.A., 1936), p. 385.

[58] Robert Edgerton, *Warriors of the Rising Sun*, p. 281.

[59] George Baer, *One Hundred Years of Sea Power: The US Navy, 1890-1990*, p. 257.

[60] Edward Beach, *The United States Navy*, pp. 474-476.

[61] Bradley, James, *Flags of Our Fathers* (New York, NY: Bantam Books, 2001), pp. 146-147.

[62] Dower, John, *Embracing Defeat: Japan in the Wake of World War II* (New York, NY: W.W. Norton & Company, 1999).

[63] Miyasato, Seigen, "John Foster Dulles and the Peace Settlement with Japan," *John Foster Dulles and the Diplomacy of the Cold War*, pp. 210-212.

[64] Walter Isaacson & Evan Thomas, *The Wise Men*, p. 698. This is a comment that does not appear to show much respect for those who served in the Korean conflict. It is, however, reflective of many in Washington who had a constant desire to prioritize geostrategic values between Europe and East Asia.

[65] Ibid., p. 477.
[66] Millis, Walter, ed., *The Forestal Diaries* (New York, NY: Viking Press, 1951), p. 14. Letter from James Forrestal to Palmer Hoyt, publisher of the *Denver Post* (02 September 1944)
[67] Eiler, Keith E., ed., *Wedemeyer on War and Peace* (Stanford, CA: Hoover Institution Press, 1987), p. 157. Letter from Lt. General Wedemeyer to General Dwight D. Eisenhower, Chief of Staff, US Army (11 March 1946).

Chapter 10: *Cold War Rising*
[1] Russell Weigley, *The American Way of War*, p. 419.
[2] Quester, George, "If the Nuclear Taboo Gets Broken," *Naval War College Review*, Vol. 58, no. 2 (Spring 2005), p. 83.
[3] Colin Gray, *War, Peace, and Victory*, p. 100.
[4] Ibid., pp. 74-75.
[5] Sun Tzu Wu, Samuel Griffith trans., *The Art of War*, pp. 113-114.
[6] Murphy, David E., Sergei A. Kondrashev & George Bailey, *Battleground Berlin: CIA vs. KGB in the Cold War* (New Haven, CT: Yale University Press, 1997). The Berlin tunnel is one example of the depth of Soviet penetration. The operation was promoted as a major intelligence success and would be under normal circumstances. However, Britain's MI6 liaison in Washington, Kim Philby, was informed of its construction before it even began. His later defection and discovery as a Soviet mole dating as far as 1930 places the value of communication gathered in doubt.
[7] Kirkpatrick, Jeane J., ed., *The Strategy of Deception: A Study in World-Wide Communist Tactics* (New York, NY: Farrar, Straus and Giroux, 1963).
[8] Haynes, John Earl & Harvey Klehr, *Venona: Decoding Soviet Espionage in America* (New Haven, CT: Yale University Press, 1999), pp. 247-249.
[9] Lewis, David, *Sexpionage: The Exploitation of Sex by Soviet Intelligence* (New York, NY: Harcourt Brace Jovanovich, 1976).
[10] Adams, James, *The Next World War: Computers Are the Weapons & the Front Line Is Everywhere* (New York, NY: Simon & Schuster, 1998), p. 257.
[11] Douglass, Joseph D. Jr., *Red Cocaine: The Drugging of America and the West*, orig. pub. 1990 (London UK: Edward Harle Ltd., 1999), pp. 37-45.
[12] Pullella, Philip, "Soviet Union ordered Pope shooting: Italy commission," *Reuters* (02 March 2006).
[13] Tyson, James, *Target America: The Influence of Communist Propaganda on U.S. Media* (Chicago, IL: Regnery Gateway, 1981), p. 127.
[14] Powell, S. Steven, *Covert Cadre: Inside the Institute for Policy Studies* (Ottawa, IL: Green Hill Publishers, 1987).
[15] Billingsley, Kenneth Lloyd, *Hollywood Party: How Communism Seduced the American Film Industry in the 1930s and 1940s* (Rocklin, CA: Prima Publishing, 1998).
[16] Blumay, Carl & Henry Edwards, *The Dark Side of Power: The Real Armand Hammer* (New York, NY: Simon & Schuster, 1992).
[17] John, Scharfen, *The Dismal Battlefield*, p. 161. Quotation by Alfred Thayer Mahan.
[18] Stephen Koch, *Double Lives*, p. 60.
[19] Ibid.
[20] George Baer, *One Hundred Years of Sea Power*, p. 133.

[21] Staley, Eugene, "Let Japan Choose," *Foreign Affairs*, Vol. 20, no. 1 (October 1941), p. 65.

[22] Whitney Griswold, *The Far Eastern Policy of the United States*, p. 472.

[23] Ibid., p. 341.

[24] Douglas Macdonald, "Communist Bloc Expansion in the Early Cold War: Challenging Realism, Refuting Revisionism," *International Security*, Vol. 20, no. 3 (Winter 1995/96), p. 163. Macdonald refers to Michael Sheng's research showing direct Soviet involvement with Mao's communist revolutionary movement between 1935 and 1937. This would contradict views that Japan's China intervention in 1937 was purely for imperialistic reasons. Active Soviet engagement in staging a communist coup in China would give Japan geostrategic motive for their invasion, especially when looking across the Pacific at Roosevelt's proactive diplomacy with Stalin.

[25] Dunn, Dennis J., *Caught between Roosevelt & Stalin: America's Ambassadors to Moscow* (Lexington, KY: University Press of Kentucky, 1998), p. 84.

[26] Ibid.

[27] Fleming, Thomas, *The New Dealers' War: F.D.R. and the War Within World War II* (New York, NY: Basic Books, 2001), pp. 14-24.

[28] Koch, Stephen, *Double Lives: Stalin, Willi Munzenberg, and the Seduction of the Intellectuals* (New York, NY: HarperCollins, 1995), p. 226.

[29] Benson, Robert Louis & Michael Warner, ed., *Venona: Soviet Espionage and the American Response, 1939-1957* (Washington, DC: U.S. Government Printing Office, 1996), p. 51.

[30] Ibid., pp. 207-212.

[31] Sherwood, Robert E., *Roosevelt and Hopkins: An Intimate History* (New York, NY: Harper & Brothers, 1948), p. 827.

[32] Ibid.

[33] Koenker, Diane P. & Ronald D. Bachman, *Revelations from the Russian Archives* (Washington, DC: US Government Printing Office, 1997), p. 654. One message, in particular, is Stalin's personal reply to Hopkins following Roosevelt's death: "I heartily agree with you in your estimation of the role and significance of Roosevelt for the Soviet Union." Stalin's message was not sent via the US State Department as would be customary protocol, but delivered directly to Hopkins himself via Vyacheslav Molotov and the Soviet ambassador to the United States.

[34] Herbert Romerstein and Eric Breindel, *The Venona Secrets*, pp. 212-219.

[35] Robert Benson and Michael Warner, *Venona*, pp. 225-226.

[36] Walter Millis, ed., *The Forrestal Diaries*, p. 58.

[37] Alfred Thayer Mahan, *The Interest of America in Sea Power, Present and Future*, p. 259.

[38] Gray, Colin S., *The Navy in the Post-Cold War Era: The Uses and Value of Strategic Sea Power* (University Park, PA: Pennsylvania State University Press, 1994), p. 67.

[39] Eiler, Keith Eiler, ed., *Wedemeyer on War and Peace*, p.153. Memorandum to WARCOS from COMGENCHINA (20 November 1945).

[40] Walter Millis, ed., *The Forrestal Diaries*, pp. 121-122.

[41] Kessler, Ronald, *Moscow Station: How the KGB Penetrated the American Embassy* (New York, NY: Simon & Schuster, 1989), p. 22.

[42] Samuel Eliot Morison, *Strategy and Compromise*, pp. 11-12.

[43] George Baer, *One Hundred Years of Sea Power*, p. 277.

[44] Ibid.

[45] Paulsen, James Cdr., USN), "The Air Force Wasn't Even Close," *U.S. Naval Institute Proceedings*, Vol. 126, no. 7 (July 2000), pp. 72-76.

[46] Dennis Dunn, *Caught between Roosevelt & Stalin*, p. 248.

[47] de Tocqueville, Alexis, *Democracy in America*, Vol. I, orig. pub. 1835 (London, UK: Wordsworth Editions, 1998), p. 170.

[48] Aldrich, Richard, *Intelligence and the War against Japan: Britain, America and the Politics of Secret Service* (Cambridge, UK: Cambridge University Press, 2000), pp. 271-278.

[49] Ibid., pp. 269-270.

[50] Schaller, Michael, *The American Occupation of Japan: The Origins of the Cold War in Asia* (New York, NY: Oxford University Press, 1985), p. 17.

[51] Thomas Fleming, *The New Dealers' War*, pp. 383-384.

[52] Clark, Mark (Gen., USA), "The Korean War and Related Matters," USS Report, ISS, Committee on Judiciary (21 January 1955).

[53] Geoffrey Sloan, "Sir Halford Mackinder: The Heartland Theory Then and Now," Colin Gray & Geoffrey Sloan ed., *Geopolitics*, p. 34. Quotation from H.J. Mackinder, *The Nations of the Modern World: An Elementary Study in Geography and History* (London, UK: George Philip, 1924), pp. 251-252.

[54] Colin Gray, *War, Peace, and Victory*, p. 22.

[55] Ibid., pp. 239-241.

[56] Koehler, John O., *Stasi: The Untold Story of the East German Secret Police* (Boulder, CO: Westview Press, 1999) pp. 73-74. Koehler notes the KGB maintained a full colonel on the staff of all eight East German Stasi directorates. Additionally, Stasi officials had society so deeply penetrated that 1 in 6 East Germans served as an informant. In other words, a family reunion or classroom of thirty people would, on average, include five Stasi agents.

[57] Associated Press, "Syria Warns U.S. Against Retaliation," *Omaha World-Herald* (15 November 1983). Article states Washington has evidence Syria helped plan the attack.

[58] Associated Press, "Reagan Boosts Funds to Embattled Chad," *Omaha World-Herald* (05 August 1983). See also "White House Tense Over Libyan Threat," *Los Angeles Times* (06 August 1983).

[59] Carlucci, Frank III, ed., *Terrorist Group Profiles* (Washington, DC: US Government Printing Office, 1988), pp. 2, 4, 74, 31, 128. Frequency of terrorist attacks shows a correlation with the state of relations between American and Soviet governments in specific regions. For example, 1983 saw twice as many staged against the US in the Middle East as any other year. In Europe, 1982 and 1983 were extremely active. A significant upswing took place in Latin America during the period 1985-86.

[60] Epstein, Edward J., *Deception: The Invisible War between the KGB and the CIA* (New York, NY: Simon & Schuster, 1989), p. 281. Quotation made by James Angleton, chief of counterintelligence (CI), Central Intelligence Agency. Angleton goes on to note that Warsaw Pact states furnished North Korea the bomb, while the Soviet Union provided highly valuable signals intelligence.

[61] Terrell, R. Emmett, Jr., "Media Consensus on the Soviets," *Washington Post* (12 September 1983).

[62] Halloran, Richard, "Some Warn New Commitments Spreading U.S. Military Too Thin," *New York Times* (10 August 1983).

[63] Mao Tse-tung, *Selected Works* (London, UK: Lawrence and Wishart, 1955), p. 130.

[64] Douglas Macdonald, "Communist Bloc Expansion in the Early Cold War," *International Security*, Vol. 20, no. 3 (Winter 1995/96), p.166.

[65] Gaddis, John Lewis, *We Now Know: Rethinking Cold War History* (New York, NY: Oxford University Press, 1998), p. 203.

[66] Golitsyn, Anatoliy, *New Lies for Old: The Communist Strategy of Deception and Disinformation* (New York, NY: Dodd, Mead & Company, 1984), pp. 107-119.

[67] Peter Hopkirk, *The Great Game*, pp. 11-15. Hopkirk describes the Russian strategic mind being formulated out of the Mongol invasions of the thirteenth century. This experience forever established the character of Russian foreign policy.

[68] Ibid., p. 15-20.

[69] The number of US military patrol craft shot out of the sky, not to mention the downing of Francis Gary Powers in 1960, is a testament to the USSR's ability to handle border incursions.

[70] Colin Gray, *The Geopolitics of Super Power*, p. 111.

[71] Robert O'Connell, *Of Arms and Men*, p. 78.

[72] Bertrand de Jouvenel, *On Power*, p. 153.

[73] Morgan, John G. (Rear Adm., USN) & Anthony D. McIvor, "Rethinking the Principles of War," *US Naval Institute Proceedings*, Vol. 129, no. 10 (October 2003), p. 37.

Chapter 11: *The Outer Limits*

[1] Colin Gray, *The Geopolitics of Super Power*, p. 143.

[2] Dolman, Everett C., "Gestrategy in the Space Age: An Astropolitical Analysis," Gray & Sloan, eds., *Geopolitics*, p. 90.

[3] The anti-American Tsunami underway throughout Latin America is an incredible geostrategic political move. See Jack Chang, "Morales' first day shows where he's taking Bolivia," *Houston Chronicle* (24 January 2006), Andrea Rodriguez, "Bolivian president-elect visits Cuba," *Houston Chronicle* (31 December 2005), Joe McDonald, "Bolivia, China look to link up," *Houston Chronicle* (10 January 2006), Mark Steyn, "If Pinochet is guilty then so is HM the Queen," *Daily Telegraph* (29 November 1998), Marc Cooper, "A woman's work is just beginning in uptight Chile," *Houston Chronicle* (21 January 2006), Sergey Sereda, "Oil Agreement Signed With Venezuela To Benefit Cuba," *ITAR-TASS* (11 March 1993), "Iran, Venezuela review expanding mutual ties," *Islamic Republic News Agency* (23 January 2006), Lowell Ponte, "Commie in Caracas," *Front Page Magazine* (10 July 2002).

[4] Conquest, Robert, *Reflections on a Ravaged Century* (New York, NY: W.W. Norton & Company, 2000), p. 173.

[5] John Koehler, *Stasi*, p. 311.

[6] Marc Cooper, a senior fellow at the University of Southern California, for example, served as a "translator" for Allende's regime. He is now gainfully employed educating America's future activist and journalistic community at the Annenberg Institute for Justice and Journalism (whatever that means). Even the daughter of W. Mark Felt, who was recently 'alleged' to be "Deep Throat," served as a member of America's left which assisted Salvador Allende in getting his regime established.

[7] Seigen Miyasato, "John Foster Dulles and the Peace Settlement with Japan," *John Foster Dulles and the Diplomacy of the Cold War*, Richard Immerman, ed., pp. 207-208.

[8] Ibid.

[9] Sarin, Oleg (Gen., SRA) & Lev Dvoretsky (Col, SRA), *Alien Wars: The Soviet Union's Aggressions against the World, 1919-1989* (Novato, CA: Presidio Press, 1996), pp. 55-59.

[10] Walter Millis, ed., *The Forrestal Diaries*, pp. 98-99.

[11] Douglas Macdonald, "Communist Bloc Expansion in the Early Cold War," *International Security*, Vol. 20, no. 3 (Winter 1995/96), p. 159.

[12] Keith Eiler, *Wedemeyer on War and Peace*, p. 182. Memorandum for the President from Lt. General Wedemeyer (19 September 1947).

[13] Ibid., p. 438.

[14] Walter Isaacson and Evan Thomas, *The Wise Men*, pp. 523-524, 469-470. In an incredible display of bureaucratic witch-hunting, both MacArthur and Forrestal were subjected to a relentless barrage of antagonism. Truman ordered MacArthur assessed, psychologically, after he made a speech criticizing Truman's disregard of Formosa. Forrestal was subjected to an unmerciful attack in the press led by Drew Pearson. Pearson later came under suspicion as a Soviet sympathizer, if not an outright disinformation agent. Contrary to the coroner's official report of suicide following his death, members of Forrestal's family publicly declared he was murdered.

[15] Keith Eiler, *Wedemeyer on War and Peace*, p. 200. Confidential letter to General Douglas MacArthur, Commanding General, Far East Command (20 October 1947).

[16] Roe, Patrick, C., *The Dragon Strikes: China and the Korean War* (Novato, CA: Presidio Press, 2000). PRC army divisions infiltrated North Korea months earlier than virtually all intelligence estimates. United Nations Command (UNC) intelligence was a great disappointment. Reports of Chinese Communist Forces (CCF) operating throughout North Korea and size of reinforcements staged in Manchuria were grossly underestimated. Following the initial onslaught and decimation of CCF's ability to sustain combat action, reports began over-exaggerating threats. As a result, UNC forces prematurely retreated south of the 38th Parallel, needlessly abandoning North Korean territory which included the capital Pyonyang.

[17] Walter Isaacson & Evan Thomas, *The Wise Men*, pp. 535-551.

[18] MacArthur, Douglas (Gen., USA), *Reminiscences* (New York, NY: McGraw-Hill, 1964), p. 375.

[19] Oleg Sarin & Lev Dvoretsky, *Alien Wars*, p. 63. Letter from Stalin to Mao, USSR Central Military Historic Archive 14/40, Vol. 116, p. 18.

[20] Patrick Roe, *The Dragon Strikes*, pp. 376-399.

[21] Colin Gray, *Modern Strategy*, p. 18. Quotation by Basil Liddell Hart.

[22] Carl von Clausewitz, *On War*, Michael Howard & Peter Paret trans., p. 92.

[23] Ibid., p. 42-43.

[24] Ibid., p. 43.

[25] Ibid., p. 42.

[26] Sun Tzu Wu, Samuel Griffith trans., *The Art of War*, p. 84.

[27] Winnefeld, James A. & Dana J. Johnson, *Joint Air Operations: Pursuit of Unity in Command and Control, 1942-1991* (Annapolis, MD: Naval Institute Press, 1993), p. 76.

[28] Colin Gray, *Explorations in Strategy*, pp. 126-127.

[29] Burke, Arleigh (Rear Adm., USN), "Burke Speaks Out on Korea," *U.S. Naval Institute Proceedings*, Vol. 126, no. 5 (May 2000), p. 72. Letter from Burke to special assistant for public relations for Navy Secretary Francis Matthews on 05 October 1950.

This all changed, as Burke warned, when the PRC stormed across the Yalu River and used Soviet aircraft _and_ pilots to challenge American air superiority.

[30] Huber, Jeff (Lt. Cdr., USN), "Nobody Asked Me, but Clausewitz is Dead," *US Naval Institute Proceedings*, Vol. 127, no. 3 (March 2001), pp. 119-120.

[31] The Saigon correspondent for *Time Magazine*, Pham Xuan An was, in actuality, an intelligence officer and full colonel in the North Vietnamese Army. His name even appeared on the magazine's masthead and he worked side-by-side with many other American journalists. See Robert D. McFadden, "Secrets and Lines: Legacy of a Reporter," *New York Times* (28 April 1997). Also Morley Safer, *Flashbacks: On Returning to Vietnam* (New York, NY: Random House, 1995).

[32] Tower, John, *Consequences: A Personal and Political Memoir* (Boston, MA: Little, Brown and Company, 1991), p. 173.

[33] John Lehman, *Command of the Seas*, p. 96.

[34] Edwards, David Edwards, *The American Political Experience*, pp. 205-213. October 2005 national debt figure obtained from the Free Congress Foundation.

[35] Lambro, Donald, "Tax Americana," *The American Legion*, Vol. 156, no. 2 (February 2004), p. 25.

[36] Anton Nugroho, "The Dragon Looks South," *U.S. Naval Institute Proceedings*, Vol. 126, no. 3 (March 2000), p. 76.

[37] Alfred Thayer Mahan, "Strategic Features of the Gulf of Mexico and Caribbean Sea," *Harper's New Monthly Magazine* (October 1897), pp. 680-691.

[38] Stuart Schram, *The Political Thought of Mao Tse-tung*, p. 413

[39] Rood, Harold W., *Kingdoms of the Blind: How the Great Democracies Have Resumed the Follies that So Nearly Cost Them Their Life* (Durham, NC: Carolina Academic Press, 1980), p. 109.

[40] Alfred Thayer Mahan, *The Interest of America in Sea Power, Present and Future*, p. 270.

[41] Fields, Damon (Maj., USMC), Bill Pope (Lt. Col., USAF) & Patrick Sharon (Lt. Col., USA), "Adventures in Hispaniola," *U.S. Naval Institute Proceedings*, Vol. 128, no. 9 (September 2002), pp. 60-62.

[42] Scheina, Robert, "Low Intensity Conflict: Does Mahan have a Place," *The Influence of History on Mahan*, p. 101.

[43] Donald Kagan, *On the Origins of War and the Preservation of Peace*, p. 487.

[44] "Putin stresses importance of US ties during Cuba visit," *Los Angeles Daily News* (16 December 2000), p. A12. The article notes in passing that 1,500 Russians man a monitoring station outside Havana to intercept US message traffic. How is this different from 16 December 1980?

[45] Robert Scheina, "Low Intensity Conflict: Does Mahan have a Place," *The Influence of History on Mahan*, p. 104.

[46] Ibid., pp. 104-105.

[47] Citgo is the North American branch name of the state-owned Venezuela oil company.

[48] Perhaps the Western press, kept busy by investigating US military interrogation techniques of cold-blooded terrorist killers, could find enough time to see what Venezuela and Cuba are doing to overthrow Colombia's government. More disturbing is mounting international political pressure to go after right-wing paramilitary groups in Colombia, while virtually no mention is made of FARC, the communist revolutionary army that has been fighting Colombia's military for decades. The killings they have

waged against both civilians and members of the military are greater than anything done by paramilitary groups. A double standard?
[49] Alfred Thayer Mahan, *The Interest of America in Sea Power, Present and Future*, pp. 310-311.
[50] Colin Gray, *The Geopolitics of Super Power*, p. 167.
[51] Mackinder, Halford, "The Round World and the Winning of the Peace," *Foreign Affairs*, Vol. 75, no. 1 (July 1943), p. 598. Quotation in Geoffrey Sloan, "Sir Halford Mackinder: The Heartland Theory Then and Now," Gray & Sloan, ed., *Geopolitics*, pp. 32-34.
[52] Robert Seager, *Alfred Thayer Mahan*, pp. 413-414.
[53] George Baer, *One Hundred Years of Sea Power*, p. 290.
[54] Costello, Robert, ed., *Webster's College Dictionary* (New York, NY: Random House, 1991), p. 761.
[55] Critics of the Carter administration focused on NATO's lack of preparedness in defense of Europe. Various estimates showed NATO sustaining a conventional defense of allied countries for 30-90 days before they would have to either be reinforced, swim the English Channel, or go nuclear. Resistance figures were incredibly optimistic but not Carter's fault. NATO staying power was always a topic of amusement among US Army personnel, whose speculation was far less rosy than civilian leaders. A common joke by members of the 82nd Airborne Division dispatched to Germany in 1960-61, for example, was four days.
[56] Sokolsky, Joel J., *Seapower in the Nuclear Age: The United States Navy and NATO, 1949-80* (Annapolis, MD: Naval Institute Press, 1991), pp. 7-16.
[57] If the Red Army was so powerful in 1947 that it could easily remove US, UK, and allied forces from Europe's mainland, then why was an invasion of France in 1944 required at all? Germany's armed forces were, by Normandy, already in a full blown retreat from the Eastern front. Geopolitics and national grand strategy made a Normandy invasion mandatory in order to prevent the Soviet Union from overrunning all of Europe.
[58] Goldstein, Lyle J. & Yuri M. Zhukov, "A Tale of Two Fleets: A Russian Perspective on the 1973 Naval Standoff in the Mediterranean," *Naval War College Review*, Vol. LVII, no. 2 (Spring 2004), p. 56.
[59] Ibid., pp. 38-39.
[60] Epstein, Edward J., *Dossier: The Secret World of Armand Hammer* (New York, NY: Random House, 1996), pp. 244-245.
[61] The nuclear disarmament protest movement confronted by Carter over the neutron bomb was identical to one started years later against the Reagan administration's decision to deploy nuclear-tipped Pershing and Cruise missiles in Europe.
[62] Fosdick, Dorothy, ed., *Staying the Course: Henry Jackson and National Security* (Seattle, WA: University of Washington Press, 1987), p. 71.
[63] Colin Gray, *The Leverage of Sea Power*, p. 266.
[64] Joel Sokolsky, *Seapower in the Nuclear Age*, pp. 69-75.

Chapter 12: *To the Gay Nineties and Beyond*
[1] Busiek, Paul, Testimony, "Gorbachev's Apparatus in the United States and The "Moscow Spring," National Committee to Restore Internal Security, Vol. XV (08 June 1988).

Notes 359

2 Sowell, Thomas, *Race and Culture: A World View* (New York, NY: HarperCollins Publishers, 1994), p. 258.

3 There are over one hundred officially recognized and supported non-voting NGOs attached to the United Nations, all pushing an agenda. Source: Perkins Library, Duke University, Durham, NC.

4 Lindblom, Charles E., *Politics and Markets: The World's Political-Economic Systems* (New York, NY: HarperCollins Publishers, 1977), p. 119.

5 Todd Buchholz, *New Ideas from Dead Economists*, p. 215. Quotation by Paul Samuelson, "Lord Keynes and the General Theory," *Econometrica*, Vol. 14 (1946), p. 190.

6 Anderson, Benjamin M., *Economics and the Public Welfare: A Financial and Economic History of the United States, 1914-1946*, orig. pub. 1949, D. Van Nostrand Company (Indianapolis, IN: Liberty Press, 1979), p. 276.

7 Ibid., p. 482.

8 Volder, Richard, "Roosevelt's Record," *Claremont Review of Books*, Vol. V, no. 1 (Winter 2004), p. 5. Volder notes figures from the Bureau of Labor Statistics (BLS) showing unemployment in March 1933 at 28.3%. Annual BLS figure for 1941 is 9.9%, two years following the outbreak of World War II. This figure dropped to 4.7% in 1942, long after America's entry into the war.

9 Pipes, Richard, *Property and Freedom* (New York, NY: Alfred A. Knopf, 1999), p. 247.

10 Tom Bethel, *The Noblest Triumph*, p. 292.

11 Bertrand de Jouvenel, *On Power*, p. 128.

12 Kagan, Donald & Frederick, *While America Sleeps: Self-delusion, Military Weakness, and the Threat to Peace Today* (New York, NY: St. Martin's Press, 2000), p. 248.

13 The number of bombing sorties over Iraq from 1991 to 2003 is a figure not widely published by those who prefer the passive hostile strategic approach. Additionally, the source of Iraqi anti-aircraft systems, which had to be knocked out on a regular basis, has not been disclosed to the public for the sake of international good will.

14 Donald & Frederick Kagan, *While America Sleeps*, p. 245.

15 Gehman, Harold W. Jr. (Adm., USN), "Lost Patrol: The Attack on the Cole," *U.S. Naval Institute Proceedings*, Vol. 127, no. 4 (April 2001), pp. 34-37.

16 The big surprise on the day aircraft were slamming into symbols of American prestige and power is that it took so long to happen. The general public are as guilty as those bureaucrats battling over responsibility. Americans are not known for their savoir faire on national security and global affairs. It is a daunting dilemma for any government in a pleasure-seeking open society. Had 9/11 occurred 50 years earlier, military recruiting stations would have men lined up for blocks waiting to volunteer. With the exception of a small spike on the recruiting radar screen immediately following 9/11, no significant increase in volunteers was noticed.

17 Edward, J. Epstein, *Deception*, pp. 289-290.

18 Joseph Douglass, *Red Cocaine*, p. 9. Cline's comment was published in 1999, not in August 1991 while being entertained by Cable News Network (CNN) reporting of one Red Army tank burning in the night. A study of the political leadership in various former Soviet republics shows all have either been in charge since the late 1980s when the USSR existed, or are products of Soviet political education.

[19] Cline, Ray, "MacNeil-Lehrer News Hour," *Public Broadcasting Service, WETA-TV*, Washington, DC (25 November 1983). Quotation in Jeffrey St. John, *Day of the Cobra* (Nashville, TN: Thomas Nelson Publishers, 1984), p. 198.

[20] Barnett, Thomas P.M. & Henry H. Gaffney Jr., "Globalization Gets a Bodyguard," *U.S. Naval Institute Proceedings*, Vol. 127, no. 11 (November 2001), pp. 50-53. According to the authors, bin Laden was good for the New World Order.

[21] Tenet, George J. (Director, CIA), "Worldwide Threat: Converging Dangers in a Post 9/11 World," Testimony before the Senate Armed Services Committee (19 March 2002).

[22] Malone, Eloise and Arthur Rachwald, "The Dark Side of Globalization," *U.S. Naval Institute Proceedings*, Vol. 127, no. 11 (November 2001), p. 43.

[23] Barnett, Thomas P.M., "Globalization Is Tested," *U.S. Naval Institute Proceedings*, Vol. 127, no. 10 (October 2001), p. 57.

[24] Foreman, William, "China shows its clout at regional trade summit," *Houston Chronicle* (30 November 2004). "China is using its huge market as a
bait to lure ASEAN countries away from U.S. and Japan and build closer relations," said Chao Chien-min.

[25] Thomas Barnett, "Globalization Is Tested," *U.S. Naval Institute Proceedings,* Vol. 127, no. 10 (October 2001), p. 57.

[26] Pomfret, John, "China Strengthens Ties With Taleban by Signing Economic Deal," *International Herald Tribune* (13 September 2001).

[27] Dareini, Ali Akbar, "Iran urges China to intervene in Palestinian conflict as leaders meet to strengthen ties," *Associated Press* (20 April 2002). The US seems to be slipping in its diplomatic attractiveness.

[28] Spencer, Richard, "Tension rises as China scours the globe for energy," *Daily Telegraph* (19 November 2004).

[29] Adams, David (Lt. Cdr., USN), "Managing China's Transition," *U.S. Naval Institute Proceedings*, Vol. 129, no. 7 (July 2003), p. 52.

[30] Barnett, Thomas P.M. & Henry H. Gaffney Jr., "Top Ten Post-Cold War Myths," *U.S. Naval Institute Proceedings*, Vol. 127, no. 2 (February 2001), p. 35.

[31] Trulock, Notra, *Code Name Kindred Spirit: Inside the Chinese Nuclear Espionage Scandal* (San Francisco, CA: Encounter Books, 2003).

[32] Ikenberry, G. John, "The Myth of Post-Cold War Chaos," *Foreign Affairs*, Vol. 75, no. 3 (May/June 1996), pp. 79-91.

[33] Prins Gwyn, "Security studies and power politics," *International Affairs*, Vol. 74, no. 4 (October, 1998), pp. 781-808.

[34] Spero, Joan E. & Jeffrey Hart, *The Politics of International Economic Relations*, 5th ed. (New York, NY: St. Martin's Press, 1997), pp. 316-358.

[35] Alexis de Tocqueville, *Democracy in America*, Vol. I, p. 170-171.

[36] Conquest, Robert, "Slouching Toward Byzantium," *Hoover Digest*, no. 2 (Stanford University, 2005), p. 100.

[37] Ibid.

[38] Dalton, Jane G., "Future Navies – Current Issues," *Naval War College Review*, Vol. 59, no. 1 (Winter 2006), p. 29.

[39] Ibid.

[40] Galdorisi, George (Capt., USN), "A U.N. Treaty We All Can Support," *US Naval Institute Proceedings*, Vol. 129, no. 3 (March 2003), pp. 74-77.

[41] Ibid., p. 76.

[42] Woodcock, William A. (Maj., USA), "The Joint Forces Air Command Problem: Is Network-centric Warfare the Answer," *Naval War College Review*, Vol. 56, no. 1 (Winter 2003) pp. 124-138.

[43] Would "further development and interpretation," for example, eventually come to include such things as inland waterways within national boundaries since those waterways empty into the seas?

[44] Wylie, J.C. (Rear Adm., USN), "Mahan and American Naval Thought Since 1914," *The Influence of History on Mahan*, p. 44.

[45] Jeff Huber, "Nobody Asked Me, but Clausewitz is Dead," *Naval Institute Proceedings* (March 2001), pp. 119-120.

[46] Laingren, Charles W. (Cdr., USN), "On War: It's Not Just a Military Affair Anymore," *U.S. Naval Institute Proceedings*, Vol. 126, no. 5 (May 2000), pp. 34-37.

[47] Lehman, John, "Captivated by the American Spirit," *US Naval Institute Naval History*, Vol. 16, no. 1 (January 2002), p. 24.

[48] J.C. Wylie, "Mahan: Then and Now," *The Influence of History on Mahan*, p. 41.

[49] Kirkpatrick, Jeane, "Law of the Sea Treaty," *Testimony before the Senate Armed Services Committee* (Washington, DC: Congressional Record, 08 April 2004). Former US Ambassador to the United Nations during the Reagan administration came out against the treaty that ironically uses the acronym LOST. Those who depend on unfettered access to fulfill foreign policy commitments are placed in a very troubling position. Those who do not rely on sea access to fulfill international obligations are, however, at a great advantage and they comprise a majority at the United Nations.

[50] Colin Gray, *The Leverage of Sea Power*, p. 290.

[51] Dirk Ballendorf & Merrill Bartlett, *Pete Ellis: An Amphibious Warfare Prophet, 1880-1923*, p. 114. Quotation from Lejeune, "Future Policy of the Marine Corps as Influenced by the Conference on Limitation of Armaments" (11 February 1922), Records of the General Board of the Navy, RG 80, NARA. Also see Robert H. Dunlap, "Lessons for Marines from the Gallipoli Campaign," *Marine Corps Gazette*, no. 6 (September 1921), pp. 237-252.

[52] Dalton, John H., J.M. Boorda (Adm., USN) & Carl Mundy Jr. (Gen., USMC), "Forward. . . .From the Sea," Department of the Navy Press Release, Navy Office of Information (09 November 1994).

[53] Harris, Clay (Cdr., USN), "The Readiness Tango of 1998," *U.S. Naval Institute Proceedings*, Vol. 126, no. 9 (September 2000), pp. 44-46.

[54] George Baer, *One Hundred Years of Sea Power*, p. 278.

[55] Ibid.

[56] Labs, Eric J., "Building the Future Fleet: Show Us the Analysis," *Naval War College Review*, Vol. 57, no. 3/4 (Summer/Autumn 2004), pp. 138-146.

[57] Alfred Thayer Mahan, "Letter to the Editor," *The New York Times* (30 January 1893), quoted in *The Interest of America in Sea Power, Present and Future*, pp. 31-32.

[58] Tonelson, Alan, "Superpower Without a Sword," *Foreign Affairs*, Vol. 72, no. 3 (Summer 1993), p. 173.

[59] Ignatieff, Michael, "The Challenges of American Imperial Power," *Naval War College Review*, Vol 56, no. 2 (Spring 2003), p. 59

[60] Carey, Merrick, "Transformation Is a Trap," *U.S. Naval Institute Proceedings*, Vol. 127, no. 8 (August 2001), p. 2.

[61] Clark, Vern (Adm., USN), "Sea Power 21: Projecting Decisive Joint Capabilities," *U.S. Naval Institute Proceedings*, Vol. 128, no. 10 (October 2002), p. 40.

[62] Ibid.

[63] Alan Tonelson, "Superpower Without a Sword," *Foreign Affairs*, Vol. 72, no. 3 (Summer 1993), p. 166.

[64] David Edwards, *The American Political Experience*, p. 209.

[65] Karen O'Connor, Larry J. Sabato, Stefan D. Haag & Gary A. Keith, *American Government: Continuity and Change*, p. 7.

[66] Johnson-Freese, Joan, "China's Manned Space Program: Sun Tzu or Appollo Redux," *Naval War College Review*, Vol. 56, no. 3 (Summer 2003), p. 59. Communist China's government-owned China Aerospace Corporation (CAC), prior to it being split in two for better facilitating space requirements, had over 270,000 employees whose salaries are far below that of comparable personnel working for private US firms. Differences in pay scales directly impacts gaps in annual defense figures.

[67] Honey, Martha and Tom Barry, *Global Focus: U.S. Foreign Policy at the Turn of the Millennium* (New York, NY: St. Martin's Press, 2000), p. 25. This work illustrates a chart from the International Institute for Strategic Studies. It shows the US portion of 1997 global defense spending at 34%. Comparing figures with Russia, China, North Korea, and Cuba is disinformation. It does not take into account currency factors, civilian labor costs, research investment, or cost of attracting and maintaining an all-volunteer force. Additionally, trusting numbers provided by a dictatorship is naïve.

[68] Knoke, William, *Bold New World: The Essential Road Map to the Twenty-First Century* (New York, NY: Kodansha America, 1996), p. 229.

[69] Seligman, Lester G. & Cary R. Covington, *The Coalition Presidency* (Chicago, IL: The Dorsey Press, 1989), p. 88.

[70] Ibid., p. 97.

[71] Bryan, Lowell & Diana Farrell, *Markets Unbound: Unleashing Global Capitalism* (New York, NY: John Wiley & Sons, 1996), p. 192. Lowell and Farrell offer a popular international market version that does not follow a Keynesian model. It still supports globally integrated economies but is based on a popular view that repressive regimes become politically free societies as markets are allowed to flourish. A big problem with such an optimistic theory is the cost of being wrong.

[72] Alexis de Tocqueville, *Democracy in America*, Vol. II, p. 358.

[73] Vern Clark, "Sea Power 21," *U.S. Naval Institute Proceedings*, Vol. 128, no. 10 (October 2002), pp. 32-41.

[74] Actions taken by Communist China have not been given a serious look for reasons that can only point to economic mating on a scale surpassing that which was done for Hitler or Stalin. Serious questions are finally being asked concerning PRC intent with its massive military build-up. Former Secretary of Defense, Donald Rumsfeld, is one of the first to officially express concern. Did Fiji declare war on the PRC and is now mounting a full-scale amphibious invasion?

[75] Bennett, Drew A. (Col., USMC), "Military Presence in Asia Is Key," *U.S. Naval Institute Proceedings*, Vol. 129, no. 1 (January 2002), pp. 57-60.

Chapter 13: *Now and Forever*

[1] Bridis, Ted, "Data-scrambling software gets OK," *Ventura County Star* (17 September 1999). Article focuses on a Clinton administration decision to allow high-tech companies to sell their most powerful data-scrambling encryption technology around the world with virtually no restrictions. This came over dire warnings and opposition by law enforcement and national security experts.

[2] Kurtenbach, Elaine, "Freedom a Taboo Word on Chinese Internet," *Associated Press* (14 June 2005), Michael Liedtke, "Google Conforms to Chinese Censorship," *Associated Press* (25 September 2005). Reports detail willful cooperation by US software and search engine providers to fulfill PRC censorship requirements, and to even act as informants for the communist government in pursuit of dissident email message traffic deemed critical of the regime.

[3] Barnett, Thomas P.M., *The Pentagon's New Map: War and Peace in the Twenty-First Century* (New York, NY: G.P. Putnam's Sons, 2004), p. 82.

[4] Somerville, Glenn, "Bernanke attempts to soothe China fears," *Houston Chronicle* (17 February 2006). New Federal Reserve Board Chairman, Ben Bernanke, testifies to Senate Banking Committee that Communist China's $819,000,000,000 holdings of U.S. assets, which are primarily Treasury bonds, are not a national security concern.

[5] Ikenberry, G. John, "The Future of International Leadership," *American Leadership, Ethnic Conflict, and the New World Politics*, Caraley, Demetrios James, and Bonnie B. Hartman, ed. (New York, NY: Academy of Political Science, 1997), p. 14.

[6] Locke, John, "Second Treatise of Government," Steven M. Cahn, ed., *Classics of Modern Political Theory: Machiavelli to Mill* (New York, NY: Oxford University Press, 1997), pp. 245-260.

[7] John Ikenberry, "The Future of International Leadership," *American Leadership, Ethnic Conflict, and the New World Politics*, Demtrios Caraley and Bonnie Hartman, ed., p. 14.

[8] Alfred Thayer Mahan, *The Interest of America in Sea Power, Present and Future*, p. 32.

[9] Rosenau, James N., *Along the Domestic-Foreign Frontier: Exploring Governance in a Turbulent World* (Cambridge, UK: Cambridge University Press, 1997), p. 71.

[10] Ludwig, Emil, *The Mediterranean: Saga of a Sea* (New York, NY: Whittlesey House, 1942), p. 64.

[11] Buell, Thomas B., (Cdr., USN), "Mao's Midnight Proposition," *U.S. Naval Institute Proceedings*, Vol. 126, no. 6 (June 2000), p. 63. Comment made to Lt. Herbert Hitch, a U.S. military observer in China during World War II. Mao goes on to state that communism will one day dominate the world.

[12] Sun Tzu Wu, *The Art of War*, Samuel Griffith trans., p. 145.

[13] Thomas Barnett, *The Pentagon's New Map*, p. 309.

[14] Clendenning, Alan, "Latin America expands Asia link," *Houston Chronicle* (20 November 2004). Article accompanies a photograph of Chilean protestors burning an American flag.

[15] Nye, Joseph S. Jr. *The Paradox of American Power: Why the World's Only Superpower Can't Go It Alone* (New York, NY: Oxford University Press, 2002), p. 110.

[16] Associated Press Wire Service, "Buffett sounds trade deficit alarm," *Houston Chronicle* (19 January 2006).

[17] Todd Buchholz, *New Ideas from Dead Economists*, p. 216.

[18] Jenkins, Holman W., Jr., "Russians Agree: U.S. Banks Are Tops!" *Wall Street Journal* (01 September 1999).

[19] Hays, Kristen, "Politics of oil will get hearing," *Houston Chronicle* (11 February 2007). Article notes 80% of the world's oil reserves are controlled by government-controlled oil companies.

[20] Accurate numbers are difficult to obtain because of tight controls over figures.

[21] Kennedy, Paul, *Preparing for the Twenty-First Century* (New York, NY: Random House, 1993), p. 225.

[22] Care must be taken in assigning blame. Companies face punitive "cost-of-doing-business" laws passed by socialist elites who would not know a profit and loss statement if it hit them in the face. Meanwhile, companies are demonized for out-sourcing by politicians seeking votes and law firms looking for billable hours.

[23] Art, Robert J., *A Grand Strategy for America* (Ithaca, NY: Cornell University Press, 2003), p. 243. In a bizarre coincidence to Art's comment, a similar formula was created by this author at the Claremont Graduate School in 1997, three years prior to disclosure by China's Institute for Contemporary International Relations. Title seems the only difference, with this author's work called Total Global Power Levels (TGPL). It shows Communist China overtaking the US in 2017 using an 8-10% annual growth rate.

[24] Omestad, Thomas, "Selling Off America," *International Political Economy: Perspectives on Global Power and Wealth*, 3rd ed., Jeffry A. Frieden and David A. Lake, ed. (New York, NY: St. Martin's Press, 1995), p. 191.

[25] Ibid., p. 195.

[26] Anti-satellite weapons can now alter the heavy reliance placed on precision-guided weapons.

[27] Brigger, Clark (Lt. Cdr., USN), "A Hostile Sub is a Joint Problem," *US Naval Institute Proceedings*, Vol. 126, no. 7 (July 2000), p. 51.

[28] Jaffe, Greg, "Risk Assessment: Plans for Small Ships Pose Big Questions for the US Navy," *The Wall Street Journal*, Vol. 238, no. 7 (11 July 2001), p. 1. The US Naval War College has used computer modeling to run various war games that enhance *Streetfighter's* utility.

[29] Hughes, Wayne P. (Capt., USN), "22 Questions for Streetfighter," *U.S. Naval Institute Proceedings*, Vol. 126, no. 2 (February 2000), pp. 46-49.

[30] Brawley, Richard (Lt. Cdr., USN), "Streetfighter Cannot Do the Job," *U.S. Naval Institute Proceedings*, Vol. 128, no. 10 (October 2002), pp. 66-69.

[31] Dimaggio, Kathy (Capt., USN), Bob Freniere (Lt. Col., USAF), Mark Landers (Cdr., USN), Bill Mysinger (Cdr., USN), Pet McVety (Lt. Cdr., USN) & Mark A. Becker (Lt. Cdr., USN), "Presence with an Attitude," *U.S. Naval Institute Proceedings*, Vol. 126, no. 10 (October 2000), pp. 76-80.

[32] Tangredi, Sam J., "The Fall & Rise of Naval Forward Presence," *U.S. Naval Institute Press*, Vol. 126, no. 5 (May 2000), pp. 28-32.

[33] A common saying in counter-intelligence circles is that "nothing happens by coincidence." Is it just "coincidence" that the attack on 11 September 2001 was within hours of the US House of Representatives opening floor debate and voting to fund and deploy a ballistic missile defense system? One location given as a possible target of the aircraft that went down in Pennsylvania was Capital Hill. This was most likely the objective based on its strategic value at that time.

[34] Corbett, Art (Col., USMC) & Vince Goulding (Col., USMC), "Sea Basing: What's New?" *U.S. Naval Institute Proceedings* Vol. 128, no. 11 (November 2002), pp. 34-39.

[35] Shorter, Andrew G. (Maj., USMC), "STOVL JSFs Put Teeth in Sea Basing," *U.S. Naval Institute Proceedings*, Vol. 129, no. 9 (September 2003), pp. 32-35.

[36] Hendrix, Henry J. (Cdr., USN), "Exploit Sea Basing," *U.S. Naval Institute Proceedings*, Vol. 128, no. 8 (August 2003), p. 62.

[37] Klein, John J. (Cdr., USN) & Rich Morales (Maj., USA), "Sea Basing Isn't Just About the Sea," *U.S. Naval Institute Proceedings*, Vol. 130, no. 1 (January 2004), p.

32. Mahan quotation from *Naval Strategy Compared and Contrasted with the Principles and Practice of Military Operations on Land*, pp. 99, 200.

[38] Jane Dalton, "Future Navies – Present Issues," *Naval War College Review*, Vol. 59, no. 1 (Winter 2006), p. 18.

[39] Nagy, Paul (Cdr., USN), "The History of Sea Basing," *U.S. Naval Institute Proceedings*, Vol. 128, no. 11 (November 2002), pp. 36-38.

[40] Herodotus, *Polymnia*, George Rawlings trans., Francis Godolphin, ed., *Greek Historians*, Vol. I, p. 433.

[41] Friedman, George & Meredith, *The Future of War: Power, Technology and American World Domination in the 21st Century* (New York, NY: Random House, 1996), p. 405.

[42] McInnes, Colin, "Technology and Modern Warfare, " *Dilemmas of World Politics: International Issues in a Changing World*, John Baylis & N.J. Rengger, ed. (Oxford, UK: Oxford University Press, 1992), p. 146.

[43] Jones, John Paul, "Testimony to the Naval Committee of Congress," *Qualifications of a Naval Officer* (Annapolis MD: U.S. Naval Academy, 1:12 26-200). Printed in Russell Phillips, *John Paul Jones: Man of Action* (New York, NY: Bretano's, 1927), p. 267.

Chapter 14: *In the Year 2025*
[1] Alfred Thayer Mahan, *The Interest of America in Sea Power, Present and Future*, p. 243.

Chapter 15: *Where to From Here*
[1] S.W. Roskill, *The Strategy of Sea Power*, p. 188.
[2] Pipes, Richard, *The Russian Revolution: 1899-1919*, Vol. I (London, UK: Harvill Press, 1990), pp. 30-33.
[3] Talbott, Strobe, "The Birth of the Global Nation," *Time Magazine* (20 July 1992). Talbott, former Assistant Secretary of State during the Clinton administration, wrote that "nationhood as we know it will be obsolete; all states will recognize a single, global authority." He goes on to add that "countries are basically social arrangements, accommodations to changing circumstances. No matter how permanent and even sacred they may seem at any one time, in fact they are all artificial and temporary."
[4] Sowell, Thomas, *Conquests and Cultures: An International History* (New York, NY: Perseus Books, 1998), p. 347.
[5] N.A.M. Rodger, *Safeguard of the Sea*, p. 75.
[6] O'Hanlon, Michael, *Technological Change and the Future of Warfare* (Washington, DC: Brookings Institution Press, 2000), p. 166.
[7] Fisher, Rand H. (Rear Adm., USN) & Kent B. Pelot (Capt., USN), "The Navy Has a Stake in Space," *US Naval Institute Proceedings*, Vol. 127, no. 10 (October 2001), pp. 58-62.
[8] Roesler, Gordon & Allan Steinhardt, "Space-Based Radar Lets the Navy See It All," *U.S. Naval Institute Proceedings*, Vol. 128, no. 9 (September 2002), pp. 56-58.
[9] Hardesty, David (Capt., USN), "Space-Based Weapons: Long-Term Strategic Implications and Alternatives," *Naval War College Review*, Vol. 58, no. 2 (Spring 2005), pp. 53-59.

[10] Bucchi, Mike (Vice Adm., USN), "Sea Shield: Projecting Global Defense Assurance," *US Navy Institute Proceedings*, Vol. 123, no. 11 (November 2002), pp. 56-59.

[11] Alfred Thayer Mahan, *The Interest of America in Sea Power, Present and Future*, p. 171.

[12] George Baer, *One Hundred Years of Sea Power*, p. 1.

[13] Ibid., p. 6.

[14] John Dalton, "Forward. . . Forward from the Sea," *Department of the Navy*, p. 2.

[15] Ibid.

[16] Editorial Staff, Time-Life Books, *What Life Was Like: When Rome Ruled the World* (Richmond, VA: Time-Life Books, 1997), p. 56.

[17] Navy League of the United States, *Centennial Membership Directory* (Purchase, NY: Bernard C. Harris Publishing, 2002), p. v.

[18] Alfred Thayer Mahan, *The Problem of Asia*, p. 124.

[19] Carl von Clausewitz, *On War*, Michael Howard & Peter Paret trans., p. 209.

Bibliography

Abu-Nasr, Donna, "Danish cartoons ignite Islamic anger," *Houston Chronicle* (31 January 2006).

Adams, David (Lt. Cdr., USN), "Managing China's Transition," *U.S. Naval Institute Proceedings*, Vol. 129, no. 7 (July 2003).

Adams, James, *The Next World War: Computers Are the Weapons & the Front Line is Everywhere* (New York, NY: Simon & Schuster, 1998).

Adcock, F.E., *The Greek and Macedonian Art of War* (Berkeley, CA: University of California Press, 1957).

_____ *The Roman Art of War Under the Republic* (New York, NY: Barnes & Noble, 1995).

Albion, Robert G., "The British Lion Afloat," *New York Times Book Review* (08 March 1959).

Aldrich, Richard, Intelligence and the War against Japan: Britain, America and the Politics of Secret Service (Cambridge, UK: Cambridge University Press, 2000).

Alexander, Fran, ed., *The Oxford Encyclopedia of World History* (New York, NY: Oxford University Press, 1998).

Alexander, Joseph H., (Col., USMC), *A Fellowship of Valor: The Battle History of the United States Marines* (New York, NY: HarperCollins Publishers, 1997).

Ambrose, Stephen E., *Nothing Like It in the World: The Men Who Built the Transcontinental Railroad, 1863-1869* (New York, NY: Simon & Schuster, 2000).

Amme, Carl H. (Capt., USN), "The Changing Nature of Power," *U.S. Naval Institute Proceedings*, Vol. 89, no. 3 (March 1963).

Anderson, Benjamin M., *Economics and the Public Welfare: A Financial and Economic History of the United States, 1914-1946*, orig. pub. 1949, D. Van Nostrand Company (Indianapolis, IN: Liberty Press, 1979).

Anderson, Fred, Crucible of War: The Seven Years' War and the Fate of Empire in British North America, 1754-1766 (London, UK: Faber and Faber, 2000).

Andrews, Charles M., *The Historical Development of Modern Europe: From the Congress of Vienna to the Present Time, 1815-1897* Vol. II (New York, NY: G.P. Putnam's Sons, 1910).

Art, Robert J., *A Grand Strategy for America* (Ithaca, NY: Cornell University Press, 2003).

Associated Press Wire Service, "Buffett sounds trade deficit alarm," *Houston Chronicle* (19 January 2006).

_____ "Chavez fuels trade relations with Beijing," *Houston Chronicle* (25 December 2004).

_____ "Chinese to ally with opponents of their enemies," *Progress Bulletin* (08 November 1977).

_____ "Reagan Boosts Funds to Embattled Chad," *Omaha World-Herald* (05 August 1983).

_____ "Syria Warns U.S. Against Retaliation," *Omaha World-Herald* (15 November 1983).

Baer, George W., *One Hundred Years of Sea Power: The U.S. Navy, 1890-1990* (Stanford, CA: Stanford University Press, 1994).

Ballendorf, Dirk A. & Merrill L. Bartlett, *Pete Ellis: An Amphibious Warfare Prophet, 1880-1923* (Annapolis, MD: Naval Institute Press, 1997).

Barnett, Thomas P.M., *The Pentagon's New Map: War and Peace in the Twenty-First Century* (New York, NY: G.P. Putnam's Sons, 2004).

_____ "Globalization Is Tested," *U.S. Naval Institute Proceedings*, Vol. 127, no. 10 (October 2001).

_____ & Henry H. Gaffney Jr., "Globalization Gets a Bodyguard," *U.S. Naval Institute Proceedings*, Vol. 127, no. 11 (November 2001).

_____ & Henry H. Gaffney Jr., "Top Ten Post-Cold War Myths," *U.S. Naval Institute Proceedings*, Vol. 127, no. 2 (February 2001).

Barnett, Thomas P.M., The Pentagon's New Map: War and Peace in the Twenty-First Century (New York, NY: G.P. Putnam's Sons, 2004).

Bastiat, Frederic, *Economic Sophisms* (Princeton, NJ: D. Van Nostrand, 1964).

Beach, Edward L. (Capt., USN), *The United States Navy* (New York, NY: Henry Holt, 1986).

Beevor, Antony, *Stalingrad* (London, UK: Penguin Books, 1999).

Bennett, Drew A. (Col., USMC), "Military Presence in Asia Is Key," *U.S. Naval Institute Proceedings*, Vol. 129, no. 1 (January 2002).

Benson, Robert Louis & Michael Warner, ed., *Venona: Soviet Espionage and the American Response, 1939-1957* (Washington, DC: U.S. Government Printing Office, 1996).

Bernstein, Alvin H., "The strategy of a warrior-state: Rome and the wars against Carthage, 264-201 B.C." *The Making of Strategy: Rulers, States, and War*, Williamson Murray, MacGregor Knox, and Alvin Bernstein ed. (New York, NY: Cambridge University Press, 1997).

Bethel, Tom, *The Noblest Triumph: Property and Prosperity Through the Ages* (New York, NY: St. Martin's Press, 1998).

Billingsley, Kenneth Lloyd, Hollywood Party: How Communism Seduced the American Film Industry in the 1930s and 1940s (Rocklin, CA: Prima Publishing, 1998).

Bird, Harrison, Navies in the Mountains: The Battles on the Waters of Lake Champlain and Lake George, 1609-1814 (New York, NY: Oxford University Press, 1962).

Blum, Howard, I Pledge Allegiance...The True Story of the Walkers: An American Spy Family (New York, NY: Simon & Schuster, 1987).

Blumay, Carl & Henry Edwards, *The Dark Side of Power: The Real Armand Hammer* (New York, NY: Simon & Schuster, 1992).

Bowen, Catherine Drinker, *Miracle at Philadelphia: The Story of the Constitutional Convention*, orig. pub. 1966 (Boston, MA: Little, Brown and Company, 1986).

Bradley, James, *Flags of Our Fathers* (New York, NY: Bantam Books, 2001).

Brandeis, Louis, "The Living Law," Vol. 10, *Illinois Law Review* (1916).

Bratton, Patrick C., "When is Coercion Successful? And Why Can't We Agree on It?" *Naval War College Review*, Vol. 58, no. 3 (Summer 2005).

Brawley, Richard (Lt. Cdr., USN), "Streetfighter Cannot Do the Job," *U.S. Naval Institute Proceedings*, Vol. 128, no. 10 (October 2002).

Bridis, Ted, "Data-scrambling software gets OK," *Ventura County Star* (17 September 1999).

Brigger, Clark (Lt. Cdr., USN), "A Hostile Sub is a Joint Problem," *US Naval Institute Proceedings*, Vol. 126, no. 7 (July 2000).

Brodie, Bernard, *A Layman's Guide to Naval Strategy* (Princeton, NJ: Princeton University Press, 1944).

_____ *Strategy in the Missile Age* (Princeton, NJ: Princeton University Press, 1959).

Bryan, Lowell & Diana Farrell, *Markets Unbound: Unleashing Global Capitalism* (New York, NY: John Wiley & Sons, 1996).

Brzezinski, Zbigniew, *Out of Control: Global Turmoil on the Eve of the 21st Century* (New York, NY: Macmillan Publishing, 1993).

Bucchi, Mike (Vice Adm., USN), "Sea Shield: Projecting Global Defense Assurance," *US Navy Institute Proceedings*, Vol. 123, no. 11 (November 2002).

Buchan, Alastair, *War in Modern Society: An Introduction*, Colophon ed. (New York, NY: Harper & Row, 1968).

Buchholz, Todd G., *New Ideas from Dead Economists* (New York, NY: Penguin Books, 1990).

Burke, Arleigh (Rear Adm., USN), "Burke Speaks Out on Korea," *U.S. Naval Institute Proceedings*, Vol. 126, no. 5 (May 2000).

Buell, Thomas B., (Cdr., USN), "Mao's Midnight Proposition," *U.S. Naval Institute Proceedings*, Vol. 126, no. 6 (June 2000).

Busiek, Paul, Testimony, "Gorbachev's Apparatus in the United States and The "Moscow Spring," National Committee to Restore Internal Security, Vol. XV (08 June 1988).

Cameron, Rondo, A Concise Economic History of the World: From Paleolithic Times to the Present, 2nd ed. (Oxford, UK: Oxford University Press, 1993).

Carey, Merrick, "Transformation Is a Trap," *U.S. Naval Institute Proceedings*, Vol. 127, no. 8 (August 2001).

Carpenter, Amanda B., "Highway Bill Spends $255 million on Bike Paths," *Human Events* (12 August 2005).

Carson, Rachel, *Silent Spring* (New York, NY: Houghton, 1962).

Callwell, C.E., Military Operations and Maritime Preponderance: Their Relations and Interdependence, orig. pub. 1905 (Annapolis, MD: Naval Institute Press, 1996).

Carlucci, Frank III, ed., *Terrorist Group Profiles* (Washington, DC: US Government Printing Office, 1988).

Chambers, Mortimer, Raymond Grew, David Herlihy, Theodore Rabb & Isser Woloch, *The Western Experience: To 1715* (New York, NY: Alfred A. Knopf, 1974).

Chang, Jack, "Morales' first day shows where he's taking Bolivia," *Houston Chronicle* (24 January 2006).

Chronicle News Services, "Rails to increase Asia trade capacity," *Houston Chronicle* (25 March 2006).

Clark, Mark (Gen., USA), "The Korean War and Related Matters," USS Report, ISS, Committee on Judiciary (21 January 1955).

Clark, Vern (Adm., USN), "Midway: Service and Sacrifice," *U.S. Naval Institute Proceedings*, Vol. 128, no. 6 (June 2002).

_____ "Sea Power 21: Projecting Decisive Joint Capabilities," *U.S. Naval Institute Proceedings*, Vol. 128, no. 10 (October 2002).

Clausewitz, Carl von, *On War*, Anatol Rapoport, ed. (Harmondsworth, UK: Penguin Books Ltd., 1986).

_____ *On War*, Michael Howard & Peter Paret trans. (Princeton, NJ: Princeton University Press, 1989).

Clendenning, Alan, "Latin America expands Asia link," *Houston Chronicle* (20 November 2004).

Cline, Ray, "MacNeil-Lehrer News Hour," *Public Broadcasting Service, WETA-TV*, Washington, DC (25 November 1983).

Conquest, Robert, *Reflections on a Ravaged Century* (New York, NY: W.W. Norton & Company, 2000).

_____ "Slouching Toward Byzantium," no. 2 (Stanford University, 2005).

Cooper, Marc, "A woman's work is just beginning in uptight Chile," *Houston Chronicle* (21 January 2006).

Corbett, Art (Col., USMC) & Vince Goulding (Col., USMC), "Sea Basing: What's New?" *U.S. Naval Institute Proceedings* Vol. 128, no. 11 (November 2002).

Corbett, Sir Julian S., *Some Principles of Maritime Strategy*, B.McL. Ranft., ed. (Annapolis, MD: Naval Institute Press, 1972).

Costello, Robert, ed., *Webster's College Dictionary* (New York, NY: Random House, 1991).

Creswell, John (Cdr., BRN), *Naval Warfare: An Introductory Study*, 2nd ed. (London, UK: Sampson, Low, Marston & Company, 1942).

Dalton, Jane G., "Future Navies – Present Issues," *Naval War College Review*, Vol. 59, no. 1 (Winter 2006).

Dalton, John H., J.M. Boorda (Adm., USN) & Carl Mundy Jr. (Gen., USMC), "Forward. . . .From the Sea," Department of the Navy Press Release, Navy Office of Information (09 November 1994).

Daniel, Caroline & Maija Palmer, "Google's goal to organize your daily life," *Financial Times* (22 May 2007).

Dareini, Ali Akbar, "Iran urges China to intervene in Palestinian conflict as leaders meet to strengthen ties," *Associated Press* (20 April 2002).

Davies, Norman, *Europe* (New York, NY: Oxford University Press, 1996).

Dean, Josh, "The Rebirth of Rail," *Popular Mechanics* (January 2006).

de Greaffenreid, Kenneth E., ed., *The Cox Report: The Unanimous and Bipartisan Report of the House Select Committee on U.S. National Security and Military Commercial Concerns with the People's Republic of China* (Washington, DC: Regnery Publishing, 1999).

de Jouvenel, Bertrand, *On Power: The Natural History of Its Growth*, orig. pub. 1945 (Indianapolis, IN: Liberty Press, 1993).

de Tocqueville, Alexis, *Democracy in America*, Vol. II, orig. pub. 1840 (London, UK: Wordsworth Editions, 1998).

DeYoung, Don, "Strategic Vision Can Be Powerful," *US Naval Institute Proceedings*, Vol. 126, no. 11 (November 2000).

Dimaggio, Kathy (Capt., USN), Bob Freniere (Lt. Col., USAF), Mark Landers (Cdr., USN), Bill Mysinger (Cdr., USN), Pet McVety (Lt. Cdr., USN) & Mark A. Becker (Lt. Cdr., USN), "Presence with an Attitude," *U.S. Naval Institute Proceedings*, Vol. 126, no. 10 (October 2000).

Doenhoff, Richard A., "Biddle, Perry, and Japan," *U.S. Naval Institute Proceedings*, Vol. 92, no. 11 (November 1966).

Dolman, Everett C., "Gestrategy in the Space Age: An Astropolitical Analysis," in Colin Gray & Geoffrey Sloan, eds., *Geopolitics: Geography and Strategy* (London, UK: Frank Cass, 1999).

Donald, David Herbert, *Lincoln* (London, UK: Random House, 1995).

Douglass, Joseph D., *Red Cocaine: The Drugging of America and the West*, 2nd ed. (London, UK: Edward Harle, 1999).

Dower, John, *Embracing Defeat: Japan in the Wake of World War II* (New York, NY: W.W. Norton & Company, 1999).

Drew, Donald (Col., USAF) & Donald Snow, *Making Strategy: An Introduction to National Security Processes and Problems* (Maxwell AFB, AL: Air University Press, 1988).

D'Souza, Dinesh, *What's So Great About America* (New York, NY: Penguin Books, 2002).

Duncan, Francis, "Mahan – Historian with a Purpose," *U.S. Naval Institute Proceedings*, Vol. 83, no. 5 (May 1957).

Dunlap, Robert H., "Lessons for Marines from the Gallipoli Campaign," *Marine Corps Gazette*, no. 6 (September 1921).

Dunn, Dennis J., *Caught between Roosevelt & Stalin: America's Ambassadors to Moscow* (Lexington, KY: University Press of Kentucky, 1998).

Dunn, James R. & John E. Kinney, *Conservative Environmentalism: Reassessing the Means, Redefining the Ends* (Westport, CT: Greenwood Publishing Group, 1996).

Earle, Edward Mead, "Adam Smith, Alexander Hamilton, Friedrich List: The Economic Foundations of Military Power," Edward Mead Earle, ed., *Makers of Modern Strategy: Military Thought from Machiavelli to Hitler* (New York, NY: Atheneum, 1966).

_____ "Hitler: The Nazi Concept of War," Edward Mead Earle, ed., *Makers of Modern Strategy: Military Thought from Machiavelli to Hitler* (New York, NY: Atheneum, 1966).

East Asia Intel.com, "China's huge footprint being felt with the rising cost of oil," *World Tribune* (22 October 2004).

Echevarria, Antulio J. II (Lt. Col., USA), "Clausewitz's Center of Gravity: It's Not What We Thought," *Naval War College Review*, Vol. 56, no. 1 (Winter 2003).

Edgerton, Robert B., *Warriors of the Rising Sun: A History of the Japanese Military* (Boulder, CO: Westview Press, 1997).

Editorial Staff, Time-Life Books, *What Life Was Like: When Rome Ruled the World* (Richmond, VA: Time-Life Books, 1997).

Edwards, David V., *The American Political Experience*, 3rd ed. (Englewood Cliffs, NJ: Prentice-Hall, 1985).

Eiler, Keith E., ed., *Wedemeyer on War and Peace* (Stanford, CA: Hoover Institution Press, 1987).

Epstein, Edward, J., *Deception: The Secret War Between the KGB and CIA* (New York, NY: Simon & Schuster, 1989).

_____ *Dossier: The Secret World of Armand Hammer* (New York, NY: Random House, 1996).

Eyre, James K., Jr., "Early Japanese Imperialism and the Philippines," *U.S. Naval Institute Proceedings*, Vol.75, no. 11 (November 1949).

Federal Bureau of Investigation, FBI Report on Albert Einstein, in File 61-7089-25 (13 February 1950).

Ferguson, Niall, *Empire: The Rise and Demise of the British World Order and the Lessons for Global Power* (New York, NY: Basic Books, 2003).

Fettweis, Christopher, "Sir Halford Mackinder, Geopolitics, and Policymaking in the Century," *US Army War College: Parameters* (Summer 2000).

Fields, Damon (Maj., USMC), Bill Pope (Lt. Col., USAF) & Patrick Sharon (Lt. Col., USA), "Adventures in Hispaniola," *U.S. Naval Institute Proceedings*, Vol. 128, no. 9 (September 2002).

Finley, M.I., *The World of Odysseus*, orig. pub. 1954 (London, UK: Folio Society, 2002).

Fisher, Dan, "Polish News Agency Surprisingly Helpful," *Los Angeles Times* (09 December 1982).

Fisher, Rand H. (Rear Adm., USN) & Kent B. Pelot (Capt., USN), "The Navy Has a Stake in Space," *US Naval Institute Proceedings*, Vol. 127, no. 10 (October 2001).

Fleming, Thomas, *The New Dealers' War: F.D.R. and the War Within World War II* (New York, NY: Basic Books, 2001).

Flemming, N.C., "Sunken Cities and Forgotten Wrecks," *Seas, Maps, and Men: An Atlas-History of Man's Exploration of the Oceans*, G.E.R. Deacon, ed. (Garden City, NJ: Doubleday & Company, 1962).

Foreman, William, "China shows its clout at regional trade summit," *Houston Chronicle* (30 November 2004).

Fosdick, Dorothy, ed., *Staying the Course: Henry Jackson and National Security* (Seattle, WA: University of Washington Press, 1987).

Friedman, George & Meredith, *The Future of War: Power, Technology and American World Domination in the 21st Century* (New York, NY: Random House, 1996).

Friedman, Norman, "Fighting Far from the Sea," *U.S. Naval Institute Proceedings,* Vol. 127, no. 12 (December 2001).

_____ "The Future of Shipboard Aircraft," *Maritime Security: Light and Medium Aircraft Carriers into the Twenty-First Century* (Hull, UK: University of Hull Press, 1999).

_____ *The US Maritime Strategy* (Annapolis, MD: Naval Institute Press, 1988).

Friedrich, Carl, *Man and His Government* (New York, NY: Wiley, 1965).

Fuller, J.F.C., *A Military History of the Western World: From the Defeat of the Spanish Armada to the Battle of Waterloo*, Vol. II (New York, NY: Plenum Publishing, 1955).

_____ *Decisive Battles of the USA* (New York, NY: Harper & Brothers, 1942).

Gaddis, John Lewis, *We Now Know: Rethinking Cold War History* (New York, NY: Oxford University Press, 1998).

_____ "The Unexpected John Foster Dulles: Nuclear Weapons, Communism, and the Russians," *John Foster Dulles and the Diplomacy of the Cold War*, Richard Immerman, ed. (Princeton, NJ: Princeton University Press, 1990).

Galdorisi, George (Capt., USN), "A U.N. Treaty We All Can Support," *US Naval Institute Proceedings*, Vol. 129, no. 3 (March 2003).

Gehman, Harold W. Jr. (Adm., USN), "Lost Patrol: The Attack on the Cole," *U.S. Naval Institute Proceedings*, Vol. 127, no. 4 (April 2001).

Gernet, Jacques, *A History of Chinese Civilization* (New York, NY: Cambridge University Press, 1982).

Gertz, Bill, *The China Threat: How the People's Republic Targets America* (Washington, DC: Regnery Publishing, 2000).

Gibbon, Edward, *The History of the Decline and Fall of the Roman Empire*, Vol. I–VIII, orig. pub. 1788 (London, UK: Folio Society, 1997).

Gildea, Robert, *Barricades and Borders: Europe 1800-1914*, 2nd ed. (Oxford, UK: Oxford University Press, 1996).

Glass, Charles, "The First Lies Club: How the Imperial Eagle Got Its Wings," *Harper's Magazine* (January 2003).

Glazer, David W. (Cdr., USN), "Breaching the Great Wall," *U.S. Naval Institute Proceedings*, Vol. 126, no. 3 (March 2000).

Glenn, Russell W., "Urban Combat Is Complex," *U.S. Naval Institute Proceedings*, Vol. 128, no. 2 (February 2002).

Goldstein, Lyle J. & Yuri M. Zhukov, "A Tale of Two Fleets: A Russian Perspective on the 1973 Naval Standoff in the Mediterranean," *Naval War College Review*, Vol. LVII, no. 2 (Spring 2004).

Golitsyn, Anatoliy, *New Lies for Old: The Communist Strategy of Deception and Disinformation* (New York, NY: Dodd, Mead & Company, 1984).

Gough, Barry, "The Influence of History on Mahan," *The Influence of History on Mahan*, John Hattendorf, ed. (Newport, RI: U.S. Naval War College Press, 1991).

Grant, Michael, *The Climax of Rome* (Boston, MA: Little, Brown, and Company).

Gray, Colin, *Explorations in Strategy* (Westport, CT: Praeger Publishers, 1998).

_____ "The Geopolitics of European Defence in 2020," Michael Duffy, Theo Farrell & Geoffrey Sloan, eds., *European Defence in 2020*, no. 2 (Exeter, UK: Britannia Royal Naval College, 1998).

_____ *The Geopolitics of Superpower* (Lexington, KY: University of Kentucky Press, 1988).

_____ "Inescapable Geography," Colin Gray & Geoffrey Sloan, ed., *Geopolitics: Geography and Strategy* (London, UK: Frank Cass, 1999).

_____ *The Leverage of Sea Power: The Strategic Advantages of Navies in War* (New York, NY: Free Press, 1992).

_____ *Modern Strategy* (New York, NY: Oxford University Press, 1999).

_____ *The Navy in the Post-Cold War Era: The Uses and Value of Strategic Sea Power* (University Park, PA: Pennsylvania State University Press, 1994).

_____ *War, Peace, and Victory: Strategy and Statecraft for the Next Century* (New York, NY: Simon & Schuster, 1990).

Gray, John, *The Canaanites* (New York, NY: Frederick A. Praeger, 1964).

Green, Peter, *Armada from Athens* (Garden City, NJ: Doubleday & Company, 1970).

Griswold, A. Whitney, *The Far Eastern Policy of the United States* (New York, NY: Harcourt, Brace and Company, 1939).

Grousset, Rene, *The Rise of Splendour of the Chinese Empire* (Berkeley, CA: University of California Press, 1965).

Grove, Eric, *Big Fleet Actions* (London, UK: Arms and Armour Press, 1991).

Gunther, John, *Inside Asia* (New York, NY: Harper and Brothers, 1939).

Halloran, Richard, "Some Warn New Commitments Spreading U.S. Military Too Thin," *New York Times* (10 August 1983).

Halpern, Paul G., *A Naval History of World War I* (Annapolis, MD: Naval Institute Press, 1994).

Hanson, Victor David, "We're Removing Saddam Hussein," *US Naval Institute Proceedings*, Vol. 129, no. 3 (March 2003).

Hardesty, David (Capt., USN), "Space-Based Weapons: Long-Term Strategic Implications and Alternatives," *Naval War College Review*, Vol. 58, no. 2 (Spring 2005).

Harris, Brayton, *The Navy Times Book of Submarines: A Political, Social, and Military History* (New York, NY: Berkley Publishing, 1997).

Harris, Clay (Cdr., USN), "The Readiness Tango of 1998," *U.S. Naval Institute Proceedings*, Vol. 126, no. 9 (September 2000).

Hart, B.H. Liddell, *The Revolution in Warfare* (New Haven, CT: Yale University Press, 1947).

_____ "Fulcrum of Greatness," *U.S. Naval Institute Naval History*, Vol. 16, no. 6 (December 2002).

_____ "Sanctions and Measures of Mutual Assistance," Panel Discussion, Allen Dulles, Chair, *Collective Security: A Record of the Seventh & Eighth International Studies Conference* (Brussels, BG: Maison Vaillant-Carmanne, S.A., 1936).

Haynes, John Earl & Harvey Klehr, *Venona: Decoding Soviet Espionage in America* (New Haven, CT: Yale University Press, 1999).

Haywood, Richard Mansfield, *Ancient Greece and the Near East* (New York, NY: David McKay, 1964).

Hays, Kristen, "Politics of oil will get hearing," *Houston Chronicle* (11 February 2007).

Hendrix, Henry J. (Cdr., USN), "Exploit Sea Basing," *U.S. Naval Institute Proceedings*, Vol. 128, no. 8 (August 2003).

Herm, Gerhard, *The Celts: The People Who Came Out of the Darkness* (New York, NY: St. Martin's Press, 1975).

_____ *The Phoenicians: The Purple Empire of the Ancient World* (New York, NY: William Morrow, 1975).

Herodotus, *Erato*, George Rawlings, trans., Francis Godolphin, ed., *Greek Historians*, Vol. I (New York, NY: Random House, 1942).

_____ *Polymnia*, George Rawlings trans., Francis Godolphin, ed., *Greek Historians*, Vol. I (New York, NY: Random House, 1942).

Holsti, K.J., *International Politics: A Framework for Analysis*, 4th ed. (Englewood Cliffs, NJ: Prentice-Hall, 1983).

Honey, Martha and Tom Barry, *Global Focus: U.S. Foreign Policy at the Turn of the Millennium* (New York, NY: St. Martin's Press, 2000).

Hopkirk, Peter, *The Great Game: The Struggle for Empire in Central Asia* (New York, NY: Kodansha International, 1992).

Hornblower, Simon & Antony Spawforth, ed., *The Oxford Companion to Classical Civilization* (Oxford, UK: Oxford University Press, 1998).

Horowitz, David, *The Politics of Bad Faith: The Radical Assault on America's Future* (New York, NY: Simon & Schuster, 1998).

Hough, Richard, *The Fleet that had to Die* (New York, NY: Viking Press, 1958).

Horsman, Reginald, *The Causes of the War of 1812* (New York, NY: A.S. Barnes & Company, 1962).

Hubbard, Charles, "Alfred Thayer Mahan: The Reluctant Seaman," *American History* (August 1998).

Huber, Jeff (Lt. Cdr., USN), "Nobody Asked Me, but Clausewitz is Dead," *US Naval Institute Proceedings*, Vol. 127, no. 3 (March 2001).

Huck, Arthur, trans., "Map of the Excellent World Situation," *People's Daily* (26 September 1968).

Hughes, e., *Churchill – Ein Mann in Widerspruch* (Tubingen, GM, 1959).

Hughes, Wayne P. (Capt., USN), "22 Questions for Streetfighter," *U.S. Naval Institute Proceedings*, Vol. 126, no. 2 (February 2000).

Hurt, Charles, "Congressional junkets picking up steam," *The Examiner* (15 April 2007).

Ignatieff, Michael, "The Challenges of American Imperial Power," *Naval War College Review*, Vol. 56, no. 2 (Spring 2003).

Ignatius, David, "A Ghost of the Cold War," *Washington Post* (20 April 2007).

Ikeda, Sogo, Kokushikan University, "American Attitude Around the Ishii-Lansing Agreement," Conference Paper, *International Studies Association, West* (Claremont, CA: Claremont Graduate University, October 1998).

Ikenberry, G. John, "The Future of International Leadership," *American Leadership, Ethnic Conflict, and the New World Politics*, Caralay, Demetrios James, and Bonnie B. Hartman, ed. (New York, NY: Academy of Political Science, 1997).

_____ "The Myth of Post-Cold War Chaos," *Foreign Affairs*, Vol. 75, no. 3 (May/June 1996), pp. 79-91.

Immerman, Richard H., *John Foster Dulles and the Diplomacy of the Cold War*, (Princeton, NJ: Princeton University Press, 1990).

Isaacson, Walter & Evan Thomas, *The Wise Men: Six Friends and the World They Made* (New York, NY: Touchstone, 1986).

Isenberg, Michael, *Shield of the Republic: The United States Navy In an Era of Cold War and Violent Peace*, Vol. I, 1945-1962 (New York, NY: St. Martin's Press, 1993).

IRNA, "Iran, Venezuela review expanding mutual ties," *Islamic Republic News Agency* (23 January 2006).

Jaffa, Harry V., *A New Birth of Freedom: Abraham Lincoln and the Coming of the Civil War* (Lanham, MD: Rowman & Littlefield, 2000).

Jaffe, Greg, "Risk Assessment: Plans for Small Ships Pose Big Questions for the US Navy," *The Wall Street Journal*, Vol. 238, no. 7 (11 July 2001).

Jenkins, Holman W., Jr., "Russians Agree: U.S. Banks Are Tops!" *Wall Street Journal* (01 September 1999).

Johnsen, William T., *Redefining Land Power for the 21st Century*, Research Document (Carlisle, PA: US Army War College Strategic Studies Institute, May 1998).

Johnson-Freese, Joan, "China's Manned Space Program: Sun Tzu or Appollo Redux," *Naval War College Review*, Vol. 56, no. 3 (Summer 2003).

Johnson, Tim, "China, Latin America getting into rhythm of good relations," *Houston Chronicle* (17 July 2005).

Jomini, Antoine-Henri, *The Art of War*, G.H. Mendell (Capt., USA) & W.P. Craighill (Lt., USA) trans. (Westport, CT: Greenwood Press, orig. pub. by J.B. Lippincott, 1862).

Jones, Archer, *The Art of War in the Western World* (New York, NY: Oxford University Press, 1989).

Jones, John Paul (Capt. USN), "Testimony to the Naval Committee of Congress," *Qualifications of a Naval Officer* (Annapolis, MD: U.S. Naval Academy, 1:12 26-200).

Jordan, Amos, William J. Taylor, Jr. & Michael J. Mazarr, *American National Security*, 5th ed. (Baltimore, MD: Johns Hopkins University Press, 1999).

Jouvenel, Bertrand de, *On Power: The Natural History of Its Growth*, orig. pub. 1945 (Indianapolis, IN: Liberty Press, 1993).

Jusell, Judson J. (Maj., USAF), *Space Power Theory: A Rising Star*, Research Document AU/ACSC/144/1998-04 (Maxwell AFB, AL: Air University Press, April 1998).

Kagan, Donald, *The Fall of the Athenian Empire* (Ithaca, NY: Cornell University Press, 1987).

_____ *On the Origins of War and the Preservation of Peace* (New York, NY: Anchor Books, 1996).

_____ *While America Sleeps: Self-delusion, Military Weakness, and the Threat to Peace Today* (New York, NY: St. Martin's Press, 2000).

Kennan, George (AKA, X), "German Strategy: 1914 and 1940," *Foreign Affairs*, Vol. 19, no. 3 (April 1941).

_____ *Memoirs, 1925-1950* (Boston, MA: Little, Brown, and Company, 1967).

_____ *Soviet Foreign Policy, 1917-1941* (Princeton, NJ: D. Van Nostrand Company, 1960).

Kennedy, John F., US Senate Speech, "The Missile Gap" (14 August 1958).

Kennedy, Paul, *Preparing for the Twenty-First Century* (New York, NY: Random House, 1993).

_____ *The Rise and Fall of British Naval Mastery*, 2nd ed. (London, UK: Ashfield Press, 1987).

_____ *The Rise and Fall of the Great Powers: Economic Change and Military Conflict from 1500 to 2000* (New York, NY: Random House, 1987).

Kessler, Ronald, *Moscow Station: How the KGB Penetrated the American Embassy* (New York, NY: Simon & Schuster, 1989).

Kiesling, Eugenia, ed., *Strategic Theories: The Essays of Admiral Raoul Castex* (Annapolis, MD: Naval Institute Press, 1994).

Kiralfy, Alexander, "Japanese Naval Strategy," Edward Mead Earle, ed., *Makers of Modern Strategy: Military Thought from Machiavelli to Hitler* (New York, NY: Atheneum, 1966).

Kirkpatrick, Jeane, "Law of the Sea Treaty," *Testimony before the Senate Armed Services Committee* (Washington, DC: Congressional Record, 08 April 2004).

_____ *The Strategy of Deception: A Study in World-Wide Communist Tactics* (New York, NY: Farrar, Straus and Giroux, 1963).

Klein, John J. (Cdr., USN) & Rich Morales (Maj., USA), "Sea Basing Isn't Just About the Sea," *U.S. Naval Institute Proceedings*, Vol. 130, no. 1 (January 2004).

Knoke, William, *Bold New World: The Essential Road Map to the Twenty-First Century* (New York, NY: Kodansha America, 1996)

Koch, Stephen, *Double Lives: Stalin, Willi Munzenberg, and the Seduction of the Intellectuals* (New York, NY: HarperCollins, 1995).

Koehler, John O., *The Untold Story of the East German Secret Police* (Boulder, CO: Westview Press, 1999).

Koenker, Diane P. & Ronald D. Bachman, *Revelations from the Russian Archives* (Washington, DC: US Government Printing Office, 1997).

Kors, Alan C. & Harvey A. Silverglate, *The Shadow University: The Betrayal of Liberty on America's Campuses* (New York, NY: Free Press, 1998).

Kurtenbach, Elaine, "Freedom a Taboo Word on Chinese Internet," *Associated Press* (14 June 2005).

Labs, Eric J., "Building the Future Fleet: Show Us the Analysis," *Naval War College Review*, Vol. 57, no. 3/4 (Summer/Autumn 2004).

Laingren, Charles W. (Cdr., USN), "On War: It's Not Just a Military Affair Anymore," *U.S. Naval Institute Proceedings*, Vol. 126, no. 5 (May 2000).

Lambert, Andrew, "The Principle Source of Understanding: Navies and the Educational Role of the Past," Peter Hore, ed., *Hudson Papers*, Vol. I (London, UK: Royal Navy Defence Studies, 2001).

Lambro, Donald, "Tax Americana," *The American Legion*, Vol. 156, no. 2 (February 2004).

Lehman, John,_"Captivated by the American Spirit," *US Naval Institute Naval History*, Vol. 16, no. 1 (January 2002).

_____ *Command of the Seas: Building the 600 Ship Navy* (New York, NY: Macmillan Publishing Company, 1988).

Lejeune, John A. (Gen., USMC), "Future Policy of the Marine Corps as Influenced by the Conference on Limitation of Armaments" (11 February 1922), Records of the General Board of the Navy, RG 80, NARA.

Liedtke, Michael, "Google Conforms to Chinese Censorship," *Associated Press* (25 September 2005).

Lenfestey, Thompson, *Dictionary of Nautical Terms* (New York, NY: Facts on File, 1994).

Leslie, Reo, "Religion and Mahan," *The Influence of History on Mahan*, John Hattendorf, ed. (Newport, RI: Naval War College Press, 1991).

Lewis, David, *Sexpionage: The Exploitation of Sex by Soviet Intelligence* (New York, NY: Harcourt Brace Jovanovich, 1976).

Lewis, Michael, *The History of the British Navy* (Harmondsworth, UK: Penguin Books, 1957).

Lewy, Guenter, *The Cause that Failed: Communism in American Political Life* (New York, NY: Oxford University Press, 1990).

Lindblom, Charles E., *Politics and Markets: The World's Political-Economic Systems* (New York, NY: HarperCollins Publishers, 1977).

Livezey, William, *Mahan on Sea Power*, rev. ed. (Norman, OK: University of Oklahoma Press, 1981).

Locke, John, "Second Treatise of Government," Steven M. Cahn, ed., *Classics of Modern Political Theory: Machiavelli to Mill* (New York, NY: Oxford University Press, 1997).

Lomborg, Bjorn, *The Skeptical Environmentalist: Measuring the Real State of the World* (Cambridge, UK: Cambridge University Press, 2001).

Los Angeles Times Co., "White House Tense Over Libyan Threat," *Los Angeles Times* (06 August 1983).

Ludwig, Emil, *The Mediterranean: Saga of a Sea* (New York, NY: Whittlesey House, 1942).

Luttwak, Edward & Stuart L. Koehl, *The Dictionary of Modern War* (New York, NY: HarperCollins, 1991).

MacArthur, Douglas (Gen., USA), *Reminiscences* (New York, NY: McGraw-Hill, 1964).

Macdonald, Douglas J., "Communist Bloc Expansion in the Early Cold War: Challenging Realism, Refuting Revisionism," *International Security*, Vol. 20, no. 3 (Winter 1995).

Machiavelli, Niccolo, *The Prince*, Luigi Ricci trans. (New York, NY: New American Library, 1959).

Mackinder, Halford, *Democratic Ideals and Reality: A Study in the Politics of Reconstruction* (Suffolk, UK: Penguin Books, 1944).

_____ *The Nations of the Modern World: An Elementary Study in Geography and History* (London, UK: George Philip, 1924).

_____ "The Round World and the Winning of the Peace," *Foreign Affairs*, Vol. 75, no. 1 (July 1943).

Mahan, Alfred Thayer (Capt., USN), *Admiral Farragut*, orig. pub. by G. Appleton and Company, 1892 (St. Clair Shores, MI: Scholarly Press, 1970).

_____ "Admiral Mahan Asserts Its Ultimate Dependence on a Navy," *The New York Times* (12 April 1912).

_____ "The Future in Relation to American Naval Power," *Harper's New Monthly Magazine*, Vol. 140, no. 545 (October 1895).

_____ *The Influence of Sea Power upon the French Revolution and Empire, 1793-1812*, 2 vols. (Boston, MA: Little, Brown, and Company, 1892).

_____ *The Influence of Sea Power upon History, 1660-1783*, orig. pub. 1890 (Mineola, NY: Dover Publications, 1987).

_____ *The Interest of America in Sea Power, Present and Future* (Boston, MA: Little, Brown and Company, 1898).

_____ "The Isthmus and Sea Power," *The Atlantic Monthly*, Vol. 72, no. 432 (October 1893).

_____ *Lessons of the War with Spain and Other Articles* (Boston, MA: Little, Brown, and Company, 1918).

_____ *The Life of Nelson: The Embodiment of the Sea Power of Great Britain*, orig. pub. Little, Brown, and Company, 1899 (Annapolis, MD: Naval Institute Press, 2001).

_____ *Mahan on Naval Warfare: Selections from the Writings of Rear Admiral Alfred T. Mahan*, Allan Westcott, ed. (Mineola, NY: Dover Publications, 1999).

_____ *Naval Strategy: Compared and Contrasted with the Principles and Practice of Military Operations on Land* (London, UK: Sampson Low, Marston & Company, 1911).

_____ *The Problem of Asia* (Boston, MA: Little, Brown, and Company, 1900).

_____ *Retrospect and Prospect: Studies in International Relations Naval and Political* (Boston, MA: Little, Brown, and Company, 1902).

_____ *Sea Power in Its Relations to the War of 1812* (Boston, MA: Little, Brown, and Company, 1905).

_____ "The Strategic Features of the Gulf of Mexico and Caribbean Sea," *Harper's New Monthly Magazine* Vol. XCV, no. DLXIX (October 1897).

_____ "Subordination in Historical Treatment," *Annual Report of the American Historical Association, 1902*.

_____ "A Twentieth-Century Outlook," *Harper's New Monthly Magazine*, Vol. 95, no. 568 (September 1897).

Malone, Eloise and Arthur Rachwald, "The Dark Side of Globalization," *U.S. Naval Institute Proceedings*, Vol. 127, no. 11 (November 2001).

Maltby, William S., "The Origins of a Global Strategy: England from 1558 to 1713," Williamson Murray, MacGregor Knox & Alvin Bernstein, eds., *The Making of Strategy: Rulers, States, and War* (Cambridge, UK: Cambridge University Press, 1994).

Mao Tse-tung, *Selected Works* (London, UK: Lawrence and Wishart, 1955).

Marder, Arthur J., *The Anatomy of British Sea Power: A History of British Naval Policy in the Pre-Dreadnought Era, 1880-1905* (New York, NY: Alfred A. Knopf, 1940).

Martin, L.W., *The Seas in Modern Strategy* (New York, NY: Frederick Praeger, 1967).

Maslowski, Peter, "To the edge of greatness: The United States, 1783-1865," *The Making of Strategy: Rulers, States, and War*, Williamson Murray, MacGregor Knox, and Alvin Bernstein, ed. (New York, NY: Cambridge University Press, 1997).

Massie, Robert, *Dreadnought: Britain, Germany and the Coming of the Great War* (London, UK: Pimlico Press, 1993).

Mbachu, Dulue, "China scores gains in Africa," *Houston Chronicle* (10 February 2006).

McCullough, David, *The Path Between the Seas: The Creation of the Panama Canal, 1870-1914* (New York, NY: Simon & Schuster, 1977).

McDonald, Joe, "Bolivia, China look to link up," *Houston Chronicle* (10 January 2006).

McFadden, Robert D., "Secrets and Lines: Legacy of a Reporter," *New York Times* (28 April 1997).

McInnes, Colin, "Technology and Modern Warfare," *Dilemmas of World Politics: International Issues in a Changing World*, John Baylis & N.J. Rengger, ed. (Oxford, UK: Oxford University Press, 1992).

McLean, Iain, ed., *The Concise Oxford Dictionary of Politics* (Oxford, UK: Oxford University Press, 1996).

Meyer, Karl E. & Shareen Blair Brysac, *Tournament of Shadows: The Great Game and the Race for Empire in Central Asia* (Washington, DC: Counterpoint, 1999).

Millis, Walter, ed., *The Forrestal Diaries* (New York, NY: Viking Press, 1951).

Miyasato, Seigen, "John Foster Dulles and the Peace Settlement with Japan," *John Foster Dulles and the Diplomacy of the Cold War*, Richard Immerman, ed. (Princeton, NJ: Princeton University Press, 1990).

Moffat, Ian (Lt. Cdr., CRN), "Corbett: A Man before His Time," *Journal of Military and Strategic Studies*, Electronic Journal of the Centre for Military and Strategic Studies, University of Calgary (Winter 2000/Spring 2001).

Morgan, John G. (Rear Adm., USN) & Anthony D. McIvor, "Rethinking the Principles of War," *US Naval Institute Proceedings*, Vol. 129, no. 10 (October 2003).

_____ (Vice Adm., USN) & Charles W. Martgolio (Rear Adm., USN), "The 1,000 Ship Navy: Global Maritime Network," *Naval Institute Proceedings*, Vol. 132, no. 11 (November 2005).

Morison, Samuel Eliot, *Strategy and Compromise* (Boston, MA: Little, Brown and Company, 1958).

Morris, Edmund, "A Matter of Extreme Urgency," *Naval War College Review*, Vol. 55, no. 2 (Spring 2002).

Murphy, David E., Sergei A. Kondrashev & George Bailey, *Battleground Berlin: CIA vs. KGB in the Cold War* (New Haven, CT: Yale University Press, 1997).

Murray, Douglas & Paul Viotti, ed., *The Defense Policies of Nations: A Comparative Study*, 3rd ed. (Baltimore, MD: Johns Hopkins University Press, 1994).

Murray, Williamson, "Corbett, Julian, 1854-1922: British Naval Historian," Robert Cowley & Geoffrey Parker, ed., *The Reader's Companion to Military History* (New York, NY: Houghton Mifflin, 1996).

_____ & Mark Grimsley, "Introduction: On Strategy," Williamson Murray, MacGregor Knox & Alvin Bernstein, ed., *The Making of Strategy: Rulers, States, and War* (Cambridge, UK: Cambridge University Press, 1994).

_____ "Thinking about Innovation," *Naval War College Review*, Vol. 54, no.2 (Spring 2001).

Nagy, Paul (Cdr., USN), "The History of Sea Basing," *U.S. Naval Institute Proceedings*, Vol. 128, no. 11 (November 2002).

Navy League of the United States, *Centennial Membership Directory* (Purchase, NY: Bernard C. Harris Publishing, 2002).

New York Times Wire Service, "Peking's Plan to 'Encircle' the West," *San Francisco Chronicle* (03 September 1965).

Noel, John V., Jr. (Capt., USN), *Naval Terms Dictionary* (Annapolis, MD: United States Naval Institute Press, 1952).

North, Douglass C., *Structure and Change in Economic History* (New York, NY: W.W. Norton, 1981).

Nugroho, Anton (Capt., IAF), "The Dragon Looks South," *U.S. Naval Institute Proceedings*, Vol. 126, no. 3 (March 2000).

Nye, Joseph S. Jr. *The Paradox of American Power: Why the World's Only Superpower Can't Go It Alone* (New York, NY: Oxford University Press, 2002).

O'Connor, Karen, Larry J. Sabato, Stefan D. Haag & Gary A. Keith, *American Government: Continuity and Change* (New York, NY: Pearson Education, 2005).

O'Connor, Richard, *Pacific Destiny: An Informal History of the US in the Far East* (Boston, MA: Little, Brown, and Company, 1969).

O'Hanlon, Michael, *Technological Change and the Future of Warfare* (Washington, DC: Brookings Institution Press, 2000).

Omestad, Thomas, "Selling Off America," *International Political Economy: Perspectives on Global Power and Wealth*, 3rd ed., Jeffry A. Frieden and David A. Lake, ed. (New York, NY: St. Martin's Press, 1995).

O'Neil, William D., "Transformation Billy Mitchell Style," *U.S. Naval Institute Proceedings*, Vol. 128, no. 3 (March 2002).

Overy, Richard, ed., *The Times History of the World*, 5th ed. (London, UK: HarperCollins, 1999).

Padfield, Peter, *Maritime Supremacy and the Opening of the Western Mind: Naval Campaigns that Shaped the Modern World, 1588-1782* (London, UK: Pimlico, 2000).

Paulsen, James CDR, USN), "The Air Force Wasn't Even Close," *U.S. Naval Institute Proceedings*, Vol. 126, no. 7 (July 2000).

Perowne, Stewart, *Death of the Roman Republic: From 146 B.C. to the Birth of the Roman Empire* (Garden City, NJ: Doubleday & Company, 1968).

Philbin, Tobias R. III, *The Lure of Neptune: German – Soviet Naval Collaboration and Ambitions, 1919-1941* (Columbia, SC: University of South Carolina Press, 1994).

Phillips, Russell, *John Paul Jones: Man of Action* (New York, NY: Bretano's, 1927).

Pipes, Richard, *Property and Freedom* (New York, NY: Alfred A. Knopf, 1999).

_____ *The Russian Revolution: 1899-1919*, Vol. I (London, UK: Harvill Press, 1990).

Pomfret, John, "China Strengthens Ties With Taleban by Signing Economic Deal," *International Herald Tribune* (13 September 2001).

Ponte, Lowell, "Commie in Caracas," *Front Page Magazine* (10 July 2002).

Pouch, Robert H., "The U.S. Merchant Marine and Maritime Industry in Review," *U.S. Naval Institute Press*, Vol. 128, no. 5 (May 2002).

Powell, S. Steven, *Covert Cadre: Inside the Institute for Policy Studies* (Ottawa, IL: Green Hill Publishers, 1987).

Prins Gwyn, "Security studies and power politics," *International Affairs*, Vol. 74, no. 4 (October, 1998).

Pullella, Philip, "Soviet Union ordered Pope shooting: Italy commission," *Reuters* (02 March 2006).

Quester, George, "Mahan and American Naval Thought since 1914," *The Influence of History on Mahan*, John Hattendorf, ed. (Newport, RI: US Naval War College Press, 1991).

_____ "If the Nuclear Taboo Gets Broken," *Naval War College Review*, Vol. 58, no. 2 (Spring 2005), p. 83.

Radio Free Europe, "Policeman Admits to faking Student's Death in 1989," *Weekly Record of Events* (06 December 1991).

Radio Free Europe, "KGB Supported Perestroika in GDR," *RFE/RL Daily Report*, No. 17 (17 September 1993).

Reo, Leslie, "Religion and Mahan," John Hattendorf, ed., *The Influence of History on Mahan* (Newport, RI: Naval War College Press, 1991).

Ricketts, Claude (Adm., USN), "Naval Power – Present and Future," *U.S. Naval Institute Proceedings* Vol. 89, no. 1 (January 1963).

Rickover, Hyman (Adm., USN), Testimony, *United States Senate Committee on Defense Preparedness* (06 January 1958).

Ricks, Thomas E., *Making the Corps* (New York, NY: Touchstone Books, 1998).

Riebling, Mark, *Wedge: The Secret War between the FBI and CIA* (New York, NY: Alfred A. Knopf, 1994).

Rodger, N.A.M., *The Safeguard of the Sea: A Naval History of Britain, 660-1649*, Vol. I (London, UK: HarperCollins, 1997).

Rodgers, William L. (VADM, U.S.N.), *Naval Warfare Under Oars: 4th to 16th Centuries* (Annapolis, MD: Naval Institute Press, 1996).

Rodriguez, Andrea, "Bolivian president-elect visits Cuba," *Houston Chronicle* (31 December 2005).

Roe, Patrick, C., *The Dragon Strikes: China and the Korean War* (Novato, CA: Presidio Press, 2000).

Roesler, Gordon & Allan Steinhardt, "Space-Based Radar Lets the Navy See It All," *U.S. Naval Institute Proceedings*, Vol. 128, no. 9 (September 2002)

Rohnka, Dariusz, "The Communist Threat," *Another Fine Specimen* (15 May 2003).

Romerstein, Herbert, and Eric Breindel, *The Venona Secrets: Exposing Soviet Espionage and America's Traitors* (Washington, DC: Regnery Publishing, 2000).

Rood, Harold W., *Kingdoms of the Blind: How the Great Democracies Have Resumed the Follies that So Nearly Cost Them Their Life* (Durham, NC: Carolina Academic Press, 1980).

Rosenau, James N., *Along the Domestic-Foreign Frontier: Exploring Governance in a Turbulent World* (Cambridge, UK: Cambridge University Press, 1997).

Roskill, S.W. (Capt., BRN), *The Strategy of Sea Power: Its Development and Application* (London, UK: Collins, 1962).

Ryan, Paul B., *First Line of Defense: The U.S. Navy Since 1945* (Stanford, CA: Hoover Institute Press, 1981).

Safer, Morley, *Flashbacks: On Returning to Vietnam* (New York, NY: Random House, 1995).

Safire, William, "Selling the Rope," *New York Times* (09 October 1983).

St. John, Jeffrey, *Day of the Cobra* (Nashville, TN: Thomas Nelson Publishing, 1984).

Sarin, Oleg (Gen., SRA) & Lev Dvoretsky (Col., SRA), *Alien Wars: The Soviet Union's Aggressions against the World, 1919-1989* (Novato, CA: Presidio Press, 1996).

Sawyer, Ralph D., *Unorthodox Strategies: 100 Lessons in the Art of War* (New York, NY: Barnes & Noble, 1996).

Scheina, Robert, "Low Intensity Conflict: Does Mahan have a Place," *The Influence of History on Mahan*, John Hattendorf ed. (Newport, RI: US Naval War College Press, 1994).

Schaller, Michael, *The American Occupation of Japan: The Origins of the Cold War in Asia* (New York, NY: Oxford University Press, 1985).

Scharfen, John C., *The Dismal Battlefield: Mobilizing for Economic Conflict* (Annapolis, MD: Naval Institute Press, 1995).

Schram, Stuart R., *The Political Thought of Mao Tse-tung* (New York, NY: Praeger Publishers, 1976).

Seager, Robert, "Alfred Thayer Mahan: Christian Expansionist, Navalist, and Historian," James C. Bradford, ed., *Admirals of the New Steel Navy: Makers of the American Naval Tradition, 1880-1930* (Annapolis, MD: Naval Institute Press, 1990).

_____ *Alfred Thayer Mahan: The Man and His Letters* (Annapolis, MD: Naval Institute Press, 1977).

Seligman, Lester G. & Cary R. Covington, *The Coalition Presidency* (Chicago, IL: The Dorsey Press, 1989).

Sereda, Sergey, "Oil Agreement Signed With Venezuela To Benefit Cuba," *ITAR-TASS* (11 March 1993).

Sherwood, Robert E., *Roosevelt and Hopkins: An Intimate History* (New York, NY: Harper & Brothers, 1948).

Shorter, Andrew G. (Maj., USMC), "STOVL JSFs Put Teeth in Sea Basing," *U.S. Naval Institute Proceedings*, Vol. 129, no. 9 (September 2003).

Shulman, Mark Russell, *Navalism and the Emergence of American Sea Power: 1882-1893* (Annapolis, MD: Naval Institute Press, 1995).

Sledes, George, ed., *The Great Thoughts* (New York, NY: Ballantine Books, 1985).

Sloan, Geoffrey, *The Geopolitics of Anglo-Irish Relations in the 20th Century* (London, UK: Leicester University Press, 1997).

_____ "Sir Halford Mackinder: The Heartland Theory Then and Now," Colin Gray & Geoffrey Sloan eds., *Geopolitics: Geography and Strategy* (London, UK: Frank Cass, 1999).

Smelser, Marshall, "Whether to Provide and Maintain a Navy (1787-1788)," *US Naval Institute Proceedings*, Vol. 83, no. 9 (September 1957).

Smith, Keith (Lt. Gen., USMC), "V-22 Is Right for War on Terrorism," *U.S. Naval Institute Proceedings*, Vol. 128, no. 1 (January 2002).

Sobel, Robert, *Coolidge: An American Enigma* (Washington, DC: Regnery Publishing, 1998).

Sokolsky, Joel J., *Seapower in the Nuclear Age: The United States Navy and NATO, 1949-80* (Annapolis, MD: Naval Institute Press, 1991).

Somerville, Glenn, "Bernanke attempts to soothe China fears," *Houston Chronicle* (17 February 2006).

Sommers, Christine Hoff, *Who Stole Feminism: How Women Have Betrayed Women* (New York, NY: Touchstone, 1995).

Soukhanov, Anne H., ed., *The American Heritage Dictionary of the English Language*, 3rd. ed. (Boston, MA: Houghton Miffin, 1996).

Sowell, Thomas, *Conquests and Cultures: An International History* (New York, NY: Perseus Books, 1998).

_____ *The Quest for Cosmic Justice* (New York, NY: Simon & Schuster, 1999).

_____ *Race and Culture: A World View* (New York, NY: HarperCollins Publishers, 1994).

Spencer, Richard, "Tension rises as China scours the globe for energy," *Daily Telegraph* (19 November 2004).

Spero, Joan E. & Jeffrey Hart, *The Politics of International Economic Relations*, 5th ed. (New York, NY: St. Martin's Press, 1997).

Sprout, Margaret Tuttle, "Mahan: Evangelist of Sea Power," Edward Mead Earle, ed., *Makers of Modern Strategy: Military Thought from Machiavelli to Hitler* (New York, NY: Atheneum, 1966).

Staley, Eugene, "Let Japan Choose," *Foreign Affairs*, Vol. 20, no. 1 (October 1941).

Steele, Shelby, *A Dream Deferred: The Second Betrayal of Black Freedom in America* (New York, NY: HarperCollins, 1994).

Steyn, Mark, "If Pinochet is guilty then so is HM the Queen," *Daily Telegraph* (29 November 1998).

Story, Joseph, *A Familiar Exposition of The Constitution of the United States*, orig. pub. 1845 (Lake Bluff, IL: Regnery Publishing, 1986).

Stubbs, Bruce (Capt., USCG) & Scott C. Truver, *America's Coast Guard: Safeguarding US Maritime Safety and Security in the 21st Century* (Annapolis, MD: Tullier Marketing Communications, 2000).

_____ "We Are Lifesavers, Guardians, and Warriors," *U.S. Naval Institute Proceedings*, Vol. 128, no. 4 (April 2002).

Sullivan, Brian, "Mahan's Blindness and Brilliance," *Joint Forces Quarterly* (Spring 1999).

Sumida, Jon, "Alfred Thayer Mahan, Geopolitician," Colin Gray & Geoffrey Sloan, eds., *Geopolitics: Geography and Strategy* (London, UK: Frank Cass, 1999).

_____ *Inventing Grand Strategy and Teaching Command: The Classic Works of Alfred Thayer Mahan Reconsidered* (Baltimore, MD: Johns Hopkins University Press, 1997).

_____ "New Insights From Old Books: The Case of Alfred Thayer Mahan," *Naval War College Review*, Vol. LIV, no. 3 (Summer 2001).

_____ "On Defense as the Stronger Form of War," *Clausewitz in the 21st Century Conference*, Oxford UK, Oxford University Department of Politics and International Relations (21-23 March 2005).

Sun Tzu Wu, *The Art of War*, Samuel B. Griffith, trans. (New York, NY: Oxford University Press, 1971).

Taft, William H., *Inaugural Addresses of the Presidents of the United States from George Washington to John F. Kennedy* (Washington, DC: U.S. Government Printing Office, 1961).

Talbott, Strobe, "The Birth of the Global Nation," *Time Magazine* (20 July 1992).

Tangredi, Sam J., "The Fall & Rise of Naval Forward Presence," *U.S. Naval Institute Press*, Vol. 126, no. 5 (May 2000).

Tayler, Arthur, *Illustrated History of North American Railroads* (London, UK: Quintet Publishing, 1996).

Taylor, S.J., *Stalin's Apologist: Walter Duranty, The New York Times's Man in Moscow* (New York, NY: Oxford University Press, 1990).

Thucydides, "History of the Peloponnesian War," Maynard Mack, gen. ed., *The Norton Anthology of World Masterpieces*, Vol. I, 4th ed. (New York, NY: W.W. Norton & Company, 1979).

Topitsch, Ernst, *Stalin's War: A Radical New Theory of the Origins of the Second World War*, Arthur Taylor trans. (New York, NY: St. Martin's Press, 1987).

Tenet, George J. (Director, CIA), "Worldwide Threat: Converging Dangers in a Post 9/11 World," Testimony before the Senate Armed Services Committee (19 March 2002).

Terrell, R. Emmett, Jr., "Media Consensus on the Soviets," *Washington Post* (12 September 1983).

Tonelson, Alan, "Superpower Without a Sword," *Foreign Affairs*, Vol. 72, no. 3 (Summer 1993).

Tower, John G., *Consequences: A Personal and Political Memoir* (Boston, MA: Little, Brown and Company, 1991).

Trotsky, Leon, "The Death Agony of Capitalism and the Tasks of the Fourth International," *The Transitional Program for Socialist Revolution*, George Breitman & Fred Stanton, ed. (New York, NY: Pathfinder Press, 1977).

Trulock, Notra, Code Name Kindred Spirit: Inside the Chinese Nuclear Espionage Scandal (San Francisco, CA: Encounter Books, 2003).

Tuleja, Thaddeus, *Statesmen and Admirals: Quest for a Far Eastern Naval Policy* (New York, NY: W.W. Norton & Company, 1963).

Tyson, James L., *Target America: The Influence of Communist Propaganda on U.S. Media* (Chicago, IL: Regnery Gateway, 1981).
United States Marine Corps, The Basic School, "Principles of Amphibious Operations," *Basic Officer Course* (Quantico, VA: Marine Corps Combat Development Command).
Van Creveld, Martin, *Technology and War* (New York, NY: Free Press, 1989).
Volder, Richard, "Roosevelt's Record," *Claremont Review of Books*, Vol. V, no. 1 (Winter 2004).
Wainwright, Jonathan (Gen., USA), *General Wainwright's Story: The Account of Four Years of Humiliating Defeat, Surrender, and Captivity* (Garden City, NJ: Doubleday & Company, 1946).
Waldron, Arthur, "Chinese Strategy from the Fourteenth to the Seventeenth Centuries," Williamson Murray, MacGregor Knox and Alvin Bernstein ed., *The Making of Strategy: Rulers, States, and War* (Cambridge, UK: Cambridge University Press, 1994).
Walworth, Arthur, *Black Ships off Japan: The Story of Commodore Perry's Expedition* (New York, NY: Alfred A. Knopf, 1946).
Wambold, Don Jr., "Sailing Through the Mountains," *U.S. Naval Institute Naval History*, Vol. 15, no. 5 (October 2001).
Washington, George (Gen., USA), Speech, *Farewell Address to the People of the United States* (17 September 1796).
_____ Memorandum for concerting a plan of operations with the French army (15 July 1780).
Weigley, Russell F., *The American Way of War: A History of United States Military Strategy and Policy* (Bloomington, IN: Indiana University Press, 1977).
Weissert, Will, "Mexico plans backup ports," *Associated Press Wire Service* (24 March 2006).
Werner, Max, Military Strength of the Powers: A Soldier's Forecast for Citizens (New York, NY: Modern Age Books, 1939).
Wheeler, Keith, *The Railroaders* (New York, NY: Time-Life Books, 1973).
White, J.A., *The Diplomacy of the Russo-Japanese War* (Princeton, NJ: Princeton University Press, 1964).
Whitfield, Peter, *Mapping the World: A History of Exploration*, 2nd ed. (London, UK: Folio Society, 2000).
Winnefeld, James A. & Dana J. Johnson, *Joint Air Operations: Pursuit of Unity in Command and Control, 1942-1991* (Annapolis, MD: Naval Institute Press, 1993).
Woodcock, William A. (Maj., USA), "The Joint Forces Air Command Problem: Is Network-centric Warfare the Answer," *Naval War College Review*, Vol. 56, no. 1 (Winter 2003) pp. 124-138.
Wright, Arthur F., *The Sui Dynasty: The Unification of China, A.D. 581-617* (New York, NY: Alfred A. Knopf, 1978).

Wright, Quincy, *A Study of War*, 2nd ed. (Chicago, IL: University of Chicago Press, 1969).

Wylie, J.C. (Rear Adm., USN), "Mahan and American Naval Thought Since 1914," *The Influence of History on Mahan* (Newport, RI: U.S. Naval War College Press, 1991).

_____ "Mahan: Then and Now," *The Influence of History on Mahan*, John Hattendorf, ed. (Newport, RI: U.S. Naval War College Press, 1991).

_____ *Military Strategy: A General Theory of Power Control* (Brunswick, N.J.: Rutgers University Press, 1967).

_____ "Why a Sailor Thinks Like a Sailor," *US Naval Institute Proceedings*, Vol. 83, no. 8 (August 1957).

Zachary, G. Pascal, Endless Frontier: Vannevar Bush, Engineer of the American Century (New York, NY: Free Press, 1997).

Zumwalt, Elmo R. (Adm., USN), *On Watch: A Memoir* (New York, NY: Quadrangle, 1976).

Index

A

Actium, battle at, 143–44
active hostile strategic channel, 78, 81, 85, 245–46
Adcock, F. E., 137, 142
Afghanistan, 61, 228, 249–50, 251
aircraft carriers
    advantages of, 284–85
    and Mahanian doctrine, 113–14
    strategic role of, 158, 188, 212, 218
    value in globalized economic world, 280
Air Force, US, 209, 237, 283
air forces, 72–73, 237, 281
air freight, 90
air power
    and Cold War, 216
    definitional issues, 5–6, 26, 59, 71–72
    and land power in Vietnam War, 227–28
    and sea power, 237, 280
Alexander the Great, 139–40
alliances, international, 78–79
all-volunteer force, 238
American Revolution, 169, 174, 175–77, 178
American War of Independence, 41–42, 165, 170, 171–73, 174
Amme, Carl, 24, 84
amphibious operations
    British vulnerability to, 159–60
    Greek vulnerability to, 134, 135
    and Mahanian doctrine, 40–42, 67
    USMC tactics, 104–5
Angleton, James, 247
anti-submarine warfare, 189
Arab-Israeli conflicts, 239
arms control efforts, 187–88, 197–98, 318
Army, US, and joint operations' effectiveness, 283
Art, Robert, 278
Articles of Confederation, 173
The Art of War (Jomini), 37
Asian power center
    Cold War in, 221–31
    European projection into, 151, 152
    historical recognition of, 22
    Korea, 153–54, 156, 212
    and need for naval power, 263
    Soviet agenda in, 211, 222–23, 225
    US-Japan alliance's role in, 221–22, 225
    See also China; Japan

missile gap, 1960s', 343n74
Mississippi River in Civil War, 179–82
Mitchell, Brig. Gen. William "Billy," 73
mobility and naval power's advantage, 284–85
Moffat, Ian, 38, 39
Molotov, Vyacheslav, 94
Monroe Doctrine, 65, 181, 185
Moore, Frank, 261
moral values
    Clausewitz on, 64, 87
    and dealings with totalitarian regimes, 250, 252–54, 291–92
    and loss of national loyalty, 288–89
    magnanimity in victory principle, 109
    Mahan on discipline to build military might, 186
    and US geostrategy, 82–83
multinational corporations, political loyalty dilemma of, 273, 277
Murray, Douglas, 95
Murray, Williamson, 15–16, 56

N
Napoleon Bonaparte, 37, 38, 55–56, 165–66
Napoleon III, 177–78, 179, 180
national grand strategy
    America's slow development of, 177
    Britain's WWII, 206
    in Civil War, 179–81
    and Cold War, 199, 200
    colonial era in America, 171
    of Communist nations, 200
    definitional issues, 5, 332n49
    and fall of Athens, 139
    flexibility of, 226
    and French threat in Mexico, 178
    and geographic domain, 199, 310
    globalization's threat to, 267, 278, 279
    internationalist threat to, 254–56, 269, 272
    and Japan's sea power projection, 156
    Mahan and Mackinder, 63
    moral values consideration, 64
    and national policy, 15–16, 18, 33–34, 78, 80–81
    and Panama Canal, 53
    Persia vs. Greece, 136–37
    Phoenicia's shortcomings in, 132–33
    and policy-strategy-tactics chain, 80, 85–86
    power generators' role in, 15, 25, 32
    power generators vs. power resources, 25–26, 64, 68, 73–74
    purposes for, 310
    Roman, 81, 141

About the Author

Wade Shol is a veteran of the United States Marine Corps and Navy. His tour of duty includes the 4th Marine Division and USS *Dwight D. Eisenhower* (CVN-69). Military service involved several overseas deployments to Europe and various locations around the Mediterranean Sea region during the 1980s.

Dr. Shol was later screened and selected as a member of Operation Deep Freeze, the 33rd winter-over detachment to Antarctica in support of the National Science Foundation. Following his two year assignment with NSF, he then served as an instructor at the US Navy's Survival, Evasion, Resistance, and Escape (SERE) School in Coronado, California. Shol's three-year appointment at SERE involved research on the craft of communist deception, indoctrination, and propaganda used effectively by regimes hostile to the West. In the process he developed counter-measures against those efforts. Additionally he created the first Chief of Naval Operations-endorsed counter-terrorism training course in 1991. Shol earned a Bachelors of Science degree in Political Science from the University of the State of New York while on active military duty.

Dr. Shol continued academic research at the Claremont Graduate School in Claremont, California, earning a Master of Arts degree in International Studies. While at Claremont he developed a model that calculates national power on a comparative global scale. The formula enables strategic analysis and forecasting of superpower growth and decline decades in advance. Shol was later awarded a Sarah Scaife Foundation research fellowship to pursue strategic studies in the United Kingdom. During his tour in the UK he earned a Certificate in Post-Graduate Research from the University of Hull, and a Ph.D. in Politics, with National Security focus, at the University of Reading. While at Claremont and Reading he was fortunate to study under the guiding hands of two eminent global scholars in strategic theory and international relations, Harold W. Rood and Colin S. Gray. Dr. Shol serves as a professor of political science and government at Yorktown University and Montgomery College.